# MOTHER'S
# LAST WORDS

*Cordially,*

*William Samelson*

# MOTHER'S LAST WORDS

A Novel

Second Edition

# WILLIAM SAMELSON

TATE PUBLISHING
AND ENTERPRISES, LLC

Published by Tate Publishing & Enterprises, LLC
127 E. Trade Center Terrace | Mustang, Oklahoma 73064 USA
1.888.361.9473 | www.tatepublishing.com

Tate Publishing is committed to excellence in the publishing industry. The company reflects the philosophy established by the founders, based on Psalm 68:11,
*"The Lord gave the word and great was the company of those who published it."*

Book design copyright © 2015 by Tate Publishing, LLC. All rights reserved.
*Cover design by Joseph Emnace*
*Interior design by Angelo Moralde*

Published in the United States of America
ISBN: 978-1-68097-415-7
1. Biography & Autobiography / Historical
2. Biography & Autobiography / Adventurers & Explorers
15.03.24

Also by William Samelson

All Lie in Wait (Memoir I)
Gerhart Herrmann Mostar; A Critical Profile
*Der Sinn des Lesens* (German text)
*El Legado Sefaradi* (Spanish & Ladino)
Sephardic Legacy; Songs and Tales from Jewish Spain
The Let's ESL Series (6 Vols.)
English the American Way (5 Vols.)
Near and Distant; Selected Poems,
View from my Balcony; Poetic Essays,
One Bridge to Life (Memoir II)
Beyond Anger; Chronicle of a Life
Reclaimed (Memoir Fantasy)
Warning and Hope; Nazi Murder of European Jewry
Celestial Messengers; Angels & Demons Among Us
World Class Assassins & their Victims
The Delight of Being; A Poetic Potpourri

*For my*
*Brother Roman Samelson*
*With Love and Affection*

*May you find peace in a better world...*


*Time is the moving image of eternity...*
**Plato**

*Time is the terminal illness of humankind...*
**William Samelson**

# Moment of Truth

MARCH 21, 1983, ALMOST fifteen years to the day when, one spring afternoon, they were married in the sweltering heat of Havana. Misha recalled those early glorious days, suppressing momentarily less happy memories, which threatened his sanity under the present circumstances. In addition, he fought gamely his doubts about the troubling past.

Misha's steps were heavy as he gazed into the distant void. Two jailers marched him to his cell. Though he knew, there were others nearby, for he heard their derisive catcalls and felt their burning eyes at the nape of his neck. He favored the intervals of silence that magnified the sounds of his jailers' steps with a resounding echo while stifling the inmates' insults in their attempt to drill an indelible imprint into his faltering soul. The two uniformed escorts dwarfed Misha's six feet frame, and made him aware of a deep sense of inadequacy. The man in front of him opened the cell door and stepped aside. The one behind touched his shoulder ever so lightly. As if that gesture had triggered an invisible, inner, mechanism, Misha stepped gingerly across the threshold of his new "home" and, before he could turn around to face his jailers, the heavy door closed behind him with a resounding whack. "Behave yourself," one of his escorts called out to him with a sardonic smile on his unshaven face, "and they might go easy on you at the trial." Both men laughed raucously. He could hear their laughter and their departing footsteps long after they disappeared from view around the bend of the corridor.

Misha sat on the edge of his cell bunk. He tested the thin firm mattress beneath him, his fingers pushing down on the taught blanket under which there were clean linens. At the head was a small pillow. He picked it up and brought it to his face. It smelled of detergent. He inhaled deeply and let out a loud sigh. It was the first sign of emotion since he had entered the massive building that carried the inscription in large black letters: INSTITUTION FOR THE CRIMINALLY INSANE above its imposing entrance.

Misha stretched out on the bunk. His figure gaunt, his one-time masculinity was all but gone. In addition, gone were the days when, on the university campus, he attracted the admiring eyes of women, students and faculty alike. It seemed so very long ago now. Meticulous in his dress and general deportment, blessed with a handsome face marked by deep blue eyes and topped with abundant, wavy hazel-brown hair. The young post-doctoral Assistant Professor from Germany was the talk of the campus and the envy of his male colleagues. At a safe distance, the whispered word "rake" could be often heard.

His cell was unlike any penitentiary cell he had imagined. Its walls were heavily padded, their exterior a rather dull-gray canvas. It had not occurred to him that this might have been the result of his lawyer's intention to plead insanity. However, he felt that there was no reason for such a plea. He had been perfectly conscious of his actions throughout. There was no need for camouflage or apology. He felt neither regret nor was he repentant. It was a sunny afternoon, and Misha wondered in his isolation how the rest of the world was enjoying the balmy weather.

The padded canvas walls, a bunk with a flat mattress, and the freshly disinfected commode in the corner—those were the modest furnishing of his new abode. There were no objects inside the cell that could be used as instruments to inflict harm.

Why suicide? He thought silently. It had never entered his mind, even during the most harrowing times of the past years, when things seemed almost hopeless. The more dismal they appeared, the more stubbornly he had clung to life. Fact was, Misha Winograd, Ph.D. with a major in linguistics, was going on trial for murder in the first degree in the death of his lover of many years, Susanna Langer; the mother of his illegitimate child; a boy named Rudi. Facing the preliminary hearing before the federal Judge, and accompanied by his lawyer, he claimed innocence. Over all, there were only few who believed him; mostly some erstwhile female admirers; suspected lovers. By now, after spending six weeks in federal incarceration before his transfer to this place, even he himself had difficulty suppressing some gnawing doubts about his sanity. He knew the prosecution would hammer away at his confession, which his lawyer claimed to have been coerced under duress. The detectives in charge had taken him repeatedly to the place where, as Misha claimed, the "accident" had happened. It was a most painful experience for him, and under the torment of suppressed, guilt-filled memories, he confessed. The interrogating detectives were astonished at the ease with which the suspect had volunteered his confession. Misha's impressive background story and his ambitious dream of success in the US were long known among all who had been exposed to him. Now, a defeated man, he tried to recall the lessons he had learned. He was weary from the ordeal he had undergone, and his only hope lay in his insistence that he had done no wrong. No one could have known this better than he could.

Lightning abruptly shatters the night. Unusually loud thunderclaps follow, as if in consonance with the irregular beat of his pulse. The echo reverberates throughout the hollow corridors. Rain hits the stone building as though delivered by the bucket. Now nature's awesome might temporarily drowns out the inmates' sporadic shouting, as they attempt to communicate, more like howl at one another with anger, from cell to cell. Misha gazes impassively through the narrow window bars and wonders: "How can I still find interest in observing this throbbing flux of nature's dynamic, while I'm well on the road to eternity?" He pauses only briefly. "Why have you left me, Susanna? Why must I pay the price?" He whispers and tears block his view, though the sound of clatter is that much more vivid. For a brief moment, he feels sorry himself, as if in tribute to the raging storm outside. "If you only knew how you've swallowed my heart, dearest Susanna. If you only knew..." He obsesses.

He does not bother to take off his shoes, as he stretches out fully clothed on his bunk, though he feels intuitively that this is a forbidden act in this place. Can this act be considered an involuntary act of defiance? He seems not to care about his present appearance. How long would it take in this state before he would pick lice from his clothes and hair? He closes his eyes, trying to retrace a past he cannot forget...

...He had a distinguished stepfather and a very noble mother. Misha was the only child, therefore quite moody and given to quick fits of tantrums and crying spells on account of which his father and mother frequently disagreed. The father used to punish him and whip him severely with a homemade leather sling he had fashioned for that purpose, whereas the boy took refuge with his obliging mom. She had always tried to get him back on track whenever she saw him drifting away in his childish manner. God knows he was trying hard to toughen up a little for his mother's benefit; to help a bit around the house, to show her that he was responsible after all. Misha remembered the stern physician stepfather only by the name of his own invention: *Herr Doktor* Horst. After all, as soon as he had come of age, Misha's surname of choice was to be that of the incidental SS man who had sired this bastard son for the Nazi Lebensborn program.

A wonder he still harbored a good measure of pride in his claim of belonging to the master race. You would think that such a demanding and monstrous father (who made it a sport to beat him and his mother often), might have caused the adolescent to lose his self-esteem and, instead, develop abhorrence to being himself. You'd also think that he would have adopted humility as a way of life. After all, he was an abused child.

Misha was thirteen when he ran away from home to seek his fortune with strangers. Blanche, his doting mother, was devastated by his absence. She became sick with grief, for she could not do without her only child; she became a living wreck. Soon, she turned into an invalid and lived by the mercy of her tyrannical husband. But *Herr Doktor* Horst felt a sense of relief at ridding himself of the burden to educate the recalcitrant lad.

On his part, Misha became a "pseudo-orphan." At first, he succeeded. He roamed about the world, unable to establish roots in any of the places he visited. Hence, he stayed a while, only to be driven out, because of his inability to adapt to his ever-new environments. As is the way with most drifters, Misha acquired many role models who had attempted to direct him, scold him, and lecture him on this or that aspect of his errant behavior. He was always in their way, all blame pointed at him; every little mischief had been attributed to him. It was his entire fault. It was no small wonder that he had got into the habit of always trying to be ahead of real or imagined adversaries. In his wanderings, he copied the manners and customs of strange people. His character was a troubling composite due to changes made impulsively. Troubling as it has been for him, his tendency to self-destructiveness led him to a weird enjoyment of the scraps he had gotten into, and even the damaging blows they earned him. Nevertheless, no matter how people knocked him about, inflicted injury, and even drew his blood, the moment they'd stopped and made some amicable gestures, there he was smiling as if nothing had happened. His behavior turned their world topsy-turvy.

It had gotten so each time people smiled at him he imagined they would accept him in their midst. However, it was not to be. They still deprived him of everything in his possession and forced him to live in dark alleys hidden from their view. Often he went hungry, but he persevered in his old ways, crept into tight places, danced and fed himself uninvited at weddings, bar mitzvahs, and baptismal rituals, until discovered and told to leave again. Though he was wild, there must have dwelt a noble disposition in his soul, and his coarseness had grown rough from living among inimical strangers. In time, he grew suspicious of everyone and cynical toward those who wished him well. He lived in a bitter and dark distress and laughter was absent from his daily endeavors. No wonder, then, that the young Misha had gotten into the habit of running away from his adverse surroundings to live in isolation, and sort of bonding with nature.

Once upon a time, there happened a wild, murky night. The sky was covered with black clouds; there was a drenching rain and hail as big as ping-pong balls, and a stormy wind howled incessantly. It was pitch dark, and it lightened and thundered as though the world were to turn upside down. The great thunder-claps and hail broke a good many windows in town about which Misha had little or no concern. The wind tore violently at the roofs. Everyone hid inside their homes or wherever they found refuge in a safe corner. In that dreadful dusky night, it was near midnight when the hail and rainstorm turned to a drizzle. There was a fork in the middle of the town, one way to the raging river and one leading out of town. He was used to taking the road most traveled, one that was easy. And he took that road. He avoided that other way, the one that led to the river, which was forbidden, as his mother would repeat often enough as a warning.

Dressed in a gray trench coat, Misha hurried through the winding street. The strong wind and the slight drizzle impeded his movements, but he managed to proceed with great alacrity. The minute drops beat directly against his face, but he seemed oblivious to his surroundings. Where was he going in such haste? What was it that could preoccupy him to this extent? He did not seem to notice the small black cat that ran across his path. He did not hesitate for a moment. The small feline disappeared quickly around the next corner. It was a subtle warning of misfortune to visit his life soon. Little did Misha suspect but that his mother's last words were to overshadow his life forever as an ominous legacy...

# Hildesheim, the Third Reich, 1941

HER SCREAMS COULD HAVE been heard above the raging snowstorm outside, had she allowed them to persist. Were it not for the presence of the hostel's head matron and Blanche's companions in labor, she might have openly despaired; a characteristic disdained by those of the matron's ilk. The cascades of snow were like a solid wall of white matter, as if nature herself had chosen to conspire with the strange events taking place in the sterilized surroundings of the hospital. The steaming windows made for zero visibility. Blanche strained to make some sense of the situation. After all, what was a seventeen-year-old French girl, with an orthodox Jewish grandfather's near impeccable upbringing, doing in this place, legs spread wide apart in a stirrup, giving birth to her first child. The physical pain, coupled by the anguish of an unwed mother, threatened to tear her asunder. She bit her lips, causing a droplet of blood to appear and slowly roll onto her chin. She longed to let out a scream, but she was certain that such behavior would have been considered a sign of cowardice or weakness or both; behavior unacceptable in her present environment. And she was not about to add humiliation to the excruciating pain that shot upward from her uterus to the nerve center in her brain.

Her young life passed before her delirious eyes while in labored breathing she attempted to aid the busy matrons in the delivery of the infant. As if it were yesterday, she could hear the voice of the heavy-set matron at the meeting of *BDM*, short for *Bund Deutscher Mädel* (Alliance of German Maidens) unit: "You *will* join the *Lebensborn* program; our *Führer* needs children to continue his glorious agenda for the Third Reich and to perfect the German nation into a super race." Her leader put emphasis on the word "will". Moreover, to mind came also a multitude of other perverse and insidious ideas hammered into the young minds until reason became atrophied. Blanche knew all too well the meaning of those words.

However, she did not understand the word "agenda". She dared not question her group leader in public. Any type of question was always taken as open defiance to authority. She would surely suffer the consequences of such blatant impertinence. Questioning superiors in particular was not a tolerated pastime. Public humiliation and severe punishment always followed such outrageous display of arrogance. Having joined the organization after the Nazi occupation of France had brought enough pain and anguish to the Claiborne family. Little did her father know that by joining the system his daughter had saved his position as Clerk of the City Tax Assessor's Office. If she had told him of her sacrifice, he would have surely quit his job to prevent his beloved Blanche from becoming one of *them*, as he referred to the Nazi thugs.

Joining the system was one thing, becoming an unwed mother, a breeder for the Third Reich, was quite another.

Blanche was unable to see the faces of the assembled girls, for the group leader demanded singular attention when she addressed one of her charges. Her blue, Aryan eyes had that look of determination only absolute authority generated, while they were focused on Blanche. The latter wanted to lower her eyes to avoid the leader's stare, but that, too, would have been taken as a character flaw. Every hesitation on part of the girls was considered a negative reflection on the *Führer's* absolute authority and his steely willpower.

"You will be well taken care of, Blanche." The matron went on, "and the children you bear for the *Führer* will bring you everlasting glory."

"Children?" The thought of bearing more than one seemed to her cruel and unusual punishment besides being absurd. But true to the *BDM* principles, Blanche remained silent. The rule was "listen, don't speak even when spoken to." She knew.

The matrons hovered over Blanche, attentive to her every wish. The food was exquisite inside the compound, in stark contrast to the rationed supplies on the outside caused by war shortages. Each day she participated in routine physical care, with an especial emphasis on aerobic routines. Her weight was checked on a daily basis, and blood samples went to the lab for careful scrutiny. She was, after all, of "pure Aryan blood." Her keepers had kept on telling her at every opportunity. If they only knew of her mixed parenthood! She shuddered at the very thought, while she tried to recall her arrival at the hostel.

The blond hair she inherited from her mom was trimmed neatly to blend with the oval face and the wide clear blue eyes. Blanche's stomach was all tied up in knots, and she felt like retching all the while when she witnessed her full, wavy tresses drop to the floor under the relentless pursuit of the barber's scissors.

"He arrives tomorrow." The matron had announced. *He* meant the chosen one for her. "He's a highly decorated hero just arrived from the Eastern front." The woman added, as if to underscore the girl's good fortune.

The young *Panzergruppenführer* knocked before he would enter the room. Even under normal circumstances, he would have caught her attention immediately. He measured over six feet in height; his blond, straight hair was neatly cropped above the ears. His gray-blue eyes shone as he smiled at Blanche.

"*Heil Hitler!*" He exclaimed with a distinct Slavic accent, his right arm raised stiftly upward.

"*Heil Hitler.*" She responded shyly, while she tried not to sound too French. "Sound cheerful." She kept repeating in her mind. He stood in the doorway, his traveling gear in hand, hesitant. It was his "first" also. That much was certain. She measured him with eyes accustomed to the scrutiny of the opposite sex. He was handsome. She thought. I could have done worse. And, oh, that black *SS* uniform made him appear so very manly and romantic. The many multicolored ribbons on his chest, and the iron cross second class in the buttonhole signified he had distinguished himself on the battlefield with uncommon valor and bravery. She promised herself to inquire about the significance of his many medals just as soon as the two of them became more "familiar" with one another.

"Come in and make yourself at home." She was well coached by the matron. "Blanche." She announced her name shyly, almost in a whisper. No surname. That was also one of the rules. Surnames implied a measure of individuality; an identity of sorts. She was, after all, just another piece of the Reich leader's property.

"*Danke.*" He said curtly. "Michael." He, too, spoke his first name. It made it simpler for all concerned. Anyway, the baby would also be the property of the Reich. That was a foregone conclusion, and surnames didn't matter within the larger picture. Aha, there was always that "larger picture" that overshadowed all personal values. Things were arranged in this manner to facilitate a higher historical purpose. Michael kept on chatting enthusiastically with references to irrelevancies regarding his frontline experiences and his great honor to have arrived in this place to meet her. There was definitely something of a mystery in his distinct Slavic accent, but it didn't occur to her to question him about it. After all, neither was "Blanche" of a purely Aryan origin, and her accent left much to be desired. Instead, she made herself useful in helping him unpack his marching bag.

His hand trembled slightly when it inadvertently touched hers, which assured her of his being a novice in this business of unusual sexual practices just as she was.

Fourteen glorious days went by as if in an eyewink. Michael's appetite for carnal enjoyment had no bounds. As the saying went,: *"L'appétit vient en mangeant."* ("The more a man gets the more he craves," translated loosely from the French.) The two "lovers" seldom left the premises of their diminutive but tidy room. Room service was exceptional, food and all. They only ventured outdoors to take long strolls in the surrounding idyllic meadows. Together. For that brief time, they were Blanche and Michael; two carefree people who, to all outward appearances, seemed happy in love.

Michael was recalled to his *Panzer* unit on the Eastern front quite abruptly. No one explained why a month's long furlough was cut in half. No one questioned. There were only rumors of reverses suffered by the "invincible" Reich forces at the hands of that "other inferior" race.

Only late into her pregnancy was Blanche able to ascertain Michael's surname; Waneczeven…Michael Waneczeven… Michael Waneczeven…she kept repeating, as if intoxicated by the sound. They did not disclose his home address or his whereabouts on the battlefield to her. "Absolutely no contact," was the order. By the time the formal notice from the Reich's War Ministry arrived, Blanche was nursing their little boy "Misha" (as she called him), because the name Adolf did not sit well with her. She was cognizant of the many "Adolfs" born at the institution each day.

*"He died a hero of the Reich, in the service of the Führer and the German people, the pride of the Aryan race…"* Said, among other things, the formal note delivered by an officer of the *Waffen SS*. *"Rejoice in his glory, mother of his child, the future of the Thousand Year Reich…"* She was surprised they took the trouble to send the official notice to her, all emblazoned with the Reich's seal of the

eagle clutching a swastika; a rubber stamped name of the great leader beneath the familiar *Heil* Hitler!

Her eyes filled with tears, Blanche was unable to finish reading. All of this was of little interest to the woman nursing an Unknown Soldier's offspring. She had learned not to weep openly. It was un-Aryan to shed tears for a hero. That, too, was a hard and fast rule in the compound. Meekly, she turned to the matron, her questioning eyes beseeching the former: "Could the child have his father's surname, please?" She asked plaintively.

"The people will decide." The matron replied. "For us, it is enough to serve." The woman folded her muscular arms on top of her huge, heaving breasts and shook her head meaningfully. Blanche knew. It was of no use arguing the issue with the matron. Hence, she decided to take matters into her own hands. There were ways to trace the roots of a family, especially in the Reich where all things were so tidily apportioned in demographic documentation and neatly recorded in all town and village registries. There was no need to hire a staff of detectives. She would handle the inquiry herself when she was ready.

Blanche stared at the floor in silence. It was the same stubborn look of defiance she had expressed on different occasions of disagreement, and the matron became suspicious. "You wouldn't try any of your shenanigans, would you, now?" She warned.

"The thought hadn't occurred to me." Blanche replied with the sound of innocence in her voice." The matron turned to go. "I wouldn't if I were you." She said with a threatening tone of voice. "But, at least, could I…" Blanche hesitated… "Could I? Could they? How about his parents?" She blurted out quickly. "After all, they're the child's grandparents."

"A child of the Reich doesn't need them." The matron said. "The Reich will be the child's family." She turned on her heel ready to leave. She stopped at the door without turning her head and said: "Don't even think about it. If you know what I mean." On that decidedly foreboding note she left the premises.

Blanche felt faint. All she could think of was that her child would grow up fatherless. The boy would have a *Fatherland* but not a father.

# Havana, Cuba, 1951

IT HAD SEEMED LIKE ONLY yesterday the newlyweds Carla and Albert Monet had left their native France, running from the Nazi hordes. The twenty-three-year-old civil engineer had barely finished his degree and embarked on a promising career with a renowned Parisian firm. Carla, two years his junior, was a talented violinist, and had a promising future ahead of her at the Paris *L'école des Beaux Arts*. They felt guilty about leaving their elderly parents behind and their many relatives. But the others wouldn't abandon their properties behind and harbored hopes things would not become critical, the allies would help, and the *Boches* would be vanquished. Only Albert insisted the time was ripe to elude disaster.

The American Embassy in Paris was reluctant to broaden the emigration quota. The Monets pleaded for their lives with one of the secretaries in vain. He dismissed their argument that in spite of being Jewish converts to Catholicism they were in imminent danger. It fell on deaf ears. As a last resort only, and with the aid of their local Archbishop, the only country that would issue them a quick visa was Cuba. Even that required the Vatican's intervention. The developing island in the Caribbean was in great need of Albert's professional talent. A fledgling civil engineer, he had joined a prominent architecture firm. His profession became their ticket to lead them out of a crisis. They barely escaped with their lives. Carla was promised a chair with the first violin section when she joined the famed National Symphony Orchestra. The young couple was optimistic about their future. "Where there is life," Carla repeated the old adage in a whisper, boarding the ship at the Marseilles harbor, "there is hope." That was the year 1941, and the Nazis occupied France.

Terrible stories followed the young couple to the New Continent. Stories verified by eyewitness refugees; confirmed by the eternal silence of the victims.

Ten years later, Carla experienced her first pregnancy. Havana has been good to the Monets through all these years. The sponsoring Catholic community accepted the refugees with open arms and generous hearts. Albert enjoyed his prominence as an up and coming civil engineer; Carla's life centered on her work with the ballet company's orchestra.

Toward the sixth month of Carla's pregnancy, Albert's anxiety grew in proportion to his diminutive wife's enormous belly.

"Is it coming?" Awakened from sleep by her discrete moans, he would ask in the middle of the night. "It is not yet the time." She calmed him with her typical stoicism. "Silly man, why would you want to subject the child to this cruel world prematurely?" She smiled. "When the time comes, you'll be the first to know. I promise."

One early Sunday morning, before embarking on their occasional weekend outing to the famed exquisite beach *Santa Maria del Mar*, Carla announced: "It is time. Kicks are more intense. I can feel it coming." She spoke through her labored breathing. "Be a dear and Call Samantha," Carla added, "We will need some help."

Carla had kept an accurate account of her progress. Attached there was a list of names of importance to call in case of an emergency. "When the great moment comes, we will be able to count on any of them." She new Albert needed reassurance. "Will you be a sweetheart and call Dr. Beato?" The moment of truth was there. But as it happened, they had to settle on Samantha, Beato's wife, herself an obstetrician.

"Don't worry, dear," Albert assured his wife through the sound of her labored breathing. "We will manage." He tried to lend his voice a heroic substance, but she knew he would falter at the sight of blood. "Yes, dear, I know you can manage," she humored him. Just then, Samantha rushed in and they were on their way to the clinic.

On the way to the hospital, Samantha cuddled the laboring Carla in her arms, while Albert maneuvered the car through the dense Old Havana traffic. His hands were shaking, and cold sweat trickled down his forehead and stung his eyes mercilessly. There were narrow escapes, as the car wound its way through the narrow medieval streets toward the Municipal Maternity Clinic. "God protects prospective fathers and drunks." Albert muttered under his breath, while the attendants wheeled his wife into the maternity ward. As its doors swung open, he had to let go off Carla's hand. "We'll let you know when you can come in." The attendant consoled the breathless father who nodded his head as a sign of concurrence.

Honestly, he might have tried to stand by during the travails of delivery, but he felt nauseous at the very thought imagining the moment the heavy breathing and "pushing" would begin. Then, the tip of the little head would appear out of its confinement, followed by a wrinkled face, and...the blood-splattered torso...He felt guilty and remorseful at abandoning Carla in time of need. She would forgive him.

After hours of waiting, Samantha came toward him, a broad smile on her face. "It's a girl." she said, "You can see your wife now, Albert."

In his excitement, Albert had forgotten to express his appreciation for all of Samantha's assistance. Anyway, he rationalized that Samantha was far better qualified as a physician to assist in childbirth than he. Now, that the ordeal was over, the little creature was neatly bundled and swabbed clean for her first bonding encounter with the young mom, and he hovered over both of them, able to play the hero again.

"May I?" He asked before taking the little one in his arms.

"Of course, silly." Carla responded with a faint smile on her face, betraying the fatigue due to the travail she had undergone moments before.

"We must think of a name, dear." He said in a whisper. The little one reminded him of no one in particular; the wrinkled face, colorless eyes, and a complete lack of hair were not inducible to the traditional ritual of naming.

"Could we...name her...for my grandmother Alida?" She asked.

"Alida is a beautiful name." He said, grateful for the reprieve she had given him during the pregnancy and delivery.

"I do love you, Albert." She whispered before falling into deep sleep.

"And I love you, my dearest." Albert responded happily. He looked back at their life together with fond memories. The little one's birth was the crowning of their solid relationship. At age thirty-four, he was a successful member of Havana's community and Carla was respected as one of the youngest concertmasters at age thirty-one for her musical contributions to the Symphony's repertory.

But happiness was not to be of long duration for the Monet family. One year following Alida's birth Albert was stricken with what their neighbor Dr. Beato diagnosed as a congenital brain malfunction.

"I'm so sorry, but there is nothing that can be done. Absolutely nothing." The doctor announced.

Carla was beside herself. "Is there no treatment? No medication?" She pressed desperately for an answer.

"He'll have to remain under daily observation at the sanatorium." Virgilio shook his head meaningfully. As a physician, he maintained professional composure. As a close friend, his eyes spoke the many unspoken thoughts of sadness. "At least, for the time being." He quickly added. Carla went into temporary shock, but was brought back quickly into the reality of having to care for the infant Alida.

Albert remained in undetermined condition and under constant vigilance of the attendants. Carla's periodic visits to her husband with the infant Alida in her arms went unacknowledged, for Albert had become increasingly oblivious to their presence with the passage of time. "He's in good physical health," Virgilio consoled the young woman. "And he's not lacking in good care. But he may never come out of the mental vacuum in which we find him at present. Even if he lives to reach a hundred years, and he may well do so, for he's without the least worry over the daily matters that harass and frustrate ordinary people. There is no stress in his condition."

Alida was one year old when Carla had decided to discontinue her visitations in the infant's company. From that day on she rejected her vain hope in Albert's return to her world. Little Alida had become a fatherless child and Carla a single mother. In time, Alida would be informed only "her daddy had tragically died at an early age." Henceforth, she knew her "diseased" father from the continual stories her mother had told her in response to Alida's incessant questioning. "Some day, we'll go for a visit to France where he lay buried." Carla hid her face in her hands, lest she betray her emotions. "And we'll place some fresh flowers on daddy's graveside."

"Yes, Mamá, we must do that," the little one hugged Carla lovingly. "When I become a *prima* with the company, we'll journey there together, won't we?"

"That we shall, my dearest...that we shall." Carla assured her.

Twelve years since Albert's confinement at the institution for the care of mentally ill, and Alida's promise as a dancer soloist with the National Ballet was the only light that shone for Carla through the dark days of failed hope and the sad, solitary, visits to her beloved Albert. The Beatos were sworn to secrecy, lest they reveal Albert's whereabouts to the inquisitive Alida. "Never! Do you hear me? Never must you reveal it to her!" Carla implored.

"You mustn't worry, dear Carla." They assured her. "As physicians, we are sworn never to disclose a patient's privileged information, ever."

Gradually, Carla's daily visits to the hospital had turned into a weekly routine of mute ritual. Though her hair was gradually graying, Albert's hasn't demonstrated the flux of time, clearly an advantage of his condition. She continued in a constant state of depression due to the helplessness of the situation. Her visits severely exacerbated her already frail physical and mental condition. Each time, on entering the establishment, she would pass by rows of patients placed alongside each wall of the hallway. They were sitting in wheelchairs, some dressed in street clothes others in their pajamas and others still dressed in drab hospital robes. Some of them slept, heads hanging limply to one side, others stared at the floor. Then, there were those who fixed their seemingly lifeless eyes on some point in a sensory-deprived daze; among them was Carla's beloved husband Albert.

He was sitting in his wheelchair very stiffly, dressed in his own pajamas and the pastel colored hospital robe. On his naked feet were the slippers Carla had brought him on one of her visits. She marveled at the handsome figure he still cut in spite of the mental void. His was a mute figure, for he did not react to her chatter and inquiries nor did he betray the slightest degree of emotion at her sight. She kissed him on both cheeks and caressed his lush wavy hair, still unencumbered by time's tell-tale grey, while whispering endearments into his ear, never relinquishing her hope that he might suddenly awaken from his utter stupor. Weather permitting she would roll him out into the yard for a stroll, and she would chat incessantly about daily occurrences, more to herself than to his seemingly deaf ears. On her visits, she would inevitably end up in tears, as the orderly took charge of the wheelchair following her unilateral farewells with her husband. It had gotten so she dreaded her return visit to more of the same, a nightmarish recurrence of her experiences. Still, she was not one to give up, in the hope that one of her visits might trigger some mysterious nerve cells (she had heard Virgilio mention the term "neurons") in that lifeless brain of a husband whom she refused stubbornly to give up for dead.

# Urbana-Champaign, Illinois, 1966

MISHA WAS IN HIS FIRST YEAR of a three-year post-doc-toral teaching fellowship. On indefinite leave from the University of Stuttgart, the twenty-five year old Ph.D. basked in the attention he was getting from the staff and students alike on the main campus of the University of Illinois. He had arrived in the US driven from Germany by, what had seemed to him, the will to distance himself from a long streak of bad luck.

He was somewhat of an oddity in his new environment. He had applied to several premier American institutions of higher learning to continue his work on the contributions of German intellectual émigrés from Hitler's Reich to the American culture and was offered positions in all of them. His selection of this university was based solely on the opportunity to work under the guidance of the renowned Professor Hans Bohmer, world-class literary critic and teacher, a native of Stuttgart, himself part of the émigré generation from the 1930's Third Reich.

During the fall semester, Misha's assignment was to teach a first year seminar on "European Politics during the 1930's and the Novel." Works such as Kafka's *"The Trial,"* Dostoyevsky's *"Crime and Punishment,"* Koestler's *"Darkness at Noon,"* and Hemingway's *"For Whom the Bell Tolls,"* expressing the strug-gle of individuals mutilated by their environment all fit nicely into the sixties *Zeitgeist* (He was unable to translate the German expression other than by saying, well, it means "spirit of the age"). Student response was a resounding success. Not only was the campus abuzz with Misha's background as a *Lebensborn* of the

Third Reich (Himmler's "fountain of life program" of pure Aryan blood); the ash-blond, blue-eyed German was the topic of conversation of much of the campus population. He was perceived, by turn, a gentleman, a rogue, and unexpectedly insecure in his boyish, childlike appearance. This was, perhaps, simultaneously appealing to women's sense of motherhood and the promise of adventure. Hence, it was more out of curiosity for the person than for the appeal of the novel that most of the students—predominantly of the female gender—enrolled in his class offerings.

The staff apartment he occupied, called the Goodwin Place, was modest but not lacking in comfort and necessities. It was there, too, that he met José Pamies, a Cuban native and professor of Spanish literature. The only bachelors in the complex, Joe and Misha struck up a cordial friendship. Neither of the two understood the American female sufficiently to build an interest in that direction. They placed a temporary hold on romantic liaisons in favor of cultural pursuits; musical evenings, poetry readings, visits to the museums, and a particular dedication to their work at hand. They held in small esteem the likes of poets of contemporary renown, such as Jack Kerouac, William Burroughs, and Allen Ginsberg, the so-called *Rat Packers,* in their passionate attempt to remove themselves from American faddism and its transitory nature.

Misha was amused at the amount of attention he'd received since his arrival on campus. He was not one to take advantage, basking in the transitory societal shallowness. He remembered how hard his mother had worked to get him through the *Realgymnasium* and, later on, the University of Stuttgart. Growing up without a father during his early formative years was hard enough. But when his mother married Dr. Horst Schweinfurt, a forensic pathologist and the city's medical examiner, life for young Misha had become almost intolerable.

The doctor was as meticulous in the home as he was over the dissecting table at the city morgue. The least infraction of his

strict house rules was met with severe punishment. Misha's cor-
poreal bruises healed much faster than those of his psyche. The
latter, he would carry late into his adult life.

*Herr Doktor*, as he addressed his stepfather, was quick tempered, frequently drunk on his return from work, and his notion
of parental responsibility was to either ignore his stepson or brow-
beat and humiliate him. "You're the bastard son of your mother!"
The doctor often shouted in his drunken rage. "I'll have you both
on the street, if you don't settle down!"

In time, Misha resisted his stepfather's insults through sheer
stubbornness and an unwillingness to submit to Dr. Horst's tyrannical behavior. Blanche meekly defended her son and, oftentimes,
placed herself between the two antagonists to absorb the blows
intended for her son. Husband and wife quarreled frequently.
Whenever Dr. Horst returned home drunk, young Misha hid in
the darkest corner of the house where he listened trembling to
the raging, drunken man's maltreatment of his mother. When
the infuriated husband slammed the door behind him as he left
the premises, Misha joined his bruised and spiritually devastated
mom in her bedroom. She pulled him into bed with her, pressing
his unclad body to hers, lavishing kisses on the boy as if he were
her pliant lover.

Such behavior on her part—her submissiveness to her husband's cruel and unusual treatment and the absence of effective
resistance in the defense of her son—met with Misha's contempt
and outrage directed at his mother. Nevertheless, he had accepted
those few pleasant moments in her warm embrace, which he
considered a reward for the affection he gave her in return. On
her part, Blanche rationalized her husband's sins as an excuse
to allow her the occasional sensual aberrations with Misha—
Michael—to probe each other's private parts in a never-ending
fantasy of desire.

On the frequent occasions of Dr. Horst's drunkenness,
Misha's posterior was covered with black and blue bruises. *Her*

*Doktor* meted out punishment with the pathologist's precision so that its traces would quickly evade visibility to the eye. In the privacy of her bedroom, Blanche applied warm compresses to the hurt, never missing an opportunity to caress or kiss away the pain with a passion suppressed during those many years of denial and longing.

Misha did not complain, but his anger grew and turned to a shared hatred of both the sadistic stepfather and his submissive mother. His school performance showed evidence of neglect as his grades suffered, and it was not because of lack of intelligence or ability to learn. His classmates avoided him, called him "bastard" behind his back and made derisive remarks out of his earshot, though he tried to appear friendly in spite of their antagonism. Early on, he was better able to make friends with boys rather than girls. He felt awkward in the company of the opposite sex and embarrassed whenever one of the female classmates tried to start up a conversation.

By the time Misha had reached the *Oberprima*—graduating class—Blanche felt it necessary to reveal to him his unique background. She was deeply troubled and at a loss for explanations. To her great surprise, Misha was the one to broach the topic before she uttered her first sentence.

"I know, mamá, I'm a product of the *Lebensborn* program." He paused. "In the people's eyes, you're nothing but a whore, a brood sow, one of those volunteers who had produced bastards for the Reich, and I am one of those little Adolfs." Misha was out of breath, his eyes unable to meet his mother's tear filled inquiry.

"B...b...but..." She stammered for the first time in as long as he was able to recall. "How did you...?"

"How did I know?" He looked away. "Everybody knows and talks about me, but you and I never do."

"It must be Dr. Horst!" She exclaimed.

"Probably, mamá," Misha assured her. "Likely he talks when he gets drunk down at the *Bier Keller*. You can leave the rest to the town's people." She wept softly. "You don't have to cry, mamá. I'm not ashamed of it. After all, the *Führer* left thousands of us around. Only some didn't have the good fortune to get reunited even with their mothers, like we did. We were lucky, mamá."

She held him to her breast. "Yes, my darling, we can count ourselves among the fortunate. We have each other." She kissed him on the lips. It was a pleasant feeling. Certain warmth pervaded his entire being, and he was unable to explain its source. They lay still, pressed against each other in a strong embrace.

"Was it not pleasant, my darling?" She asked.

"Oh, that it was mamá. That it was, indeed." He whispered, as if afraid someone could overhear. "But...what if...?"

"Hush, now, my darling." She admonished. "Would you rather have someone else show you...? It's all right, my dear. It's all right." She assured him.

They slept that night in a tight embrace till the morning sun entered through the curtains. She woke him with a kiss on his lips. "You had better leave before he returns." She said.

"Once a lewd woman, always a lewd woman." He thought silently, getting dressed. "Hitler's whore." He threw mental insults at his mother. What's she afraid of? She can't be worse off than she is already. "Stand up to the horrible drunk." Misha's silent sarcasm was bitter. Not at all as clever as he'd have liked it to be, like his girlfriend Susanna's, for instance. But even though her conversation could be stimulating at times, in a way, he'd occasionally get tired of it. His conscience reminded him that he was a hypocrite just trying to be someone else. It was no good. He disliked putting on an act. He knew he was a victim of her manipulations. And he fell hopelessly in love the more she refused him, for such was her designing nature.

Blanche regarded her son with a mother's concern and a lover's hunger. She was still very much hung up. And going to bed with more than one man didn't prove she could cope. As far as sex was concerned, she would say anything and do anything that would shock, to prove she could do it with no qualms. But all things considered, she was still very uptight. Anyone trying to talk sex with her, she'd drop her teeth and be very slow about collecting them. In her attempt to remedy the situation, she could be quite Victorian at times. It was obvious why. It carried back to her mother. Ever since "those days"—she never mentioned them by name, though everyone was aware she referred to the Hitler days—she never quite forgave her. Blanche always rebelled against her mother and the constant innuendoes. But she'd be the first to defend her and agree with her. That's why she'd have to be so very careful about her own activities. She was quite judgmental, and more severe toward herself than others would ever be.

Blanche was part of her mother's ideal little dream, a dream of a pure, innocent, beautiful life. She could pretend it was still there, and only she had taken the wrong road. Now, that Blanche could not practice what her mother preached, she questioned it. Dear mamá. She must have had a terrible guilt complex. It was killing her to know she was unable to steer her innocent little girl in the *right* path.

Misha looked at his mother with guarded compassion. To him, even long after her death, as he remembered her, he knew full well that matters pertaining to her son's welfare were of utmost importance, almost sacred. Society's malicious interference in their lives made him sick. What right did they have to ruin people's lives in spreading vicious gossip? Well, he thought, it'll never have that warped pleasure with him. Mother would be so pleased to know that she'd succeeded in doing what other women had failed time and again. That alone would justify her own existence. It's not everyone who can make life a living hell for someone else, all in the name of righteousness and goodness, of course. It had just occurred to him that his mother was one of the best examples of a good Christian or Jew or Muslim, you name it, after what she'd just done for him. And it made him wonder why there was any claim to the expressions "good Christian" or "good Jew" or "good Muslim" as a benevolent concept. Poor mamá will now be stuck with the dual role of both martyr and shrew. He wondered if she'd be able to play them both like a pro. As for himself, would he be able some day to bowdlerize his psyche as he would an offensive literary passage? Only time would tell.

# 1.

AS A SMALL BOY, Misha had a vague picture of his biological father. It was only when his mother had come to claim him at the orphanage at age seven did he dare to begin probing, trying to bring the picture into focus. At first, there were evasive answers: "Your father fell at Stalingrad." Or, "There is no record of your father's whereabouts." But as time went on, and the boy's inquisitiveness had turned into a teen's challenge, partial clues had begun to emerge, reluctantly at first, but soon more spontaneous, candid.

She was unable to gather some courage and say: "As you well know, you are a product of the *Lebensborn* program, *mon chèr.*"— Blanche chose to intersperse some French phrases whenever nostalgia took hold or she felt a sudden intensity of hatred for all that was German welling up inside her.—she only said: "There are no records available regarding your father's roots or, at least, a gravesite we could visit. God knows, I've tried to trace his beginnings, especially since the time I had found you, but I've run up against a bureaucratic vacuum."

Misha did not understand what she meant by that expression, even though she quickly added: "I've hit a stone wall, Misha. I've run against a stone wall." The mystery only increased his determination to find himself in his father. "I swear mamá! I will not rest until I know who I am!" He was a young adult of fifteen when he had made that promise. Since then, he was only exposed to rumors.

Landsberg was a small town, and news got around very fast of their arrival. At school or social functions usually attended by both parents, only Blanche accompanied her young escort. She never left his side, and it got so that girls avoided coming near him for fear they'd experience his mother's rejection. Still, the handsome, tall Misha was the envy of his male classmates. They marveled at his popularity with the girls on the one hand, but were astonished on the other at his refusal to succumb to their persistent advances. Only during socials, did the reason become obvious. Blanche was relentless in her obsession with Misha's "safety" and would not leave any of his social contacts to chance.

"I think I'll hate your past with all my heart for as long as I shall live," Misha once told Blanche during their private moments.

"I feared you would, my darling," she stroked his hair gently. "They were circumstances I could not alter." She paused with a deep sigh and then went on. "My past is neither yours to hate nor to live by. It is not your enemy. It is mine. Despise your enemies, but do not hate them. Hate lends them undeserved dignity while it wastes yours as well as precious energy that can be more profitably spent."

"Mamá, don't tell me you don't hate *them* for what *they*'ve done to you..." He paused. "And to me." He added quickly, as if in afterthought.

"I used to hate them very much, darling, but that was before I'd found you." He kissed her cheek, and he felt the saltines of her tears. "Finding you has given me reason to live. It taught me love."

"I'm not the image of Jesus, mamá." He said with sadness in his voice. "I can't bring myself to love my enemy."

"Trust me, my dear boy, and avoid those who would draw you into their circle of half truths. They're all liars. They'll do anything to attain their goals." She reflected gently. "I am deeply convinced that you are going to benefit from my words, dearest Misha." She looked at him with that unique gaze only a mother can grant her son. "I hope this will help you understand whatever manifests itself to you in the years to come." She paused for breath expecting his immediate reaction. But he was silent, more out of pity for the dying than respect, and she added: "Long after I'm gone, my dear; long after I'm gone." She repeated and he regarded her with puzzlement in his eyes.

"I'll try to remember, mamá. I promise I'll try." He enfolded her in his arms.

"A person desperately in love is soon devoid of a meaningful existence," she added. He nodded without enthusiasm. "You must remain focused and put things in their proper perspective between your tough current reality and a shining life that will open up to you in your future endeavors."

"Difficult." He murmured as if to himself.

"Enemies are useful." She went on. "Appreciate them for what they show you to avoid." Mother and son spoke in the dark of the night often, and their passions rose for the things denied them in real life. Now and then, she would disengage herself from his embrace and spoke with a feverish impulse, as if she felt the imminent end approaching that will silence her. "I have always known you will leave a beneficial imprint, a luminous trail of enjoyment in the space-time continuum of your life. And by improbable chance you shall touch deeply the lives of those who will cross paths with you."

"Incredible." He whispered under his breath again.

She would bring her hand up to his face, to caress, to pass her soft fingers over the ridge above the eyes to push the hair away. He felt headachy and feverish, but her gesture had a soothing and tranquilizing effect on him. It would be hard for him to replace those precious moments. Later, much later in his meanderings, he'd experience a strange longing that for lack of another expression he would call homesickness. And he had hated the thought of it as he had hated the dark side of his heart.

He knew full well that in every life there are some regrets concerning the choices we must take. Or, even if you don't truly regret those choices, you ask yourself if your life would have been happier if you had taken a different road at the proverbial multiple forks. And he expected a number of emotional relationships to come and go during his prime, and some won't even happen because the burdens of everyday life outweigh the impulses of the heart. What will he do when he finds himself face-to-face with a hope of love that he had thought was lost or impossible to achieve? Will he be able to develop a lasting affection based on true feelings that challenge the test of time? He glanced at Blanche, and his face expressed doubt.

He knew, too, that every person had a dark side. He would always argue that point. You can see it in their faces. He would gaze into the mirror; hold one hand over one half of his face, and then the other. Which side was the harder? He tried to determine. Which one is the colder, the softer?

That other side keeps most people safe from themselves because most people don't listen to their hearts anyway. It's the heart that gets you in trouble, they know. Because a heart's like a woman—in the end, it rules. It's the dark side of your brain that makes you think the evil things. But it's also the dark side of your heart that makes you love them.

He believed what his mom had been telling him. He believed that the night was a dark time. In a way it was true. Things happened in the dark that couldn't happen while the sun shone brightly. He believed there were dark places. His birthplace was like that. Hildesheim was such a place. You'd have never heard of it, if you hadn't been there yourself. But if you had been there, you'd have felt it. You couldn't quite know the name for what it was you felt, but it was the darkness. A chilling darkness in your heart.

They had told him he was born in that small town. He believed them, never having seen his birth certificate, if there ever was one. The time of his birth he made up himself, because the exact time would cast his horoscope.

The woman who had given birth to him was just another girl whom the system had fashioned into a common whore. His wasn't an ordinary birth in an ordinary hospital. His was an anonymous one, without fanfare, without love. An antiseptic kind of birth. It might just as well smelled of sewage and excretion, of vomit and garbage—of all the discarded things.

Misha had come to that place later in search of his past, when he'd found the names of the old man and hers, his wife. He came to the big dark house that stood like a tomb under the huge poplar trees. The poplars Napoleon had planted one hundred plus years ago to trace his Eastward expedition in his intended conquest of the Tsars. The old man looked at Misha with suspicion, but there was blood between them, he had told him. The old man denied knowing the whore, who bore Misha; else he would have paid the price for his son's pleasure. So he told him. He only knew that his son was Misha's father.

"You were an unwanted child," the old man spoke haltingly; "You had no blood family that wanted you." Misha wept quietly. "You shouldn't ought to cry," the old man went on. Tears were strange to the young man. And he was now certain that no one would be able to do his life-chart right—calculate everything from noon—only by assumption, all these things about himself he'd never really know for sure.

Had it not been for Blanche, Misha might have remained ignorant and coarse. She was the one who cared. The others petted him sometimes like you pet a dog. He had never confessed his dreams to anyone. There were too many people around, always other people, and he felt like that he wasn't in the room. They smiled slowly and laughed softly and smelled strong and sweet. And they were all afraid of each other. Sometimes he thought the strong, sweet smell on them was their fear.

He loved his mother with a pain like a fist in his heart. All that fear and wanting and loving and hating wrapped up tight in a knot so he couldn't tell it apart anymore. He knew, from the love he experienced, how he hated, too. And he hated himself for loving her—like a dog, lapping at her feet—and he promised himself time and again never, never to touch her again bodily. Because he wanted to do it so much.

Misha looked forward to his mother's death. She would sweat her life away on a high, hard, narrow bed in some dark corner bedroom. After that, he would find peace. He'd go to the cemetery to bury her, which was like a little toy city—row after row of little toy houses, white cement houses just like the one he used to live in. And he'd hoped that the darkness would fade from his heart.

# 2.

FRAIL AND SICKLY from the frequent beatings and bouts of depression, Blanche died a year after Misha's graduation from the university. He was glad she had lived to see him receive his teaching diploma, which she had held to her breast even as the priest was giving her the last sacraments. "She died happy." The priest remarked on leaving the premises. "What nonsense! Only a fool's credo." Misha thought. "Whoever dies 'happy'?"

The funeral was a modest affair. She was put to rest in a remote corner plot, away from the "righteous" people. He could have returned home from the burial in a big black Mercedes Benz the funeral director provided. But he hated that symbol of his mother's past—and of the manufacture of cost-effective concentration camp crematories—and preferred to walk. They were all milling around the room, talking, and there was Dr. Horst's face conveying his profound and pious grief, accepting condolences. All those people seemed to have known his mother, yet in her lifetime Blanche had no friends.

"Misha...Misha...we must talk." Dr. Horst addressed him.

"Talk? We must talk about what? What's there to talk about, *Herr Doktor?*" Misha asked. His tone of voice was unforgiving.

"About your future, my boy." The doctor replied, smiling.

"It's my future." Misha responded obstinately. "I'm old enough to plan it for myself."

Misha had been feeling sick and hateful for days during the decline of his mother's health. He watched her die, fast but too slowly, sweat and energy poured out of her relentlessly, until she was just wet sheets and bones. The sweet stink of the house was symptomatic of her dying and of his fear. Where was *Herr Doktor* Horst all that time while she had been turning into a shadow? He hid the whole time in his taverns and whorehouses. And when he'd return home drunk, he wouldn't climb up the staircase and visit her room. Occasionally, when Misha walked past him as he sat in the big, dark living room, *Herr Doktor* would ask: "How's she doing?"

"She's dying," Misha would say. "Why don't you go upstairs and see for yourself. You're a doctor, aren't you?"

The doctor just shrunk into his easy chair and kept repeating after Misha: "She just keeps on dying...keeps on dying."

But when Misha walked back into the house after the funeral, down the hall into that house that always seemed to go farther back than he'd believe, he could feel the doctor's foul breath on him; his bulging eyes pinned to the step-son's face. It was as if he were to feel his hands imminently, touching his innards. And Misha was no longer afraid of that man he'd call *Herr Doktor* though he now spat contemptuously on his title. Misha felt something else; he felt growing strong, and he knew that now *he* was the one whom the good doctor watched and feared. That sweet stink of fear was for him.

"Just don't you ever touch me again," Misha made a threatening gesture toward the doctor. "We talked. She warned me before she left. I know what my rights are. Don't you ever!"

Misha heard Dr. Horst's spasmodic breath catch once... twice. There was something awful about hearing someone gasp for breath; something too close about it. Misha kept on walking, until he put the place behind. When he looked back, it was all gone; the house, the stench, the doctor, the liquor and the whores. Only the memories remained.

That was the way Misha was growing up. He had always derived strength from adversity, hating those who needed hating without once revealing his thoughts.

"There's something wrong with you, Misha." He recalled Dr. Horst saying after the funeral. "Everyone needs to be loved."

"Not I." Misha answered, and the old man saw in his obstinate smile and the sarcastic gleam in his eyes that he relished the opportunity to make the statement. Indeed, Misha loved to stand close to the aging man, smell the fear rising off him like smoke or incense. Misha relished letting Horst—that was now the way he addressed his step-father—smell the no-fear on him from close proximity. The old man knew he loved the evil in it, and it made the old man love and fear him more, as if to make up for lost time and wanton abuse.

"You watch out for Horst and people like him," Blanche had warned him before her final sigh, as she looked at him for the last time, before closing her eyes forever. "The doctor has a sinister heart. He loves what he doesn't have, and he envies those who have it. Watch out for him and the likes of him, they'll try to take it from you."

"Take what?" Misha asked. "What is it you're talking about, Mamá?"

"He'll want to break your will, Misha." She whispered almost inaudibly. "He'll want to see you broken in spirit...spirit..." With an ear to her lips, her last words would remain indelibly in Misha's thoughts. "...And no matter what happens you'll give no one the power to hurt you..."

"Not a chance, Mamá." Misha assured the dying woman. "I know it all too well. And I feel it. I feel it as firm as the bones under my skin." He stood very still now and felt his strength. He knew she had given it to him. Blanche had taught him life's substance, the dos and don'ts through example. She gave him all she possessed and more. Her fingers stiffened in his. It had all suddenly come to him in one brief moment of introspection. "Mamá!" He exclaimed. "Mamá!" He squeezed her lifeless hand. "I love..." It wasn't meant for her to hear his declaration of love;

that precious word she had always hoped to elicit from his lips but never succeeded.

He let go off her hand. Years of living with her passed through his thoughts. Their secret get-togethers, early mornings when the dust danced, trapped in the bright sunlight, which burst through the window shutters. Those nights spent in her arms, blood thundering through his veins, and her loving eyes always on him, feeding him, making him strong. Then, there was the awareness, the transcendence of time. It came like a silver flash of a razor sharp knife with a faint feeling of helplessness that started in his stomach and traveled down to his testicles and made him groan with unspeakable pain. He was resolute. He would walk the wire, for he knew there would be those who would wait for him to fall. Wait to see him ridden, like all of the others; wait to see darkness overwhelm him.

He would be in control. Love it. Use it. Grow stronger with each passing moment. He would not allow darkness to subdue him; he owned it. Others would love him for that. And he would love no one.

# 3.

MUCH AS HE HAD TRIED, Misha was unable to bring himself to thoughts of mourning. Blanche was dead, period. He was done with that segment of his existence. He could no longer think of her as "mother." The central issue now was to find the man who was his "father." Or, was it? He was confused. He questioned his motives while waking and deep into the sleepless nights. Why should he care about that part of his life? After all, no one went searching after him. Was it a passion that consumed him temporarily? To be let go when things are done? When he'd find that missing link to his past, if only to rip his soul apart from its dependency? Was it worth the risk he was taking? So many unanswered questions cluttered up his mind. Ulysses must have been torn by similar thoughts before embarking on his perilous journey.

Misha's search had begun. In his mind at first, then, after painful reflection, he ventured forward. There were so many departments with which to start his inquiry that they threatened to overwhelm him at first. How does one follow the traces of a mysterious *SS Panzergruppenführer* (Tank unit leader) with the name of Michael Waneczeven, who was a native of Poland who had served in Hitler's elite ranks? With no photos to identify, no records of reference, no place of birth, the quest seemed doomed before it had begun. He would search one department at a time.

"I'm going with you," Susanna insisted. They've been together since Blanche's death, with no one there to interfere in their relationship. Dear Susanna had to put up with awesome odds while

Blanche was still alive. "This woman will betray you." Blanche hissed into Misha's ear, while she hugged the youth. "She's no good." His mother's warnings rang vividly through his memory, but failed to touch his conscience.

"This one is a solo act, honey." He said with determination. Give me space.

"*Einsatzgruppe II*," (Special Action Groups—euphemism for *killing squad*—) the archives clerk at the Federal Authority for SS Research and Identification in Bonn placed a heavy box of documents before him, "this is where you'll most likely retrace the activities of your subject." He said without emotion.

"Huh?" Misha was puzzled.

"There were four *Einsatzgruppen* in the territory of the General Government. That's the one that had the largest contingent of *Volksdeutsche*." (It was the English equivalent of "National Germans," which comprised "inferior" nationalities seeking to serve the Nazi "master race.")

*Aktion Majdanek*, Misha read the title of the top file. The clerk looked over his shoulder and said "uh-oh?" His voice stumbled between syllables, and it sounded like an indrawn breath or a hiccup. All the while, Misha had hoped for some photographs that might be found inside the binder.

Misha turned to look behind. The man's eyes stared at him. "Uh-oh, I think you ought to try the next file." He suggested in a hushed voice. "You did say the subject was a casualty at Stalingrad. Didn't you?"

"I did." Misha sounded annoyed. "What's that got to do with my search?" He took exception to his anonymous father being called a "subject."

"Simple." The elderly clerk shrugged his shoulders. "That's where *they* usually ended up."

"By *they* you mean the *Volksdeutsche*?"

"Exactly. That's what I mean." It was now the clerk's turn to show a degree of irritation. "If you don't want my suggestions, just say so."

"Sorry," Misha hesitated, and then he pulled the next file from the box. "Is it this one?" The file read: *Aktion Sobibor.*

"Yes...yes...that's the one." The man walked back to his desk. Only now, while examining the files, Misha had realized the magnitude of the task before him. Where does he start? Which is the beginning, the middle, and which is the end? He had done serious research before, in the course of his academic pursuits, but this looked now as sheer detective work. Was he cut out for it? He'd soon find out. Several hours later he felt like he was ready to venture out "into the field," as he would say.

He placed the files on the clerk's desk and readied to leave for now. He'd be back later. But before he'd left the premises, the clerk motioned Misha to approach. "Young man," he started, and his manner was markedly friendlier than when they'd initially met. The old man even managed a faint smile of confidence. "Just thought you ought to know." The man paused, carefully studying Misha's face, as if to enjoy the effect his sudden change of manner affected.

"Know what?"

"Well, these files have been opened before," the clerk continued, his voice dropping to a whisper again. He looked over his shoulder, as if in fear of being spied on or overheard. "And ransacked." He added in a whisper.

"Well? Go on...go on!" Misha urged, while his impatience grew.

"Another person...persons..." The man hesitated again.

"Who might they be?" Misha urged, desperate for a clue, any clue, for he had noticed that many of the personal details describing the "subject" had either been extracted from the file or inked over to become illegible. What was most significant was the absence of photos in a file of such personal detailed and intimate file.

"Who were these persons?" Misha pressed for answers. "And why there are so many pages with an absence of photos that obviously have been extracted from all of those blank spaces."

"Can't tell," the clerk hesitated, "can't tell who was the one, maybe a man, maybe a woman…" he paused briefly, touching his knuckles to his forehead, as if trying to evoke some deeply hidden memories.

"Now, that's not very helpful," Misha controlled his tone of voice, afraid his anger was showing. His disappointment was obvious. The clerk's ambiguities intended or not confounded him. He felt anger push its way up to his consciousness from which he had locked it away. Ordinarily, Misha was timid when dealing with bureaucrats, yet focused always of his desired goals and his helplessness without their services. He was fully aware of their power to obstruct due process. He tried usually to hold his tongue, to smile, not to antagonize, lest he drive them even further in their inherent arrogance. He remembered the lessons of the past. The *system* demanded respect and servitude.

He looked at the clerk with a burning intensity, and he weighed his response on a delicate scale. "Well, then, we don't really know, huh?"

"To be sure…to be sure…" the clerk repeated, "only, when you've found who you're looking for, be sure to look up the birthplace. First, the place he came from, then, and only then, go to the places where he had gone. Every person leaves tracks. It just takes a good tracker to follow them." A rather loud "harrumph" followed by the laconic *"guten Tag,"* were indicative of the meeting's end.

"So there is, after all, a human side to the wooden automaton." Misha whispered to himself. "I appreciate your candor and your help." He thanked the clerk, and added the abbreviated greeting, *"'Tag."* As he was leaving the premises, he almost bowed, as was the erstwhile custom.

# 4.

SHE HAD LUSTROUS BROWN eyes with a tinge of gold in the corners and softly freckled cheeks, and she wore her chestnut brown hair short. You would expect her oval face to be sunbrowned due to the native climate of the Gulf island. Yet it was pale and in stark contrast to the hue of her eyes and her lustrous hair. The present haircut, she was quick to explain when reproached about the disappearance of her once shoulder length tresses, facilitated movement in her pursuit of becoming a great ballerina. Indeed, at age fourteen a soloist with the renowned Cuban Ballet Company, Alida had come a long way. Her career at that point looked most promising, having been singled out to perform parts seldom entrusted to dancers of her tender age.

Carla beamed from ear to ear, while watching her daughter perform *jettés*, pirouettes, and assorted combinations of steps on stage. She was her daughter's constant companion; classes with the ballet master; rehearsals with the corps de ballet as well as the soloists. Early morning piano lessons were mandatory. Carla projected her personal ambition into that of her daughter's with the self-effacement of a saint. It was of no surprise then, that the applause and praise showered on Alida was gratefully received by her mother.

"Oh! My darling! If only your father were here!" Carla often exclaimed. "He would be so proud of you!"

"I'm sure, he's watching over us, wherever he is." Alida assured her mother, while the other avoided her daughter's inquisitive eyes. It was a painful charade she played, and Carla's conscience was heavy with the collected guilt of years during which the initial lie had grown into a monstrous spiritual burden. She was going to tell the little one the truth some day. When this "some day" would come she couldn't tell. But this was not the proper time; a time of development and learning; a time when everything was going so well for the two of them.

Carla's visits to the institution of Albert's confinement continued through the years unabated. It was always during Alida's ballet activities that she was able to get away to be with her beloved Albert. Only he was never with her. He would sit opposite Carla, stiffly, his inanimate eyes staring into the void, while she spoke softly, endearingly, occasionally touching his cold hand. She had maintained her activities in the belief that what was helpful in the cases of prolonged coma patients would also work for her Albert.

She never gave up hope that one day her Albert would suddenly awaken, like one who had suffered a comma, smile at her, take her in his arms as in the past, and whisper: "I love you, my dearest." She saw it happen in her dreams, in her daily musings. But it hasn't happened in the real world. Meanwhile, Albert looked fit, not a gray hair on his scalp, while Carla's brown tresses had been gradually transformed into the salt and pepper kind. His skin retained the healthy glow of the thirty-four year old, while hers had shown the wear of years and worry.

Over the years, suitors knocked at the Monet household to invite her out. But Carla was true to her one and only love Albert. At one time, during a masters golf tournament, a prominent US golfer was entertained at the social club. He was attracted to the pretty, intelligent, Carla who happened to be present with one of her lady friends who was a club member. The pro approached and asked Carla to be his date. He was surprised at being rejected.

"Mamá, why don't you go out with men and have some fun?" Alida asked on many occasions. She did not understand why her mother would remain a widow in spite of her beauty, intelligence, and availability.

"Not yet, my darling," Carla responded, "it's still too early."

"But it's been years since papa died." Alida insisted. "I won't mind if you do, really, he wouldn't mind either, Mamá, I wish you would get on with your life."

At moments like those, Carla wrestled with her conscience. But she was unable to garner the necessary strength to deal with the truth. Back in her room, she buried her face in her pillow and sobbed bitterly. Fate had dealt her from the bottom of the deck for the second time in her young life. It was easier to deal with it when Albert was there with support during those difficult times of the war. In her present conflict, she was alone with a child, no one to turn to for counsel, burdened with this terrible secret and afraid it may somehow surface and be revealed to Alida before the time was ripe. Would the little one forgive her for the years of deception?

How long will it be before Alida realized her mother's subterfuge? After all, the last thing Carla wanted was to affect negatively the relationship with her precious daughter. Lying had never been Carla's strong side. It was especially painful when all she had desired was to be always up front with her child, an example of sincerity with the only person in her life that mattered. The person whose role model she was.

"Albert, my beloved," Carla spoke into her husband's deaf ears. "What shall I do?" She squeezed both his cold hands, while looking lovingly at the perennial, imbecilic smile on his face. "What shall I do?" She repeated. Even the tears that rolled down her cheeks made no impression on her Albert. "I cannot abandon you, and I cannot reveal our secret to her." Carla wept softly, while glancing over her shoulder, lest someone sees her emotional outbreak. "If you intend to respond, now is the time, my dearest." She spoke into thin air. His bright smile, the shiny, black hair combed back as always, the handsome face before her, it was all there but for the realities of life. At moments like these, Carla implored the good Lord desperately in blessed memory of her martyred parents for help. But help was nowhere near. Evidently, she reasoned that she would have to wait a while longer. Perhaps…perhaps time would reveal the way, as it always did in the past.

"Why don't you have some fun, Mamá?" Alida's persistent question woke Carla from her reverie.

"Yes, my child, I'll try." She said, to mollify Alida's anxiety and concern.

"You'll have to do more than just try, Mamá. Besides, I'm no longer a child, so don't treat me as such." Alida replied with the assurance of an adolescent conscious of her own direction. It put fear into Carla's heart. It was the fear of every parent cognizant of the changes in the psyche of their maturing children. No wonder then that her worries grew proportionately to Alida's mental and physical growth. They grew in number with the flux of time, as there was the ever-present, unresolved issue of the absent father. She contemplated how a sudden awareness of reality might affect Alida's presently cheerful personality; what with the continuous tension and distance between the memory of her father and herself, and the shadow of doubt it might throw at mother-daughter relationship? Up until even a year ago, at thirteen, Alida's self-confidence and uncommon maturity have been exemplary. The occasional child demanded her mother's undivided attention, and only Carla was able to understand her every wish in silence. Whenever their eyes met, Alida's radiated an inner peace. Carla knew then that for as long as they'd remain part of each other's lives she wouldn't mind if they'd become occasionally separated. The thought that her concealment of reality might breach Alida's absolute trust for her mother and cause irreparable damage to their relationship had given her great concern and alarm.

Her wavering and recurring conscience bites caused Carla immeasurable pain, despite all of her rationalizations. And each time she was near to confessing the truth, Carla took refuge in her primary conclusion: He was a good father. He loved Alida like no one else will be capable to love her. He shall live in her memory through the power of Carla's narratives, those beautiful imaginary tales. Now he was gone from her for an indefinite time, and no one should dare take the place and role of a loving father away from his daughter. Carla found herself wishing at times that Alida might have sprung from her forehead, like some mythological goddess. They'd both be happier and without ties. People seem always happy when they have no obligations to face. Only now, Carla seemed to want the impossible; to share this lovely creature with the only man, albeit absent, who could bring them both happiness.

Until that wished for day would come, Carla was certain she could fulfill all of Alida's needs. But if that were so, then why did the little one urge her to find another? She was puzzled. Why did Alida long for her father, talk about him so often? It troubled Carla's heart when she saw this happen, and she remained alert to every nuance of Alida's mood. She saw herself guessing at every interplay between her and her precious child/woman. Was her "baby" more aware of the situation than she had let on? Was each trying to fool the other?

"Dance on, my darling," she'd often say, "and be not concerned about the worldly happenings that cannot be changed." She lacked the courage to engage in another sortie of unanswerable questions.

Albert was her one and only friend. Their offspring Alida had affected an even closer bond between them. But now, she felt it choke and strangle her when, in her recurring doubts, she began to question her persistent celibacy. She kicked against these thoughts and resisted all she could. But there was also a suppressed anger that kept rising inside against the gross injustice of it all. Resentment throttled reason. She could see no way to free herself from him, nor did she want it. They were locked together by the small sweet creature that was Alida. Their hearts beat in unison inside their beloved daughter.

Carla had always loved Albert. Always. Since they were teens. She was certain that his love for her carried an equal intensity. Why? Because even though he had gradually drifted away in his eternal stupor, she kept falling in love with pieces of him all over again, each day, as she watched Alida grow into a beautiful woman.

She was fearful that the love that shone brightly through her eyes burned as much for Albert as it did for Alida. That, too, frightened Carla.

It had begun on that day when they took Albert away, and Carla still cradled Alida near her heartbeat. The thoughts of him were tender then. She heard his voice often. It was low and warm, she remembered. And she felt the gentleness of his hands on her body. Gentleness mixed with authority; the hardness of absolute ownership, of right, when needed be. She felt it when her body swelled and grew heavy or when she fell asleep every time they lay together like animals in the field. She would wake up and be happy she'd find him nearby, find his eyes, and they would dream long sweet dreams together that way.

She could never feel as comfortable with another. She knew, though they had only spent two such perfect years together. In that very brevity of time lay the great injustice against which her conscience rebelled. Why such a brief time, when all was going so well? Couples that hate each other with a passion are given eternity to submit to their misery. She remembered well the time they were together, she had felt so easy in her body and all was primitive, function fulfilling, mysterious and pure. It was all good in her love for him that was beyond need, transcended passion and words. They were both completely un-self-conscious, void of fear. For her, it was all power, all womanly strength, all female magic and darkness and grace. She wished that same feeling of liberation someday for her little Alida.

And it was all going well, so it seemed. Dance on my ballerina dance.

# 5.

THE NAME OF THAT NEARBY country, "Poland", kept reverberating in Misha's mind. The very concept had grown into a mysterious fascination. He knew he had to commit to go there, yet he could not incline to look forward to that experience. How would he go about—with his limited knowledge of that country's native language—to convey the idea that he was in search of his own past when, all along he searched for information concerning the background and whereabouts of someone who had caused much grief to his own people; a potential turncoat.

In a rented BMW, he had set off for Poland almost to the day of his twenty-fifth birthday—the morning of May 29, 1966. He obtained his entry visa on the premise that he was to continue his doctoral research on the Activities of the Mercenary SS units, as part of the *Einsatzgruppen* in Nazi occupied Poland. He would have to work fast, if he were to accomplish his task before he was due to depart for the United States to pursue his studies on his post-doctoral stipend.

Blanche had often mentioned the Silesian City of Sosnowiec, and Misha decided, on a gut feeling, to visit that place first before he embarked on his journey to the various Nazi killing factories and the main archives.

Between the towns of Katowice and Sosnowiec, Misha was told, lay the erstwhile labor camp, *Arbeitslager*, now a museum. There was a modest library, holding among other archives the diaries of former inmates. "*Dokumenta,*" the hostel clerk had informed him after receiving a generous twenty Złoty gratuity.

Most importantly, he was told in broken German, he ought to speak with the curator, an old Jew, *stary żyd*, allegedly a former inmate whose life's mission it had become to inform visitors about the camp's history and the tragic truth buried under its blood-soaked earth.

As it turned out, the curator, Josef Kraitman, a native of Sosnowiec and Auschwitz survivor was more than merely a curator of the museum. He was a veritable encyclopedia, a living register of the Jewish community there. One simple question set off a litany of answers, spoken in the singsong of a Hassidic scholar.

"Ah, so you wish to know about the Jews of Sosnowiec?" Josef asked. "Any names? Do you have photos? I can identify any one. Just name them."

"No, Mr. Kraitman, unfortunately, I have none." Misha admitted.

"Well, then, we'll have to do with my memory." Kraitman said. "Perhaps it will be just as useful."

"Was there an *Einsatzgruppe II* unit around these parts?" Misha asked, and felt himself trembling with anticipation.

"You ask if *they* were here?" Kraitman answered with a question of his own. "Most certainly. And when they got through, there were virtually no Jews left in these parts. Thousands were murdered mercilessly...thousands..." Misha saw the old man doubling up before his very eyes. His lips kept on moving soundlessly. To defuse an impending collapse, Misha hastened with another inquiry: "How about your local cemetery? Could you direct me there?"

The man nodded absentmindedly. "Sure, I can. But it'll do you no good. Most of the victims lie in mass graves outside the city."

"Uh-hu. I'm sorry." Misha said with genuine sadness in his voice. "I thought I might find some familiar names. Ancestry, perhaps of the man I'm looking for."

"Do you have a name for that man?" Kraitman inquired, now composed.

"My mother thought it was Michael Waneczeven...or something like that." Misha said with hope in his eyes.

"Ah? You know, I recall there was a person looking for the same name only months after the war." Kraitman thought a moment. "Yes, I remember. It was a woman. Slender built, clear blue eyes, brown hair..." he smiled triumphantly. "I don't forget a pretty face. Good, uh?"

"Mother!" Misha thought to himself. "Did she look through the archives?" He asked.

"That she did. Copied some documents. Went to the cemetery." While he was speaking, Kraitman set a large metal box in front of Misha. Dusty from apparent disuse, the papers didn't seem to be in any particular order, and Misha knew what he was up against.

"I'm looking for a man who may be my father. He abandoned my mother even before I was born. Never returned. I'm trying to find out who he was, so that I can live with his surname. Whatever he was." Misha said in one breath.

"You might not be so eager when you know the truth." Kraitman said with an devilish twinkle in his eye. "Sometimes the truth is not what we expect...nor desire."

"I know, and I'm prepared." Kraitman smiled at Misha's resolve. He looked the man in the face and produced a faint smile. He didn't wish to alienate a sympathetic soul. Alienations create setbacks, and a smile is not a great price to pay for the desired cooperation. "Tell you what." Misha said. "Later on, you can take a good look through the documents the woman had examined and let me know who the man she sought was. I'll do the rest. But first go on with your visit to the cemetery..." Misha wanted to continue, but Kraitman interrupted.

"Won't do you any good going there alone and not knowing what to look for. So, here..." Kraitman scribbled a name on a scrap of paper. "Look for this name on the grave markers. When you return, we'll have a lot to talk about."

Misha glanced at the slip of paper handed him. Printed on it was in capital letters: MOTELE WINOGRAD. For a long while Misha regarded the name in silence. "Strange", he thought. The name evoked a measure of anxiety. He read the name, alphabetizing it over and over, as if to invoke some sort of triggering device that might allow him recognition. It was all to no avail. It was all to no avail. With a puzzled look on his face, he held on to the scrap of paper. On his way out the door, he turned to the smiling curator: "I'll be back...I'll be back later." He said. "Good bye, now, my friend." He didn't quite understand the sudden inclination to call this stranger a "friend," nevertheless, he felt a unique sense of kinship with his newfound acquaintance. The old man regarded Misha with an intensity capable to pry the pain present in the young man's eyes. He would never forget these eyes eyes, but add them to the multitude already nestling restlessly in his soul. Misha, on his part, was looking forward to seeing the old archivist again with a strange anticipation of new developments.

Even from a distance, the ancient Jewish cemetery signaled wanton long term neglect. Weeds ran rampant. Their random growth had by now covered the narrow passages in-between lots. It had reached the markers and made the reading of the etched testimonies well nigh impossible. Misha was overwhelmed at the state of disarray the overgrowth affected. It was maddening. Decades, centuries of Jewish history, of lives lived to the fullest, others cut down in the turmoil of war and prejudice, lay before him. Was it possible that some of his ancestry lay buried here under the many layers of foliage and earth scattered here and there in a chaotic manner?

The scant knowledge of the Hebrew alphabet from his studies of the Bible came in handy as he tried to decipher the names on some of the headstones. Here and there, he read a surname; saw the sign of the *Cohen* (Priest) as expressed by two hands joined by the thumbs and each hand forming a V-shape sign by spreading its middle and ring fingers to one side. Could we have descended from a long line of *Cohen*s? He deliberated silently. Did Mamá keep the truth from him? Why would she have done that? Again, some puzzling questions.

Much as he tried, he was unable to decipher the name Winograd, on any of the grave markers. He had by now beaten a path through the tall weeds, taken some pictures with his Leica for his travel album, and read the inscriptions over and over. He had attracted a small crowd of youths and a scattered number of adults. They remained at a safe distance at first. Then, he heard a boy's voice, calling to him from beyond the graveyard, reminiscent of the cat-calls of the not-too-distant past: "Hey! *Brudny żydzie!*"

Misha was startled and reacted with fear. From his limited Polish vocabulary, he surmised the meaning of filthy Jew. Why now? He wondered. After all that had transpired, they still spoke of the Jews with derision. Frankly, there weren't enough Jews left alive to inspire in the Christian Poles such an abundance of hatred. "Take your treasures and go to Palestine, Jew!" An adult voice shouted in German now. Others followed suit mimicking the first caller. An object fell near him, and Misha realized they were tossing rocks at him. He had better leave, he thought, without challenging their marksmanship. He would not run. They'd give chase. He remembered his grandfather's admonition of long ago in reference to canine behavior: "If a dog barks at you look strait at the animal and withdraw slowly. Never run or the dog will chase after you and bite." His grandpa was a wise man. Though he would not look the mob straight in the eye, he would walk away slowly without looking back.

He understood. They thought he'd come to dig up some buried heirlooms hidden there by the deported ghetto Jews. The silent victims of the Nazis dared speak from their mass graves to the surviving few. They revealed their secret clues, and now this intruder dared return to claim what's rightfully his. He would deny the vultures these buried treasures, the booty they'd waited to collect for such a long time. Their shouts became louder the greater the distance he had put between them. And Misha knew full well: were he to bathe in the sacred waters of the Jordan River for the rest of his life, he could not wash away the venomous filth of their remarks.

"Ah..?" The curator voiced his kind of comprehension when Misha expressed his astonishment at the strange behavior of the cemetery mob. "I should have forewarned you of this peculiar illness from which these people suffer. It is a congenital malady; carried from father to son, from mother to daughter, from generation to generation. It is such a baseless hatred they carry in their hearts for the Jewish people...such a terrible sickness..." Kraitman stroked his goatee gently as he reflected. He shook his head sadly, and Misha was not about to interrupt. After all, he did not come all this way to talk but to listen. He would wait.

"Even as the Nazis were loading us onto the freight cars like cattle—more than one hundred into the limited space—we peered through the small wired windows, and we saw our assembled neighbors who came to bid us a not so fond farewell. And we heard their shouts of '*Jude! Jude!*' ('Jew! Jew!') Words they'd learned from their Nazi friends. And they yelled: 'You had it coming to you!' With great elation, they shouted insults and derision." The old man breathed heavily.

"I dared to return, a remnant of a once vibrant Jewish community, and my good neighbors would not forgive me for not having perished along with the countless others. It seems my presence here has greatly inconvenienced their collective memory, mixed with guilt and wishing for collective amnesia..." Kraitman was now spreading some documents before Misha, while he gathered his thoughts to continue. As the old man spoke, Misha felt the sorrow of years of suffering and redemption weighing upon the curator's bent back. And he wondered how this old wreck of a human being was able to sustain such an enormous abundance of sorrow before it spilled over and drowned the whole of humanity. Two schools of old wisdom reflected the old man's philosophy. On the one side, there was the wisdom of the Jewish tradition, that to remember is the secret of redemption. Coupled with it, was the wisdom of George Santayana, so often quoted in relation to historical fact that "those who forget the past are condemned to repeat it." On the other side, there was the profound insight of the historian Ernest Renan—author of *The Life of Jesus Christ*—that every nation is a community both of shared memory and of shared forgetting. "Forgetting," Renan stated, "and I would say even historical error, is an essential factor in the history of a nation." The old man paused. "I only hope that our good neighbors will in time forget their hatred and renew their acquaintance with love." He paused again and added laconically: "Generations...it will take generations."

Misha recognized the wisdom on both sides. He also knew that the two theories could not easily be fused, reconciled with one another. The closest fusion they would be able to achieve was a prescription in several stages; he would investigate, record, reflect, and move on from there.

"We lost count of time." His host's somber voice startled Misha from his reverie. "Darkness and the stench of terribly crowded bodies caused nausea. Lack of food and fresh water, the cries of children, the wailing of the elders and their constant but unanswered prayers, drove many to madness. On some occasions it rained. Scraps of paper were quickly fashioned into narrow tubes that gathered drops into makeshift repositories: pots, pans, glass jars, and even the palm of a hand, objects that fit between the barbed wire enclosures.

"Using a large nail extracted from the wall of the freight car, someone succeeded and carved a relatively large hole in the floor. This had become the place where one could relieve oneself. Those nearest had an advantage. Those farther removed from the makeshift latrine were soon covered with excretion and got wet with urine. The stench was indescribably nauseating. Everyone wanted to be near the opening, and that caused people to argue and led to physical confrontations. The rule of the stronger prevailed. This was the first legacy we had inherited from our Nazi rulers. The animal concealed within human skin had surfaced. There was little chance conditions would improve. Cattle led to the slaughter fared better conditions." He paused.

"Am I trying your patience, young man?" Kraitman suddenly asked.

"Of course, not." Misha was caught off guard. "I try to understand."

"How could you, if I myself don't." Kraitman retorted gently.

"If it takes a lifetime, I'll try." Misha assured the old man.

"You may have to give it more than that…yes…more than that." Kraitman mused loudly, shaking his head.

"Go on, now, Mr. Kraitman, don't let me distract you." Misha urged.

"I won't bore you with the details. They are history." Kraitman waved his hand in front of his nose, as if to swat a nuisance. "Only, we thought we were the lucky ones when liberation came. At that time, we had no idea we'd be condemned to forever recall, to see the events in minutest details; to remain a memory capsule is a hard task. Damned to remember; to relive; like the proverbial Sisyphus in his nightmarish task of pushing the bolder upwards only to see it tumble back into the abyss."

"If you had been foretold your fate, would you have craved survival?" Misha asked.

"By all means. If only for the satisfaction of seeing the Nazis in defeat, Germany humbled and humiliated!" He almost cried out.

"Do you still think it was worth it?"

"In retrospect, yes. I do now what has to be done. What many of the survivors do as well. We have no choice." He paused to collect himself. "But, let's get to the matter at hand. Here, take a look at these files." Kraitman pointed at the thick dossier. "You will find some things that may interest you."

The file was under the name of Motele Winograd, a.k.a. Michael Waneczeven. Large letters in bold print announced, *SS II.* For what seemed a very long time, Misha was silent. When he spoke, his voice was almost inaudible: "This is *my* father?"

"I'm almost sure, young man." Kraitman sounded sympathetic.

"But...how do you know?" Misha was incredulous.

"The woman." Kraitman said with that now characteristic twinkle in his eye. "She followed the same pattern you do."

Misha opened the dossier. PART II was stamped at the top of the first page. "What happened here?" Misha inquired.

"It's not unusual for us to lose part of a file." Kraitman spoke resignedly. "Many people come through these doors. Visitors of every kind. Some are genuine historians. It is hoped they wouldn't stoop to theft. Then, there are journalists who look for a story everywhere they can find one. Finally, there is family." He shook his head meaningfully: "They're the worst. They would steal files for their own reasons. Sometimes to learn, other times to protect their own."

"Are you quite sure he was a collaborator?" Misha hoped against hope.

"Yes, quite." Kraitman assured him.

"Did you know him?" Misha asked.

"I knew of him," Kraitman evaded the issue. "We have learned never to be sure of anyone. You never know what people will do under pressure. Never judge unless you find yourself under the same circumstances. Circumstances," he repeated hastily, as if to assuage Misha's presentiments, "they make you do crazy things."

"What was he like?" Misha asked.

"Just another youth in another ghetto, trying to survive."

"Yes, but what was he like?" Misha repeated his question impatiently.

"About your height, ash-blond crop of hair, eyes clear blue. Passed for Aryan." Kraitman evaded opinion making. "Those were the days when no one really knew anyone. Every person was a loner. For themselves. Motele started out as a ghetto militia member. Like all of the other strong boys." He used the Yiddish expression the *shtarkes*, which bore similarity to the German, and Misha understood. The old man continued his narrative as he sat in his chair, eyes focused into the open window over Misha's left shoulder.

"At first, he went through the motions like all of the others, delivered his daily quota for resettlement, *Umsiedlung*, they called it. It soon became easier for him to deliver, with each committed victim sent off to the killing factories. He got caught up in the weird excitement of it. But, then...but then..." Here Kraitman choked as if unable to collect his thoughts.

"Go on, go on, Mr. Kraitman, please..." Misha pleaded.

"One day, it appeared, there were no longer strangers to be tapped for transport. Motele faced the inevitable. Took his grandparents on both sides, then some uncles and aunts, cousins distant and close. For his efficient work, he was awarded the status of *Volksdeutscher.*"

"A Jew? Incredible." Misha whispered.

"Still, it is true." Kraitman assured him. "You'll find the rest of the story in the Krakow archives. You will go there, won't you?"

"I must." Misha looked a defeated man. "Can you tell me, why did he do it?" He asked, dreading the response.

"At first, to survive. Then, partly for excitement in the feel of power and the rewards that came with it." Kraitman took a deep breath. "No one can really say why. It wasn't ideology, that's for sure. And it wasn't loyalty to the cause of the Third Reich." He stopped for a moment to rest again. "Maybe the Krakow files will tell you more." He added. "He was tried in absentia, you know. Death by hanging. But he never returned to stand trial. And they never found him. No one knows what has happened to Motele to this very day as we speak." He let out a deep sigh. "Seems he got off easy. Killed in action. So it was officially reported."

Misha was silent. Mother kept secrets. Father was a common assassin. Worse still, a Jewish assassin of Jews. All of them Jews.

He left the premises of the museum deep in thought. The old man followed his young guest outdoors, visibly disturbed about a son's distress over his father's sins. "Go in peace," he said, "and remember. Memory is the secret of redemption. So says the Talmud." They shook hands. "Good bye and thank you." Misha turned to go. He didn't look back. Only when lying down to sleep that night, he retraced the day, the revelations, and the uncertainties yet to be verified and the whole mess of a lifetime to be unraveled. Were there any more surprises? He would soon learn.

# 6.

EARLY NEXT MORNING MISHA was on his way. Moving on, he was unable to rid his mind off the old Holocaust survivor. The latter lent his inquiry a renewed impetus at the very moment Misha had thought his pursuits were in vain, well nigh quixotic, having hit the proverbial wall. The man was, after all, a living part of the tangible feel of the past, a storehouse of memories and a generator of new ones. Some of the old man's phrases reverberated in Misha's mind to the sound of the tires grinding into the rough gravel road. "When they knew of someone dying, they would come and steal his belongings." Then, another morsel of information: "The wealthy, in great numbers, were leaving for abroad to escape in anticipation of Nazi persecution and worse. Their fortunes entrusted to the Swiss banks preceded them. Only the poor, the despondent and those without a solitary choice, had remained sanguine and trusting in the Almighty. But even the Almighty Lord God was seemingly disinterested."

Ah, the wealthy Jews. Misha mused. Why did they choose to stash their loot in hiding places soon to be discovered and pillaged or in safe-deposit boxes of neutral banks? Why wouldn't they use it to save some of their less fortunate brethren? Was it greed? After all, most of them perished, unable to use their fortunes in order to avert the assassin's murderous zeal.

This was once Nazi territory. Misha continued. Many years after, there were still road signs in German. Nobody bothered to take them down, it seemed. A small town, Tarnów, was just off the road a bit. "Don't stop in Tarnów," Kraitman had advised, "nothing worthwhile remains there. It used to be a women's camp. They disconnected the cars marked WOMEN there, the rest of them went on their way to Auschwitz."

Small villages and towns flickered in the corner of his eye. They resembled picture postcards. In the distance he spied contours of the great Tatra Mountains, splendid forests, rivers, meadows, peasants in the fields, straw-thatched huts with smoke billowing out of the chimneys, barns in the background. This was Poland. Why hadn't the beauty of this land influenced the character and nature of its people? Misha wondered. Can such natural beauty live side-by-side, with a people void of heart and soul? Will that, too, change in time for the better? Misha wondered.

A road sign indicated only 24 Km to Kraków. In favorable traffic, he should be there in twenty minutes or less. "You will find a chuck full of information there, if no one had plundered it before you." Kraitman assured him." He trembled with anticipation of the surprises his visit might offer.

Kraków was the medieval capital of Poland under the Jagiełło dynasty. The first of the monarchs, Casimir IV, had issued an invitation to the Jews who were running at the time from repeated Inquisitions. He welcomed them into his realm. It was an enlightened period in Polish history, both intellectually as well as economically. But it was short-lived. His successors had none of Casimir's refinement nor did they intend to keep the promises he had made to his guests. What ensued through the coming centuries were series of persecutions during the takeover of Poland by the Great Russian tsars, many violent pogroms sanctioned by the empire and the church, which culminated in the Nazi Holocaust.

Kraków was once again the seat of great learning, boasting its revitalized, ancient Jagiello University and many satellite institutions of higher learning. It was also the center of the National Archives, where Misha had hoped to find his lost father.

He was in luck. Inside File No. 1432, marked CRIMES AGAINST HUMANITY, he read the name of Michael

Waneczeven, a.k.a. Motele Winograd. It contained detailed reports and descriptions of the *Aktionen* in which Motele took active part. In all, there were some 734 information-packed pages for Misha to study.

"*Mein Führer* must have been running out of manpower, what with his reverses on the Eastern front and the advances of the Western powers after the Normandy landing." Misha whispered to himself. Page 543 offered a glance at some of Michael's activities:

*Survivors reported SS Gruppenführer Michael Waneczeven participated in the murder of 20 Jewish children and 20 Russian POW's. The forty victims were hanged during the night of January 20-21, 1945, allegedly on final orders from Hitler's bunker in Berlin. Reason: they had been used in medical experimentation and the Nazis did not want to leave any trace of their atrocities behind as they retreated...*

Misha let out a quiet whistle through his teeth. Damn! This is as late as January 45! His "killed in action" notice to my mother must have been an official cover up. Misha thought. His hands trembled. He must go back to the beginning of the archives. There ought to be more. He wasn't looking forward to it, though. He read on, his face buried in the palms of both hands. He turned the pages with a heavy heart. What will he read next?

Among other feats chronicled in the dossier marked "Michael Waneczeven, a.k.a Motele Winograd and Mietek Vino":

*...The murder of eighty-four Soviet prisoners and the exemplary and brutal punishment of inmates in the concentration camps Sachsenhausen, Buchenwald, Natzweiler, Majdanek, Ravensbrück, Peenemünde, Vught, Drutte, Dessauer Ufer and, finally, Neuengamme...*

"Almighty God! How much more must I endure?" Misha whispered under his breath. After hours of reading, it suddenly came to him: He's alive! My assassin father is out there somewhere, and I must find him! I must bring him to justice! He was glad the Polish authorities concurred with his view in spite of the German Ministry's communiqué to the contrary, announcing Michael as a casualty of the eastern front. *Gruppenführer* Michael Waneczeven was arraigned to appear before the Polish Supreme Tribunal in Kraków, which deliberated on the issue of crimes against humanity in January 1964. Former Buchenwald concentration camp victims, Rudolf Gottschalk and Dorothea Morgenstern appeared as prize witnesses and their testimony against the SS officer influenced the verdict *in absentia*. Other former camp inmates came forward and offered damning evidence as well. Michael Waneczeven was found guilty on all counts as charged. His sentence: death by hanging.

Back in his hotel, alone with God as his witness, Misha wept nonstop. The night had gone and the morning sun had risen. He was like a man in a daze. "My father, a murderer of children... my father a murderer of innocent people..." he kept repeating. Tears rolled down his cheeks, their saltiness bit into his tongue. He had missed his breakfast and lunch, but he felt no hunger. Unshaven and disheveled, he finally came down into the lobby, where a polite porter took pity on the haggard man.

"Cup of coffee?" The man asked.

"Yes, please." Misha said in a nearly inaudible whisper.

All he could take in was a strong, black cup of coffee. He felt as if all his strength had been drained out of him. He sat there and his shoulders shook spasmodically. He had come to believe now that the hope he'd felt for the many months was on loan only. It was Michael's soul inside of him that he pretended was his own. But when it finally left him, it took his courage away as well. He saw it now clearly, shining through him like a light. He understood only too well that he had never known before what loneliness really meant. He was alone and overcome with grief. Could he ever reach beyond his own mourning and conduct discourse movingly about universal emotions? After all, he was a decent person. None of his alleged father's character traits seemed imbedded in his psyche. Didn't he devote many months to carrying for his ill mother?

When they were together, his mother and he, he didn't want to be told what to feel, to have her rattle off the common points like a checklist. That he formed his own thoughts, independent of hers, was his mystery and his moment of truth, and he didn't want it reduced to the level of everyday experience; rote memory, ice chips, a piece of blank stationery scotch-taped to the wall above his bed.

The glory and revelation of his own worth had been the knowledge that his body, misused and misunderstood from childhood onward, had a bland, implacable wisdom of its own. That wisdom of blood and flesh was exhilarating and calming all at once. It was the animal nature of the thing that he found so enthralling that let him sink deep into his bones and inhabit them in a way he'd never done before. He desperately wanted to trust this, to rely on instinct and the wisdom of his body and mind. He wanted now to get as far away from all of the archives, fluorescent lights of library carrels, the smell of humidity permeating the pages that embodied the putrid tale of murder and mayhem abounding on their parched surface.

There was that and then he felt this overpowering urge to *know*. If only Blanche were alive, he thought, she'd agree with him. He knew he could tell that she wasn't comfortable with the life of lies she'd led. He would return home on the nights he had class, arrived at the door flippant and hard in a way he'd almost forgotten, a way he hadn't been for a long time. The moments were tense and silent and, once there, he could actually see her tightening up, shrinking away from him, retreating behind a wall of pretense and cynicism.

One night, when he had come home, he told her he was leaving. He had tried to explain how he'd felt, how he'd wanted to trust her, if only she'd confide in him, his capacity to understand, to forgive. But his words fluttered and stuck in his throat and his eyes grew more and more contemptuous in his disillusionment, as his silence settled in like a third person were present in the room.

And now it was too late. For then, on his way out, he turned toward her: "I wish you'd have had the courage to tell me all that before, if only out of consideration for my sanity." He well nigh barked the words hoarsely at her as he was out the door. Exiting, he saw his mother double up as if to retch. He was unable to find even the smallest crevice of compassion in his unforgiving heart.

In his room, he spread the map of Poland on the bed. *Kraków, Rzeszów, Majdanek, Puławy, Siedlce, Treblinka...*his head was swimming, and he felt as if he was going to retch at any moment. He must go to these places. He had to see with his own eyes the killing places his father had contaminated with his presence. This done, he could leave this unhappy land behind, never to return.

# 7.

HE LAY CLOTHED IN HIS bed, his eyes wide open though it was way past midnight, and he planned to get going early morning. That way he would avoid commuter traffic, even though it was mostly bicycles and motorcycles. Cars were still a rare commodity in Poland. Only the very wealthy were able to afford such luxuries, which gave the impoverished good cause to cultivate hatred and envy.

He missed Susanna. He should have allowed her to come along when she asked, nay, pleaded for him to let her come along. But there were things here for his eyes only. Things she might have found radical. After all, she came from an affluent upper class family, her father owner of a splendid vineyard; mother mistress of the household servants. This was between Misha and his father. Unusual things; strange and incomprehensible things happened, which were better left in the family. His eyelids felt heavy. He closed his eyes and imagined he was...

...*Back in high school, the* Realgymnasium *in his hometown during the formative years of his life. He met Susanna at* Tanzschule Bier, *a famed dancing school, where all of the boys and girls of the senior class would attend ballroom dancing lessons. It was a good arrangement. This way, contacts were made without constraints. The opposite served to imprint in their minds formal, socially accepted norms of etiquette as well as provide dancing partners. She caught his eye, as she sat shyly on a corner bench, pretending to be brave. He was immediately drawn to her. There was something about the young woman that had told him she would be a good partner in more than one sense, if not a great one.*

"May I? Misha." *He introduced himself briefly with an outstretched hand. He held his breath, lest she refuse. But she didn't hesitate.* "Susanna." *She responded likewise. She offered him her hand with a soft* "danke" *and they were off waltzing, fox-trotting, and doing the routines endlessly, it seemed, together. They became inseparable in their daily life as well. It was reminiscent of his chemistry professor's poignant analogy in class in reference to studies related to the properties of mercuric oxide;* "at times," *Professor Lenox carried on in his melodic tenor voice,* "the substance would remain as one, however on occasions each molecule might capriciously decide to go its own way."

*Misha knew then and there. He was going to have her, quite like the mercury united with oxide. Damned good analogy, Professor Lenox. He chuckled inwardly. He scrutinized her carefully. Though she wasn't one those* "drop dead" *beauties, she was quite handsome and extremely sexy. They danced and she talked incessantly. She did so, perhaps as a cover up for her inherent shines. She told him about her family and their age old tradition of growing the finest champagne grapes of the Saar Valley.* "My dad is so proud of his champagne." *She said with a tremor in her voice. You must taste it sometime soon." He sensed the family pride.* "I'm sure I shall." *He whispered in her ear.* "You must have heard of* Hänkel Trocken, *no? It is world renowned." He nodded. Yes, he'd heard of it, but was never privy to the taste. He wouldn't admit to his poverty. He would tell her eventually, when they'd get to know each other better. Truth was, he could not afford a bottle of this* "nectar of the affluent." *She noticed the slight tightening of his features.*

"Oh, dear!" *She lowered her dark-blue eyes, and he gazed at her fiery red hair all bundled up into a bun above the nape of her neck.* "You seem sad, Misha. Have I talked too much?" *Susanna expressed concern. She reached up and touched his cheek.* "Don't worry, Misha," *she said with a faint smile curling up her full, red lips." She paused.* "Whatever it may be you're concerned with, I'm sure daddy can fix it."

*He did not respond verbally. Only his arms tightened round her lithe midriff gently so as not to cause her to panic. They continued to dance, their bodies very close. He felt the rhythm of her heartbeat, and he became aware of her firm breasts weighing against his chest. And he had a pronounced sense of her large nipples so hard they sent clear signals all the way to his pubic region.*

*"That's really dancing!" His mind exploded with boundless pleasure.*

*Susanna and Misha had remained a couple. They shared things; scorn for everyone who was not like them, certainty, smugness, idealism, and immortality. They went to college together and shared things; love and disillusion, responsibility and fear. They got too close, knew each other in the Biblical sense, knew too well how to hurt, where to hit and to drive the other away. Six months of silence and they would wander back into each other's lives with smiles as pure as if the anger had never existed. It might have taken them years to come to a place where they could have stood together and weathered the storm they'd created, dealt with the anger and the fear and stayed at each other's side. But they took a shortcut.*

*Now, it was three years later, in the dead cold of winter. They sat cross-legged on the floor of their modest apartment. Yellow lamplight splashed warmth across the polished wood panels. It was a housewarming. Another reunion.*

*The peyote made magic in their minds. They were in each other's eyes, watching for reactions, directions, "where are you going? I want to come along." He was slipping away from her, or she from him, receding motion, slow and inexorable. And he reached unthinking hands across the widening gulf, felt her warmth on the sliding tips of his fingers. And they were suddenly, immediately close, knees overlapping; her head dropped over his shoulder, tangled together, and his voice was behind her eyes, under her heart, love words.*

*"I didn't know..." she started to say. Colors wheeled, sound overflowed. "I never knew..." He took her thoughts out of her head and answered them, also without moving his lips.*

*"Always..." the sound receded now, again stretched away, darker and darker, it left her.*

*"Always..." his voice came from the bottom of a well.*

*She followed him down, and it was cold there, but he was warm, so warm. She butted her head against the underside of his jaw, rubbed her face against the tender heat of his neck, felt the pulse and roll of his blood beneath the surface and suddenly she was inside, under his skin, warmth and light around her like an envelope.*

*She felt everything he felt and, at the end, she cried with him, their tears mingled, released with the rest of it.*

*Although early in her pregnancy he spent the nights often at her house, the last few weeks he stayed almost completely away. He was never far from a phone, though, on purpose, and she called to tell him she was in labor. He came and drove her to the hospital.*

*He remembered so little of it now, only flashes and fragments of thoughts, like disrupted spasms of memories. He remembered helping her into his truck, his hand hard and cold against the aching small of her back, and he recalled the image that came over him then. He saw himself from behind, small and distended, in a pastel-colored hospital gown, entering a long, black tunnel. He remembered being clearly aware that there would be no going back, that the only way out was to go through that darkness, through the pain, trusting that there was a painless light ahead.*

*Then, he entered the tunnel, and the darkness crashed around him. The darkness was red, and the pain was shut in with him.*

*Faces were swimming in and out of view. Hers did least often. There was now something terrible in her face; something that filled him with fear. "She's leaving you," a still voice whispered in his mind. "Don't leave me," he wanted to say, to scream, but the current sucked him under, while she looked on with an eerie smile round her lips.*

*Something told him "scream, don't be brave." He wasn't sure who it was, but he knew it wasn't him. He could see her, though, little and dark against the light wall, too little, too dark, so far away. The screams magnified, rushing at her like trains. Now she, too, screamed.*

*"It will not come into the world like that,"* she seemed to say. *Not to the sound of my pain. When she couldn't stop it anymore, she yelled, "I love you!" Around clenched teeth, over and over, for both of them, the first words* it *ever heard…*

…When he heard her cry, reality washed back in. It woke him and he sat up, soaked in cold sweat. It felt to him like the way your ears pop after the plane has landed. Sounds, colors, smell, everything was suddenly immediate and close. And he was diminished; so empty and weak and afraid. The helpless, overwhelmed love, he now felt for the tiny screaming little thing that was part of him and part of her, humbled him.

"Happy birthday, little girl," he muttered under his breath. How he wished he could bury his face in the warm, meaty smell of her and cry. This time, though, she wasn't there for him. Had she been there, she might have told him how she abhorred being left out of his life when it mattered most. How she had sacrificed all, her dissident parents, the family tradition for him. He laid his heavy head on the pillow and closed his eyes, unable to face the light of day.

*…Suddenly, she was hysterical again. They came and took her away to the hospital and gave her a shot, a sedative maybe or something to ease the pain. Then they wheeled her to recovery. He floated along, a few inches above the gurney and passed her in the hall.*

*It might have looked comic (*were it not a dream), *him spreadeagled there, his cheek and flat open palms against the pale green wall, his closed eyes only narrow black slashes on white skin. They stood out like scars, and in his stillness was a frightening intensity, as if by pressing hard enough he could be inside the wall, in the cool and the dark, and the safe.*

*A nurse's hand reached out, long and elastic, a white blur, to touch him, his bunched, knotted shoulder, and in slow motion he turned around…*

Sleep washed over him, her eyes were still on his, he fought to focus, to follow as the gurney wheels clicked and rolled, fought the drowsy undercurrents as he receded and receded. Suddenly, he heard her speak:

… *"I'm so scared," her lips moved without a sound, but he 'heard' her well. "Misha, my darling, I'm so very frightened." She used the word* frightened *for greater emphasis. "I'm sooo…" the sound drifted, until he lost her under the waves. He watched her carefully, but there was only lip movement, there was no sound…*

He packed for the trip, Susanna on his mind. There were her favorite things he had taken along to keep him company: her pink silk underwear; her Curious George magazine, the picture he'd taken from the wall in her living room of her when she was a mere teen-ager, even before they'd met on the dance-hall floor. She was pretty even then. With the wavy red hair spilling over her shoulders, the deep blue of her eyes smiling at him, though there was no visible crease behind them. As he packed the things into his backpack, it had occurred to him that he might be con-sidered frivolous. She followed him, like a shadow he'd invented, from the nightstand into his backpack and back to the nightstand again. Her full, red lips parted a row of white, even teeth in full view, so very much alive he could almost see her suck her thumb, as she often did. It made the packing a slow process.

He had to get going. Untangle his thoughts from her image, lift her thumb from her lips in order to kiss them farewell. "We'll have so much fun when I return," he whispered more to himself than to her. She'd heard that before, many times. He knew. But she couldn't help hoping it might come true one day. He imag-ined her, as she listened gravely, unmoved. "We'll go up in a plane, and you can look down and see the little buildings from up high in the air, just like a bird," he continued his imaginings, "and the grocery store, and, yes, the insignificant minuscule people milling around like ants." He cracked a faint smile. He knew how many times he'd promised her to travel together and never made time to fulfill the promises. He must make one promise to himself.

Once this is over, yes, once it's over and done with, he'll devote more time to his Susanna.

He remembered that she didn't ask too many questions before he'd left. Her eyes wide and infinitely blue, she was mistrustful of such easy love. She only looked at him with sadness. She didn't even ask why he had to go on his journey. In retrospect, he placated himself with the belief that what she never had she will not miss, but will she? Will she one day remember that her fondest wish had been denied?

He was dangerously close to tears. How he bent over in front of her, face to face, meeting those wise eyes a moment longer before departure, he drank that love, let it swell his heart until it ached. It was that ache he remembered now, even when he slept, and was awestruck by just her sight. She patted his cheek softly with one open palm. Leaned forward to kiss the tip of his nose. She was at times taciturn, but basically kind. And Misha hoped nothing untoward had happened to her in his absence, and she wasn't in any danger.

There was a knock at the door, but he couldn't pull away from her. Those gentle hands that touched him with so much authority, so much tenderness, with the hardness of absolute ownership, of right.

"You called the concierge, Sir?" The voice called in.

Time to move on. He followed the bellhop down the stairs.

# 8.

IT SEEMED THE TRAIL would not end. At least, not soon. Misha felt suddenly persecuted by loneliness, in the middle of a blind alley, torn asunder and falling, unaware of direction. What could have been under different circumstances a historical pilgrimage, a trail in search of his roots and personal identity, had now taken on the nature of a journey of sorrow, each step awash with tears. Kraitman's gentle admonition reverberated through his mind: "Be careful, young man, else you might follow a trail of blood..."

It had gotten so each time he would encounter a new challenge shrouded by mystery, his breath got shorter, and his entries into his daily journal aphoristically brief in his attempt to explain the incomprehensible. He tried ever so hard to enlist the registered revelations of his daily search as the key to his father's retrograde activities and motives. How Misha succeeded in his task depended largely on his momentary frame of mind. In his quest, he had listened to so many diverse voices that, in the end, he failed to distinguish their owner's lips, eyes, and the hue of their skin or the days that spawned the information and who had revealed what.

Thus the unanimity of the many occurrences seemed, on first glance, factual enough to him, though they were not presentable in any syntactical order in which they had occurred only as a succession of events without their real dimension.

It was becoming clear to him that *his* reality had to appear subjective if he were to retain his sanity. He was now entering an emotional state in which he was incapable to maintain any form of an objective reality. The truth was a series of fragmented elements of banality that renounced clarity, as though they had become a function of sight and sound without meaning; an enumeration of many voices, expressions of uncertainty and helplessness.

"It is all so dark today, dreary, stupid, and dull," Misha told his hostess in the village of Sobibor, where he had gone on his trail to seek the truth. Maria Kuras listened, while she swayed back and forth in the old rocking chair. In her late sixties, thinning gray hair fell quite disheveled to her skeletal shoulders; her once pretty face now leathery and worn and only her deep, dark, penetrating eyes still shone brightly as she spoke.

"They were comrades, your papa and my Piotr," she grimaced in her attempt to smile, showing a scarce remainder of tobacco-stained, uneven teeth. Misha listened, fascinated by her candor and homegrown wisdom. "Everything happened so fast," she continued, "there was no beginning, no end, nothing continued, it made no sense whatsoever. We got caught up in this thing, the killing and slaughter, the self-deception. And we couldn't help ourselves." She paused and took a deep breath.

"And you, *Pani* Maria," Misha addressed the woman with the formal *Lady*. "You looked the other way?" He controlled his voice for fear he'd shout.

"What could I do, young man? It was a time without sunshine, nothing made sense, and the sun would neither rise in the heavens nor in our hearts. It was an indescribable situation, and nobody said that things would become increasingly bleak those days, so cold and dark and no longer tolerable."

"But...but...all that killing, *Pani* Maria," Misha whispered, "You must have known."

"Ah, the killing," the woman repeated. She held out the teapot toward him, "more tea?" She asked. "No, thanks," he responded impatiently, eager to listen.

"Well, they didn't see it as...as...what you say, that it was outright random killing." She spoke now with great resolve. "For example, one Saturday, when all of the Jews were at prayer, it would start out with a roundup. It all seemed so orderly and proper then. The Jews followed orders without the slightest resistance—even to their own militia—stepped into the gas vans, were taken for long rides..." Maria's voice faded into the past. She stopped rocking for a brief moment and resumed her soliloquy. "After all, what could one do? It seemed so *right*. It was hard on my Piotr, doing the same thing all day long, but he endured and learned to look at it in a different way."

"Different?"

"Yes, indeed," her voice became animated, "it was more like... like he saw the good he was doing for society, you know? Like getting rid of..."

"Vermin?! And my father?!" Misha shouted. "Did he think likewise?!"

"You don't have to shout, young man." Maria sounded indignant. "After all, we are among civilized, law-abiding people." She suddenly broke out into a sporadic giggle. "*Wunder über Wunder,*"—wonder of wonders—she said in German, and it appeared eerie and not at all the right emotion in which to express it. "See here," she continued, "there were people gassed, and there were some burned or shot into a ravine; some stood in the howling wind and others hung from the trees; sometimes it rained, other times things fell from the skies that no one saw. But everyone knew that things were going on. Unholy things. And no one disturbed their conscience. They turned a deaf ear and a blind eye, not to hear, not to see..."

Misha wondered how it was possible for this woman to narrate without the least sign of emotion or remorse, to speak the unspeakable with such lack of empathy, to spice her narrative with an occasional giggle.

"*Tak, tak,*" she said in her language, "yes, yes, Hitler extinguished the new cities, made them into old ones, ruins. Once again, the snow lives, and the wind sends its voices into every house..." she pointed to her chest..."and this heart no longer beats. Yes, yes, *tak...tak* " she repeated, "some paid, others got away...some paid, others got away..." she grew silent, pressed her thin lips together as if to terminate her discourse.

"You mean...?" Misha stopped in mid-sentence.

"My Piotr paid with his life." She placed the fingers of her right hand below her scrawny chin round her neck. "Hanged till the death." She indicated the interview was over, rose from her chair and walked toward the door.

"And my father?" Misha asked, already in the doorway. "Tell me what has become of my father?!"

"You'll have to find out for yourself, young man." She shut the door unapologetically behind him. Misha knew, for him there was no turning back.

At least, Misha knew Michael aka Mietek a.k.a Motele was somewhere, alive. After the hanging of his comrade Piotr, he had disappeared somewhere near Warsaw, perhaps under another alias; he was nobody's fool. It was a mark of irony for Maria Kuras to deny him the truth, though she didn't state categorically that his father was no longer alive. Had he been caught, he would have paid. He would have shared the fate of his comrades. Was he sitting somewhere on a remote riverbank, fishing rod in hand, smoking his favorite pipe and enjoying the countryside?

Misha imagined Michael wearing blue, sun-blocking eyeglasses, for his eyes must have suffered during his war experiences and were now sensitive to light. A woman sat next to Michael on a thick blanket with assorted foodstuffs spread and ready to be consumed. She held an open magazine on her knees and occasionally read passages for Michael to hear. She read in a calm, soft voice, so that anyone passing by would not be able to discern the nature of her topic. Then again, it might have been poetry she read. No, anything but poetry. Misha wanted to doubt an assassin's appreciation of the fine arts altogether, but he remembered the sentimentality of the *SS* and the Hitler Youth engaged in their romantic kitsch moments before they tore into a crowd of "sub-humans" in a killing frenzy.

Together, the man and the woman present a serene picture. It is a rainy, acrid, though relatively clear day. The pair sits there, unconventional, aging, and alone with one another, wrapped in heavy, rustically stiff waterproof woolen overcoats. Any accidental passer-by might discretely withdraw in the presence of such an intimate solitude. It is a dark, brief encounter of two beings in need of one another. She has been to the doctor only a couple of days ago to learn that she had consumption. "With luck and good care in the country, you've got another year or so," he told her, "perhaps an additional half, on condition that you remain in the country." She spares her husband the news, and they soon move back to the city, where the pollution will surely exacerbate her condition.

# 9.

TWO DAYS OF TRAVEL had brought Misha to the quarry at Babi Yar near the city of Kiev in the Ukraine. His head bowed, he stood silently and read the inscription on the modest granite monument, which underscored the terrible tragedy of the not-too-distant event, but failed, nevertheless, to present a true profile of its victims:

Russian citizens died here in this quarry, killed by the German assassins and their surrogate collaborators. Buried in a common grave, nameless but forever remembered...

Though the inscription went on to describe details of the mass killing, nowhere was there mention of the Jews who were the sole victims. That fact remained a well-kept secret among the Kiev community, testimony to a sort of collective amnesia for which human beings can claim an astonishing capacity. The Soviet Corps of Engineers erected a dam across the end of the ravine, filled it with pulp, which turned it into a muddy lake. Several years later, in the spring of 1961, torrential rains had rushed down toward the ravine and filled the lake to overflowing. The dam was unable to contain the fury of the rushing waters, which rushed over its top.

It was a flood of human remains that spilled down into the streets of Kiev. The mud spewed the skeletal remains of the victims as it did the shredded clothing and occasional personal belongings. The ravine had its own way of relating the truth of an event suppressed by human conscience or lack of it. People talked in hushed voices about the "revenge of Babi Yar," fearful of security police reprisals. Would another generation someday erect a worthy memorial to the Jewish victims murdered here? Misha wondered silently.

Misha stood solemn, his sight impaired by the flow of tears, his thoughts fused with those of his father, Michael. He tried to feel the emotions of the latter on that first day of slaughter, when the hollow ravine was filled with a sea of blood, hear the sound of the persistent rattle of machine-guns...rat-tat-tat-ta...rat-tat-tat-ta...the children's screams of anguish and fear, the pleadings, the unanswered prayers...His ears pealed, his senses at their highest pitch, Misha was able to hear them now, feel the victims' pain, and experience their despair.

He would give it a try. Why not visit the old city and absorb its sinister spirit? Imagined this way, it wasn't inconceivable. He might yet comprehend. Keep away from the labels, names, and anachronisms. After all, life continued in this modern age, with the latest accoutrements of history's memory, but nothing had really changed.

He was aware of it; he had come to this *new* yet *old* land. A place where covert prejudices as well as overt superstitions worked in concert to keep its own people in discord and strangers away from its borders. Even a change of a person's religion and surname—common and easy enough procedure—was no guarantee of immunity, and no one could foresee where that might lead.

Of the fifty thousand surviving Polish Jews, Misha was told most were leaving for Israel. "Zionists," he thought. "Nah," he concluded on second thought that Zionists were those Jews who financed other Jews to go to their "promised" land, when it still was Palestine, and now Israel. "Colonize!" Those affluent Americans and Britons and South African diamond dealers had told the hapless immigrants. But even then, Israel's total earning capabilities could not sustain her needs nor was she able to invest in itself. Her continuous well-being depended largely on that time-tested "honor code" among Diaspora Jewry—particularly affluent Americans—in need of self redemption with a remorseful view of their bystander status during the European Holocaust. But that was not new either; already in antiquity, Jews dispersed among Roman and Greek cities contributed *shekels* toward the restoration of the Great Temple in Jerusalem.

Time and again during his stay in Kiev, Misha was drawn to Babi Yar on the outskirts of the ancient city. Painful silence was interrupted by those wistful cries only he could hear. Though heaped randomly into that mass grave, the victims were indelibly marked. Somehow, they were known. Even in this place, *their* city. There were places with names, liquor permits on the wall, owners who hired bands, counted inventory, paid taxes. Places located on streets with familiar names that could be pointed out on maps. *This* place is very different.

It haunts. It is marked. Somehow you find yourself here, here particularly, it calls to you. It summons you and your kind, and it warns the others; the ones who crave the hunt, those who acquiesce in some secret chambers of their hearts. It calls your willing prey.

This place has a name: *Babi Yar*. It even has an address on the fringes of reality, somewhere in the twilight of reason. But these facts tell you much less than the truth.

How did he get there? Better yet, *why?*

Misha wandered through the dusk-washed city, as shadows grew and muddled, and quenched the blazing sizzle of the cobble-stoned streets. He felt restless. The city steamed and bubbled like a frying pan would swirl with boiling water. Eventually he would end up there again, on its sinister quarried outskirts, darkened through circumstance and steaming with the sweat of skeletons, the untold numbers of bodies, strangers fused like lovers in the orange glare of the moonlight doing their macabre dance of the dead who refuse to die.

He wandered through wasteland; scorched earth and rubble left of buildings crackled beneath his feet. In his recurring dreams the sky was gray and motionless, the ground was black and hard. He walked through a thin rain, over a landscape that was not really a landscape at all. The devastation around him was also inside him, what was left of who he was. This wounded land was, in final analysis, his soul. Though he waged a long and fierce battle with the demons inside, this was one war he could not win. And in his dreams he would wander and inspect the damage and know that these were hills where green would never grow again.

Morning came and his body felt lazy and waterlogged. He slept late, though he knew the time had come to move on. But he dared not disturb this feeling of comfort—temporary though it was—he knew. Since childhood, he had wanted to be happy. And if he had known then how easy it was, he probably would have followed a different dream. There was no glamour in happiness. And the things he thought would guarantee it did not. He also thought he was so clever when he was young, to answer to that question, "what do you want to be when you grow up?" only "happy." He'd thought this response meant that he was a simple person, but all it really meant was that he was naïve. Along with his "happy" went thousands of things, marriage, children, and a rewarding career; good looks, fame, money, and writing a best seller someday. If he had known happiness could be found in solitude and in a modest house on a secluded beach, he would have despised himself for the paucity of his dreams. When he was young, he wanted glory and passion and pageant. Now, he would gladly settle for peace.

Misha Winograd, son of Motele Winograd, a.k.a. Michael Waneczeven, in the prime of his life, thought himself now old and worn. He felt, even on his best days, that his life was no longer what it seemed to be. Instead of pursuing all it had to offer, he was on the lookout for solutions where there were none. Early on, he concluded that life lasts and lingers, and there is happiness in small things, in the finding and the living of a life. His consuming passion, compelled by a gnawing need to expiate the sins of the father, and the abounding hatred for the one who gave him life and caused him pain, offered him peace neither in his nightmares nor in his waking hours.

Misha knew his life would not be a liturgy. It would merely be a lesson, and small parts of it would be lovely. But he was also aware that someday, instead of streaming into sunlight, he will step back softly into darkness. The tunnel would be his last place, his softest place of all. There was a long journey between here and there, and he was no longer afraid to undertake it.

"I will find him," he murmured stubbornly to himself, "if it takes the rest of my life, I will find the murdering bastard…"he paused, breathing heavily, "and I'll do the right thing. Yes, the *right* thing."

# 10.

THE FIRST RAYS of the rising sun flirted with the last departing shadows of darkness, when Misha opened his eyes and glanced at his wristwatch. "It's late," he murmured sleepily, "I had better get going." Little did he know at the genesis of his Odyssey that there was no hiding from the light it might shed. Though dim at the outset, brighter as he progressed, his long journey was leading him into the abyss of the deepest night.

Belzec, Majdanek, Sobibor, Treblinka, the killing factories that had become to him silent reminders of his father's trail of blood, opened no doors to Michael's whereabouts. "Warsaw, Warsaw,"—"*Warszawa, Warszawa*"—people who knew kept repeating the name of the capital, in answer to his inquiries. The time for his departure neared, and he had to make up his mind whether to let the ghosts lie or to continue in their pursuit.

"Warsaw it is, then," he resolved. "*Warszawa*," as the natives call her.

Misha wandered aimlessly through the streets of the ancient city. They were carnal, tactile; they assaulted him from every hidden corner. He reeled through scents thick as fog, the pulsating life of the city settled on his skin like soot. He slid through it, will-less, drawn from one seemingly random turn to another, wallowing in the sink and stink of the city; he tasted it as he moved through its variations. He was led, at least he felt like it. But he was prepared for the worst.

He passed first through the dark streets quietly, reverently. Though he saw no one, he felt their presence. He sensed their presence in the absence of any other sensation. The square-shaped, fading, Victorian structures leaned against each other like rotten teeth, seemed to whisper secrets one to the next, watched his progress through windows blank and dark as the eyes of aging soured widows. There seemed a feeling of pervading evil in these streets, of backyards gone to seed and worse. But he passed unscathed. He was part of this, this dark, macabre, carnival winding its way through the heart of the city. He walked safe in the sleepless night, through the cruel, crazy-making heat. Yes, he felt at home here. Strangely powerful was the feeling of belonging, a looming sense of lurk and leer under the swollen crimson underbelly of the sky. Thick, damp clouds lit from beneath by the lights of an emerging city.

He went from door to door. They looked at him with blank eyes, embarrassed perhaps, but he would not let them forget he was there on purpose, an integral part, not a frightening accident. No one there knew him, but he was expected. His place was waiting for him, a table, vacant in a sea of faces, he sank down there, leaned back against a cement pillar, felt its roughness poke through the back of his shirt like fingers, peppered his shoulder blades with dry, gritty stings. He kicked off his shoes underneath the table to feel the cool kiss of the moist floor on his skin. A small band was playing, and he could feel the bass line throb in the balls of his feet, from the tips of his toes, through his testicles into the pit of his stomach. He ordered a drink, and when it came it was strong and sweet. It felt like cold candy in his mouth.

"Thanks," he said in Polish *dziękuję*, to the waitress, in an attempt to ingratiate himself. "*Nie ma za co,*"—"you're welcome"— the waitress replied with a smile. Several couples appeared on the dance floor. They were close enough for him to feel the heat coming off them, smell the perfume and powder, the sweat dew on fresh-washed skin, the mist rising off of fresh-washed hair. It was a sweet, thick, cloying smell, riding high on the wave of human heat like icing on a cooling cake. His hunger whipped up and up, but he waited. He would let the night spiral up to meet him. He knew that from experience; as the witching hour came and passed, clothes would loosen, shoes would pile up under tables, people would dance with more and more abandon, in ones, twos, and threes, on tables. Sometime, then, the choice would be made. For now, he waited, and he watched.

Misha was not the only one waiting. There were others there. He avoided looking at them, but he felt their presence. He sensed them as cold spots in the human warmth, as dark corners in the bright-lit, shifting crowd.

It was dusk at the watering hole, and the animals were gathering. Still wary, still alert, but relaxing. They felt strange comfort in their numbers; inconspicuous, they lowered their heads. Somewhere there was the prey. The willing ones would make themselves known to him, as they always did. He would linger a little behind the pack, drink deeply, be slow to startle. The willing ones would soon come forward.

The waitress refilled his drink. Her name was Matylda, and her eyes met his with the blank contempt of absolute knowledge. Misha was at first uncomfortable in her presence. Like cats, they were each other's mirror reflections. She was pale; pale skin, pale hair, pale eyes. She was pale and perfect and eerie, and the bottom of her skirt seemed to float and swirl constantly, revealing the shapely thighs in motion, it seemed to ride on its own unknowable breeze even when she was standing still.

She moved from him, weaved between the tables, the dancers, but her image, the illusion was different. Misha seemed to see the dancers, the furniture, bending away from her, making her room. She could be walking across the spreading, empty floor, so sure and smooth and straight in her path. Heads turned to follow her progress. Eyes glared. Misha was familiar with those kinds of looks. It happened to him as well. Too far removed from their senses, the watchers reacted to the disturbance they felt and called it lust; some may have called it love. They didn't seem to realize it was fear sounding the alarm inside them; its resonance had caused them to tremble, to ache and flush.

He followed her path across the dance floor, and she resembled a Gypsy dancer, a can-can performer. Only tonight she was dancing in a lace bed jacket over a loose, flowered sundress like white trash. The points of her bony hips made crisp, perfect figure-eighths, like a stripper's. And yet, her turns were funky, fluid and slow, under the white arms that twisted languidly in the air as she balanced her tray, her head held high.

She returned to his table and flirted with him. Her long, cool neck, the way she stretched it out, tilted back her head, an offering. She was ready. She had that dreamy blankness, that certain allurement in her eyes. Her hair, which hung straight and dark and long, was like curtains parted on the cool, white room of her face, a face that hung so still and sweet in its dark frame, looking out through the half-closed eyes of a sleepy lizard. He wanted to possess her that very moment. But he knew when it happens she will struggle, she will protest, the "no" like a chuckle in the back of her throat. She will always know what she was doing. Always know what he was. What he urgently needed. Wanted.

The music died away, and she dropped into the chair next to him. She smelled strong and sweet. He realized that she was there now for some time. He was staring.

She looked back at him, her eyes half-dazed, half-amused. Some spark of defiance looked out at him from the familiar black well of surrender.

"You have been watching me," she said. Her voice was not as thrilling as he would have imagined it, but everything was lost in the rush, the swooning unreality of the conversation.

"I like the way you move," he said for want of anything else he might have said at the moment. All he could think about was that this woman will be his guide in those difficult surroundings.

"Do you want to dance with me?" She leaned forward in her chair, revealing her full breasts, half-braced to stand, sure of herself. Sure of what she'd wanted.

"No," he was not sure he wanted it to sound as a rejection, and he quickly added: "To talk, can we talk?"

She continued to smile for a beat or two. Slowly, she stopped smiling. She was cautious now, but still interested.

"You…American, yes?"

"No, German." Her expression lost the smile. "Well, more like French, really," he added quickly.

"Don't you dance?"

"No."

"What do you come here for then?" She challenged.

"I come to have a drink and watch." He replied.

"Ugh, that's boring." She shook her shoulders and glanced away from him, out over the sea of dancers, as if looking for someone else who might be watching her. He felt like saying something quickly to rivet those eyes on him again.

"Can we go somewhere? To talk? When do you get off work?"

She didn't look at him. "I don't go out with strangers."

"Make an exception in my case. I'll make it worth your while." She turned, quizzical. He tried to read her eyes, she surely wrote him off, pigeonholed him. Her face read determination and she was about to leave.

"I can be a lot of fun." He said, and then he added, "I'm not half as bad as you think me to be." He tried to laugh, but only a short cough came out of his dried throat. She surprised him and laughed. Her laughter was shrill, relieved. The amusement was back in her eyes. It was a kind of cockiness that signified her obvious half-contempt toward him. He had to wonder if she'd heard that line before. She must have.

"What is it you want with me?" She asked with the candor of misplaced innocence.

"I need your help. Important help. I'll pay." He was desperate.

"Let's go." Without another word, she led the way toward the back door and into the dark yard.

# 11.

AFTER A NIGHT WELL SPENT, Misha felt the intensity and suddenness of change when morning came. The phenomenon was a direct product of his passionate need to pursue his goal; that of finding his father.

"You might try their cemetery," Matilda suggested from the comfort of her bed, as he was readying to leave. *Their* meant Jewish.

"Cemetery?" He asked puzzled. By now this directive was quite familiar.

"Surely, you've heard, that's where they go to visit first when they return." She paused. "Some to say the mourner's *Kaddish*, others to dig up the loot they'd buried before they left." She giggled wildly. He looked at her quizzically, and she added: "Only a month ago, Moshe Feiner, the former owner of *Feiner Textiles*, came back and recovered three pounds of gold he'd buried under the his grandfather's grave marker."

"You don't mean…"

"Didn't live to enjoy it, though…"

"How's that?" Misha's curiosity got the better of him. The moment he'd asked the question, he knew he shouldn't have.

"The police found Moshe in a local hotel room strangled with his telephone cord the morning after." She declared, emotionless.

"You mean…people still pursue them, even after what they've gone through?" He was appalled.

"It's become a sort of industry," she giggled, "and it's called 'waiting for the rich Jew's return'."

"Things haven't changed much." He said.

"And never will." He detected sadness in her voice for the first time. "Go now," she urged, "the earlier you get to the place, the more of a chance to meet someone. And come back when you're through."

As a result of the great uprising and subsequent destruction activities of the German Nazi "conquerors", the Jewish Warsaw cemetery was reduced to a state of chaos. Virtually, not a single grave marker, vault or grave was left intact. It seemed so deliberate a barbarism, next to which only a hurricane of great force could have inflicted such heavy destruction. There was nothing left of the once sumptuous cemetery, a final resting place remarkable for the centuries of its great variety of structures and rich panoply of landscaping.

Misha wandered through the havoc perplexed and helpless. Here and there, he would clear the debris or weeds that had taken over a site. Kneeling, he read the grave marker inscription. All this to no avail. The latest dates on the stones were carved in 1943. Only some of them showed a semblance of efforts at restoration; the debris had been removed, a stone halfway cemented together to its original dimensions, occasional bundles of withered flowers gracing a site. Misha regarded the latter with restored hope. "Someone must have laid them here," he reasoned.

"What do you want here!?" A gruff voice thundered behind him. Misha jumped to his feet, frightened to hear an angry voice coming out of nowhere. He turned. A tall, haggard looking man, in his late fifties perhaps, towered over him. A heavy black beret covered the man's head above the skeletal face whose fiery eyes spewed hostility at the intruder. His hands wielded menacingly a shovel, the emblem of a gravedigger.

"You don't belong!" The man thundered.

"No need to worry," Misha's voice shook with emotion, conciliatory. "I'm not doing any harm."

"Go on, beat it!" The man shouted into the stillness. He motioned toward the gate with his enormous hand. Misha noticed the poverty of the man's clothing; a thin shirt, sorely in need of repair, pair of dirty pants with holes worn through the knees, and rustic military boots that must have seen better days. Beyond their fierceness, the gravedigger's eyes showed anxiety over the intruder's presence. Some fear, perhaps, as well. Misha knew a tried remedy, as his hand reached into his pocket.

"Now, keep your hands where I can see them." The man growled. Misha kept his hands clear off his pockets.

"My good man," he addressed the gravedigger, "I mean you no harm," he smiled, "will you permit me to share some money with you?" Misha's eyes squinted in his attempt to penetrate the man's thinking. "I'm willing to pay for your help," he reached into his pocket again, now without the man's protest, and withdrew a fifty Złoty note, at the sight of which the fire in the gravedigger's eyes was almost extinguished. He put down his shovel, relaxed his demeanor, and reached for the note. Misha breathed relief.

"Not so fast." Misha pulled back. "First some information."

"All right, all right." The man barked. "What's on your mind?"

"Is there a grave site around here with the name Winograd?" The man was silent, and Misha trembled with anticipation. "If there is one, point me to it, please." He waited. The gravedigger's lips moved without sound. He was in deep thought.

"Winograd...Winograd..." He repeated. "I couldn't tell. So much killing. So many graves. Many are nameless. So many dead..." He brooded and spoke in monosyllables.

"Can you think of anyone who knows?" Misha insisted. "It's important."

"You might try...the..." the man was hesitant, his eyes directed at Misha's hand, which held on to the fifty Złotys banknote, "well, I would look for it at the *shul*, you know, a small room in which the Jews congregate for their daily worship. That's where they get together now that the great synagogue was torched during the uprising." Misha handed the man the money as he readied to leave.

"Here, take it." The gravedigger swiftly pocketed the money. He cracked an artificial smile. "To think that I took you for some Jew come to dig up his loot." He chuckled. "Sorry...sorry...I didn't mean to make joke. You had better go now and visit their community." He hesitated. "They're in the Old City"—he used the Polish equivalent *Stare Miasto*—"some of them survivors, some that got away before the war, to Palestine, you know." He turned to go. "Hope you'll find the one you're looking for." He picked up his shovel and vanished into the thicket as mysteriously as he had emerged earlier.

Misha had finally gotten directions from the most unlikely source. He had come here, to this soft place. And it had shown promise of leading him in the right path. Would he be happy? There was a subtlety to happiness, a texture to it that seemed to escape the young. When he was younger, he wasn't happy. Really happy. He was elated, devastated, uplifted, and emptied out. He was tempest-tossed and storm-ridden. What he'd believed of his life was that it was passionate, creative, and impetuous. But he had learned that strong emotion is opposite to happiness; as serenity is the other side of youth.

Now, that he approached the end of his journey, Misha felt unsure, a little hesitant about the future.

Not far off to the north, the hurricanes whipped the beaches, the thunderstorms pounded the rooftops, the hail and snow cut the power lines, and Misha shivered in starless darkness at the mere thought of it. He had a foreboding of things to come. And when the sun came out again, there was a crisp, hard edge to everything, as if the world sparkled in sharp light. And in this new world it was meant to be a joy to breathe, and stretch, and feel the sun on one's face, and touch the walls of the houses that lived nearby, stood in and around you like a long-lived lover. In that new world, the old fears should lag behind as dreams of those long dead, and they had no place there and their dreams even less so. He thought.

They huddled around the small lectern, the prayer shawls wrapped round their shoulders and over their heads—only the initiated would see the phylacteries under the cloth on their foreheads and the left arms—they prayed. Their rapid delivery transported Misha centuries back. This was the core of their faith. Misha thought as he observed the swaying figures. After all they went through, loss of loved ones, torment, hunger, humiliation, constant fear and the absence of *their* God in all that, they stubbornly returned to His fold. This must be the epitome of trust. Misha thought.

Someone handed him a yarmulke and a prayer shawl while his lips kept moving and no sound emerged. Misha placed both in the right places. The *shamus* (beadle) called out names, and those called came forward to recite the prayer before the Torah portion was read. Misha prayed his name would not be called out. He dreaded their embarrassment more than his own. They did not call him. He was relieved when there was shaking of hands and the services ended.

"You must be new in town," someone addressed him.

"Yes, I am only passing through," Misha answered. It was the *shamus.*

"Looking for someone?" The man inquired.

"Why do you think that?" Misha admired the man's perception.

"Well, you, obviously, didn't come only to join the *minyan*, did you?" There was a well-intended humor in the man's eyes.

"I must confess, I'm looking for a man named Winograd. Do you know anyone by that name?" Misha looked anxiously at the bearded, old man.

The old man thought in silence. Misha could feel a sense of effort on the part of his host. "Winograd...Winograd...?" He repeated, stroking his beard. "That's a tough one. You know, most of us try to blend in nowadays. Many have changed their surnames. Difficult to say what his name might now be." He mused.

"Any idea? Any at all. Even a guess would be helpful." Misha knew he was grasping at straws.

"I'd say your best bet would be putting an ad in the *Excelsior*. That's our major paper. If you don't get a response from it, you just won't get one anywhere else." The man shook his head. "Our people, the few that returned home, are now scattered all over the city. Not all of them are, how should I say, card-carrying Jews. Some don't even come to worship on the High Holy Days, *Rosh Hashanah* and *Yom Kippur*." He sighed heavily. "Ah, the price we still pay for the hellish events of the past."

"I want to thank you for your help." Misha said quickly, reluctant to enter into philosophical debate with the eloquent *shamus*. He clasped his hand cordially, "good bye, good bye," he said to the startled man.

"Good bye, young man," the *shamus* responded. "If you need our help, you know where to find us." He called after the departing Misha. "How quaint," Misha wondered, "after all they went through, they still have trust in random strangers. How unusual, indeed."

The entry into the personal ad section of the *Excelsior* read:

*Urgent—seeking family of Michael Waneczeven or Winograd. Anyone with information please call 62-568. Ask for Dr. Misha Winograd.*

Two days had gone by. Misha had all but lost hope of making contact. His deadline for departure was imminent, and there was no response. He was certain that he had traveled the wrong path on his tedious journey. Only Matylda's sincere encouragements gave him a semblance of hope. Then, on the eve of his departure, the phone rang:

"Dr. Winograd?" A shy, anxious, female voice inquired. Matylda handed him the receiver. "It's for you." The blood in Misha's veins surged with a singular excitement. Could it be? He asked himself silently. He was speechless. "The voice on the other end repeated the inquiry: "Dr. Winograd?"

"Yes, this is he." He responded and hated himself for sounding hoarse. That revealed his excitement. "Do you speak German or French?" He asked. God, let it happen. He prayed silently.

"Yes, I prefer French." She said. "I'm calling in reference to your ad...in the *Excelsior*, you know. We need to talk. Can we meet?" All this gushed out in one breath. She, too, was excited. He knew.

"Uh...yes..." Misha was composed. "Where and when?"

"You tell me, please." She waited silently for him to make up his mind. He indicated Matylda's place and she agreed. "Will it be all right to meet during morning hours? Ten a.m. would be fine with me." The woman insisted that the meeting take place during "working hours."

"That will be fine." He said, and he was glad she agreed to meet at Matylda's, just in case there were some language problems. The woman's French was not altogether up to par. He replaced the receiver to its cradle.

Moments later, the phone rang again. "It's her, again." Matylda said. And she added: "She wants to talk to you."

"Yes?" Misha felt some trepidation. "What is it?"

"My husband...Zbyszek..." her words were labored, "he wants you to come see us at our place..." She breathed heavily.

"Are you certain?" Misha asked. Zbyszek? He was surprised.

"Absolutely." She let out a sigh of relief.

"Where and when?" He asked.

"Poznańska 24. For dinner, at six. Yes?" She was anxious. "Look for apartment 12. Janina and Zbyszek Ładziak."

"Thank you. I'll be there." Misha hung up the receiver and threw a quizzical look at Matylda. "Janina and Zbyszek Ładziak? What do you think? Dinner at six, at their place. That might not be the man I've been looking for. Will you come along? Please, do, dear Matylda!"

"I don't think that's a good idea, Misha." Said Matylda. "You've been waiting for this moment, and you deserve to savor it on your own. Face to face. Don't you think?" She paused. "And, as far as names go, you know, name changes, they are quite commonplace."

"Please come along, as a witness." He begged.

"I'd rather stay away. If you should choose to kill him, I don't want to witness it." She let out her usual giggle. "But, if you should find it in your heart to forgive and forget, let it be to your credit entirely. I'd rather have it this way."

"I've been looking forward to this meeting for such a long time, Matylda. Now, that it's here, I have my doubts. It makes no sense." Misha tried to explain his mixed feelings and presentiments. He shook his head. "It makes no sense at all."

Misha tossed and turned through a restless night. Instead of taking refuge in the arms of the sensuous Matylda, only hysterical symptoms had found their place in his soul. It was his typical "flight into his illness," which had little or nothing to do with the erotically frustrated woman lying next to him.

On her part, Matylda felt hot flashes appearing like a stammer, as though the menstruation disturbances had arrived sooner than expected, and in their wake a hysterically founded "false pregnancy." How long these symptoms would now last, she dreaded to guess. Days? Weeks? Months, perhaps, as a result of one wasted night. It was the longest night of her young life.

# 12.

THE ANCIENT MERCEDES taxi—a far cry of the erstwhile conventional horse-drawn carriages that were still in occasional use—delivered him to the designated address; a drab, Soviet-built apartment high-rise in the new city. Misha rang the outdoor bell and Janina came down the three flights of stairs to fetch him in the entry hallway. She had asked that he come through the back way. "People talk. This way you'll attract less attention," was her reasoning. The courtyard was empty. There were some trees, obviously planted here and there after the deluge of total destruction, and he walked in their sparse trail. He savored the evening cool, though the gravel underfoot gave up the familiar summer heat collected from the daily sun. Colored lights strung from the trees scattered shadows all around in the semi-darkness, soothingly; helping him rid himself of the anxiety he had felt during the sleepless night and on his way here.

They walked the three flights up, and she led the way. He observed her wide hips, in contrast to the narrow, flat chest when she greeted him with a slight curtsy. "So nice of you to come." She said, before commencing ahead of him up the steep staircase. Her graying, chestnut, hair was combed back tightly into a bun. Her full, round, face was punctuated by a pair of laughing blue eyes. Overall, she'd made a positive impression. Misha wondered how this wide-hipped, narrow-chested woman with the laughing eyes would taste. Was it like thick, light cream, vanilla froth over bitter honey? The crisp crunch of bones as delicate as the bird's. Was he ravenous for her? *He*, his father?

The door was open, and they entered. She showed him to the living-room sofa, and he sat down. She excused herself with another curtsy and walked toward the corner room. Misha observed that it was a four room apartment, a rarity in any of Poland's cities, except among small elite.

Janina returned and sat down opposite Misha. "He'll be with us soon." She said, her eyes downcast. "We are registered at City Hall as Holocaust survivors and qualify for a small government pension. We also collected a tidy sum of restitution moneys from the Federal Republic of Germany." She said, apparently to justify the appearance of their modest wealth.

Misha was silent. He wanted to tell her that this wasn't necessary, that he understood that she shouldn't worry. But he was unable to speak. He wasn't even sure this was the right place and the people he had sought. What if all this was in vain? He thought, when, he saw Zbyszek appear out of the corner room.

Suddenly, he saw this man before him; the stranger he'd imagined to be his father in his weird nightmares and daydreams. A frail man. His feet shuffling laboriously, shoulders hunched over forward over the chest cavity, with fear in his empty eyes, the narrow lips expressing time spent in solitude and silence. He bowed his naked head with a soft *"dzień dobry"*—"good day or hello"— and sat opposite Misha next to the woman called Janina.

Bear hugs were unnecessary. They would be completely out of character, even though this has been the very first meeting and, most likely, their last. The Third Reich had brought them together. Its legacy would also keep them apart. They sat silently opposite each other, each drawing the other to open the conversation. Misha couldn't help but think of the comments he'd read in the archives about this man who might be his father. *"Efficient ghetto and camp policeman, Michael was rewarded by being given a* Volksdeutscher *status. To show his appreciation, he turned his brutality on his own people…turned out more zealous than his masters, the Nazis. He beat inmates to death with blows of his rifle butt; he forced many to crawl on all fourth or sit on their haunches until they lost consciousness. Of all this he was very proud and oftentimes boast-ful...* There followed much more of the same.

"Have you killed people?" Misha suddenly asked. He was now certain it was the right place and the man he faced was the father he had sought.

"*Tak, tak,*" Michael responded absentmindedly, "yes, yes."

"How many?" Misha pressed, while he contemplated killing this thug. How proud and arrogant he must have felt in victory. How meek he was in defeat like all of them.

"Plenty, it was war." Michael's reply was clear.

"Were they children? Women? Jews? Priests? Gays?" Misha's rage was evident. The blood ran to his face and escaped it intermittently.

Michael seemed to have, finally, understood what Misha was driving at, cracked an imbecilic smile, wagged a finger at his inquisitor bastard son, and said with a raised voice: "Enemies of the Reich, Bolsheviks!" Janina walked behind her husband and placed her hands on his shoulders. Her fingers dug into his clavicles. She said: "Calm down, Michael, calm down." She addressed him by his given name. No more charades, neither pretense nor deception. It was the first time she had used it, and he looked up at her serene face and became calm himself. Only his left hand, curled inward, a gesture he habitually used to hide his trigger finger deformed during interrogation by his captors, the partisans. It twitched imperceptibly off and on. Never again would he fire a shot. Misha regarded the frail frame of his father and thought how easily he could snuff out that miserable life. Suddenly, Michael spoke with a measured but monotone voice:

"I was doing them a favor. I killed them to save them from all that suffering. Sooner or later they'd be humiliated, tortured, only to end up gassed and burnt in the ovens. I knew that, and I knew they would suffer before they were put to death. I had mercy on them. That's what it was, mercy." He paused and took a labored breath. His left hand now shook spasmodically, and he no longer tried to hide his deformity.

"Dear, maybe you shouldn't get excited. Remember what the doctor said." Janina cautioned.

"I must tell him," Michael insisted. "If it's the last thing I do. He must know. I can't hide it any longer. I'm done. Let him be the judge."

"I didn't come to judge you." Misha heard himself say, although it was contrary to what his thoughts and intentions have been. "I only wanted to see you, Motele Winograd. To see the monster who abandoned my mother and caused her immeasurable pain and, surely, her death." Misha spoke with an even cadence; his eyes never left those of Motele, while the latter sat still, his own eyes directed into the void of an open window. Suddenly, Motele spoke again:

"You have to hook up with somebody in life, don't you?" He posed a rhetorical question, which he himself answered in the next breath. "I was caught up in the middle of that movement, and it was great power the Nazis had at that time. It was, it seemed, limitless. Nothing, nobody, could stop them, and it felt good to share their destiny. To be a part of their glory was exhilarating. I did not hesitate to do my duty. If I'd have refused, there would have been many to replace me. I don't doubt that for a moment. And when their luck ran out, things took a turn for the worse, it was too late." He spoke haltingly, almost apologetically, with sadness, though without any sign of remorse. Misha listened silently, incredulous. Was it possible? Was this the person from whose sperm he had been conceived? Was he?

For the first time, Misha felt himself overcome with great, totally genuine hatred toward the father he never had, and thoughts of homicide reentered his mind. He resented the arrogance, the very smugness of Michael's confession. "Just like so many others of his ilk," he thought in silence, "willing assassins of innocent children consumed with a sense of entitlement and possessed of unlimited power during the height of their conquest." His eyes bored into Motele's with such hatred it made the other turn sideways. "But in his defeat he grovels in exaggerated humility, denying individual responsibility, his own complicity." Misha concluded.

"I wish...I wish..." Misha trembled violently from head to toe, tight-fisted, the whiteness of his knuckles evident, while Motele sat rigid in his chair, without expression. "I want to kill you!" Misha shouted at the man before him, while he took hold of his shoulders and shook him violently. "But that would be too easy a way out for you!" Misha let go and regained composure. "I want you to go on with this eternal fear, an imprisonment of your soul and spirit, in complete darkness and a total absence of hope. That's a fitting punishment for one of your kind. You must expect the final blow every moment, look over your shoulder, but you mustn't know where it will come from or when." Misha stepped back to his chair and sat down.

Motele's face paled. He showed emotion for the first time since Misha's arrival. "Son...please, hear me out, please, have mercy on..."

"Like you had mercy on the victims you murdered?!" Misha was relentless. "And don't you dare call me your son!" He stood up and approached Motele with both his hands high above his head as if to strike a blow. Janina came between them.

"Please, Misha, for God's sake!" She implored.

"Which God? Whose God?" Misha mimicked. "Your God? His God? My absent God? Is there one?"

"Don't blaspheme." She implored in a nearly inaudible whisper.

"Me? Blaspheme?" Misha asked. He pointed at Michael. "There's the man who invented blasphemy!" He shouted. Motele cringed under the sound of Misha's voice. His upper body hung limp from the chair, his eyes lifeless, directed still into the void.

"I'm dying...soon I'll be gone...cancer of the pancreas...it has spread to the bones..." Motele, the recalcitrant Nazi, recited these words as if in solemn prayer. "Forgive a dying sinner. I need your forgiveness. Say you forgive me." His hand reached out for Misha's.

Misha put both his hands behind his back and moved away from his seat. He was silent. "I need you to say *Kaddish* when I'm gone..." Motele, the eternal Jew, agonized.

"You must ask forgiveness of the many victims you murdered and wronged, they alone have the right to forgive you." Misha readied to leave. "I wish you long life, Motele." He addressed the erstwhile *Waffen SS*-man, now aged beyond his age, degenerate in body and spirit. "Enough time to prepare yourself for the final judgment. As for me, I'm done with you. I had no father, conceived of a virgin mother, victim of her times. I'll have no memories of him. So be it." He approached the door. As he reached for the doorknob, Misha turned with his last hard look at the bent over frame of the surviving Nazi. In the ancient Jewish tradition, he spat toward the latter three times. Through the open door, he'd heard Janina's spasmodic sobs even as he descended to the lower flight of stairs. He felt a sinister satisfaction within. He chuckled hoarsely.

Misha's heart pounded like those hurricanes that whip the beaches, the thunderstorms that pound the roofs. He would now be free of the specter that held him captive all those years of lamentable growing up. He cut out his past, as the hail and storm cut the power lines, and left the "old" man to shiver through moonless nights. He stepped out of the building and into a new world where it was a joy to breathe and stretch, and feel the sun on his face. In this new world the old presentiments lagged far behind, like dreams in the head of someone who'd lived long ago. In his new world there was no place for that long dead person.

It was a day of renewal for Misha. Everything was new. Liberated. The cool breeze made love to him, it cleansed him. This was not a dream. He felt as if he stood naked, and the cool ocean waves swept up and around him, first from one side and then from the other. They teased the hair around his face with their fingers and then, losing patience, gathered it all up in a tail and flung it back from his neck. Misha raised his face to the wind, and it took his breath away. It slid up from the ground, along and between his legs only to vanish into the distance, to sneak up on him some other way.

Misha remained still in his trance for as long as he was able, his arms wide, and then, when he could stand it no more, he ran through the courtyard and out onto the street. Every breath he took in the June air, the wind stole away from him, until he stood still, panting and dazed.

Life lasts and lingers, he thought. It is virtually indestructible. In bed with Matylda that night—the last on that continent for him—in the glow of the many candles she lit, came the realization. Sleek and soft and smooth as water, life pours around you, engulfs you, and drowns you in reality. An unglamorous reality, but a comforting one. Where there is enough to eat, and a roof overhead, where there is freedom from want and physical pain and some sort of exercise for the mind, where these things exist so can we. Love and laughter, passion and prayer and poetry, all these are luxuries, lovely luxuries. Life does not always include them initially or well. These are things that are not to be taken for granted, but things for which room must be made.

Not the most romantic view of life, but Misha was comfortable in it. Though in his chase for his past, he thought he was chasing something noble, and he became an apostle to pain. He remembered, as a little boy, Blanche had introduced him to another axiom of life: "If it doesn't hurt, you're not trying hard enough." Early on, he was obsessed by it, and as he grew, in his pursuit of the unknown, he embraced pain as an indicator of going in the right direction. Things did not come to him easy then, and the pain toughened him, not only was he tolerant of it, but he gloried in it. The pain of denial was the closest he could come to having in abundance. He would not give it up even to "save his life," as they say. And he didn't.

Suddenly, an excited vendor's voice shouted a daily headline. He waved a copy of the *Excelsior* high above his head for all to see: WIFE OF ELDERLY HOLOCAUST SURVIVOR ZBYSZEK ŁADZIAK VICTIM OF MAIL BOMB!! Misha bought a copy and read with great disbelief: "...*A seemingly harmless letter arrived this morning at the Ładziak residence. It was addressed to the Ładziaks and the sender was an alleged attorney in Hamburg—the police was unable to decipher the name from the leftover fragments—Janina opened the airmail envelope, which contained the triggering device. Her face and hands were instantly mutilated and she was left totally blind...*"

The article went on to further embellish the circumstances, but Misha tossed the paper into the trash bin. He'd read enough. Commentary was superfluous. "This one was meant for you, dear papa." He whispered under his breath. "You'll never figure the timing of the next one." A bitter smile on his face, he turned to his companion.

"Good bye, sweet Matylda," Misha embraced her tenderly.

"Come back soon, love." She surprised him with the sound of the "L" word they had never used before.

"I'm not the same person that I was coming here, Matylda." He said, and there was sadness in his voice.

"To me, you'll always be the same," she said, and he knew she didn't understand what he had implied.

"I've fulfilled the dream...perhaps the nightmare of my lifetime." He said more to himself than to her. "Since childhood I'd wanted to feel free of it. Now, that all this is behind me, I don't quite know whether to climb to ecstasy or wallow in despair. All I know is that this is no place for me."

"Uh?" She clung to him.

"You'll just have to come to my world, Matylda." He smiled sadly. "Only there we can live harder and faster, instead of dying every day slowly. We will leave this planet glowing whiter and whiter, hotter and brighter, until together we'll stream out into sunlight and become one with its energy. Burn out, flame out, flare out!" Misha laughed loudly, for he knew Matylda hadn't a clue about the meaning of his soliloquy. He was wont to explain its meaning. Then, softly, he added, as if in afterthought: "My life might yet become a paean or a modest poem. A short poem at that. Then who knows, it might even become an important novel. Perhaps even a saga, to be transmitted through generations by word of mouth, though sometimes I think it will suffice it to be a haiku."

He stepped up to the ticketing counter, handed his tickets and passport to the official. The morning news was still on his mind. With that explosion, he knew, Michael or Motele a.k.a. Zbyszek, had become a public figure. He was now in the forefront of an altogether public enterprise. Auschwitz, Maidanek, Sobibor, and other killing factories, were such a public enterprise.

Before he entered the carrier, he turned to wave goodbye, and he saw the puzzled look on Matylda's face. He burst out in loud laughter to the astonishment of those near him. It felt good to be alive.

# 13.

THEY WOKE HIM at the exact moment when the explosion tore Janina's hands into shreds and was made her totally blind. He could clearly see the hollow sockets of her eyes and a thin trickle of blood as it made its way down both her cheeks...

"Wha...?" He sat up on his bunk at the sound of the loud knocking at the door and tried to rub the sleep from his eyes.

"Misha Winograd!" He heard the bailiff's voice. "Get ready for the hearing!"

He looked around him in a daze. Much as he tried to collect his thoughts, they still came to him only in fragments. His drab surroundings seemed so familiar by now that he was, for the moment, under the illusion they were part of his dream. Only when he saw the bailiff's eyes peering at him through the tiny, square spy-window in the door did Misha wake up to the reality of the moment.

"In half an hour! Misha! Get ready!" The voice was unmistakable. He must do what they say; else there will be reprisals. How was he to get ready? He'd like to shave his face clean, but all of his toiletries were confiscated save the bar of soap. Not even his hairbrush or a comb was left him. Dangerous instruments. They said. His street clothing, too, had been put on hold, and he wore the drab pajama-like uniform of the institution day and night.

He splashed some cold water on his face. The liquid felt refreshingly good. He was completely awake now, and he paced across his cell impatiently. Why don't they come? He was ready. Wasn't it half an hour yet? He had no way of telling. They confiscated his wristwatch early on. "You'll have no use for it here." He was told. "Time is irrelevant for the likes of you." He didn't understand what they meant by that, but he let it go at that. What's the use of asking for explanations?

He wished they'd come for him now. The sooner the better. He was weary of the monotony of his routine. If he could at least light up a cigarette. He'd acquired the habit during the long hours of research when he worked on his doctoral dissertation, even though he knew that cigarettes were more harmful than smoking his pipe. He'd had too much trouble lighting and re-lighting the latter. The tobacco inside the confounded thing kept going out all the while.

Misha stepped up to the door to have a look through the spy-slot. There was no one in sight. Have they forgotten him? Was this, too, one of their ways to torment him? Wasn't it half an hour yet?

He counted the cadence of their steps that echoed against the tile floor. They don't forget anyone in this place. Everything happens as if rehearsed. Even the screams of the inmates resound at certain intervals; the lamentations; the derisive cat-calls and endless cynical commentary from inmate to inmate.

Two huge, athletic attendants accompanied him to his second interrogatory. The first one took place after his arrest, and it was a complete disaster. Everything went well initially, until they put *that* question to him about *that* night, facts which he had tried to push into the farthest recesses of his memory. He preferred not to think about it now. This time, it was going to be different. He had hoped.

The sun was shining in a cloudless sky when they left the building and stepped into the courtyard. Spring was nearly over, and the pleasant weather conditions played well on Misha's psyche. Had he not lost count of the passing time, he might have known that his birthday had come and gone a few days ago, on May thirtieth. It was his first birthday away from Alida.

Though he hadn't any idea what to expect from the court proceedings, he felt relieved at the mere thought about getting on with it. Anything was better than being cooped up in his small cell day in day out. Over these hot, languid nights and days without seeing daylight—his room had no windows leading to the outside—he had come to despise the place.

He remembered vaguely what had brought him here. Some disjointed facts he had tried to put together in his mind and make sense out of them. There were muddled fragments of his past etched in his memory like some sort of a story of which he was an integral part. Like a tale told by wandering minstrels in smoke-filled pubs and meeting halls. Or it might have been a story intoned by a wizard in a dark mysterious cavern deep in the forest? Lorelei might have sung his story, wafting to the sailors over a midnight river. His was a long, strong tale. Of that he was certain.

Some day, he promised himself, he would write that story. He would write what he knew well. Doesn't everybody? This story that he knew so well, it breathed inside his soul and beat thunderously in his heart. This tale whispered its words into his as he spoke them, it lived in his eyes, and he saw it in his nightmares and dreams. He knew it too well, almost too well to write it. Suddenly, one of the three Judges spoke to him:

*"Have you got anything to tell us? Facts, young man. The court wants facts. What happened on that night? Do you remember? Susanna...*

*There was no name more terrifying in this tale than that of his Susanna. It was so, because most of the time he could not remember the details. There were times she appeared to him and he could hear her speak, though no words were spoken. Vaguely, as if through a mist of time, he remembered...*

She was loving and pliant on his return from Poland. She made him feel comfortable in her place, and he stayed not as a welcome guest but much more than that. Significantly more.

"Is She in love with me?" He often asked himself. His mind labored very slowly. He was never at his best in such matters. He was never like her. Her mind reacted instantaneously. Especially in the dark of night when they lay in bed in a tight embrace. As a child, Misha remembered, he was afraid of the dark and sought refuge in his mother's bedroom. He recalled obsessively the scene with great clarity. He saw that bedroom, which she had all to herself, and it got so she used to wait until her drunken husband was asleep and then had Misha crawl in next to her. He would inch his way under the sheets (no finger or foot was left uncovered), barely breathing, careful not to wake his stepfather, the sinister *Herr Doktor* Horst. He always remembered to get up early and sneak up back into his room. He would be severely punished when caught.

It was different with Susanna. Where it was once fear that kept him awake, now he loved the darkness. He felt safe in it. In fact, well-lighted rooms made him feel vulnerable at times. Not darkness. In a lighted room, he felt as if invisible eyes, beyond the blank, black windows, maybe only a few feet away, were watching him. And though both of them had friends, they preferred to share their moments of relaxation with one another.

Misha had gotten a teaching position at a private trade school. Susanna worked as a mannequin at the exclusive *Prima* department store. Through all the time they were together, Misha and Susanna had developed a mutual trust even without the bonds of matrimony. "We don't need a piece of some bureaucratic stationery to remind us of our fidelity." She'd say, with a twinkle in her bright blue eyes and a smile on her lips. "All we need is good sex," Misha would conclude for her and they'd laugh uproariously, irreverently. Susanna used to tease him about the pretty coeds who were after him, but he had a way of dismissing it: "That's the fantasy you live with, my darling." He said, and would suddenly become very serious: "You're all I can handle." To defuse what might have become a source of sadness for either of them, their lovemaking intensified; a lot of it. When they were not making love, they engaged in incessant conversation. And they never lacked for interesting topics. He shared his knowledge with her, and she proudly made it her own. They read to each other from the works of great poets, some serious works like those of the classics, Goethe, Schiller, and some foreign greats, Balzac, Maupassant, Zola, to name only a few. Other times they enjoyed humorous verses of Wilhelm Busch and Gerhart Herrmann Mostar, that brought tears to their eyes, they laughed so hard.

There were times, however, when the authority from above had made itself felt, and caused Misha to fall into fits of profound remorse and depression; oftentimes, to the point of punishing himself. After all, ever since he could remember, first at the Sisters of Mercy, where he was placed as an orphan, and in later years reunited with Blanche, who insisted on a sound Jesuit education, his only wish was to become a priest. He accepted all authority without question, and his present behavior was tantamount to rebellion against those time-worn principles and dictates. He puzzled over what became of his ideal to join a mission somewhere in the darkest regions of Africa where he would help to educate the natives and their underprivileged children? His lofty goals had weakened when they met—Susanna and he—at the dance school as graduating seniors. From then on his animal instincts had taken over; his attraction for her had become stronger than the furtive drive to remain celibate.

They had lived in wedlock for nearly two years when he was offered the post-doctoral stipend at the University of Illinois. "Of course, you must accept it, Misha," Susanna was adamant, equally as excited about his good fortune as was the recipient. Her calmness belied a deep anxiety. What she would not make known to him was that she was already well into two months with his child. She feared such news would most definitely become a hindrance to his career outlook.

"I do not feel good about it," Misha said, "leaving you here alone like this while I am on the far end of the globe." In the cool of the evening, they walked by the river, held hands, fingers intertwined, and talked about mutual concerns. The following day, he had purchased a modest engagement ring as a symbol of his devotion and the seriousness of his promises. "I'll send for you as soon as I'm well situated there, my darling." He said. She avoided his searching eyes. She accepted his pledge and was proud to be engaged to him. He would be a good 'catch' for any of the girls chasing after him. Wasn't it every woman's dream to be a wife with a husband of her own, and a bunch of children clinging to her apron?

Susanna did not complain. She considered herself especially fortunate. Theirs was an intense and passionate relationship. Though they knew little about his background, her parents, her entire family and their relatives, had come to accept Misha for what he was. They surmised that he was terribly in love with her or so it seemed. And Susanna most certainly worshipped the ground he walked on.

When the time of his departure approached, there were moments she wanted to reveal her condition to him. Each time, she retained her cool manner and her own brand of cynical humor to make him feel free and without obligation toward her. It was only after he'd left that she spent many night hours awake, helpless under the pressure of her thoughts and worries. Her anxiety grew as time passed and there was no word from Misha. She tried to rationalize. He was getting settled into his job; after all, different environment, strange people, another language. But the passage of time and the great distance between them was deeply troubling. Her friends had shown concern as her belly presented tell-tale signs of a new life stirring inside her. The sixth month was upon them and still no word from her betrothed. She tried in vain to hide her anxiety from the family and close friends.

Her feelings overflowed spontaneously. They were all too volatile to remain concealed from anyone, least of all from her mother's keen eye. She sought refuge in the latter's loving embrace more often than ever. Her once pervading high spirits seemed completely extinguished, and she seldom smiled, rarely letting out her characteristic giggle, resisting all her friends' attempts at humoring her.

"Perhaps he's ill and there's no one to let you know." Her mother suggested. "Why don't you catch a plane and surprise him?" She pressed.

"He'll let me know when to come. He will, he will." Susanna repeated stubbornly, staring dully in front of her. She would wait.

The details of Susanna's pregnancy soon became public knowledge, hard as the family had tried to conceal them. Although she said nothing, Susanna had made her own arrangements to have the baby delivered at a private clinic in Baden-Baden. During the following weeks, there were times she wanted to write Misha and summon him to her side. She had no idea where he was at present and, besides, even if she had known of his whereabouts, she would not compromise her pride. If only he'd write. There was still a possibility that her pain might suddenly stop, just as a dream or a nightmare is capable of coming to a sudden ending. She had always lived with hope and wasn't one to abandon it during this trying time.

With each passing day, her hope receded as in a puff of bitter disillusionment during her agonizingly sleepless nights. Was it her pride that kept her from taking the only step to be taken boldly? Or was it fear of the unknown that prevented her from seeking the truth?

Time and again, she'd begin *"My dear Misha..."* and abandon the project before she could gather her thoughts further. Though, she wrote him daily, she kept the letters locked in a small strongbox, occasionally opening it to read her own thoughts that she dared not bare to him. Finally, she could hold out no longer. One each day, she mailed the letters to the address Misha had given her on his departure.

Almost one academic year following his arrival in Urbana, Misha had yet to communicate with Susanna. His first few months were rather hectic, and he was unable to write, but as time went on, his procrastinating nature had been the main hindrance. After a while it was his overwhelming sense of guilt that prevented him from getting in touch with her. What could he tell her caused the delay? How would she react? How about the letters he had now got from her almost daily? Why hadn't he replied? These and many other questions persisted unanswered and the letters remained unwritten. Summer of the year 1967 was imminent, and he had to make up his mind concerning vacation plans.

"What am I to do, Pedro?" He asked his Cuban friend. Pedro smiled. He was by now well informed about Misha's relationship with Susanna. Divorced, the thirty-four-year old professor of Spanish literature considered himself the last person qualified to render advice in matters of the heart. He cut a fine figure with his six feet four inches stature, his tanned, pleasant face, and deep gray eyes that would melt away anyone's distrust or resistance. His hair had begun to gradually recede from his forehead when he was in his twenties, and it was his habit to stroke and twist the small remaining curl on his forehead between his fingers when he was deep in thought. He smiled again and looked at Misha with an expression of empathy but not without puzzlement.

"You ask *me* what you ought to do."

"Have no one else to ask, Pedro, my friend." Misha said.

"Let's take a vacation in Cuba. Give it a little time and relaxation. Clear the air and come to the right conclusion." Pedro suggested with a smile.

"In Cuba?" Misha was surprised.

"Why not? We've both worked very hard this year and deserve a vacation. Don't you think?" Pedro looked at Misha inquiringly. He continued to smile. "Well? Uh? What do you say? It'll give you a chance to meet the whole Pamies clan at our family *finca*"—they were the owners of one of the largest sugar cane farms on the island—"in Santiago. Perhaps even my ex, if you promise to behave."

Misha smiled and looked and Pedro fondly. "Funny you should suggest it," he said, "I had recently gotten some other offers as well."

"Anyone I know?" Pedro asked.

"You might. It's possible." Misha didn't satisfy Pedro's curiosity. He was undecided and playing for time.

From their initial meeting during the get-acquainted party for the Humanities Division, they'd hit it off well, having found much in common. Immigrants both, in a host country, their backgrounds resembled one another, their friendship continued to thrive and grow strong during the academic year. They rented adjacent efficiencies in the faculty Goodwin Apartments complex that fit every detailed description of a monastic setting. Pedro's vintage '49 Plymouth Sedan with a rebuilt Dodge engine came in handy on weekends, when they'd take a drive into the countryside with or without the company of others.

They would occasionally venture into the 'windy city' to do some shopping. Chicago held a special fascination for them both as the main hub of cultural activity west of New York City. Pedro had a keen appreciation of quality; he was an *aficionado* of the arts, especially sculpture, with a highly developed sense for natural beauty. Misha loved to watch his friend as he examined some fine pieces of sculpting, and rubbed his sensitive fingers along their subtle contours before every purchase. The pieces he liked best turned out to be the most expensive ones in the studio. He would modestly step aside and say: "That's not quite what I'm looking for. Not quite." He often repeated with a smile. Now he turned his inquisitive eyes toward Misha again.

"Well? How about it?"

"How about what?" Misha smiled, knowing full well what his friend's question implied.

"Our Cuban vacation, *Hombre!*" Pedro feigned exasperation.

"Oh, okay, if it means this much to you." Misha acquiesced. "Let's do it!"

They left early to travel through the many states on their way to Key West, Florida. "We'll take the ferry to Havana there," Pedro said, "It takes about nine hours to cross." He paused. "If the weather's fine, we'll have a pleasant crossing."

Misha showed some excitement. Most of the time, he used to sleep soundly and effortlessly. But now, during the entire journey southeast, he volunteered the many hours of night driving—there was less traffic then—while Pedro slept. And when it came his turn to relax, he was unable to fall asleep, talking and navigating for his friend, perhaps under the press of his thoughts and in an uneasy anticipation of things to come. He tried to hide his troubles from Pedro, but it was not possible. His feelings were too volatile, and too obviously displayed in his features, to be concealed from his friend's sensitivity for too long. Pedro was especially aware of Misha's changing moods and sudden fits of depression.

"Come on, Misha, something's on your mind. Can we talk?" He urged Misha to confide in him, but the latter shook his head. It was not in his nature to bare his soul to others, even untested "best friends." He would do it on a 'need to know' basis. He had to be ready. "I can guess," Pedro said, "it's Susanna, isn't it?"

"You're clairvoyant, my friend." Misha said gloomily.

"Hey, what are friends for?" Pedro chuckled, using the old adage. "Besides, you may not know it, but you're an open book, Misha. Make clairvoyance easy." Pedro joked.

"I can't help it." Misha whispered. "Am I so hope-lessly transparent?"

"You sure are *amigo*." Pedro intoned, now with a serious demea-nor. "What's the use of worrying, when you can't do a thing about whatever it is that bothers you." He paused. "What do you say, we have a good time now, and worry about things later. As soon as we'll return, I'll remind you to start worrying again. Deal?" He smiled, and Misha reciprocated. Pedro was right. After all, there was little Misha could do at this point. Wasn't he supposed to be moving away from trouble? He thought. In the direction of relaxation and fun. Why worry?

The ferry docked in the Havana Harbor past midnight. The sight of *La Habana Vieja* or Old Havana, as the natives called it, was impressive. Divers, milling around in the murky harbor waters, called out to the arrivals on deck for coins. As soon as one was tossed into the water, they would dive after it, and soon, after a mad scramble, the victor emerged, coin between his teeth, smiling broadly. "*Gracias, Americano!*" An exuberant call from deep beneath the ferry's bow acknowledged the guest's generos-ity, while encouraging more of the same. Disembarked, the two friends drove through the streets of the old city. From time to time, Pedro would point out some worthwhile sights to his guest, unable to contain his native pride.

This is the most densely populated city in Cuba,"Pedro boasted, and Misha had no reason to doubt. People milled around and garnered every inch of pedestrian space and spilled onto the nar-row streets making passage well nigh impossible. They were the night people, the street people of the ancient city. They walked swaying rhythmically, dance-like, smiling, humming popular folk tunes. Every darkening doorway spit them out onto the already clogged streets. Filmed lightly with the grime of poverty, they smelled thick and damp; they crowded together in small pockets of heat. Pedro's Plymouth labored slowly behind the dense traffic of people who crowded into its path whenever, with a unique abandon, and unexpectedly. Only Pedro's manipulative agility behind the wheel averted imminent tragedy.

You could see raw life vibrating in the undulating mass, those *Habaneros* and *Habaneras*, the sullen red glare through their dark skin, their flimsy, rag-like clothes they must have worn all year long. There were street musicians playing the marimbas and drums with a passion only present in people whose pulse beats out their ancestral melodies. Their noise was a buzz, a fever in Misha's head. Salsa bands drove writhing dancers through the streets. Misha felt their quest, the need, cycling up inside him. It was infectious. He felt the hurry-hurry thunder of the blood in his veins. For those few moments he forgot Susanna and those nagging forebodings. They were, as if replaced by the old men in the pleated shirts—the islanders called them *guayaberas*—and the dark-skinned, fiery-eyed women in loose cotton dresses that embraced their well-formed limbs and deliciously pronounced bosoms. And there were easier ways. The hunting ground. The feeding ground, thumped like a heart, all pink neon glow and pounding music. Out of the hot, damp dark, Misha came into the noise and glare. The stringy, almost-pain, the restless tug that led him there eased. In its place the tide of the hunger started to rise.

This feeling was rare, wild, and tart. The time when it came was sharp-edged, savage and sweet. Along with the hunger and it's sating, Misha felt a lump in his throat, the swimming, the swooning, the dying-away of Susanna and the traces of love. A part of him wanted to save that. It was the part not blinded by anxiety. Something to dream about as the summer steamed itself out. To delay and delay. Bring himself to the razor-edge of desire, smelling her high, sweet heat night after jungle night, and then swerving away.

"Well, my friend, how do you like my country?!" Pedro shouted through the din. Misha held his answer momentarily.

And just then, there was a pink smear of neon—half worn for lack of replacement—in the corner of his eye. It glimmered down a dark alley on his left, when Pedro had already turned right. He knew it was always like that, an accident, a whimsy, an almost-missed, at-the-last-moment kind of chance that had brought him there, at the point of utmost urgency, on the delicate edge between hunger and control. There it was, *La Floridita*—though the neon lacked the *'l'* and the *'t'* and, therefore, read *La Foridia*—Havana's most exclusive hangout, regarded almost a shrine, where Papa Hemingway consumed countless daiquiris and *Cuba-libres* served him across the bar. Above it hung photos of the great author, at the bar with his friend Gary Cooper, in another Hemingway toasting Spencer Tracy or in yet another chatting with Ingrid Bergman.

"He was a great man of letters," Pedro said almost with obvious reverence. "If I didn't know where he came from, I'd think him to be native Cuban."

"You may as well," Misha remarked, "he belonged to all of the people. He would be the first to tell you that." Misha paused. "All great individuals transcend national boundaries." He added, as in afterthought. "And that's how it ought to be with all of us." Misha concluded.

Just then, the Pamies farm spread out before them as far as the eye could reach. It was an awesome sight and left Misha breathless.

"Nice little spread of land, uh?" Pedro laughed.

"I'd say it's nice," Misha agreed.

"Though we share it with Fidel," Pedro added with a bit of levity. When asked why the government hadn't sequestered the property altogether, Pedro was quick to explain: "Papa was with Fidel in the *Sierra Maestra*. Gave blood and money for the revolution." He let it rest at that.

The Pamies mansion squatted on the very outskirts of the gracious landscape. Painted hugely on part of the whitewashed, low stonewall and ornate iron fence surrounding the mansion was a mural. It meant to commemorate the 30th of *Diciembre*, 1959; Fidel Castro's triumphant descent from the *Sierra Maestra* mountains. The enormous greenish face of an old man glared down at the viewer, swinging a length of chain above his head. Long white fingers of hair blown back from his temples by an invisible wind, he resembled some half-mad Dickensian denizen of the damp, thick streets of Victorian London. From his expression, he might have just turned some dark, cobble-stoned corner of the city and come upon evidence of the eternal truth—hunger will be satisfied.

To the left of the rich mansion stood shacks that were in stark contrast to the sumptuous villa. Shriveled into living quarters, they served to house the hired help. In the dark of the descending sun, they crouched behind shuttered lights. Their dim glow said two things; there was life inside, and it was not accessible to anyone. Well, with the exception of the *patron*, who had access at any time of day or night. These people would not answer a knock; there was no ring of the bell. They would crouch inside, in low light, and wait for morning. They were present-day people, now seemingly emancipated, but they knew the old truths. They knew that the night was different. Darkness freed things to show their true faces. They were animals too, these humans, some dark part of them could still scent the wind. Only the ones who ignored that darkness would open the door in the night.

Misha heard a low, almost imperceptible laugh, and turned to see a woman walking out of the shadows. She came from a boarded up, strange shack next door that was used to store some broken farm equipment, extra parts, an occasional bunk bed or two propped up against the wall. She stopped a little way in front of Misha, who only now noticed the woman at Pedro's side; her arms held limp at her sides, a wood chip from a packing crate caught in her short, and white gold hair.

"She's yours for the night," Pedro said, and Misha stood still with incredulity. The woman's eyes were on him, they were hot, smug, satisfied. At the corner of her pale sliver of a smile was a hair-fine bead of blood. She watched Misha watching her, smiled more broadly, and touched the tip of one pale finger to the corner of her lip. Held it out to him. The blood smear on her pale skin was faint and tiny. He stood still, revolted and fascinated, as she ran her thumb across his lips and slid her finger into his mouth. The faintest, smoky tang, the echo of her meal, disappeared into the bottomless well of his hunger. Prideless, he moaned, sucked and pulled at her finger, craving more. She laughed again and pulled herself free.

Her eyes mocked him. No longer blank and pale, they blazed with contemptuous pity. Don't be like all the others. Her gaze commanded silently as she pirouetted round him gleefully. Her colorful cotton skirt danced upward and revealed her shapely thighs and slender limbs. Don't confuse what you feel. Their fear is not love. Your hunger is not love. It is only hunger. And there is only one way to satisfy it. It was desire raw and unrefined. What's required is pushed through the thick, humid darkness, back into the bright throb and pound of music.

"Go now," Pedro urged, "*hasta pronto.*" His voice was commanding, like that of a feudal lord of yesteryear. Misha glanced at Pedro, and he saw the distorted face of his stepfather, Dr. Horst. He looked at the woman. She was unmistakably his mother Blanche. He hesitated.

"Go!" His voice commanded.

They went inside. Things became frenzied. Faces shined. Wet hair lay in spikes on her cheeks and forehead. Her arms waved in the air. Her face was now flushed, dreamy, entranced.

Misha knew then and there that he was a monster. He noticed everything with a keen awareness. It was a place that whets appetites. In his mind, dancers clustered under colored lights, looked like multi-colored bon-bons in a box, jumbled and disarrayed. He wanted to move among them, in a wasteful, wanton frenzy, graze up one and then another, chew them lightly, savor the flavor, and scatter them like light.

He saw the girl. She sat on a high stool at a bar-like table, stretched backward, the hem of her short top swung out like the rim of a bell above the dusky flesh of her taught stomach. He felt the heat come off that curve of her skin. It would bake his hand. He imagined how it would yield, like pudding that he could reach inside, her screams lost in the throb and pound of music, and bring some jelly-like part of her away with him, as a memorable souvenir.

He crossed the floor, let the way part before him, accept it as his due. The gypsy girl danced up to him, danced in front of him, her eyes feverish and bright on his. "Eaten anybody yet?" She asked in a loud, shrill voice, for everyone to hear. Her smile was dazzling. She shimmered in front of him. She pulsated. His mouth was dry, his throat thick. Misha felt hot, dizzy. His head reeled. She was taunting him now, weaving in front of him, her skin sweat-slicked, flushed, and craning toward him. "You want to devour me?" Her stare was brighter, hotter, molten brass. He felt its weight in his stomach. He was mindless now, beyond control. The hard hand of hunger rode him.

She smiled at him, led the way toward the back door. The dark yard. The place next door, under colored, swinging lights. She was thinking of the mattresses, leaning there.

He smiled back at her...

"Misha...Misha..." a tap on his door woke him, and he, vaguely, heard Pedro's voice. "You've slept all afternoon, and we've got a million things to do." Misha's eyes squinted slightly and then closed to the glare of the afternoon sunshine entering the open window.

"Wh...a...t...?" Misha rubbed his eyes, trying to put dreams and reality together.

"We have a big date in Havana tonight, sleeping beauty," Pedro teased.

"A…date…?" Misha seemed to search his memory.

"Yes," Pedro assured him, "the ballet. Finest in this hemisphere. Pride of Castro's Cuba."

Misha sat up in his bed. "What's tonight's fare?" He asked.

"None other than *Sheherazade* or *Arabian Nights*, on which the ballet is based." Pedro informed him, "What do you say, we get ready. Eh?" Pedro prodded his friend.

"Wouldn't miss it for anything." Misha assured his friend.

# 14.

IT HAD BEEN RAINING uninterruptedly for several days. The judge's chambers were situated on the second floor across the long covered walkway of the courtyard, and Misha could hear the big drops pound its tin roof. He wasn't looking forward to the tedium of another courtroom session. It only heightened the depressing atmosphere. What can they ask me now that they haven't already asked? Misha thought. What can I tell them? His thoughts turned toward the sympathetic social worker Diana. Though in somber surroundings, her cheerful, dark-brown eyes offered him some solace. "Don't be afraid," they seemed to say, "I'm here for you." Misha understood.

They were closing in on the judge's chambers, and Misha suddenly became aware of his disheveled appearance. He wished for one brief glance into a mirror. Perhaps a slight trim of his now prematurely white hair and the full-grown beard? He would have liked to trim it neatly into a Van Dyke. His pajama-like apparel left much to be desired. By now, it was crumpled and unfit to be seen in public.

The doors came ajar, and the bailiffs inside the chambers took over from his two escorts. They practically carried his limp body underarms to the witness chair. There were no others present. No attorneys to represent him, except for the social worker, Dr. Diana Ferrucci. During their long rehabilitative sessions, he'd wandered about her ancestry. Was she first generation American or did she arrive from her native Italy as a small child? Why this sudden preoccupation with nationalities? He didn't know.

She did what she could to make his confinement bearable; provided reading material, brought news from the outside, gave him strength and courage to persevere. Especially dear were those letters from Susanna...yes, those letters that began with the very first one she'd sent back in...

*February, 1967, Baden-Baden*

*My dear Misha,*

*So many months have gone by since your departure for America, and I have been awaiting word from you, given you time to settle your things, hoping I'd hear from you one of these days, but you are still silent. Sometimes, I fear you've taken ill and don't want me to know. I worry more. Would it be too much to ask? Just a postcard, perhaps? To let me know how things are, when you might be coming here or when you want me there? All I ask is for a sign of life. If that is too much, please let me know, and I won't burden you anymore. Love, Susanna*

That was the first of many unanswered letters he'd received from her. His conscience wouldn't let him sleep at night; his guilt grew each waking day into unspeakable torment. That is, until that day when, for the first time, he saw Alida...

...The performance on that memorable night was a mix of fairy stories and the plot of *Sheherazade*; a beautiful woman—who happens to be the sultan's wife—keeps her husband from killing her by telling tales over 1001 nights. The queen's role, as portrayed by prima ballerina Alicia Alonso, supported by an excellent corps de ballet and a delightful group of soloists offered an evening of enchantment. But it was one of the soloists especially, Alida Monet, who had caught Misha's eye from the moment she had entered, more like floated onto center stage. An aura of her hypnotic charm, her graceful movements, the supple beauty of her body and her performance immediately smote him. Her role exuded candid innocence, velvety strength and boldness; a capacity to show love and compassion without sentimentality. "I think, I'm in love." Misha whispered in Pedro's ear. And, after a brief moment: "No, I *know* I'm in love." Pedro smiled. "Alicia's taken.

Married to the Ballet-Master, Fernando." He paused, "besides, you're one of a multitude. The whole world's in love with Alicia."

"No, my friend, it's not her. It's that little one over there," Misha pointed at the *pas de trois*, performed center stage. "Alida Monet is the one I'll marry. I'll surely marry her." Misha repeated during intermission.

"Don't you think she'll have something to say in the matter?" Pedro said with a mischievous twinkle in his eye.

"I'm sure, I can convince her." Misha said loudly enough for all nearby to hear. "Can you arrange a meeting, Pedro?" He asked his friend.

'Why, of course." Pedro whispered mysteriously. "It so happens, she's my little sister's dearest friend. They've attended ballet school together initially." He paused. "Alida went on to bigger and better things." He continued with a trace of sadness in his voice. "Little Margarita had other things on her mind. Mostly boys." They laughed. "Mother was devastated." Pedro said with empathy. "To see her daughter center stage is every mother's dream." He added. "But it wasn't meant to be for Margarita." He concluded.

"Let's put her influence to good use." Misha pleaded.

"Yes, let's." Pedro agreed.

From the moment they'd met at the informal party arranged by Margarita, Misha and Alida became inseparable. He had met her grandmother, Sra. Acadia, and her mother Sra. Carla. Those he had not met were the patriarch of the family, Grandfather Manuel, and Alida's father Albert, whom he had assumed were both deceased, an assumption confirmed by Alida on his inquiry. Decorum had prevented him from pursuing the issue. He would come back to it another time, perhaps. For now, he was transported into his own private paradise. Why ruin a good thing?

Misha spent the last fortnight of his summer vacation in Havana with the Monets. Granted, they lived in a modest, two bedrooms, apartment with little room to spare for a guest, but he was made to feel welcome on the living-room sofa. The little discomfort was a small price to pay for Alida's nearness. Early each morning, he was awakened by the sounds of her upright piano, as she practiced her assigned lessons through countless repetitions. Bach fugues, one after another, each louder than the previous, resounded like a reveille through the premises. Though they had turned in late the previous night, after a day on the town, much sightseeing and a bit of shopping, Misha would have preferred to snooze somewhat longer, but Alida's relentless pounding on the keyboard could have awakened the dead.

Routinely, after an early breakfast, Misha accompanied Alida to the rehearsals at the ballet academy, which took up the better part of the morning. He sat in the front row of the auditorium, transfixed with the movement on stage. His eyes followed the rhythmic motion of Alida's pliant body, every curve of it, oblivious to all others near her. Even the great Alicia took second place to Alida.

A light lunch followed, after which they sat holding hands in a listening booth at the music shop and hummed to the beat of Latin melodies he was beginning to love; notably *La bella Cubana* and *Quiere me mucho*—Beautiful Cuban and Love me a Lot—were to remain *their* very private melodies for years hence, and Ernesto Lecuona had quickly become their favorite Cuban composer. And always, mother Carla wasn't far off, her observant, keen eyes fixed on the young lovers, for she had taken leave from her task with the orchestra to accompany the young couple wherever they went. Misha was cautious, lest he be seen in public caressing this almost half his age girl. But most of all, he'd wanted to impress mother Carla with his honorable intentions.

One of the two weekends he'd spent with them, the family decided to go swimming on *Santa Maria* Beach, a mere twenty-five km from Havana. Sunday early morning they left on their journey. It was a gloriously beautiful day; the sun was shining in a cloudless sky, its blue merged with the clear blue waters of the Gulf on the far horizon. Under those pleasant conditions the place was crowded, but Alida and Misha swam out into the deep, seemingly beyond the reach of inquiring eyes. There they bobbed on the waves, dove into the oncoming surf, and touched for the first time those intimate parts of their bodies with great abandon, impervious to thoughts of remorse or feelings of guilt. They laughed loud when they came up for a breath of air, simply to indicate to those on shore that all was well with them.

"Your mother, she'd be angry at our behavior." He broached cautiously.

"If she knew, she would." Alida giggled happily.

"And I'd get my walking papers immediately," Misha said. He was well aware of the fact that at age twenty-six, and his professorial appearance, he was much too old for Alida in the eyes of onlookers.

"Walking papers?" Alida was not familiar with the Americanism.

"Means, I'd be kicked out." Just then, as he spoke, a big wave caused him to swallow some of the salt water. He coughed violently. Alida was amused.

"That you would be, for sure." She giggled again. "Banned forever."

"What do you say we make it good and proper?" Misha held her in a tight embrace, his lips touched hers. "Will you marry me, Alida?" He suddenly blurted out, and it seemed just what it was, spontaneous and from the heart though weighted down with impetuosity.

"What...?" He caught her by surprise, but she did not try to free herself from his hold. "First, we will have to ask permission. Then, there is the formal engagement. After that, you will be presented to the family. They must approve, not I alone." In so few words, Alida explained the procedure leading to matrimony in her culture. But she didn't say "no". That was encouraging. And she lingered in his embrace a bit longer. "Now it is time to come ashore," she said with resolve. "You might want to share your idea with the others."

"Who? Mother or father?" He asked. His curiosity peaked concerning the whereabouts of Albert Monet, the always-absent father, away "on business" for the most part, he was told. He had been informed about grandfather Manuel's passing not long ago with cancer of the pancreas. Alida glanced at Misha, as they walked to shore holding hands. "I'm sure, when papa returns, he'd be happy to listen to your proposal. Meanwhile, Mamá and Grandmother Acadia will have to give us their blessings."

When the news of their intended engagement reached the ballet Academy, Alberto pointed to the holstered 9mm Browning he was wearing on his belt: "You see this?" He asked Misha. "I ought to shoot you this instant and be done with it!" He raised his authoritative, ballet masterly, tone of voice. "You're trying to make a housewife of the most promising ballerina of my company!"

"I...I..." Misha stammered, taken completely by surprise by the Ballet-Master's attitude.

"There's absolutely nothing you can say to persuade me, old man," Alberto's attitude made him feel much older than he was. "Her destiny is not to spend the rest of her life bearing children and cooking choice meals for a demanding husband." He waved his hands through the air dramatically, as if improvising movements resembling some intricate choreography. It was as if he were ready to strike out at some invisible object, perhaps even at Misha. He was known for his violent temper outbursts, especially when totally frustrated. "Ah, what's the use?!" He shouted. "Take her! Make a domestic animal out of her! Expect no blessings from me!" He turned to go. Then, as if on sudden impulse, he turned toward them both, as they stood speechless and embarrassed in the presence of the giggling members of the corps de ballet, and said: "I see no good in it at all. Only regrets a few years down the road. Beware!" Before they were able to utter one word, he was gone.

"Whew!" Misha exclaimed on leaving the premises. "For a moment there, I really thought he might shoot me."

"His bark is worse than his bite," Alida said with sadness in her voice. "Besides, he considers your intrusion an assault on his traditional domain."

"Don't dancers ever marry?" Misha asked.

"Not frequently. The exceptional ones seldom allow mundane life to interfere with their ambition to excel, to succeed in their careers. They're married to their *profession.*" She explained. Though her eyes were downcast, Misha felt her sadness.

"And I thought only the Catholic Church exacted such strong demands on individuals." He was truly astonished. "That's why I didn't pursue celibacy."

"You? Celibate?" Alida laughed softly.

"It was my mother's wish that I become a priest." Misha said, his eyes lowered to avoid hers. "The nuns had been preparing me for a lifetime in servitude to the Lord." He hesitated. Should he continue? Reveal all? He wasn't sure he'd want her to know his deep past. Not just now. Not before some sort of commitment on her part. He glanced at her smiling face. Beautiful. He thought. Why burden her with those sordid details. Another time, perhaps.

On the eve of their departure, Misha asked Pedro to be present at his formal proposal. Pedro's presence served as a kind of endorsement of his intentions, he felt. On the way there, Pedro coached his friend as well he could. Interspersed in his English address were some simple Spanish phrases—like *la quiero muchisimo* and *pido permiso,* "I love her very much" and "I ask permission"—Grandmother Acadia and mother Carla had both been impressed by Misha's intentions and his credentials. He was a good catch for their little Alida. At sixteen, she was somewhat young for marriage. But they gave their blessings, nonetheless. After all, in the old days girls were known to have married at that age and younger. Besides, they hoped, it would be another year before the wedding day.

"Will you be able to support a wife and children?" Grandmother Acadia asked.

"I'm sure, I will." Misha responded. She seemed placated. She turned toward Pedro, and he nodded. The Pamies family prestige buoyed the Monets. They would now travel in good company, Acadia and Carla exchanged glances. *Asi que sea*—"so be it"— they shook Pedro's hand, then Misha's. It was a done deal.

Their courtship was brief by any standard; it lasted one academic year, and was punctuated by daily correspondence, which rivaled that of the great romantics. He read her long, declaratory, letters, repeatedly. They were filled with expressions of longing and love. He even placed them under his pillow at nighttime initially. Soon, however, he would glance at them cursively, dwelled slightly longer on the more appealing expressions, and then discard them as he would any extraneous materials, such as his old notes or his students' old compositions.

Alida, on the contrary, read and reread his brief—and gradually briefer—notes, tied them in multicolored ribbons and placed them in a special, ornate box. Daily, as she would miss the arrival of an expected letter from "her Misha", she drew some of those precious slips of stationery from her "love reservoir" and spent half the night totally absorbed by his "company." Toward the end of five months, Alida was in possession of an impressive bundle of letters from the man she planned to wed on June 12th, on a hot Havana afternoon during the coming summer.

When Alida reminded him about the brevity of his letters, tactfully, of course, he'd make excuses; "busy with research," or "terribly involved with my students," or any other reason that sounded legitimate. What he hadn't told her was that he had taken a particular interest in a seventeen-year-old Chinese American student, born in San Francisco, a daughter of immigrants, endowed with the intriguing name Xin-Xin, jet-black, shoulder length, hair and a pair of mischievous brown eyes that gazed at the world from behind not too narrow eyelids. In addition, her beautiful, four feet and seven inches, well-proportioned body rivaled his vision of Alida.

# 15.

XIN XIN WAS TAKING UP much of Misha's office time under the pretext of "being tutored in...whatever." However, he soon found her breasts irresistible to his touch, and she reciprocated in kind by favoring his erect member. He was negligent in his duties toward his other students, and their persistent knocking at his office door during his frequent encounters with Xin Xin only made him shift his activities to the privacy of his apartment.

"What am I to do, Pedro?" He confided in his friend. "I am so terribly drawn to her. Obsessive-compulsive, I guess."

"You're playing with fire, *amigo*." Pedro mused. "You should know by now the adage: You don't play at your work place," He smiled sadly. "Besides, the only honest thing would be to tell Alida the truth. You know, I have a stake in your engagement. It was through me that you met her, wasn't it?"

"This is just a passing thing, my friend," Misha pleaded with Pedro, "nothing to be worried about. Like the Gypsy girl on your *finca*. No more than that."

"Much to worry about when you're caught." Pedro warned. "A thief that runs free is an honorable man." Misha understood the implied analogy, but tried to turn his friend's attention away from the serious theme.

"We take safety precautions. She insists. We both know it's only a sexual thing." Misha avoided his friend's eyes. "And I feel great remorse and guilt at what I'm doing. Believe me." Friendship is friendship," Pedro mused, "but this Gringo has no idea what

Latin honor means to us." This was serious business. Something not to be trifled with.

"I'm not a priest, Misha," Pedro said. "Go to confession."

"Why haven't I thought of it sooner?" Misha said. It was his way of trying to assuage his friend. "I can't wait."

It felt strange to sit in the confessional and hear himself say: "Father, forgive me, for I have sinned…"

The Priest was his usual patience and kind counsel. He, too, advised Misha abstinence, especially in view of his impending marriage. "Either you reveal the truth to your betrothed, my son, or begin to act responsibly with your students."

"I shall, father, I promise." Misha assured his confessor without spelling out his sincere intentions. It was hard to ignore Xin Xin. In class or outside, she demanded attention. The struggle he underwent with himself had become very stressful. He was unable to work or sleep. Soon, his phone calls to Xin Xin had become more frequent during late night hours.

"What are you doing?" He asked.

"Trying to go to sleep." She replied.

"No, I mean, what are you wearing?" He insisted.

"Nothing." Xin Xin answered in her straightforward manner.

"Nothing?" He almost cried out in anguish.

"Yes, nothing." She was silent for a long time. He listened for another sound.

"…Ouch!" She said softly after a long pause. It had gotten so she was impossible to talk to on the phone. When she was in high school, one of her boyfriends used to stay on the phone for hours just to listen to her breathe. It was driving him crazy, but she didn't mind. She watched the TV or did her homework or painted her toenails with the phone wedged between her shoulder and her ear. Sometimes she would rub her neck in the mornings and complain about the soreness. She liked to tell people she had a stiff neck or a pulled muscle or a headache. She liked to appear fragile. But that was then, and now she didn't say things like that to Misha; he was aware of her playfulness.

"What's wrong?" Misha asked. She was quiet again. He couldn't tell if she had really hurt herself, perhaps stubbed a toe against the chair leg in the dark, or if she just didn't want to answer his question.

"The dog is biting my toe." She said in a whisper.

"Why are you whispering?" He asked.

'Because I don't want to scare him away."

She toyed with him. He could picture her, curled up in the chair by the phone. Her bare toes were hanging off the edge of the cushion, and the dog was nibbling on them gently. He was a very good dog, really. He understood pain. When she said "ouch" loud enough, he would stop.

"Is he in love with you?" Misha came to the point. He knew Xin Xin was not the type to remain lonely for very long. She didn't answer. "Is he in love with you?" Misha asked again. He had decided she was just evading the question. Talking to her sometimes was like talking to a sleepwalker. She would answer a direct question usually, but her answers didn't always make sense. They made sense to her, but the connections were too vague for him. And sometimes she wouldn't answer at all.

She never did walk in her sleep when she was a little girl. She told him so, and she told him she didn't even dream. People used to ask her what she dreamed about, and she would answer "nothing". Misha always thought she was lying, but he didn't care to challenge her. He thought she just didn't want to talk about it. He knew for sure she didn't sleepwalk, though. She was awake at night. She would climb out the window and walk the dog in the woods at night, and return to the room she shared with her older sister. By then, the sun was rising, and there was the smell of dew and fallen leaves. And later on, when she'd reached thirteen, it was the boys she walked with in the woods. Come early morning, she brought their smell home with her, and the smell of wood smoke in autumn, and crushed wildflowers in springtime.

"When Javier makes love to me, I can feel him in my heart," she whispered suddenly, and her candor shocked him. She was angry with him, but she did not use the f… word. He was prying. He was also puzzled. Why did she not use that coarse but sincere expression at this time?

"Is that supposed to be an answer?" He feigned boredom. He was tired and sleepy, and his bladder was exploding.

"No. It's supposed to shock you and make you shut up and leave me alone."

Oftentimes, she did this, too. Answered a question so briefly and honestly that it took his breath away. She never explained anything. To never explain would make him nervous. He'd be afraid people would think he was lying, "walking around the truth," he remembered his mother called it. He had always been that way. He'd elaborate explanations prepared for the simplest things. Why it took him five minutes longer to get from the doctor's office to the grocery store. Why he didn't take a short-cut when there was an accident on the highway. But Xin Xin never explained anything, and he'd never questioned her before. Somehow, by being vague, she attained a certain degree of cred-ibility. He knew he should have hated her, if only for that reason alone. But he was unable to hate the very thing he desired with all his passion.

"It doesn't shock me, Xin Xin. That word doesn't shock me. All it is, is just plain vulgar. I haven't taught you that. You've always been vulgar." He said, taking his turn to be mean.

"…Ouch," she whispered again.

"The dog's biting you again?" Misha asked.

"No, you are." She was also very perceptive. And when she was like that, it nearly drove him crazy. He was unable to sleep, eat or perform any normal function without thinking about her. Pedro wasn't much help either.

"You're becoming irrational, Misha," he said, "and it doesn't become you."

Misha was aware of his hopelessness. There was no one that turned him this passionate before, that drained his blood the way the mere mention of her name affected him. There was neither sentence nor paragraph, neither a page full of words that, put together, could describe the sensation he felt touching her breasts. The very prospect of writing it down, wrestling each word onto paper in an attempt to limn out her face for others to see, when he could see it effortlessly everywhere he turned, drove him to agony. The strength it would take! And he was fresh out of strength those days.

Writing was no catharsis for him, it was actual reenactment. He did not wish to live through that again. Whether he could or not didn't enter into it. He would not. He knew that with a certainty. To go back into that tunnel would be an act done in full knowledge that he would never again emerge at the other end. He would remain in there forever, talking with the echoes and wandering in circles, thinking he was progressing. What really frightened him was how attractive that prospect sometimes seemed. The mere thought that someone else's fingers—at present it was her Venezuelan lover Javier—caressed her body drove him out of his mind. Caressed or, as Xin Xin put it plainly, "had his way with me."

He knew. She was deliberately being exasperating. She has always known how to do this well. Once, during a long car ride, she whispered to him that every time she looked at him she was thinking how stupid he was to have such a crush on her. He tried to argue, invoke his own logic. "Xin Xin," Misha would say, "I give you something no one else could give you."

"Yes?" She challenged. "And what's that?"

"Knowledge." Misha said softly.

"And I give you my youth." She said defiantly. "You couldn't give that to me, try all you want."

Misha listened. Defeated.

"I have an older sister that you would probably like to meet. But she would surely dislike you even if she met you..." she laughed at what she was going to say next "...because no one will like you if you like them first." Her unintended aphorism was reminiscent of his mother's dictum he remembered well. For the rest of the car ride she would, every now and then, rest her eyes on him with a significant look, and he would want to cry. He couldn't, though, because if he did he would admit to writhing under every glance of hers as if it were a whip.

Now it was late morning, and the phone rang. It was Xin Xin. He listened to her breathing into the phone.

"You called me," Misha said, "just remember that, please. I didn't call you. You called me, that's why I'm here for you."

"...Ouch," softly.

"I didn't mean it nasty." He was apologetic.

"No, that's not that. The dog's biting me again." She liked the analogy.

By now, she was waking up. Her voice was less husky, her speech less slow. Soon, he knew, she would be impossible. She slept away as much of the light hours as she could, and wandered groggy out of bed at eleven. She was still up as the moon waned, and he could picture her now, sitting up straighter in her chair; her oval, baby face and medium round eyes. She resembled an owl in the dim light. She never turned any lights on at night. Her big old room always looked deserted after sunset. At times, he went up on the rickety porch and peaked in the window in the hope of catching an alluring glimpse of her naked flesh. Instead, he saw the dim glow from the TV set flickering on the bare walls. The room looked worse than deserted. It looked haunted. The little green lights on the stereo were on, and maybe a candle here and there. He remembered she always had some scented candles lit in the bathroom. How he loved taking baths with her! She told him she did that to set the mood. But she didn't say "mood", she said "ambiance."

She wasn't smoking yet, or he would hear her. There was a rhythm to her talk when she was smoking, a soft cadence, a rise and fall meant to accommodate the slow inhalation of the smoke. The best times to talk to her were when she was still half asleep or when she was stoned. That's when she would tell you the truth. But you had to be up to it. Her truths, some of them, were bitter enough to make his teeth hurt. She stripped the veils from everything.

"How can you live with yourself? How can you think like this all the time?" Misha asked.

"I sleep a lot." She replied.

She called him to tell him that Javier was leaving. Moving to California. They had lived together for three months. Last year when her grandmother died and Xin Xin inherited a small fortune, she moved into an apartment alone and, when they'd met, Javier moved in "for only a couple days." He didn't have a stove or an air conditioner in his place, he said. The floors flooded when it rained. Every time she had gone to his place, she returned looking wrung out and sticky. She hated the heat. She liked cold, dark places. Like a snake.

"Why are you telling me all this?" Misha asked, exasperated, half hoping she'd beg him to come back. "I didn't even like Javier much, and I don't care." His longing for her body weighed him down like a dark cloud. He hated Javier, as he would anyone who had closed her doors to him. From early childhood, he was accustomed to solitary play. Now, that he had savored the company of others, it was more difficult to deal with his solitude.

At times, he imagined Xin Xin lying in the grass, in the front yard of her apartment. A shrill yell for help came his way, and he ran to her aid. A huge dog had attacked her. A bloody froth sputtered from the dog' mighty jaws, which held on to Xin Xin's left breast like a vise. "A rabid dog," came through Misha's mind immediately, "I must help her. She's in mortal danger." With his bare fingers, Misha tore a large rock from the nearby flowerbed. He smashed the rock into the back of the dog's skull. Blood spurted onto Misha's hands, but the dog released his grip on Xin Xin's breast and turned, growling madly against Misha. Another blow at the dog's snout, and the animal ran off with a loud yelp. Misha carried Xin Xin in his strong arms into the house. He had to stop the bleeding. The left, mutilated, breast hung lifeless from her chest. He rushed the injured woman to the emergency, where surgeons worked for three-and-a-half hours to restore her breast to its original form. He waited in the hall close to the emergency area, and when she finally opened her eyes, they were filled with gratitude. "I'm here for you…I'm here for you," he kept repeating. "It doesn't matter," he said quickly noticing concern in her eyes. "Your breasts will look splendid again. Don't worry."

"What really happened, Xin Xin," Misha asked. "Why did you call?"

She didn't respond for the longest time. Finally, she said, softly, as if to herself: "He was good for me, that's all. Having sex with him cleared my head."

"And with me, it doesn't?" Misha blushed and was grateful she couldn't see his face. "Thank you." He said with a degree of sarcasm, but he was sure it was lost on her. She could be very sarcastic when she wanted to, but she ignored it in others. And she was far down inside herself, he knew. She dealt with pain well most of the time, he had to admit. She understood it. She even taught her dog about "ouch."

Misha endured three months of solitude after that last encounter. He counted the days when he would leave for Havana and… the wedding. What he had realized was that he never understood about Xin Xin. She broke the pattern. She was the only person he'd ever allowed to touch him, not only in a physical way but there was the physicality of it too. When he put his hand on her arm, you could see her bones shake. She caused him to gaze at her starry-eyed, literally. He would come back from being with her, and his eyes would be exalted, like an angel's. They touched each other all the time, like animals in the field. He would tell her he slept with other women, but she didn't mind. Rather, she wouldn't let herself mind.

"How can you stand it?" He asked her once.

"I sleep a lot, too." She answered. Or maybe that was another conversation. Then, after a moment of hesitation, she added: "I'll stop when I can't stand it anymore. Not because it's too much of an upset for me, but because it upsets you."

She was able to *read* him. She knew he was concerned. That he was trying to help. But Xin Xin always believed that you show concern for someone by leaving him or her alone. "In India or some place like that," she used to say, "to touch someone's face is the worst sign of disrespect."

So, when he couldn't stand it anymore, he took refuge in his thoughts of his engagement and the impending marriage. It made him feel safe. He could love Xin Xin, but he could never trust her. His other women meant absolutely nothing to him, but he counted on his relationship with Xin Xin to be something very special. Part of the problem was it couldn't turn out that way. She would have to alter her sense of values. And that would mean the beginning of the end for them. Things still held together those few months in some kind of fashion. He was glad he didn't get her pregnant. That would have created complications. Misha didn't like complications. In that regard, they resembled each other. Xin Xin shunned complications, too.

What was strange was that he still craved her. Often. Much of the time, he felt tempted to pick up the phone, just to hear her voice; to listen to the silence and her inevitable "ouch". But he didn't let it happen. It depleted the reservoir of his will. It debilitated him. That's when the tunnel felt attractive. He was alone there. After the months of all the pain and passion, there was finally just solitude in that tunnel which could take him anywhere he wanted to be. And though his subconscious self drove him to her, without whom life felt empty and meaningless, he restrained himself.

He was safe now for some months. Outside, the sun shone hot and bright on sand and flesh and sparkling water, while the tunnel was cool and the darkness was easy on the eyes. Sometimes he had dreamed of going into that darkness, going deeper and deeper, going a long way. And in his dream he found her there, and lay down beside her in the coolness and the safety. In his dream he searched for her, she was somewhere far away, and he knew that when he found her, her skin would be smooth and sweet, and they would sleep the way they used to dream of sleeping, together and forever.

When winter came, though, the darkness and the cold were all around him, and he felt closer to the tunnel, and to her, who disappeared into it. At that nearness, it lost its pull, its undertow. There were winter nights when he looked right into the mouth of the tunnel, and he saw her eyes there, and they were not happy. Those were the nights that dragged out long. Nights when he thought if he closed his eyes and then opened them again she would be beside him.

There were times he thought he'd never be happy again. How does one measure happiness? Perhaps to be well is to be happy. Being well is such an easy thing. Even if you lose it, you can get it back again. There are rules. There are guidelines. And getting it all back will make it all the more precious. To become well again, they say, is to be truly well.

And so perhaps that, too, is the secret of happiness. To have lost it; and to be grateful for small things. In his better moments, Misha was grateful for the small things; the sun and the fresh air, and every day they kept him out of the tunnel. He once thought that life with Alida would be the greatest, most fulfilling work of all. To wake up every morning to the sounds of Bach's fugues, to everyday learn something new about her, about one another; to fight away the demons of jealousy, faithlessness, and boredom. To be truly *one*.

But there was a challenge greater than that one. There was a lover more jealous, more strident and strong than ever he was. The lover inside him. The sickness takes up the room that is necessary for other things in life. Misha knew that everyday that he stayed well was a miracle and a blessing. He looked in the mirror and waited for that dark, wild, gleam to appear in his eyes; he walked about and touched the walls and waited for them to open into darkness. The mouth of the tunnel was everywhere, behind the furniture, underneath the floor. Someday he would slip into it and get lost or, perhaps found, found by himself or someone, something. Perhaps it will be a lovely thing and perhaps it will not. That *perhaps* was what had kept him fighting; kept him sane, perhaps.

It had dawned on Misha at last that the way things seemed to do lately, he wasn't sure that love existed at all. That what happened was one of the small tragedies of life. It would be hard to view such shows as "Love Boat" or "Fantasy Island" and believe in love and goodness and happy endings. He recalled the sighs and the silences and the angry/sad words exchanged through the telephone line between Xin Xin and himself. Maybe nobody else wandered about those things, but he did.

On the eve of departure on his journey to Cuba, Misha made that "last" call to Xin Xin. He felt like he owed it to her, maybe for no other reason than that of common decency.

"For good?" She asked.

"What?" He didn't align the frame of reference.

"Are you leaving for good?" She repeated her question. "Moving to Cuba?"

"You mean am I coming back here?" He hoped she would beg him to return.

"Yes, with your wife?" She emphasized *wife*. "What about me?" She asked in a challenging manner he didn't expect from her at that point.

She is getting annoyed at me. He thought silently. Her voice was getting that edge it sometimes got, a low, angry rasp, like the buzzing of a bee. But this was just annoyance, not real anger. When she was angry, her voice was low and even and her face was very white. Misha saw her get that way once. He stood at the door, unannounced, she opened it only a crack. She was in her nightgown and he heard a voice calling from the bedroom. It was the voice of a man. She stood very still, and Misha could see her sinking deep inside herself, where the pain couldn't follow. When she spoke, she was low-voiced and even-toned and rational: "I can't see you right now, Misha. We can talk later, if you want to," she said, "but not right at this moment." She hesitated, looked back into the bedroom. "We...we...were right in the middle of... of...something..." She didn't finish her sentence and shut the door close in his face. He managed to notice that her knuckles were blue with clenching and her face was gray and dead.

He remembered it well. Her behavior shattered the image he'd held of her. In his mind's eye, Xin Xin was gossamer and bird's wings, and she was always able to live quietly inside herself with wisdom and a courage that he had envied. He knew, she may never be happy, but she will, nevertheless, have a braver life than his.

"Didn't he love you?" Misha asked in reference to her breakup with Javier.

"Oh, sure, he loved me and I loved him. It was very cozy." She chuckled giddily.

"But if you love..." Misha started to say. He didn't understand.

"Love doesn't always matter," she cut in. She was quite upset. "Love isn't always what's important. You've been reading too many fairy tales. 'Happily ever after' and all that sentimental garbage. Just because you're living with someone who makes a mud turtle look quick, you think you know all there is to know about making it work. Hell, anybody could make it work if they tried hard enough and knew how to deceive themselves. Just say as little as possible and spread your legs as often as demanded during TV commercials."

"That's very mean," Misha heard himself say, and his voice sounded weak and breathless. "That's so mean."

"Love won't save you, when it comes down to it," she said, grimly. Her voice was low and even now. He heard the silence on the line as something clear and true, a bell-tone. He knew she was not pretty when she was angry. Anger made her eyes very narrow, her mouth a tight line. He knew she wasn't angry at him, but at something he couldn't see.

"Love won't save any of us." She repeated.

"Won't you miss him? Me?" Misha asked without expecting a reply.

"...Ouch," she said loudly. Loudly enough to chase the dog away.

"I'll make the best of it," Misha whispered to himself. After all, the ancient gods themselves had great strength and passions as well as frailties. Humans should resemble them in many ways.

"Good bye, Xin Xin." He said into the speaker. "See you."

# 16.

MISHA HAD LOST COUNT how many times he had appeared before his judges. Those confrontations seemed endless and made absolutely no sense to him. Did they know something he was unaware of? He wondered. If they did, he was sure he would learn soon enough. Distant memories seemed rather intact in his recall, but the more recent past was blurred, obstructed by a fierce struggle of demons inside him. Sure enough, they weren't there all of the time, only when he tried so very hard to remember the events that had brought him to this place, he drew a blank.

"You seem to have set yourself up pretty well," one of the judges began in his severe tone of voice, and Misha looked quite forlorn and intimidated. The severe gentlemen on the bench were wearing some of those stand-up collars that fit round their necks like low, symmetrical dog-collar without corners or points, so as to look almost like priests. And with it a clip-on bow tie. Oh, no! Misha thought in silence. Not another one of these.

"Now, let me see what we have here." The judge continued. There was a large folder in front of him on the desk, and he proceeded to open its covers, lined with red velvet, and leaf through its contents slowly, almost caressingly. While there reigned a deferent silence around him, the judge emitted brief, grunt-like, throat-clearing sounds of "hum...hum..." from time to time, as he progressed through the file. "Well, Dr. Winograd," he said finally, addressing Misha with a stern look on his face, "I can see from the literature before me, you have your mind full of quicksilver." He paused and Misha's head hung very low. "And it weighs heavily upon you." He added as if on reflection.

To be reprimanded like that by this mild-mannered man of the law made quite an impression on Misha. "Do you know on what charges you have been brought before me?" The judge asked. Misha was quite at a loss for an answer. He looked pleadingly in the direction of Diana Ferucci, but received no response there. It was apparent to him that he would have to stand on his own, at least temporarily. Why do they make such a to-do about his modest person? He asked himself silently. What was he to tell the judge in answer to his question? Misha was at a complete loss. He traveled back into his past once again, as he did habitually when in trouble, especially in view of complications as reflected in the prevailing circumstances...

...It was past mid-Summer 1968, a scorching July afternoon, and the small parish named *Virgen de las Mercedes* in the center of Old Havana was standing room only. The overcrowding wasn't so much due to the presence of family and friends—not to mention the presence of some dozen secret police, who tried to look as inconspicuous as possible, notwithstanding their hip holsters bulging under their sweaty *guayaberas*—as it was because the entire Cuban ballet and the *prima* Alicia Alonso was present, well, save Fernando, of course. The overriding curiosity that had brought them there was: why would this promising almost-seventeen-year-old ballerina agree to marry a man ten years her senior—*el viejo* (old man) they called him—for an existence tied to an apron of domesticity? Was he worth throwing away a lifetime of fulfillment and public adulation on center stage? If so, why this hurry?

There were prayers—too many to recount—and there was music. The music was requested by the newlyweds. The band played their songs—*Quiere me Mucho* and *La Bella Cubana*—all very romantic, and Misha drank his share of Cuba *Libres*, which made him oblivious to the giggling and gossip mongering activities of the corps girls behind his back. The festivities went on throughout the night, and when daytime arrived, Misha and Alida bid farewell to the few stalwarts who had endured even beyond the departure time of the secret police before they embarked on their ten-day honeymoon at *Varadero* Beach.

The other guests at *Casa Happiness* must have wondered about the newlyweds in their total absence from the dining table. Had they eavesdropped at the door of the bridal suite, they'd have been privy to the sounds of passion rarely heard within those walls. Their virginal bliss lasted three days and four nights—sparse food treats and drinks were delivered to the door—after which they emerged to a world with stars all around on a dreamy night voyage. Beyond their opium visions of fishlike iridescent clouds, they saw the diamond-shaped blue moon, swimming in a colored glass atmosphere. They listened to music, walked the beach, swam in the gulf waters, and had eyes only for each other. The rest of the world didn't matter much, if at all. Everything was under control. They seemed contented with nature, with themselves, and at peace within their own selves. They gave the impression of two people in harmony with the universe, liberated and enjoying high self-esteem.

"Darling," Alida sighed, "I hope this will never come to an end."

"It won't, my love, it won't," Misha assured her.

The time to say goodbye had come. Never having left the security of her family surroundings, Alida's confidence seemed on the verge of collapse. Were it not for Misha's loving support, her losses might have seemed far greater than her future prospects. It wasn't easy. As the only child, she felt a feral attachment to Carla—she had promised herself never to reveal her knowledge about her father's whereabouts. Grandmother Acadia swore her to secrecy. After all, Albert would have made it to her wedding, regardless of business obligations—and she was sure to miss the patience and wisdom of grandmother Acadia. "I shall write you...I shall write you often," she kept repeating.

Taking leave of her ballet companions was much easier, though interspersed with sentimentality. Hugs and kisses and many promises. Even Alicia was present at the going-away-party to wish the couple happiness. Fernando, Alida's stern ballet master, carrying his inseparable sidearm, was busy elsewhere and was inconspicuous in his absence. "Remember, my little one," Alicia whispered in their embrace, "if Misha maltreats you or if you change your mind, there's always a place for you in the company."

"I shall remember, I promise," Alida whispered in return. She looked up through her eyes swimming with huge tears that ran down her cheeks and left silvery, shining lines all the way down to her neck. Misha observed the entire ritual with some dark foreboding. His jangled nerves sent a sharp, white, pain through his entire body. The feeling settled in some corners of his soul, together with the last traces of an evaporating intoxication from the past few weeks, which, here and there, had not yet gone away. Above all this was an empty space, roughly between the midriff and his heart; it was, so to speak, gaping open and ready to receive an uncertain future. In the back of his mind, he could feel the powerful thrust of his present, genuine affection for Alida, which was what really lent a proper emphasis to his outlook on the future.

A sudden thunderstorm covered the area at the time they boarded the taxi for the airport. Pedro had offered them a ride, but Misha insisted they would be fine alone. The rain was like a solid gush of water. It streamed down on the windows and blocked all vision. And while it pummeled the metal roof, the rain made a steady strumming noise. "Sounds like bongo drums," Misha said, trying to sound cheerful, and Alida managed a faint smile.

In spite of his attempt to feel upbeat, Misha became agonizingly conscious that something or other would await him, something that hitherto he knew to have been delayed by his euphoria for a tiny space of time. That certain something he could not as yet grasp, but which was now present and ready to force its incisive way into their lives.

It was late August, and the reception Alida had received from Misha's Urbana colleagues was much friendlier than that from Mother Nature. As if heralding an especially severe Illinois winter, the northern wind embraced Alida's tropically attired body and breathed a cold chill through her bones. Why hadn't he warned her? She might have worn something more appropriate. Alida thought in silence.

The small Goodwin Apartments efficiency, once sufficient for Misha's needs, seemed at first glance inadequate for the two of them. She made a mental note of it. They'd discuss it later. For the moment, she was anxious to investigate the possibilities in her line of endeavor. Misha had briefed her about his research responsibilities. The library stacks would be his home away from home, and Alida wasn't overly enthused about spending her days in idle solitude.

The Champaign City Ballet Academy received her with open arms. Not only would she teach advanced ballet and choreography but also head the fledgling dance ensemble as its soloist. She was happy. Misha, too, sighed with relief on hearing the good news. He felt guilt ridden about withholding information from Alida; about his work, the cold northern climate, and the eventual pursuit of her vocation. Now, all of a sudden, he was freed from the dreaded or imagined responsibilities.

On her part, Alida was happy to have gotten the opportunity in pursuing the dance. It had been the major theme of her life ever since, as a six-year-old, her mother started taking her to performances of the Ballet de Cuba, solo recitals of Alicia Alonso, Martha Graham or Helen Tamiris, both visiting artists at the academy which she attended. Following the performances and recitals, little Alida was rewarded with a visit to the ice cream shop on the *Malecon*, but gradually the images seeped and shaped the ideal of beauty and dedication that led to count-less hours of dancing lessons and concerts. Eleven years later, and the enchantment hadn't worn off, Alida had acquired such an intimate knowledge of the dance world, that even when fed up with the big egos—commonly accepted as "narcissistic personal-ity disorders"—and small minds of some of its artists as well as the insipidity of many of its products, she stubbornly clung to her only solid love affair. She had realized that the investment in background was too large to discard.

Now, they had something in common; things to discuss dur-ing their weekends together away from work. He, voiced his fears and achievements of research; the direction in which it progressed; its strengths and weaknesses. She, confessed that the quality of the dance in Champaign fell short of that in Havana; even that of the touring groups that visited the university during their months in Urbana, especially the San Francisco Ballet with Nureyev as soloist—albeit past his prime and brilliance—was not what it was touted to be. "You'll learn to be more tolerant, though I wouldn't want you to lower your personal standards," Misha said, a smile on his lips, "alas, you've been spoiled by the demands of perfection among your teachers and peers."

"It isn't that," Alida wasn't sure there was a total absence of sarcasm in Misha's statement. "I just wish they'd allow the audi-ences some credit to recognize the finer points of the art." She paused for reflection. "The dance, as the rest of the arts, should not remain at the mercy of dilettantes lacking professional zest and dramatic energy. It should not indulge itself in a petty contest for mere entertainment and personal glory. As an art, the dance ought to strive to rise above the mediocre, and reach great spurts in artistic level that warrants public interest and adulation."

"Give it time, darling," Misha smiled again. "This is a young country. Only an infant compared to yours or mine. They'll develop yet, give it time...and tolerance."

"Yet, this infant country, as you say, had managed to hone all of the physically aggressive arts to perfection, such as boxing, wrestling, martial arts of all kinds. I can't help but wish they'd follow the fine examples of such famous immigrants as Valery and Galina Panov as well as..."

"Alida Winograd..."Misha interrupted, and both burst out laughing.

"Well, now that you say it, I'd be the first one to admit that, beyond all personal rewards and glories, there is satisfaction in making a genuine contribution to a developing society." Alida became reflective again. "Can you imagine a group of serious dance students who have never had the opportunity to see a first class performance of Swan Lake or Sheherazade? In showing them my video tapes, and pointing out the fine features of style and composition, I know I'm adding to their understanding."

"And I'm sure they appreciate you..." Misha put his arms round Alida's waist and planted a passionate kiss on the back of her neck. "And so do I, darling."

"Ah! What's the use? You and your jokes, every time I try to strike a serious note." She said coquettishly. She returned his affection in like manner, and they indulged in an afternoon of passionate love making reminiscent of those not too distant days at Varadero Beach.

What he hadn't told her that afternoon was that problems and frustrations beset him as well along the academic way. He stumbled over superiors whose world views were fixed in the light of past glory—and tenure—and who did not, willingly, move aside to make room for more imaginative people with fresh approaches. That this country attempts to shield its citizens with protective institutions that allow no one—or nearly no one—to go hungry or die for lack of medical care. Yet, at the same time, it insures a dead weight of job-safe parasites, whose tenured unproductivity impedes every impulse toward forward motion. There exists even a degree of inertia or, call it, lack of dynamism, among the students, who regard education merely as job preparation and show little or no interest in exploring ideas and widening their prospects of creative speculation and thought. Misha knew that this was all part of his challenge. He was unable to realize his visions immediately or even in their complete shape. Only with persistence, energy and tact, could he begin something important and see it develop and grow. He'd hoped.

"What do you say, we eat out tonight," Misha asked. "I believe we've both earned it. Maybe we could even take in a movie, huh?"

"Movie is fine," Alida said reflectively, "but we've got to be careful with my present diet." She paused to glance at Misha only for a moment. "You see, I'm pregnant with your child."

"What!?" Misha's reaction startled her. She lowered her eyes.

"You're not pleased, darling?" She asked with anxiety in her trembling voice.

"Well...no...it's...just...so sudden..." He stammered clumsily, unable to put his violent astonishment into proper expression. "How long have you known?"

"Only in the beginning of the last two months. When I had missed my period." She paused again. "I waited to make sure. It's official now. I called Havana; spoke with Samantha Beato two weeks ago. She suggested I select a good obstetrician. I went to see Dr. Sylvia Briar, on Pedro's recommendation. Hope you don't mind. It's all confirmed now. I'm fine. The baby's fine. We're going to..."

He cut her short. "Why haven't I been told before?!" Misha shouted. They were having their first marital fight, and it looked like it was going to be a lulu. It was his reaction to the sudden news, he knew, and he wished he hadn't overacted that violently, but the harm was done already.

"You...you...aren't...happy...?" She asked, and he knew without looking that her eyes were glossy with tears.

"No, not at all," Misha lied, "I only wish I'd been the first to know. Even before Samantha and Pedro. After all, I had something to do with it, haven't I?" He tried to make light of his unwarranted behavior, but he knew it was too late. Hasty behavior as well as words spoken lightly lingers indelibly in the listener's memory.

"You mustn't worry, dear." She assured him. "The baby won't be in your way, I promise. And I'll keep working for as long as I can."

"No, no, my dearest Alida," he protested, "you mustn't think of it. I know we'll manage." Her head was resting on his chest now. Her hair smelled fresh and crisp. It was so full of life it forced him to contemplate happiness against his impulse judgment. Though both were referring to an important event in their lives, their paths have diverged markedly. His lips brushed against her ear, and he kissed it ever so tenderly. She was calm, and they remained still for a long moment, both absorbing the impact of the past few moments.

There was no movie that evening. They had called for Pizza delivery and served it with a salad and a glass of tart Merlot, after which they spent a pleasant evening at home. Two hours later, her body was comfortably curled against his. They lay still for a long time, and he thought she might have fallen asleep, while he was absorbed in his own thoughts. He felt her regular breathing against his chest and nearly drifted off to the rhythmic in and out motion. But he remained awake, in the hope that the stillness of the moment had its healing effect on Alida, inasmuch as it didn't pacify his torment.

Suddenly, she moved for the first time and brushed her hand through his hair, as if inadvertently. "I love you," she whispered.

"I love you, too." He said, unsure as to the direction of their conversation. He expected it to pass as suddenly as it began.

"You must," she said, "if you take such good care of me."

"I do my level best," Misha said.

They lay in silence. It was well past midnight, but the sunrise still seemed in safe distance. Alida seemed peaceful. As peaceful as could be expected, but Misha was quietly weeping. She was the strong one in the face of this momentous event to come. He was still unsure of himself and not quite the man he thought himself to be. He worried now that his outburst might have widened the chasm between them. Surely, she understood his concern and anxiety. He tried to reassure himself. Why didn't he show the steely resolve of a grownup when the situation called for it? She did, and that was not what he'd expected. She will revel in the comfort of his body at night but, in the morning, she will brush herself off and march on more or less without him.

Even though he was doing his best to concentrate on Alida's condition, he was overwhelmed by the prospect of his loss of freedom; his inability to love her for herself and for the new life she was carrying inside her womb. "I'm sorry." He whispered softly, hoping she wouldn't hear.

"It's okay, Misha dearest," she responded in a whisper, "just hold me." He realized then she somehow read his thoughts all along. He held her tightly. He enjoyed the moment for itself, naively hoping it would last forever, like he had done so many times in the company of women. He kept her close, so close to himself, he acquired a sense of oneness in their entangled form.

Through the open window, there was the first hint of light in the sky, and he decided to shatter that illusion they have created. It was likely that the sun wouldn't rise on the horizon for another couple of hours or so, but Misha didn't want to lie there and wait for the slowly increasing light. He wanted the moment to remain oddly fixed and endless.

"Alida," he whispered, wondering whether he'd have to repeat it because she was hard asleep. But she was alert.

"Yes, dearest?" She responded. He was surprised that she had been awake for all that time after what had occurred earlier that evening. He considered, for the moment, telling her that it was nothing, to go back to sleep, so he could cradle her some more.

But, with new resolve, he stuck to his original plan. He leaned down and kissed her forehead.

"I love watching you when you sleep." He said.

"Yes, it was a beautiful night." She said dreamily. Misha stretched his arms, and then proceeded to play with her hair. He hoped they would rise at the same time and leave together. He hoped she was all right.

"Alida," Misha pronounced her name and let it hang in the air. He put his hand on her breasts, and then ran it down to her belly, where he let it rest. "Still so very quiet there." He said.

"Wait another month, dearest, and you'll feel life stirring." She lifted his fingers to her lips and kissed them ever so tenderly.

# 17.

"EVERYTHING IS NORMAL," Dr. Briar was saying. "Just lie back and relax." Her voice echoed in Alida's ears from far off distance and seemed more like a shout than a mild whisper. "Just breathe in and breathe out. Leave the rest to me."

With the first "signs" of Alida's growing pregnancy, they had rented a modest, two-bedroom home not far from the campus and a block from the doctor's office. Alida went for checkups at regular weekly intervals, while maintaining her schedule at the ballet academy. Only when she reported noticing seemingly insignificant, tiny blood spots on her undergarments, did the doctor suggest that she take temporary leave from her routine teaching. "You may do some choreography and Labanotation drills," Dr. Briar noted, "but dance is presently out of the question."

"Is there a danger to the baby?" Alida asked. Her anxiety was obvious.

"Not that I can foresee," Dr. Briar observed her patient intensely, "should there be anything, we'll just make sure that we keep things under control." She paused, while scrutinizing Alida's sad expression. "Is there anything you're keeping from me? Anything you might have left out when responding to questions in reference to your family background? Your own profile?" Her index finger under Alida's chin, the doctor met her patient's eyes with a kind smile of encouragement. Alida was hesitant.

"Well...perhaps...I should tell you..." Alida paused, "in confidence..."

"Everything you say to me is in the strictest confidence," Dr. Briar assured her, "privileged information, between doctor and patient."

"Not even Misha, my husband, must know." Alida said, her eyes downcast.

"Promise." Dr. Briar smiled encouragingly.

"My mother lost her first baby to umbilical strangulation," Alida confessed.

"Is that all?" Briar inquired. "Are you the only child?"

"Yes, it's me, alone." Alida breathed heavily.

"Why? Didn't your parents try again?" Briar asked.

"No. Just me." Alida repeated. She fell silent, without an answer to Dr. Briar's inquiry.

"Is there anything else?" Briar pressed on. Gut feeling had told her there was more. "Any reason why your parents wouldn't try again?" The grimace on Alida's expression was evidence of her great anguish and pain. Briar took both of Alida's hands in hers and squeezed them softly, endearingly. "Come, child, you can confide in me. Let it out, and you'll feel better."

"Mother doesn't know it! She hadn't told me herself, but I finally found out the truth! From my grandmother!" Alida, uncharacteristically, raised her voice. "My parents couldn't have another child. My father was confined to a mental institution at age thirty-four, a year after my birth."

"Do you know the reason? When was he released?" Briar wanted to know. She suspected there was more.

"He's still there. He suffers from congenital brain damage. They say it's incurable." Alida's response sounded hollow, like an echo of herself and without the slightest sign of emotion. "It's a dark cloud I've lived under from the day I'd found out." She began to sob, wiped her running nose with a tissue in an attempt to regain composure. "For years, they wouldn't tell me."

"Who kept it from you?" Briar asked.

"My mother and my grandmother," Alida spoke softly. "They've tried to spare me the anguish of knowing the truth. I've led a sheltered life, yet the deception had done me more harm than the truth would have. I even learned about the facts of life eavesdropping on the older girls at the academy who were obsessed with sex. Some extolled its virtues. Others rejected it as something demeaning and filthy. In the end, I couldn't make up my mind either way. I can understand my mother's and my grandmother's concern. But now, having found out through sheer coincidence about my father's illness, I must deal with it as best I can, alone, for I cannot turn to anyone for guidance."

"You may, my dear, we shall confide in one another from this day on. Won't we?" Dr. Briar continued to hold Alida's hands in hers. "Let me become your sounding board and friend as well as your physician."

"I'll try. I promise." Alida whispered in gratitude.

It was now a question of making up her mind: to tell Misha or not to tell? Not to tell meant, in a way, deception, and she wasn't altogether satisfied with that. To tell meant to risk his anger at having been deceived thus far. But while doing so, she couldn't help but try to guess his behavior either way. The whole business of telling the truth or concealing it from the one you love was so very complicated. Was there another alternative? What were her options? She was at a loss for an answer to her dilemma. Suddenly she felt an aversion for it all; her mother's lack of candor for so many years was now playing havoc with her own life. It seemed as though her mother's sins had come to visit her daughter at the most inopportune moment. Alida remembered Dr. Briar's counsel: "Worry less about the past. You can't help what had happened or turn back the clock. Think about the future and the new life you're carrying. It needs your total strength of body and mind."

It was good advice. Alida knew. Yet each evening that she spent alone, with Misha working in the library stacks pursuing his research, she was torn every which way. Lying wasn't going to embellish her situation. Not telling it up front to the man she loved was tantamount to lying. Was it going to become a way to stay alive? Her lifestyle? But when they were together, she was unable to overcome her innate fear and face the truth with him. It was a question now of how to pluck up enough courage and start to climb up those steep stairs and walk through the door into an open relationship.

"How did your visit go with Dr. Briar?" Misha asked before bedtime.

"Oh, everything went very well." Alida was glad the conversation had turned to the child voluntarily. She didn't have to contrive artificial chitchat after all. "The baby's doing fine. Beginning to stir a little. But that's to be expected at this point. All's normal." She was happy to report.

During her January checkup, five months into the pregnancy, there was a look of concern in Dr. Briar's face. "What's wrong?" Alida asked anxiously. Somehow, she felt a cold chill run down her spine. She'd been predisposed to bad news lately. Misha has been busier than ever with his work away from home, and that left lots of time for her to think. She spent lonely nights immersed in negative thoughts. They hadn't enjoyed each other lately, what with her belly grown to the size of a big melon, and her face usually pudgy and tired. She hadn't even taken the trouble to put on her usual make up; to try to look a bit more alluring for him. In a way, Alida dreaded the arrival of the child. She already felt isolated and left out of Misha's life.

Misha didn't seem to care either. On his frequent trips to "meetings" or the "work" at the library he was, as he said, too tired to be concerned about sex. All he did at home nowadays was eat and sleep. His indifference had affected Alida's behavior severely. There was no laughter when they were together. "I am very lonely," she'd confess to him. "What is it you wish me to do? Quit my job? My research?" He reproached her. He seemed constantly angry with himself. After a while, she stopped complaining. "There should be no lack of things for you to do," he admonished. "Now, that you're not working anymore, you have a lot of time on your hands." Was there reproach in the tone of his voice? She wondered silently.

"Yes, but the things I'd be doing, I'd rather not do at all by myself." She responded, and he became sullen at such moments and cut off the conversation before it could become more serious, confrontational. She began writing to those dear friends she'd left behind, trying desperately to feel their presence across space and time. It has been difficult for her to strike up a cordial friendship with her American acquaintances. Their sense of values differed radically from hers. And though she often wondered whether she wasn't taking life all too seriously, she couldn't quite force herself to understand the Americans' passionate quest of trivial pursuits and their superficial concerns of everyday life.

"The baby is ready to exit." Briar's voice brought Alida to the present.

"But...it's only..."

"Yes...my child...I know," the doctor stroked Alida's hair gently, "it's only the sixth month...it must come out." Briar stated matter of factly.

"What's the alternative?" Alida asked pleadingly.

"That's a big question mark, my child." Briar replied softly. "And I'd rather not second guess it."

"What will I tell Misha?" Alida was concerned.

"I wouldn't worry about that just now," Briar smiled. "Let's take things one at a time. Okay?"

"I suppose, then, we must set the date." Alida said resignedly.

"Next Tuesday, 9 a.m., my dear, confirm an appointment on your way out."

Alida put on a mystified face while dressing to leave, but Briar kept silent and busied herself with the folder before her. "I'll be here then," Alida said in leaving, "and I hope I can persuade Misha to come along."

"That would be lovely, if he could!" Briar called after Alida as she exited.

Misha took the news placidly. "You may call your mother and brake the news to her and your grandmother as well, if you wish." He told her, and there was a rare smile on his face.

"We're going to have a baby!" Alida called out into the phone joyfully," she caught her breath, "next week Tuesday!"

"Congratulations to both of you," Carla responded happily, "let it be a healthy baby!"

"God willing, Mamá, it will be." Alida prayed.

They named him Albert, after her father. He had come into the world on the 5th of January at 11:13 a.m. after a brief hour and a half of induced labor. The tiny creature weighed all of four pounds and 8 ounces. Misha stood by, held Alida's hand throughout the ordeal, and her eyes expressed gratitude. She even caught, she thought, a twinkle of pride in her husband's eyes.

"The baby will remain in an incubator for the time being," Dr. Briar said. "Just to make sure, you understand." She added as if to allay the parents' fears. Little Albert remained in hospital care for over a week until his release to the proud parents. Now it was up to them to attend to all of the infant boy's needs according to the strictest instructions of the head nurse and Dr. Briar.

The boy gained weight rapidly. But there were unexpected complications. His lungs, for one, periodically filled up with fluids. His fingertips and lips had the tendency to turn blue. "We will not worry yet," Briar assured Alida. "You'll bring him in for observation daily. If we can control it, he'll quickly grow out of it."

"You mean 'when' not 'if' we can control it." Alida remarked, as she looked anxiously from Misha to Briar and then to Misha again. She had been breast-feeding the infant. Well, not directly. At first with a dropper, then she used a bottle with a small nipple provided by the hospital. The chore of caring for the baby was terribly demanding, as the infant had to be fed every two hours round the clock. Misha tried to be of help during the night. Still, they were both exhausted come daybreak. She was nearing stress exhaustion, and Misha was unable to function normally. Their only consolation was an occasional smile on the infant's face.

Albert reached the age of six months when their happiness ended abruptly. They were awakened by the boy's faint cry in the middle of the night. His tiny fingers and lips turned completely blue. They called Dr. Briar and rushed the infant to the emergency at the children's clinic. Soon, they had learned the worst. A chest x-ray revealed that Albert's lungs had filled with fluid. No sounds of pain. Only an occasional whimper escaped the child's lips. They felt utterly, desperately helpless as they observed the pain and suffering of their firstborn.

"Why?" Alida asked no one in particular. "Why would God grant us joy one moment only to take it away so quickly?"

Misha hugged his grieving wife without words. The last few months have been too harrowing for the both of them. They were incapable of thinking clearly, and he wasn't going to give it even a try at explaining Alida's poignant question. Not at his emotional state of mind, unsuited as it was for philosophical speculation.

For over ten days, Albert's fragile grip on life was sustained by a tangle of breathing tubes and intravenous lines. Alida would not leave the hospital and slept only at brief intervals of complete exhaustion at her child's bedside. Misha managed as well as he could under the circumstances, while he prepared an important paper for delivery at a soon to take place conference. In spite of all their efforts and the best possible medical attention, Albert's life ended on the morning of July 6th, only two days after the national holiday festivities.

At the funeral, the priest's words were drowned out by a compressor-concrete mixer duet from the next street. The infant's body lay in a tiny casket, covered by an array of flowers. Members of the church choir chanted responses to the priest's prayers that followed the eulogy. Why a eulogy for an infant that hasn't been given a chance to savor the circumstances of life? Misha wondered silently. Just then, it had occurred to him that he hadn't been to confession for quite some time, and the old guilt crept into his tormented almost-Jesuit mentality. Four men lifted the diminutive casket effortlessly and lowered it into the small grave. One of the attendants placed three large, rough flat stones on top of the casket and then shoveled on, with typical lack of emotion, a pile of rich earth, accompanied by the intonation of "Hallelujah… hallelujah…*in excelsis Deo…*" which brought the ceremony to its conclusion, with all those present throwing a handful of earth on top of the casket as they filed by to the sound of responsive prayer.

Though both were silent, Alida and Misha must have shared thoughts about the vulnerability of the human body, as they imagined their firstborn stretched out inside the tiny casket, now almost invisible under the smothering weight of the stones and earth; the plaintive, unadorned melody of the choir, and the last homage of the falling rocks and earth. It all moved them to feel strongly the presence of death and sorrow. What else is aesthetics, if not the striving for expressive beauty and appropriate form? Presumably, some would have preferred the good-mannered pretense that death is not terrifying—as communicated by the banal choir melodies, the polished coffin, and the carpeted halls of the unobtrusive motel decor of the funeral home. As for the noisy building machines nearby, the priestly message, and the responses of the choir and the mourners, these were crude, honest reminders that life continues.

Dr. Briar met with Misha and Alida following the funeral. "We believe Albert had something called severe combined immunodeficiency—SCID," Briar said. "I know it's of no consequence to you if I tell you that babies with this genetic defect are prevented from developing a normal immune system. Hence, SCID babies are susceptible to infections that normal babies fight off and seldom live beyond their first year." Alida didn't want to listen. "Genetic defect…genetic defect…" These two words echoed in her mind persistently. She thought back to the discovery she'd made of her father's genetic illness, his confinement in the sanitarium, her family's secretiveness about it. It all added up now. Grief-stricken, she wept inconsolably in her solitude for days.

"Please, darling," Misha implored, at his wit's end, "we'll try again. We'll have another baby," he put his arms around her and pressed her gently to himself. "It's the only thing that will ever heal us."

"But what if we have another baby with the same illness?" Alida asked.

"We'll just have to take that chance." Misha said stubbornly. "After all, we can't be that unlucky twice in a row." Alida didn't argue. If this was what Misha wanted, she'd go along. Their marriage was showing signs of stress. If another baby was to save it, she was more than willing to take that chance. "All right, then, we'll try once more." She said briefly. She knew, their future together was weighed in the balance of a successful pregnancy that would result in a healthy baby.

It was at about that time, letters from Susanna had arrived more frequently. A few months had passed since little Albert's death, and both Misha and Alida seemed happy and involved in their own affairs once again; he in his research and she with the ballet. At first, Alida managed to ignore the mysterious letters that kept arriving from Germany, and she rationalized some urgent academic relations Misha might have maintained in his native country. Soon, however, she had noticed a certain degree of edginess on Misha's part whenever she tried to engage him in innocent chitchat about the nature of that foreign correspondence.

"Nothing important," he would say, dismissing her inquiry, "just some old acquaintances trying to keep in touch." More than that he didn't say, though when alone and out of Alida's scrutiny, Misha opened the letter and read:

*My dear Misha,*

*I know, this might be added to the many unanswered letters that have come your way, but I can no longer spare you the news of your son. He's a wonderful and happy baby, approaching his third year, in good health and well taken care of. I've had to ask my mother to stay with him during the day, as my job can not afford me the services of a day care, though I would much rather have him there. Mother is the typical grandma. She spoils Rudi no end, and I can foresee trouble in the future. But it can't be helped, my dear.*

*In case you wonder, I haven't gone out with anyone nor have I sought male relationships. It got so, my girlfriends suspect me to be a closet lesbian. That's a joke! If only you were here to set them straight! But you won't even give a sign of life, and I do so much want to hear from you and so does little Rudi. I show him your photo, and he points to it and says 'dada...dada...' In fact those were the first words I taught him. 'Mamá' came after that, I'm sure. Next letter you'll get a photo of your son, okay? I hope you don't mind my letters. I miss you so.*

*Love, Susanna*

Misha's reluctant reply was brief:

*Dear Susanna,*

*I regret my long silence and the anguish it had caused you. Needless to say, I was not at liberty to communicate with you for personal reasons that I don't care to discuss at this writing. Of course, I am astonished at the news that I am a father. If, indeed, the little boy is mine— and I don't doubt that what you're saying is true—I shall fulfill my responsibility. Enclosed, you will find a cashier's check to defray some of your expenses and buy a little something for little Rudi. I am looking forward to receiving a photo of the little tike.*

*Love, Misha*

Whether he'd intended it or not, Misha's response to Susanna initiated a flow of correspondence unlike the sporadic arrivals of letters in the past. Soon, the letters had become more personal, delving into everyday occurrences, photos as well as expressions of an intimate nature. With the fine instinct which a betrayed woman possesses for her husband's private emotions and indiscretions, Alida sensed Misha's ongoing involvement with another. She bore her suspicion in silence. But her pain and anguish became harder to conceal each day. She would not be sent back home, a woman spurned. Her Latin spirit, a sense of pride—*orgullo*, in her language—did not permit her to confront the reality of Misha's relationship with another woman. She preferred to ignore the facts, in the hope that, somehow, he would soon come to his senses and return to her. Problems come and problems go away in time. She reasoned.

But that was not to be. Encouraged by Alida's seeming ignorance—whose need to take matters into her own hands lay dormant under a fatty tissue of contentment with the status quo—Misha not only intensified his exchange of letters with Susanna, but also renewed his frequent visits to Xin Xin. He was received there with open arms albeit with some astonishment. As was commonplace in her life, Xin Xin was experiencing one of her 'transitional' periods; between sleep-in boyfriends.

"I'll take you, on condition that there will be no attachments," she said in her uninhibited manner. "When the time comes to part, we part."

"I have no problem with that," Misha assured her. He would have promised her the stars for another night in bed. He had missed the uninhibited sessions of sex they'd enjoyed in the past, what with Alida's changing moods and his preoccupation with Susanna. He was amply rewarded with nights of unremitting passion and such pleasures, which had left him totally exhausted but exhilarated and without stress when morning came.

During Alida's routine physical several months after the death of little Albert, came the discovery of a large ovarian cyst. "When it rains, it pours." Alida thought, using the old cliché.

"It may not be as bad as we imagine at present," Dr. Briar tried to allay Alida's concerns. "We'll have to keep you a few days at the clinic, take some tests, and send samples to pathology. Meanwhile, don't worry yourself over it."

"Not to worry?" Alida was beside herself. "You tell me not to worry in one breath, Dr. Briar, and in the following you're sending samples of my flesh for biopsy." Her composure gone, Alida sat in her chair opposite Briar in total defeat.

Her brief life passed before her eyes in rapid succession. The happy childhood; her intended career; Misha's arrival and their tumultuous relationship that culminated in a storybook wedding; the discovery of her father's illness; the loss of her first and only child; Misha's apparent infidelities. She felt very much lost and thoroughly unhappy. Would it all have happened the same way, had she heeded *Maestro* Fernando's words? She asked herself silently. If it hadn't been for Misha she would have continued with the company. But then, she realized that even if things had gone their "normal' course, it wouldn't have changed the state of her condition. "Congenital" was the word they used for little Albert's rare illness. That fateful word had imbedded itself firmly in her memory by then. Now she questioned the state of her mother's health; her grandmother's as well. How far back does "congenital" go? All the way back to her ancestry?

"Why me?" She suddenly asked the perennial question.

"What do you mean, child?" Dr. Briar seemed startled by Alida's question.

"Well, what have I done do deserve all this unhappiness?" Alida spoke almost in a whisper. "Only yesterday, my life seemed all in place. I had a career, a new husband, a baby boy..." She sighed heavily. "Now they're all gone. My baby is dead, my career in shambles, my husband..." She stopped in time not to reveal the most intimate of her fears.

"This happens to millions of women all over," Briar explained, "and it isn't the end of the world."

"Please explain." Alida's eyes tried to meet those of her physician, but Dr. Briar lowered hers onto the folder before her.

"Let's leave the explanations until the time we have some concrete evidence of complications, the results come to us from the lab, okay?" Briar tried to delay the inevitable. She had taken a liking for this gentle, innocent patient, and it was hard to maintain the customary objectivity characteristic of her profession. She was going to be careful not to say things that may be unwarranted, not even infer. To hurt irrevocably was not the task of a healer. She would keep that foremost in her mind.

She knew it all along. Alida's worrisome nature was able to neutralize part of the effects the news was to create. That, too, she'd inherited from her mother. X rays pinned to the fluorescent lighting before her looked larger than life. Muddled images appeared; some too dark to discern the details, others too light and transparent to be of great significance. Amidst all that imaging mystery, Dr. Briar, aided by one of her colleagues from pathology, attempted to interpret for Alida the incomprehensible.

"What we thought was a cyst," Briar began, while the other pointed at a spot, which seemed to be the uterus, "we have concluded to be a small tumor." She stopped, noticing Alida's eyes, widening in fear. "Now, there is nothing to be alarmed about, my dear," she patted Alida's trembling hand, "as of now, we know the tumor is benign. It hasn't spread, but that doesn't mean it won't grow." By then, Alida was in tears. Where has she heard such ambiguous assurances before? She thought. Only to be told that her darkest fears had come true. What if they come true now as well?

"We have to remove the growth, my dear." Dr. Briar hugged Alida with motherly affection. "The sooner the better." She paused. "You can depend on it, trust me, child."

In her sheltered life, there was much love and it was based, in part, on trust. But the very people she trusted had betrayed her in the past; are betraying her now. Once betrayed, it was hard for her to regain trust in human integrity. Yet, she urgently needed to trust somebody, anybody. Alida weighed her alternatives; trust was an issue she hadn't questioned until now. Besides, there was a basic need to trust strangers every passing moment. She regarded Dr. Briar with teary eyes. Has this woman betrayed her in regard to little Albert? Can she entrust her own life into Briar's hands as well? Become dependent on her professional expertise and integrity?

"We must schedule surgery," Dr. Briar's voice had a hollow echo to it. "It is urgent…urgent…urgent…" The voice repeated in ripples of warning in Alida's mind..

Alida hesitated. Silently, she weighed her options. True, she suffered pain and irregularity during her menstrual period. Excessive loss of blood. Larger than normal flow. She had to make up her mind quickly; weigh her options and take responsibility for her own decisions. "What's the earliest we can proceed?" She asked with surprising resolve.

"A week from today," Dr. Briar answered. "You must inform your husband."

Alida was silent. She pocketed, without comment, several sheets of instructions on the procedures and preparations leading to surgery. She would inform Misha when he returned from his latest conference in New York. He'd been gone five days and hadn't called once. Where were the affectionate postcards of yesterday? She mused. *Ni modo*—no matter—she would attend to the issues at hand. She had no time to waste on matters that she couldn't alter in the foreseeable future. Her awareness of the crisis she'd faced lent an added urgency to her resolve. After all, when it came right down to it, the one person you could really rely on and trust in this world is *yourself.* Alida had opened her eyes to reality. She had also come to understand that her first duty was to herself.

And then she knew. She recognized, with the most stunning clarity, what her agitation and tension and restlessness were all about. What a fool I've been. What an utter fool. She thought. And her reaction to her sudden self-knowledge was quite reassuring. By exercising her ballet-learned iron self-control, she had presently managed to retain a self-possession that was quite remarkable under the circumstances. Nonetheless, Alida was growing conscious of a significant silence between her and

Misha, and she sensed his disquiet even in his frequent absence. "He has things on his mind." She reasoned. She knew what that something was without having to hazard a guess.

Of course, she needed time to explore, which meant making Misha understand that she needed his support as well. She should communicate this to him, not allow her pent-up anger to get the better of her reason, so that with his understanding she would no longer feel trapped and abandoned in her situation.

# 18.

ALONE AND WAITING Misha's return from New York, Alida had realized for the first time that her life might, from then on, take a sudden turn. Strange things were going to happen to her, she'd never suspected would come to be. To a great extent, she was no longer the Alida of yesterday; the naïve teen married at an age other girls dared dream their romantic fantasies; a person who had forsaken a promising career and a life accented by acclaim, for the obtuse existence of an ordinary housewife.

She found herself rummaging through thoughts she'd never believed herself capable to entertain. Like: "I don't want to die on the operating table or while I'm in a coma. If I died just then, I wouldn't know how I died." The very quality of life had become an issue, not the act of dying and the ultimate finality of death.

It had suddenly struck her that, if she needed the "surgical removal of the womb," as Dr. Briar put it, it would mean strange instruments, made of cold, sterilized steel, were going to intrude into the sanctity of her body. She shuddered at the very thought of such a violation. How primitive humanity continues in this era of developing high-tech, she mused, the knife still remains its basic, nay foremost, instrument dealing with questions of life or death.

Tests were conducted immediately to determine the causes for the irregular but persistent vaginal bleeding. An initial cell-smear—which involved a microscopic examination of secretions obtained from Alida's genital tract—was unable to give conclusive evidence of cancer being present. It was followed by CT scan, bone scan, MRI's, and you name it…

"Does that mean…?" Alida was unable to finish her question, but Briar was aware of the expression of hope from the tone of her voice.

"Let's hope it means that things aren't as critical as we had supposed earlier." She said. "We cannot take any chances, however," Briar continued. "The most trusted method of detection is the taking of samples of tissue to conduct a biopsy. This will allow us an accurate diagnosis. It'll only take a few minutes, while you're here. So, let's do it." She proceeded to administer a local anesthetic and, within minutes, extracted samples needed from the area in question.

Alida lay on the small surgical table in total silence. The procedure made her feel not only more than uncomfortable; it was downright humiliating. Even though she had developed a certain intimacy with Dr. Briar, the intrusion of the sharp metal into her private parts had made her feel violated, as she'd expected. If only Misha were here. She thought on the verge of tears.

"It will take a couple of days," Briar remarked, while Alida was readying to leave. "I'd like to see you then. Have the front desk set up an appointment." A brief "good bye," and Alida, deep in thoughts, left the premises.

Misha returned late that evening and, to her great surprise, she welcomed his return without a word of reproach. Should she tell him about the frequent calls she'd received during his absence? They mustn't have been of an important nature; else the calling party would not have hung up after hearing her voice. Or was it someone that wished to remain anonymous, to speak only with him? Well, *ni modo*, Alida thought in stoic silence. Why spoil his homecoming with trivialities? She needed his support not a confrontation. Her eyes followed Misha across the room; her gaze somewhat preoccupied, her face wreathed by attempts to conceal her concerns.

But suddenly her full attention was riveted on him. He was reaching across and over a large potted plant—it was her favorite hollyhock genus—to open the window, and his body was at an oblique angle. The silk shirt stretched tautly across his broad back and shoulders and forearms. His exceptional physique was apparent through the fine fabric, his muscles rippling as he moved with his usual lightness. It had suddenly occurred to her that much time had lapsed since a last touch was exchanged between them. How she had missed his naked embrace; the feel of his skin on hers; the press of the two bodies entwined. Her heart ached and the pain seeped into her eyes like black ink, staining them to the deepest of browns.

"Briar took some samples of tissue, and we'll know more when the results of the biopsy come in." Alida informed Misha.

"What is she looking for?" He asked.

"She suspects some complications," Alida said. She tried at all costs to avoid the dreaded "C" word. "Dr. Briar doesn't think it's anything very serious. She told me so herself." Alida attempted to make eye contact, but Misha seemed unable to face his wife squarely. After a long moment, he picked up a decanter of port wine, which was her favorite, and poured two glasses, which he carried toward her. He looked at her now and smiled weakly. "Won't you join me, darling," he said his voice at a whisper. "It's not fun drinking alone." He handed her one of the glasses.

"Thank you," Alida said, returning his smile.

"Forgive me for behaving so rudely during my absence," Misha said, settling in the sofa. "It was terrible of me to let the worries over my work get the better of me, neglect being in touch, while you were trying to put up with this...this..." He didn't complete the sentence, but it was obvious he had tried to exonerate himself and put her at ease.

"You don't have to apologize, honey. And my shoulder is always here for you to lean on when you need it," Alida said softly, It was her turn to reassure Misha. She gazed at him with all the gentleness she was able to muster.

"Yes, I know that, darling," he responded. He leaned over and picked up his drink from the coffee table. The front of his unbuttoned shirt sagged open and revealed his chest covered amply by mats of ruddy-blond hair—she had always wondered why it differed from the hair on top of his head. Alida regarded the scene over the rim of her wine glass. She felt herself blush unexpectedly, and her heart missed a beat. She dropped her eyes quickly; afraid he'd notice her embarrassment. If he did, he managed not to reveal it.

He was visibly weary and breathed deeply as he shifted slowly closer toward Alida. All these "female" complications disturbed him deeply, and he didn't know exactly how to react. He was unaccustomed to express concern, even during her frustrating monthly menstrual episodes. For him it meant an unnecessary deterrent from having sex with his wife. Nothing more. All this talk about "biopsies" and "complications" only added to their already troublesome relationship as far as he was concerned. He immediately tried to change the topic of conversation. "Let's not bore each other with our problems tonight. Take things one at a time." Misha went on quietly. "Let's make this a pleasant evening. You know, this place is becoming a veritable tomb. Try to inject some laughter into our daily schedule, good fun, and gaiety. Things ought to be different from now on," he added as if to himself, his eyes avoided hers. She observed him thoughtfully. Why would he try deliberately to avoid the issue at hand?

She had once seen in Misha every quality she most admired and respected. His intellect and his cultivation had been a constant revelation. He was handsome and had the distinction and grace of his profession. And he had such beautiful, deep blue eyes; large, widely set and lucent. He was so different from every man she had come in contact with. He used to be attentive and concerned. Could that have changed, though the physical attributes remained? He had a way of tuning her out.

"Honey?" Alida tried to reach him. "A penny for your thoughts."

"What do you want me to say, darling?" He was evasive, a faint smile on his lips. "I suppose, even if I tried, I wouldn't know where to begin." He paused and, finally, their eyes met. "Anyway, darling, you're in the very capable hands of Dr. Briar. Aren't you? And in spite of the present situation, you're still a young woman, and beautiful at that. I'm sure you'll overcome the temporary setbacks." He'd hoped this would end their conversation, but she wasn't satisfied with his attempt at disengagement.

"Don't you want to speak with her? To find out more about it?" She insisted. She gave him a long, probing look.

"What in heaven's sake gave you the idea that I would want to know more about such an abominable thing as that?" What was it that possessed him to speak to her in that manner? He saw her reaction to his words, and he realized the error of his approach. It was too late. Alida was instantly in tears, her shoulders shook convulsively and, though he had tried to show some of his latent sensitivity, she pushed him away in his attempt to embrace her.

"You don't care! Do you?" She cried. "Whether I live or die, you don't really care." She sobbed. "All you care about is your precious work and..." She wanted to continue, to tell him that she knew about his infidelities, his continuous philandering in his betrayal of their marriage vows. But she stopped herself in time, though it had taken a great deal of will power. This isn't the appropriate moment. She thought. After all, she was Mrs. Winograd, and the others were only his fleeting interests. Whores all. She hadn't felt imperiled by the attention he had given them from time to time. After all, men are like that. She remembered the mother's teachings. Hers were severe admonishments. A woman must be prepared and know how to deal with a "situation." Clearly, her mother would call it that. It was a situation, and nothing more. She dried her tears. Composed herself quickly. She had been brought up in the spirit that loss of composure was vulgar, a characteristic of fishmongers and streetwalkers.

"Oh, honey," She said to the departing Misha, "this'll affect both of us, and, therefore, both of us should know all there is to know about it."

"What is it that you want me to do?" He turned before leaving the room.

"I need your help." Alida said.

"Be specific." He said with annoyance.

"I want you to be here for me in times of crises."

"Crises?"

"Yes. Wouldn't you consider this dreaded disease a crisis?" She seemed shocked he questioned the validity of her concerns.

"I'm truly sorry, darling." He became apologetic, remorseful. Once again, he chose to engage in his favorite charades. He was good at it.

"I can't fight this alone," she whispered. "Oh, God, what's happening to us?" Alida shook her head and began to weep quietly.

"Stay calm, darling Alida," he hadn't called her in that endearing manner for quite some time, and now he implored her, "we must both approach it with calm hearts." He took her into his embrace, and she did nor resist. But she could feel the stiffness of his arms and the cold of his heart. Still, she didn't allow it to come between them, to influence her feelings toward him. She was willing to go on like that, to share his affection, to look away, if only she'd remain *the* Mrs. Winograd; wife of Dr. Misha Winograd.

"When the time comes, darling," he was careful with his words now, "when I must know about all that, I'll learn." He paused. It was one thing, he knew, to make a statement, but quite another to substantiate it with a real reason. "Well, what I'm trying to say is that, be it as it may, there is nothing certain about it at the moment. Why torment ourselves with the uncertainties when we can wait for some concrete data to which we shall react appropriately. Together." He added the last word quickly, to assuage what seemed to him Alida's unnecessary anxiety that could have easily turned to genuine fear. He looked at her intently. She even managed a faint smile. It had been so long since that expression of contentment had well nigh disappeared, that it now caught him by surprise. She did have a pretty face. He thought to himself. God, what kind of a mess had he wrought upon the two of them with his behavior? "Agreed?" He asked.

"Yes, honey," she pulled him to herself, "whatever you say. I'm such a spoiled ninny, aren't I?" She tried to appease him, keep him in her embrace longer, while he was anxious to disengage himself in the pursuit of some well-earned sleep and his precious solitude. And while he retreated to himself, Alida whispered: "My dear Misha, no one was ever so loved or more needed than you are at present." As he closed the door behind him, she'd realized that she had spoken into the empty space that had grown increasingly larger between them. She felt a great loss within herself. But she was quick to recover her inherent stoicism. An old aphorism came to mind: "You mustn't stay busy remembering what you've lost or you won't have time or energy to hold on to that which you have," she thought aloud, "life's too short to dwell on the negative past."

In the days that followed, Alida looked sullen, her lips began to slack and her eyes were swollen from lack of sleep and occasional bouts of crying. Her once luxuriant chestnut brown hair was straggly from the neglect of not being brushed lately. Still and all, outward appearances bore little or no testimony to her characteristic strong will power.

The meticulous discipline of the ballet had forged Alida into a woman of extraordinary patience. It was now, during her stressful time of awaiting the biopsy results that she had to reach deep into its reservoir. For the first time in her adult years, her solitude was filled with loneliness and self-contemplation. But with great resolve, she decided no longer to listen for the phone to ring to hear Misha's voice or for the door to open and perceive his approaching steps. She chose, instead, to spend her time in meaningful reading.

Alida familiarized herself with the details of the dreaded illness she suspected of carrying inside her. No more surprises. She would be prepared next time she visited Dr. Briar. To this end, she'd visited the medical center library on a daily basis and searched out the books and periodicals necessary for her enlightenment in that area. It was also then, by what seemed sheer coincidence, an important book caught her attention. It would exert a riveting influence on her attitude from the moment she'd opened its pages. It was *The Guide for the Perplexed,* by the renowned twelfth century Jewish physician/philosopher Moses Maimonides. Inasmuch that she had found the horrors of the physical world in her readings about ovarian cancer, she drew comfort from the philosophical approaches to life as expressed by Maimonides.

They sat in silence a long while after hearing Dr. Briar's graphic description of the operational procedure. "Nowadays, this type of surgery is quite routine," the doctor explained. "Though you have experienced a decline of appetite and suffered from weight loss, it hadn't caused you pressure or pain, other than the annoyance of frequent urination and vaginal bleeding."

"Which is indicative of cancer, isn't it?" Alida interjected. Misha stared at her, unable to speak. Dr. Briar was, likewise, surprised at Alida's directness.

"Indeed, it is," Briar answered, "and that is why surgery is recommended by all whom we have consulted thus far in this matter."

"Can we get it over with as soon as possible?" Alida asked matter of factly.

"Yes, my dear," Briar turned to her, "I've scheduled surgery for a week from today. That'll be...let's see," she examined her calendar carefully, "...on the twenty-first. Will that be all right?" She addressed Alida, with a gentle expression on her face. The latter was silent, staring out of the window into the distance. All previous thoughts were swept entirely out of her head, and only one remained. Surgery. She was ready for it.

"And the time?" Misha cleared his throat in embarrassment. He had to seize the initiative now. "How ungrateful of me not to have acknowledged all you have done for us, Dr. Briar." He breathed easily. He was proud and vastly relieved to have handled the situation with a degree of adeptness.

"7:00 a.m." Briar indicated the hour without responding to Misha's apology. "The nurse will give you all the necessary instructions as to your diet before and after the operation. Is that okay?" She addressed Alida. But Alida did not answer. She continued to gaze out the window. A tiny frown appeared and wrinkled her smooth brow, and her once perceptive dark eyes seemed to have lost their luster. Yet, she was in absolute command of herself. The perfect lady, as always.

Alida underwent surgery on the morning of October 21, only three days from her twentieth birthday. Those who knew it, went out of their way to prepare a few pleasant surprises for the day to compensate for her pain. After three-and-a-half hours of anguished waiting, Dr. Briar entered the recovery waiting room to face Misha who was deep in thoughts about the future prospects of his marriage.

"We have succeeded in removing the ovaries, the uterus, and the fallopian tubes," she commenced unceremoniously. "While we have done that, much of the grossly visible cancer has also been removed."

Misha's heart sank to its lowest ebb. Cancer? He thought silently. Isn't that supposed to be the illness of people in the middle age? Why should as young a person as Alida suffer from this dread disease? His worst presentiments have been confirmed. He was stunned and unable to utter a word, ask the myriad questions crowding his mind.

"Do you have any questions?" Dr. Briar asked.

"Questions...? Yes...I think so..." Misha responded slowly, as if in a daze. "How...? What...was...the...? Why...?" He whispered almost inaudibly the three disconnected interrogatives.

Believing to have understood his concern, Dr. Briar once again informed Misha: "We have performed radical hysterectomy. Though rare in as young a person as Alida, it had to be done to prevent further spreading of the residual cancer."

"Cancer...cancer...cancer..." Misha kept repeating mechanically, record-like, more to himself than to his informant, without making eye contact. "And what now, Dr. Briar?" He asked.

"Chemotherapy is the usual procedure in these cases," Briar said. "There will be a follow-up examination performed frequently, to make sure the cancer hadn't spread."

"Has it not been removed in surgery?" Misha asked, while he labored to regain composure.

"We'll know the answer to this question when we start postoperative therapy. Right now, we must hope for the best and treat what we know is there."

"How's she going to feel after the operation? Will she have pain? Will she be able to lead a normal life?" Misha shot the questions, which crowded his thoughts in rapid succession. "Will Alida be able to bear children?" He added quickly before Briar could answer his previous queries.

It was now Briar's turn to be startled. She kept silent for a long moment, which seemed like eternity for Misha who wanted ready answers. He observed the doctor intently, the veins on his forehead and neck bulging, as if trying to pry the responses out of her. She sensed his desperation.

"Women who undergo radical surgery such as Alida has undergone this morning, are generally unable to bear..." she paused to choose the right words, concerned about the deep impression her statement played on Misha's fragile condition. He sat motionless, wordless, his face enfolded in the palms of both his hands, soft moans emanated from within. He was in deep pain.

During those long hours before the surgery, Misha had read every bit of material dealing with ovarian cancer he was able to put his hands on. Though he asked the questions—as one would who wished to hope against hope itself—he knew most of the answers. In younger women, when the ovaries are removed, the body's natural source of estrogen is lost and menopause sets in. Symptoms of menopause are likely to appear soon after surgery. Hormone replacement therapy is commonly used to ease such symptoms as hot flashes and vaginal dryness.

"Good God...dear God..." Misha invoked a distant, almost forgotten, call of faith. He needed strength to cope with the unexpected. "The use of hormone therapy has not been studied in women who experienced ovarian cancer." He heard Dr. Briar's distant voice. "There are certain risks, and there are benefits. We should discuss them."

"Side effects...benefits..." Misha repeated mechanically.

"It's not easy to live with a serious disease, both for cancer patients and those who care about them. They face many problems and challenges." Briar continued. "Mainly, how to cope with those difficulties will be easier when people are well informed and are able to be supportive of one another." Briar paused, a look of deep concern directed at Misha. "The patient may worry about holding a job, getting on with her life, or even keeping up with minimum daily activities."

"Only the patient?" Misha asked. "And what about me? Don't I have the same concerns? Don't I have a life?"

"Quite so...quite so..." Briar repeated. She was happy to perceive signs of genuine excitement in Misha's behavior. "You will have to fight it together. *Together* is the key word, Misha. Mutual support is a must." She added for emphasis.

He didn't respond. What could he say? Even during the best of times, he had kept very much to himself, his work, and the extra-curricular activities. How was he to change all that with a young woman who had become old before her time? What about her? Would she see through him and his duplicity? After all, she was nobody's fool. "May I see her now?" Misha asked suddenly.

"Of course, you may." Dr. Briar said with a smile. "She's still under sedation and might not respond to your presence, but you may talk to her, and she'll most likely hear you."

Misha walked into the recovery room and stood still at Alida's bedside. She lay peacefully, it seemed, her eyes tightly shut, oxygen tubes led into her nose, and IVs protruded from both arms, the narrow tubes snaking their way to the plastic bags attached to the back of her bed. Behind her, machines made all sorts of beeping and humming noises as they faithfully measured her vital signs. There was a pungent smell of sterile equipment and medication, which made him nauseous. Misha hated hospitals. They made him sick. It took all of his will power to refrain from retching, as he contemplated Alida's frail form, her face pail as the sheets which covered her up to her neck. "Good God...dear God..." he whispered almost inaudibly under his breath. "Why her? Why us?" His eyes glazed over. "Why us?" He repeated. He knew difficult times were on the way. Could he cope with the physical aspects of their situation while he battled his conscience simultaneously? He questioned silently. Only time would tell. That was the only aspect of the circumstances of which he was certain.

Three days following surgery, Alida was to be discharged from the hospital. Come morning, she could hear Misha's steps in the hall, as he strode swiftly in the direction of her room. He entered, with a deceptively nonchalant and carefree air. He was wearing his white tennis sweater under the professorial corduroy coat, matching corduroy pants and his favorite moccasins. He looked taller, broader, and more grown-up to her than ever. How handsome he is, Alida thought, and her heart leaped to her throat. She felt a sharp stab of pain, and she knew full well it was the bittersweet pain of love.

Within moments, he was bending over her, his face lit up in a wide smile, his clear blue eyes reflecting his obvious delight at seeing Alida well enough to leave the depressing premises of the hospital. Alida thought her heart would burst. He lifted her from the bed, and his arms felt strong and protective as ever. She now stood on her once firm legs, forced to lean against the bed frame, unable to trust their ability to support her. Misha kissed her passionately and ran his free hand down her back caressingly. She blushed, conscious of the eyes of strangers upon them. Then he stood a step away, his strong fingers gripped her shoulders tenderly, and he gazed deeply into her face as if seeing it for the first time. Good God, she is a beauty, he thought, and excitement trickled though him.

"I've missed you much, dearest Alida," he whispered softly in her ear, his ardor apparent on his face. "I couldn't wait to have you back. Did you miss me too?"

"Oh, yes, my darling Misha. I did, indeed." She responded. "I was so very lonely without you."

He laughed for the first time in so many weeks that it seemed strange. "You do believe me. Don't you?" She inquired anxiously, not knowing why he would laugh at her assertion.

The look that crossed her face made him come back quickly: "Oh yes, my sweet Alida. Surely, you know I believe you. My laughter attests to my happiness." He paused. "Now, let's not delay it any longer." He gathered some of the flowers in the room, carried them in one hand while the other supported Alida—she had refused the use of a wheelchair—as they walked toward the exit accompanied by the well wishes of the nursing staff.

On the way home, in the car, he glanced at Alida's face from the corner of his eye. Her eyes looked seriously ahead. They drove in silence when, suddenly, he spoke: "You look very pensive all of a sudden, my sweet."

"Just thinking." She said. "Nothing serious."

"Must be," he said. "Can it be that you no longer love me?" He jested.

"How can you even suggest that?" Even in jest. He thought he spied a tear as it rolled down her cheek. "Misha...my dear Misha..." Alida hesitated and swallowed hard. The words she knew had to be spoken were lodged in her throat.

Misha touched her shoulder tenderly. "Well then...say what's on your mind and be done with it." He encouraged.

"Misha, dearest, I'm never going to have another baby. You know, don't you?" She blurted out harshly. She didn't know how to tell him the news more gently. Glad not to carry this worrisome burden alone, she was nearing tears again.

"Of course, I know. Whatever do you take me for, I'm not an ignorant boor."

Alida felt great relief. He knew, and he was still affectionate and loving. She was excited—if that was a form of happiness—and she clasped her hands together to stop their trembling. In that tortuous moment of truth that hung between them like a lead curtain, Alida's heart beat to bursting. It was her turn to spy his face and try to detect traces of doubt, perhaps even rejection. But she could see none. As well as she had known him, could he still disguise his feelings? She wandered. She bit her lip, eyed him, and tried to assess his attitude.

Sweet Jesus! She cried within. I should have listened to Fernando. Never married. Never bore a child. Did the birthing exacerbate my dormant malady? A smothering feeling enveloped her. I'll never dance again! How can I perform with a bloated belly full of incisions and scars, the skin once stretched to the utmost in childbearing, now a sagging parchment? It's his entire fault. She suddenly thought.

"Misha, I'll hate you to my grave!" She exclaimed in all seriousness. Her facial expression reflected her thoughts. He examined her very carefully from the corners of his eyes. Are sudden mood changes inherent to her condition?

The sudden change in her behavior frightened him. Was it the first dose of the hormone treatment? He agonized. Quickly,

he tried to dismiss it as an attribute of her Latin temperament. "What in God's name are you talking about?" He asked.
She wasn't making much sense. Now he, too, fell silent, as they
approached their apartment, his mind floundering, a thousand
thoughts pounding in his head. He had never contemplated the
eventuality of Alida turning against him, rejecting him. What
an imbecile he had been not to think of such an eventuality, the
most obvious and natural consequence of his behavior coupled
with the unfortunate course of events.

Now Misha racked his brains. He invoked all of his native
intelligence to help him deal with the turn of events. He cleared
his throat, somewhat nervously. His voice was shaky. "Look, darling," he started, "true, we've never faced such crisis before. But
I'm sure we can overcome whatever adversity, if we only remember
to do it together. Isn't that what Dr. Briar had counseled? Alida
was silent, and Misha continued to observe her from the corner
of his eye with utter bewilderment. His mind was in chaos. Did
she know? How could she have kept it all to herself for so long
only to hit him with his guilt all of a sudden, so unexpectedly?

The decent thing to do was to confess and beg forgiveness.
Make a new start. Would she go for that? He wasn't sure. But no.
Didn't he follow the old dictum "what they don't know won't hurt
them," and didn't it work all of the time? He wasn't one to abandon tried and proven formulae, the pseudo-scientist that he was.

And so Misha swallowed hard and remained silent. He bit
back the confessional that he was almost ready to utter. And that
was a decision he would live to regret, for had he spoken up, told
the truth and reclaimed her as his own, braved his innate cowardice, Misha's life would have been so very different.

Alida saw with unmistakable clarity Misha's pretentiousness
on his face and was bitterly aware of the hypocrisy reflected in
his eyes.

The day Alida came home from the hospital, she'd decided to
occupy the second bedroom. Misha, patiently, helped move her

and furnished the room with all of the amenities she asked for. From that day on, they saw each other during breakfast, which she insisted on preparing for both of them, and on occasions that he would be home for dinner that was ready as always. They greeted each other with a cool "hello" in the morning and bid one another "good night" before bedtime.

Alida spent her worrisome hours in prayer at St. Andrew's Church in downtown Urbana, while Misha found solace in the arms of Xin Xin as often as his time permitted. Alida's thoughts wandered across the great distance to her mother and to her friends in Havana. A distance that was intensified by self-doubt and a fledgling agnosticism. She lived in a state of unreality, a sort of delirium, no longer quite alive and not yet dead. She wished with all her heart to continue her religious upbringing, keep her trust in a merciful and omniscient God, but her recent experiences gave her reason to meander through an interim between partial faith and total disbelief. Her mind was at odds with her heart. She felt totally aimless, adrift and somewhat at a loss to think clearly.

She tried to find solace in her dreams. But when the dark of night embraced her into a restless sleep, she had a recurring vision of an hourglass filled with minuscule granules of gold. It was Misha's gold, she knew. Slowly, the gold would run out of the hourglass, while Alida tried vainly to scoop it up with her hands, only to see it vanish between her trembling fingers into nothingness.

She found no sleep, and when she did fall into an uneasy slumber it was then only with heavy palpitation. Love no longer permeated the body; it had only become insatiable. Just then, three to four letters weekly kept arriving from the "other" woman in Germany addressed to Misha. One restless night, she held one of the sealed letters in her lap, as if she'd hoped it would somehow open itself and the words—written in that strange language—would jump out at her with some sort of lucidity. She had to know, once and for all, what that persistent communication between the unknown from overseas signified for her. Daily she would let her thoughts wander absent-mindedly, unable to gather courage, not daring to ask forthrightly, to have the source of her anguish revealed once and for all.

At certain periods, she remained in her room for days, and boredom descended on their household like a dark cloud. It had gotten so Misha hated to get up in the morning to face the new day. He was beginning to take his solitude for granted, and Alida's infrequent appearance at their breakfast table did nothing to encourage a resumption of a meaningful relationship.

On her part, Alida had decided to take refuge in the spiritual reawakening through daily readings of biblical passages and some treatises on the human condition she had found in Maimonides' *Guide*. When in doubt about her marriage, she recalled that it was taken for granted by all who knew her—except of course the stern Fernando—and the family in particular, that she would one day marry. She wasn't absolutely certain at present; in fact, she doubted the merits of having pursued matrimony at such a tender age. She had least of all expected her failure to satisfy Misha's needs as a wife and lover, not to speak of becoming a potential mother. And one day, she had come upon the passage in the Bible that addressed the issue of her own failings, in similar terms to those of Rachel in her relationship to her husband Jacob in the following manner:

> *"Here is my slave-girl Bilha;"* said Rachel to Jacob,
> *come in to her,*
> *so that she may give birth upon my knees,*
> *so that I too may be built-up-with-sons through her.*
> *She gave him Bilha her maid as a wife,*
> *and he came in to her.*
> *Bilha became pregnant and bore a son.* (Genesis 30:3)

Maimonides brought home the realization that she had placed too much importance on material possessions. Maybe she thought that, somehow, property would protect her. She must tell Mamá how wrong they had all been in their belief.

# 19.

*THE JAILERS FOUND Misha curled up in the far corner of his cell floor. He has retreated to his fetal position—one that he had so often assumed when punished by his abusive stern stepfather—now in view of the threat posed by authority. It was all that was left him from his early pubescent relationship with his mother and the stepfather* Herr Doktor Horst...

*...The Judge studied Misha's unshaven face; he then addressed the social worker Dr. Ferucci, in his imposing voice: "Would you like a recess now, so that you could discuss some of the testimony with counsel and the defendant?"*

*"No, your Honor," Ferucci replied. "Let us continue with the testimony." She hesitated, "If it's all right with your Honor?"*

*"By all means," the Judge said, "let's continue."*

Misha's eyes reached beyond the courtroom into the distance, perhaps trying to recall, to put things into their proper perspective. Outside, they were experiencing a mild, snow-less, winter; the skies were azure blue overhead. Only in the shop windows of department stores that advertised toys could one see glittering paper-snow.

*Where will I spend Christmas? Went through Misha's mind. He mustn't let sentimentality distract him. He corrected himself instantly. Concentrate on the relevant issues at hand. He must try harder. There was a great deal at stake.*

"Listen to me, Alida," Misha said one rare morning of breakfasting together, and his voice was cold, calculating, without accent or tone. "There are things happening in the Middle East.

Israel is threatened with annihilation by her Arab foes. There is saber rattling so loud that it can be heard around the globe. Many people are arriving in Israel from distant countries. They want to be there in case something does happen, to help anyway they can." He paused and studied Alida's face. If she felt any emotion at all, she didn't let on. Suddenly, she fixed him with her penetrating glare, and her fierce pride rose up inside her.

"Are you asking my permission, Misha?" She said.

"Not really. I've decided to leave for Israel as soon as possible," he stated matter of factly. He wouldn't try to explain his real reason for going. Fact was he'd been plagued by thoughts of remorse and guilt for the injustices wrought upon the Jews by *his* people. This feeling of profound personal guilt grew especially strong ever since he had met his father. Deep inside, Misha had harbored the belief ever since then that his act of contrition would, at least partially redeem his father's dark soul for the murderous life he'd led, while it would also ease his own conscience. Then, on a sudden impulse, he added, as if parenthetically:

"Besides, a brief separation might do us both some good, offer us a chance to regroup, reflect on things. We need some space."

Alida didn't comment. He stood up, shifting nervously on his feet, obviously anxious to be gone, to escape further inquiries. They would be inquiries without real answers. She looked at him, as he stood there, embarrassed by her indifference. She realized how tall and handsome he was on the outside. Inside that beautiful frame he was still a weakling, a scared little boy with the physical attributes of a mature man. She would not regret his leaving. He wasn't worth it. Not now. Not ever. She decided hastily.

In a way, she was glad to see him leave. Misha's absence would enable her to invite Carla for a long overdue visit. She did miss her mother profoundly during those hours of solitude and need.

"Would you mind if I invited mother to stay with me during your absence?" Alida asked and, without waiting for his reply, she added: "I've missed her, you know. Yes, I believe that's what I'll do. It's been such a long time." On saying that, she got up from the table and retired to her room. They would not see each other for some time to come.

Misha had become aware of the impending danger to the State of Israel by way of one of his departmental associates, a young Sabra—Israeli-born—exchange professor of physics whom he had met at a faculty function. The twenty-four year old Shoshanah Eden, a woman of stunning beauty, whose jet-black shoulder length hair and equally fiery dark eyes had attracted him for more than cerebral reasons.

"The very existence of the State of Israel makes it inconceivable that it can be destroyed," she said in response to Misha's suggestion of "another Holocaust." She smiled with an impressive measure of self-confidence almost bordering on arrogance when Misha uttered those words. "Impossible," she said, "for not only does her army, navy, and air-corps protect her from would-be conquerors; the whole nation stands united against that possibility." There was a kind of native spontaneity in Shoshanna's attitude, an expression of faith in her country's destiny that defied every argument.

He was awed by Shoshanna's inner strength and desired to become part of it, if only for a brief moment in his life. That was precisely when he sensed his opportunity to atone for his father's sins. "I am leaving tomorrow," Shoshanah went on, "most of us belong to the armed forces reserves. Wherever we are, when the country faces a crisis, we must answer the call."

Shoshanah left the university the following day on "emergency leave," and the day following her departure, on the morning of Yom Kippur in Israel, explosive headlines appeared in all news media, electrifying the world with sketchy details about the surprise massive Arab attack on the State of Israel. It was quickly dubbed the "Yom Kippur War." One eyewitness report from Tel Aviv in particular captured Misha's attention:

*It (the war) began on the morning of Yom Kippur—the only day of the year in this noisy city that blaring radios, the car motors and the horns of impatient drivers are still—a stillness penetrated only by the voices of children, birds and dogs. In a 1970 survey of non-orthodox Israelis, the Jewish holidays were rated in order of their significance. High on the list were Passover, Hanukkah, and Independence Day. The least meaningful was Yom Kippur. I wouldn't be surprised if the Arabs changed all that in 1973. The air raid sirens, reminiscent of the* shofar's *(ram's horn) ancient warning sound, may come to be a symbol for Yom Kippur, more potent than the flaming torch for Hanukkah or the matzoth for Passover.*

Four days into the war, before dawn, Misha's phone rang. Haunted by vague images of dying soldiers, civilians on city streets and kibbutzniks on the farms, Misha was restlessly awake. The bell in the darkness startled him from deep sleep. It was Shoshanah, calling from Beer Sheba. She was now a Lieutenant in the Israeli Army.

"Misha, is that you?" He heard Shoshanna's voice as clearly as if she were speaking from her office on campus.

"Who else? My dear Shoshanah," he replied enthused. "I must go and help in the war effort," he added quickly, afraid his intentions might be rejected.

"You understand, Misha, we don't want you to fight for us," she hastened to explain. "You will replace the soldiers in their peace time duties." She waited for his response. It wasn't coming, so she added quickly: "No previous experience required. This is the typical 'on the job learning.'" She laughed, and he was astonished to hear her carefree laughter. They're either collectively insane, he thought silently, or else they have the courage of the innocent. "Take the next *El Al* flight out of New York. They've been shuttling volunteers on the hour. *Shalom.*" With that singular word in Hebrew that signified everyday greeting as well as the word 'peace,' Shoshanah hung up.

216

Misha was convinced more than ever that a person couldn't be considered well educated unless he has lived in at least three different cultures. He has experienced two thus far. Even in this satellite-TV-linked age, the world could not be considered one global village, Marshall McLuhan to the contrary. Variations in outlook, expectations and traditions—all seemingly etched into a person's DNA—that separate one people from another. They are as pronounced as the human condition they all share. In a jet-shrunk world, these variations must be taken very much into account, if people are to attempt rational planning for the survival of the human species; their only common denominator.

While Misha was airborne, events had been developing in Israel of great significance, propelled by their own momentum, to continue, it seemed, to their bitter end.

At 7:00 a.m., an Army jet hurtled low across the sky. It ripped through the gauze of tranquility and sent people running in curiosity and fright to their windows. Nothing else followed, and the viewers dismissed the incident as an isolated patrol. Later in the morning, as streets started filling with pedestrians, police jeeps, private cars bearing black military license plates, and army vehicles were moving rapidly through otherwise quiet streets; their headlights on as a sign of emergency. A bus stood empty, its motor idling. Something was obviously afoot, but what? At 2:00 p.m. the sirens wailed their alert. People poured out of doors of houses and synagogues. Almost immediately, the radio stations, shut down for the holy day, began to broadcast brief bulletins of the double-pronged Egyptian-Syrian attack. There was no need to panic. There had been many rehearsals in the past.

Life proceeded in its normal course. If, in fact, there was any concerned discussion about the war, it might have been regarded as would have an earthquake in a distant land. The only difference here was that most of the able-bodied citizens had left their duties in field and office, as if collectively abducted. All bus drivers, doctors and nurses, and police had been ordered to report to their buses, hospitals, and stations respectively. Wavy, high-pitched signals broke into the announcements that were followed by strange phrases repeated three times: *Sea Wolf—Woman of Charm—Thread of Wool*. Each was a code name for a reserve unit. Every Israeli citizen from age 21 to 55, not in the regular army, belonged to one of those units. When they heard their code name, they knew exactly where to report. Buses started moving through the streets. They picked up groups of reserves at street corners.

Shoshanah greeted Misha at the Lod Airport. She now wore uniform fatigues. The greeting was brief but cordial. "I'll be moving out with my reserve unit tonight," she said matter of factly, "but before I go I'll get you settled in my flat. You'll be contacted later in the week concerning your job." He was silent. "You came to work, didn't you?" She asked more in jest than seriousness.

"Oh...sure...what do you mean, did I come to work?" They broke out in laughter. He was surprised laughter could still be heard in a nation under siege. "I simply can't get over it, how absolutely dashing you look in uniform." He added, his arm rested on her hip. She gently released his hold.

"My dear Misha...this is no time for...what do they call it in America? Fooling around?" She rebuked him gently. And so Misha swallowed hard and remained silent for a long moment, biting back the words he had originally been ready to utter. In the past, he would have considered his response rather puerile. But time was not the same here. Nor were the circumstances.

"Sorry, I couldn't help myself." He blushed embarrassed.

"Always the boy." She smiled at him, and he knew she had forgiven his indiscretion. By then they had arrived at Shoshanah's modest apartment on Ariel 9, in the middle of Tel Aviv's residential area. "I trust you'll feel comfortable here."

Misha looked around the living room containing some essential furniture: a small sofa, some recliners, and a charming coffee table on top of a 6x4 Tabriz that seemed genuine. An efficiency kitchenette and an adjacent bedroom completed the furnishings. "Very much American!" He exclaimed.

"What did you take us for?" She smiled. "Savages?"

Once again, he felt embarrassed. "No...not at all...I...only..." He stammered like a small boy caught with his hand in the cookie jar. Why was her presence so intimidating? Was it the uniform? Her manner of commanding authority?

"This is the second time I've managed to embarrass you. Obviously, I'm not a very good hostess. Allow me to redeem myself, let me take you out to a fine restaurant. It's my treat." Shoshanah said. And before he could respond, she added: "Yes, we even have those around here." Both burst out with carefree laughter. Arm in arm, they arrived at an elegant restaurant reminiscent of any Misha had experienced in Europe or America. They dined splendidly, talked about issues he'd never been concerned with before, with great intensity. "How can there be peace between the Arabs and their Jewish cousins? Their hearts had been filled with the puss of hatred that festered within them from the day Sara drove Hagar, and her son Yishmael from Abraham's household to wander in the desert." Shoshanah said with deep concern in her voice.

"As I see it," Misha suggested, "peace will come through intermarriage."

"We shall lose our Jewish identity, if that happens." Shoshanah replied.

"Is identity worth the terrible bloodshed and disproportionate loss in lives?" Misha asked. "Didn't your God make a covenant with Abraham to make equally great nations of both Isaac's and Ishmael's seed?"

"Time has cut deeply into that promise." Shoshanah said softly. "The All Mighty cannot be concerned about trivialities, it seems." She continued. "And there are forces at work to prevent reconciliation between our people."

"What forces are you speaking of, Shoshanah?" Misha asked.

"The great powers, my dear Misha, they are the ones in whose best interest it is to create chaos, destabilization, and distrust among us." She paused. "You must remember, when God struck the covenant with Abraham, He made the promise to make Abraham's seed 'a blessing to all nations.' That was one of the tenets of that covenant."

"I don't understand," Misha said.

"Think, my dear Misha, how powerful a united Arab/Israeli nation of this Middle Eastern periphery would become if the people learned to live in harmony with each other? Needless to say, the democratic State of Israel is a great threat to the tyrannical rule of the Arab despotic rulers. Only a dream of democracy's rule will awaken the Arab populace to a revolt that will bring peace and harmony in the Middle East. There is much to gain from it on both sides of the spectrum."

"Oh, I see, I see indeed." Misha marveled. "The resources, both natural and intellectual are beyond measure."

"You have discovered the source of our conflict, Misha."

"Oh, yes, how very clever these Americans and British as well as the Russians and the Saudis are, as they play their little power games at the expense of many innocent lives." Misha remarked.

"And how very frightened to lose their supremacy in the end, uh?" Shoshanah smiled. "Well, enough for one evening of geopolitical speculation. Time for me to report to my unit is at hand. Stay out of trouble, my dear friend."

"You do the same, Shoshanah."

"Shalom, Misha."

"Shalom, Shoshanah."

When they parted company, the sun was rising in the east, and Misha wandered when he would see Shoshanah again. If ever. Misha stood in the window, his eyes toward the great metropolis, the likes of which he did not expect here. Tall, shimmering glass and steel skyscrapers glowed in the faded twilight of the rising sun. They seemed to reach upward to claim the sky for themselves in behalf of the dormant city, lit only by the amber glow of lights lining the periphery of the broad avenues. This could be Berlin or Los Angeles or any city in a technologically progressive society.

The Yom Kippur War hastened Misha's coming of age. Up to that time, life had been a kind of *Decameron* epic—a mad debauchery of women, wine and song—and the heat of the war burned the tinsel trappings off his "adventure in hedonism" and bared his soul to himself. Here he experienced a huge well-oiled contraption of delicately balanced powers set to explode at the touch of any one of a hundred panic buttons—a unique, self-generating crisis machine that emerged always stronger from each devastating explosion. Deep down, he was certain many confrontations would take place, each more threatening to the global stability.

Misha was awed by the realities around him. A wiser person was needed to do justice to the interplay of leaders and nations; to armies, torn bodies, and war prisoners; to the ordinary lives flung at random by the roulette wheel of history—in short, to explain *what* had happened, the *why* and *how* of it. Thus far, he was convinced, humanity continued on that tired vessel called *The Ship of Fools*, so aptly described in the medieval novel by the German author Sebastian Brandt he had read during his senior high school year.

People were trying to learn the details of the attack, but few were revealed. Everybody seemed in high spirits nonetheless. The war was a time of excitement and anxiety, so packed with intense emotions that it seemed much longer than the 17 days it would last. People helped each other with preparations and gathering of necessities. From his bedroom window, Misha watched an elderly Arab watchman at a construction site across the street, surveying the scene with uncertainty. He, like everyone else, was trying to comprehend what was happening. In the evening, people gathered around TV sets for speeches from worried-looking Prime Minister Golda Meir and confident Gen. Moshe Dayan, who summed it up: "We expect a *Khatima Tova*—"good signature or seal"—the same wish that all Jews bestow on one another for the Yom Kippur, Day of Judgment, on which the Angels close the *Book of Life* with a full report on every mortal's conduct.

Each night Misha fell asleep certain that he would wake up to news of an overwhelming rout of the attacking enemy. A few hours later, his conscience prodded him awake with the first sickening realization of the battles, and the lingering thought that for many young soldiers the B*ook of Life* was at the moment being slammed shut forever. If only he could share his thoughts with Alida! Would she want to hear? He agonized. Maybe tomorrow.

All day Sunday and well into Monday, soldiers continued to move out of the city in buses, tenders, and private cars. Friends Misha had made on the day before disappeared as suddenly as they appeared in his life. Some remained. Radio and TV sets were on all the time, transmitting news, music, *Ironside* and *Dr. Welby.* The Israeli High Command released only limited information tidbits. Most of what the people at home learned was sifted from the Jordan news in English. One release from Cairo via the BBC told how the Egyptians had liberated the town of Kantara, on the East Bank of the Canal, and how the population turned out en masse to greet their Egyptian brothers. Kantara had been a deserted ghost town since 1967. Jordan would give accurate accounts—out of context. For example: "The Israeli government has just announced that all schools will be closed for ten days." They did not add that the regularly scheduled Succoth vacation had just begun.

Everyone was waiting, hoping, for the announcement of a conclusive Israeli victory. But euphoric optimism gave way reluctantly to a subdued acceptance of a difficult struggle. No one doubted for a moment that Israel would best the attackers, but no one was unmindful of the cost. The word was out—not just in the foreign press, but word of mouth from soldiers, that the first days had left hundreds of widows. A persistent rumor circulated that Israel had lost more soldiers on Yom Kippur than during the Six Day War.

In the middle of the night, Misha would make a roll call of acquaintances that might be at the Canal or on the Golan Heights: Shoshanah Eden, the only daughter of his Tel Aviv friends. She was in the commandos. (Israeli army regulations discourage an "only daughter or son" from joining such a dangerous corps, but at her insistence, Shoshanah's parents used their influence with a general to get her in.) Misha's next door neighbor, Ariel Shimshon, a new immigrant from South Africa, with a pregnant wife and one small son; the husband of two weeks of his other neighbor, Nurit, who was in the Golan Heights with an artillery unit. There were others. How many would never return? And those who did come back from the front spend their first few days attending funerals and paying condolence calls.

On Monday, Misha joined the children from 10th, 11th, and 12th grades at the post office to sort mail and deliver it all over the city. They lent a hand in grocery stores. They did orderly duty in hospitals, where beds were emptied of all but the seriously ill, to await the wounded soldiers. Misha folded newspapers at the offices of the Tel Aviv *Times*, for distribution overseas, and taped windows against the possibility of air raids. Everyone tried to respond to the urge to "do something," but found for the most part that there was little left to do. Misha felt useful for the first time in his life. He volunteered, and his work was appreciated. When he went to give blood, he found an unbelievable crush of people, pushing to donate.

Scenes around town were orderly and ordinary, if a little unnaturally quiet. Buses and cars were operating everywhere, though fewer in number than usual. Offices were open and stores selling as always, although on the first day of the war there had been some panic buying food. There were not many young men to be seen. Children, women and older men, as they gathered inside for cakes and wine on the holiday eve populated the Succoth—outdoor tabernacles or eating booths—.

On the ninth day of the war, the Egyptians opened a major attack along the East Bank of the Canal. Gen. Herzog, Israel's chief military analyst, commented: "We've been expecting that, of course. It opens many possibilities." Misha wondered what that word meant: possibilities, for whom? Them or us? He was proud to think in terms of "them" and "us". His distant heritage was gradually emerging. On BBC, a former British ambassador discussed Egypt's intentions: "Egypt's President Anwar Sadat hopes that the attack will enable him to continue negotiations from a stronger position." Negotiations? What negotiations? Misha thought with surprise. Sadat hasn't been talking to the Israelis in the past, not now, publicly. Were there some deals made behind the scenes?

After the initial shock of the attack and mobilization, people in Israel opened channels of communication in every conceivable form. They tied every civilian, every soldier, and every government official one to the other and to the outside. Meanwhile, in Arab countries, aloof rulers determined the fate of their subjects in isolated fashion—isolation not conducive to a sense of community and high morale seasoned with patriotism.

The enemy collected all radios from their soldiers, while almost every Israeli soldier possessed one. TV had an important function other than the presentation of the news. In the first nine days, Misha noticed, Golda Meir appeared before the people three times; Defense Minister Moshe Dayan twice; Chief of Staff Elazar once; and army spokespersons at least daily. Not only did they address the nation, but they permitted detailed questioning from the press about their aims, strategies, and expectations in the military and political arenas. Here, Misha was astonished to observe how the people round him examined the faces of their leaders as well as each word they uttered and commented on them: "Golda didn't look so worried tonight, did she? Why was

Moshe perspiring so heavily? General Yariv seemed confident... etc...etc..."

For the Arabs, there had not been a single appearance by Egypt's Sadat or Syria's Assad, or any of their top officials. While the Israeli cabinet had been continually in session, after ten days of fighting there was an announcement of the first Egyptian cabinet meeting. The Israeli leaders asked for feedback from the citizens concerning trust in the government and the official news or about the aspects of the war that most worried the people.

For personal communication, Israel's telephone lines were vibrating day and night with anxious calls of inquiries from relatives and friends, and from soldiers who called home. For families with no phones, message centers were set up, operated by volunteers who carried news from soldiers on the front lines. There was a special mobile van line in the service of the Communication Ministry that followed troops to the front lines and provided direct dialing from Israel to Syria in service already the second week of the conflict. The Postal Service, now operated by volunteers who worked around the clock, gave top priority to letters, cards or scraps of paper, to and from soldiers. Underwater cables unceasingly buzzed with overseas calls, most of which were transmitted almost immediately—much faster than in peace time—with their morale boosting assurances of affection and interest on one end, and well-being on the other.

It was revealed that, for some reason, Cairo telephone exchanges were having great difficulty in making any contact with the outside world.

Except for a brief period at the outset, Israel's International Airport was open through the war, and El Al's planes carried thousands of home-rushing Israelis, news people, Jewish and non-Jewish volunteers, and outgoing tourists and diplomats. Cairo Airport was closed down for the duration, as was Jordan's.

The rumor network had messages zigzagging with deadly efficiency through the country. In the '67 war, no casualty figures were released until the fighting stopped. This time, numbers were announced after nine days, in part because rumors were more demoralizing than the facts. One story spread of 30 female soldiers captured, raped and murdered at the Canal. Misha heard that story from at least three people. His thoughts were with Shoshanah.

But word of mouth wasn't always false. News of individual soldiers killed, missing in action or wounded often spread before official notification. These channels also drew people together—no widow was left alone in her grief; no wounded soldier languished in a hospital bed lacking personal attention from family, friends or relatives; no parents mourned their child alone.

Misha was painfully aware of the smallness of Israel. It was frightening in contrast with the attackers' immenseness, and it was that smallness that made the Israeli people feel close. It also led to some peculiar ties between the home front and the battle lines. On the evening of the twelfth day, Misha received a long awaited call.

"Hello, Misha?" He could not contain his joy at hearing Shoshanah's resonant voice. It was clear and seemed very close.

"Shoshanah!!" He shouted into the receiver.

"Control yourself, Misha," she said calmly. "They might hear you in Damascus."

"This is no time for jokes, my dear." He reprimanded her. "Are you on your way home?"

"Not yet, Misha. Perhaps in a few days." She paused. "Only calling to ask that you pay the newspaper delivery at the end of the week. I don't want them to discontinue. Okay?"

"Of course, it's okay." He was impressed at the spontaneous form of communication as exemplified by Shoshanah's call. He would not tell her, but he felt a strong urge to embrace her warmly so as to render her invulnerable to enemy bullets, pain or cold. But it was not to be.

"Good bye for now, dear Misha. I appreciate all you have done for our country as well as for me." She said softly.

"I want you to know, my dear Shoshanah, that I expect you to repay me soon in kind." He joked. Suddenly, there was silence.

Misha never learned the details about Shoshanah's fate. Does it really matter how a person dies? The finality of the event was underscored by the void that followed in its path. On hearing that Shoshanah had become the latest casualty of the war, Misha experienced great pain in the pit of his stomach. "Why couldn't it have been me? Why couldn't it have been me?" He repeated time and again as he wept bitterly, like one who had lost a most precious possession. As high as he felt during the war, so low he had fallen when he heard the dark news about the lovely Shoshanah. His face hidden in the palms of his hands, with the entire body shaking unhaltingly, he cried himself to sleep that night.

The shooting had stopped soon thereafter. He felt his personal loss each moment of the day. Everywhere he went, he looked at faces of women in uniform—just returned from the front— hoping to find Shoshanah among them. He felt himself floating in a void; the war had exploded all his feelings of ambivalence about his self as well as his past complacency about the position of nations.

He struggled to come to terms with what he'd felt was the terrible failures in judgment and preparedness of the Jewish State. So were the Israelis. They kept saying: "How could Mummy and Daddy—Golda and Moshe—had let us down." For a long time he had thought with the others that Israel had been defeated militarily, since the Arabs had been crowing in victory and no one was contradicting them. Then, gradually, the extent of Israel's military feat became known. After being caught off guard by a two-front attack of unbelievable magnitude in men and arms, the Israeli army not only held the enemy from the centers of her population, but advanced deep into the territory of the invaders; surrounded and threatened with extinction a mammoth Egyptian army; only to be held back by the intervening super powers—among them one of their Machiavellian spokespersons, Henry Kissinger—who had arranged a cease fire in time to prevent the humiliation of the Arabs.

Misha spent countless evenings with friends and neighbors. He listened to war stories brought back by the homecoming soldiers. There was no glory in these achievements. The shock of war and the illusion of defeat did not wear off easily because of the widespread mourning and the appalling stories that were being circulated. The worst rumors became confirmed reports. Israel had come perilously close to being overrun in the north. At times, during the first two days, one Motti or one Amir in his tank, surrounded by wounded or dead comrades, maneuvered for endless hours to hold back dozens of Syrian tanks, the spearhead of a huge force set to pour down into Safed and Tiberias and other towns and settlements of the Galil.

Every newspaper story brought to light new nightmares. Misha stopped reading them after a while. He refused to dwell on those horrors as he had always avoided studying details of Nazi death camps. Here, he was afraid to run into Shoshanah's last moments. There, he feared learning about his father's complicity in the crimes.

The TV ran and reran videos from the front, candid pictures of the Israeli army during the war. There was a grim-faced tank driver on the African side of the Suez Canal; a disheveled officer sitting on the turret of the tank while he flicked ashes down on someone's head as he described his battle experiences. The man underneath grinned and waved at the camera. The camera caught another soldier as he read a book in his tank, wearing a prayer shawl—a page of the Sanhedrin a day. There was a wedding, somewhere in the Golan: a beautiful dark bride in white lace; four soldiers supported the corners of the *chuppah* (wedding canopy) with their guns. Misha loved them all.

Many of the soldiers stationed at the Canal when the war burst upon them were Jerusalemites—mostly reserves. Some of them got their first inkling of the attack when they emerged from their bunkers in slippers—religious observers don't wear shoes on the Day of Atonement—to get a breath of air on that Saturday afternoon, and found themselves under Egyptian fire. Later, their decimated units were moved to bunkers in the Jordan Valley for a rest.

At the conflict's end, before their departure, the volunteers were invited to visit a unit in November, to reward them for their volunteer work. They rode from Jerusalem to Jericho along the modern highway—built in 1967 for Jordan by the United States—past miles of sandy hills criss-crossed with camel paths and dotted with scattered flocks of goats. The visitors saw recent additions to the landscape: miles of wire, unwound along the road in triple strands, trailing off into hills as telephone hook-ups for small patrol units; a tent popping up around a curve that shaded two soldiers from the strong sun as they passed part of the afternoon with a game of shesh-besh; a group of uniformed men sitting cross-legged like campers resting from a hike at the side of the road; a split through the pavement filled with dynamite charges, to be set off in the event of an attack from the east; an avant-garde theater vignette: behind a hill, out in the open air, a single desk with an officer seated in front of it, matter-of-factly filling in forms. The most frequent sight, however, was that of destroyed artillery pieces and what was left of countless enemy tanks, marking the dunes and hills of the countryside like some surreal sculptures.

Past Jericho, the buses drove across a deserted waste land, through three gates set in barbed wire—at each of which the driver in an accompanying jeep got out and opened a lock, and closed it behind the passing buses again—until they reached the post. The soldiers welcomed the volunteers warmly. It was a well-earned interruption of their routine day. They handed out gifts and engaged in popular games.

The hosts gave the visitors a guided tour of the elaborate station. They led them through a tunneling underground from kitchen to sleeping quarters to observation dugout, where a powerful telescope brought close, sharp images of the sleepy Jordanian villages across the river. The soldiers were not so young, and behind their casual jokes about the joys of living away from wife and job, Misha saw sad weariness. Their comradeship was deep but subdued. No outsider would ever know what they really went through nor understand the terrible secrets they shared. As the volunteers were leaving, to be out before twilight, the soldiers were organizing a game of volley ball.

Despite the closeness of the nation, there was a chasm between the men and women who had been under fire and those on the home front. Unlike during the Six Day War of 1967, where there were battles in the streets of Jerusalem and around many settlements, the fighting during the Yom Kippur War was "far away." More than one returning soldier expressed dismay: How could life continue as usual? How could people concern themselves with cars and the price of cheese? Surely now they must put aside all essentials and work together to build a morally strong society.

Leah, the only Israeli in the room, sat on the floor next to Misha on a damp Saturday night in November, on the eve of his departure for America—and they were listening to an immigrant from America complain about the cold apartment. She could not keep silent and cut in.

"I'm so glad to see that there are people living normal lives here. All we talk about is death. My brother Avi came home on leave and told me: 'this one died. That one was killed.' This was a judgment on us, maybe a catharsis. We are being punished for our sins. We were living corrupt lives, like the Americans. Why am I bothering with philosophy studies at the university? What has it got to do with us?"

"So, what do you suggest should be the Israeli policy from now on?" Misha asked.

"When they come to the bargaining table, we shouldn't give back a millimeter of the territory we have acquired at the expense of our blood." Leah stated flatly.

There was a desperate need to grasp what had happened. Everybody tried, each started from a different premise and many reached different conclusions. Turmoil was reflected in all reactions. Every focus had been blurred or shifted. Gila, another Israeli neighbor, once told Misha, in the heroic manner of the Biblical Hannah: "I plan to bear many children. Israel needs them for her security." Now, she wondered aloud: "Am I becoming a pacifist?" Mark was a recent émigré from Mexico, a TV engineer who came to the apartment one evening, pale; men with whom he had been working the previous week would never be back at the station. They were on the list of casualties. There was Victor, a mathematics teacher from Brazil who argued not long ago that Israel should unilaterally return conquered land to buy peace. Now he was terribly upset: "Maybe they are just out to destroy us after all, and no concessions will make any difference." He stated sadly. *They* meant the Arabs.

As solidly as they had held together during the war, now people were concerned with fixing the blame, with second-guessing and with endless questions: Why the Yom Kippur surprise? Was the failure in intelligence services, preparedness or both? Had there been a political decision to sacrifice a certain number of troops? Would a pre-emptive strike have been less costly in lives? Would America have made good the threat not to stand behind Israel if she struck first? Was that threat just a rumor? Should Israel have withdrawn from all or some of the territories to try and mollify the Arabs? Should Israel annex all of the territories outright, since only in size lies security and only aggressive action will gain her respect and therefore peace? What can be done to interrupt the senseless cycles of killing?

The butcher around the corner, a tall, handsome Sephardic, had been killed on the Golan. Gila's co-worker at the Institute of Social and Behavioral Research had been killed at the Suez. His wife, a mother of two little girls, couldn't sit Shiva (solemn seven days of mourning) because his body hadn't yet been located. A neighborhood pediatrician, who came from Seattle, recently, lost his only son. A professor's son had been offered the chance to complete his studies on a scholarship at an American university before he joined the army. He insisted on returning to Israel to complete his military service. He was killed in action.

The cliché that war consumes the best was borne out hundreds of times as it had been throughout history. When the cease-fire took effect, Israel had lost over 2000 men and women, and the reckoning continued. On a Saturday, Misha drove a young woman and her three children to visit her husband in a Beersheba hospital. Burned in a tank explosion, he had had three skin graft operations, and she could talk to him only through a window. On that day, after a month in the hospital, he would be able to greet her in person and kiss her.

"I'm so happy he is safe where I can see him and touch him." She sighed.

The government had appointed the Agranat Commission to investigate the military side of the mess. It would yield no results for a long time. Meanwhile, generals leveled charges at one another; returning soldiers made accusations from personal observations; and many civilians had their own versions of where to lay the guilt. An election was coming up, and opposition politicians were not averse to exploiting the nation's misery in an attempt to bring down the party that had led every coalition since 1948.

Misha watched with great sadness as frantic parents held up snapshots before the TV camera, pleading for information about missing sons and daughters. Had anybody seen them alive or captured or fallen? The Syrians would not release the names of their prisoners.—weren't these echoes of the nearly forgotten Second World War? Didn't the Nazi forces condemn to death any uniformed or civilian Jew who decided to resist and fight? All they had intended was to die with the dignity of a struggle for survival.—But now, voices were raised through all the media demanding that the Israelis purge themselves of material pursuits; castigating the Israelis for their despondency and demoralization as a sure preface of surrender to the enemy; condemning the Israelis for their cocksure self-confidence—they called it chutzpah—as causing the war in the first place. There seemed to be no one in Israel or abroad without a sermon for the Israelis, though there weren't two alike.

One by one, European nations "even-handedly" called on Israel to withdraw from every inch of occupied territory—except for the magnificent Dutch—and nations in Asia denounced Israel for her "aggression". While African nations, one after another, broke off diplomatic relations and expelled Israel's dozens of industrial, agricultural, and educational advisors who had worked through the 1960's and shared Israeli know-how with the developing societies in an elaborate Peace Corps program. The impression derived from UN speeches, diplomatic conferences, and oil blockade meetings was that only Israel's stubborn refusal to die or leave Arab land stood in the way of peace, harmony, heated homes, and amply fueled vehicles throughout the world.—Where had all these voices been when virtually all of the Arab nations attacked the newly formed State of Israel in 1948, as they tried to prevent the implementation of the UN resolution calling for the formation of a new State? Where had they been during the betrayal of Czechoslovakia in 1938; and where, indeed, were they when the Nazis exterminated one third of the world's Jewry during the Second World War? Here, Misha became familiar with one of the many Israeli sayings: *"Col ha olam negedanu* (The whole world is against us").—No one could disprove it that time. Misha was infuriated by what he saw as unfair treatment of Israel, and he promised to bear witness, no matter how crazy and callous the world's ugly history had proved the nature of humanity.

On final analysis, it seemed to him that reliance on reason had little to do with the prevailing circumstances. On the contrary, he saw in it the whole thrust of Beckett's plays: by pointing out the absurdity of life, he was affirming some sense in his own exist-ence. Otherwise, why bother? The alternative was suicidal despair.

Nowhere can there be a more logical place to contemplate issues than suspended 35 thousand feet above earth's gravita-tional pull. Misha said goodbye to his new Israeli friends at the airport, and now he was waving farewell to the tiny State below him. In truth, he, like many Israelis, felt cheated in his reaction to the superpower-imposed cease-fire. Now, from the objectivity of distance, he took out his diary and made the following entry:

*We had expected a decisive victory and were frustratingly told the fighting must stop. The Soviet Union, who less than two weeks earlier had exhorted the Arab nations to join in the battle against their com-mon enemy, Israel, while dumping tons of weapons into the Middle East, now was playing the role of the peacemaker. America, who had generously helped Israel with weapons and money, allied herself with the Soviet Union in sponsoring a Security Council resolution for a cease fire just when the Israelis were knocking at the gates of Alexandria, poised for a decisive victory.—It is 1945 all over again... the Allied forces are at the doorstep of the Reich's Chancellery, where Hitler and his thugs are holding out...their defeat is imminent...sud-denly...a voice thunders through the din of battle...it is God's voice... "I demand that you cease your fighting immediately!!" The sound of battle fury is overpowered by the supreme demand...the scoundrels get away once more...as they did many times before...*

*The irony of this farcical performance lies in the disappointment not only of the Israelis. The Arabs had been fed lies by their govern-ments into believing they were victorious. Both Jews and the Arabs could be forgiven for feeling worried: had the superpowers united to sell them out for other interests? Oil? Geopolitics? Try to intellectu-alize casualties.—It is 1938, Munich, the Third Reich...Hitler and Britain's Chamberlain meet to contemplate some options, other than all out war...after some deliberation, they hack up Czechoslovakia in the name of peace...*

*With the lightning cease-fire, all of the Semites of the Middle East glimpsed the chilling truth that small nations survive and prosper only at the pleasure of the big ones. Like most Israelis, I tried to form a for-eign policy for their government. After much soul searching and intel-lectual gymnastics—even trying to penetrate the logic of Kissinger's Machiavellian manipulations of* Realpolitik—*the more background I read and the more I followed reports and speeches and negotiations in the daily press and broadcasts, the more it became obvious that there was no formula for genuine peace that Israel could pursue unilater-ally except, of course, perhaps to dissolve itself. She was not about to do that. After all, the State of Israel was forged in the fires of Nazi crematories; like steel, its people acquired the character and endurance of the element... (More later).*

Misha concluded his entry for the day. He leaned back in his comfortable seat of the Boeing 747 El Al aircraft and closed his eyes. For the first time, he was truly glad of the diminishing distance between himself and Alida. He had missed her more than he cared to admit. He felt truly safe for the first time in so many weeks. Almost asleep, he woke suddenly and reached for the diary in which he scribbled wearily...*well, perhaps there is a solution to all of this madness...I can see peace...and miscegenation is the only answer...*

When he awoke, the sun had barely made its appearance over the distant land body, and Misha recognized the contours of Manhattan Island. The shell of the jumbo aircraft trembled as the engines were shifted into retro power for the landing. Moments later, its mammoth wheels touched down on the tar-mac of Kennedy Airport.

"How fortunate are these people," Misha whispered under his breath, "to live without the threat of invading forces spilling across the borders of their vast land…" It was then he knew where he belonged. This was his home. He was free to stay.

Suddenly, a shiver traveled through his spine; will this nation sustain her moral fiber to avert her decline?

# 20.

*THE PRESIDING JUDGE scribbled a few notes onto the notepad in front of him. Misha studied the man's expression with concern, uncertain that his fragmented testimony had thus far contributed to making him seem credible in the eyes of the presiding Justices. Why were they intent on asking those many questions concerning Susanna? It just didn't add up. Why would they suppose he'd bring harm to the person who bore him his only son? The son who will no longer...*

...Alida greeted him with cool indifference and a strained smile. She submitted rather meekly to a half-hearted hug at the doorstep and withdrew unceremoniously to her room. Disappointed, but not surprised, Misha carried his suitcases into his bedroom and tossed them on top of his bed. They could wait to be unpacked. He wanted to talk; he had so much to tell Alida about the imprint those few days had had on him during his journey to the Holy Land. Surely, she would want to know how he had changed in his outlook on life and how it would affect their relationship. Silently, he prayed that it wasn't too late.

"Darling," he spoke behind the closed door of her bedroom, "we ought to talk." He waited, but there was no reaction. "Please, Alida, come out. There's much I want to tell you. You won't regret it, I promise."

"It's no use, Misha, no more talk." Her voice sounded hollow, though the words issued forth were resolute. He had imagined or hoped he'd detected some tenderness. Or did he think the unthinkable?

"This one more chance, Alida, dearest…" he pleaded. The door opened a crack. Alida's face appeared her eyes downcast. She hesitated, and Misha stepped back and out of her way to let her through. She walked toward the living room, and he followed her. They sat opposite one another, their eyes avoiding contact. "I've changed, darling," he spoke softly. "Can you forgive me?"

She was silent, for what seemed eternity to him. He dared not interrupt her concentration for fear of spooking her into solitude again, as he had done on so many occasions in the past. When she began to talk, it was in a whisper, still without eye-contact, as if to herself: "I only wanted five percent of you; didn't want to monopolize your time; take you away from your precious work." She paused, not sure she was going to reveal her suspicions—more like knowledge—about his indiscretions. Better not. At least, not yet. Let him think she doesn't know.

"But you didn't even let me have the five percent," she continued. "Now, it's too late. It'll never work." A brief moment of silence followed. Then, quickly she added: "Even if we find some common ground at this juncture, it'll never be like it was before."

"Don't say never, honey," he fought for her now, realizing what he'd lose, were she to abandon him. "We'll make it work."

"And how do you propose to do that? To make it work?" She repeated his words with emphasis. "Without reproaching me daily about my being too demanding?" She added, and he didn't respond immediately. He now weighed his thoughts, responses, carefully, not to commit an error he couldn't retract. This was a very sensitive area, he knew. She waited patiently.

"We'll just have to compromise, darling. Won't we? Isn't it what marriage is all about? Compromise?"

"The way you've treated this marriage, my dear Misha, you'd probably expect me to do all of the compromising, become a millinery employee and spend my days in the sweat shop." He was startled by her forthrightness; her direct approach to their relationship.

"How...can...you...?" He stammered and fell silent. What Misha didn't know was that Alida had made up her mind long before his return from Israel. She would continue in her solitude, she told Carla during the latter's visit with her. In spite of her mother's arguments and pleadings, Alida would not yield from her designated course of action. Now she recalled the day clearly...

...Outside, storm clouds had gathered, and a fierce wind started to blow. Mother and daughter were both confined to Alida's little room. Alida was looking out the window and saw litter whooping past pedestrians who were running for cover. Nature itself was trying to put her raging emotions in perspective. Alida thought. She tried to quiet the demons inside her, fighting that deeply moral wind that converged on her from every direction.

When she finally turned her eyes toward Carla, she felt as though her brain was cleansed off toxicity, imbued with new meaning; as if she had washed free all the dirt out of her thoughts and brushed the grit off her soul; tried every rational way to retract, but decided in the end to keep it all. The next time I have a near death experience, she thought, I'll be prepared for it. She turned to her mother.

"Whenever I was filled with doubt and nausea, where was Misha?" She finally asked her startled mother, and Carla listened carefully. "When heart-grief crept into my soul, where was Misha?" She continued softly, as if to herself, trying to compromise even in her harshest thoughts of him.

"You're being too severe with him and also with yourself, my dear." Carla argued. "You must learn to forgive. Be less demanding."

"I've tried, mamá. Believe me, I've tried. I even tried to look the other way." Alida's eyes glazed over as she argued against her own dark thoughts, as a last resort to keep her marriage whole. "Misha's been in search of something...something I could no longer distinguish or identify, hard as I tried. It seemed nondescript and gray." Hands folded in her lap, tears rolling down her cheeks freely, she barely spoke these words: "He can have her here, Mamá, and I won't interfere. He will have his German whore. When she arrives with his child she can give him what I'm not able to give him."

"What are you talking about, Alida?" Carla was beside herself. "How can you think of suggesting such a thing?!"

"You need not be surprised, mamá." Alida now kept her composure. "Misha can—not just come in and go out of my life at will. Learning to trust after having been betrayed—not once but repeatedly—is hard. I don't know if I can give him that…if I have the will…or the energy…"

…Misha got up from the couch and walked toward the window. Alida's eyes had followed him across the room, her gaze preoccupied, her face wreathed with concern. Suddenly, her full attention was riveted on him. He was leaning into the open window—as if something had caught his attention below. His exceptional physique was still apparent through the fine fabric of his favorite silk shirt wide open to reveal the curled dark brown hairs on his manly chest. The intruding sunlight reflected from his suntanned face, now appearing to her more mature than she ever remembered it to be before his journey. There was an air of self-confidence and openness about him now with a tacit promise of understanding and overt compliance. His muscles rippled as he moved about the room with his usual lightness. This was, most likely, one of his characteristics, perhaps, that attracted her to him in the first place. Yes, it was the muscularity and elasticity of a ballet dancer. Her eyes glazed over with certain tenderness she still felt for him, and it was at that moment something deep within her whispered: "My darling. My true and only love." Her heart responded with a deep ache and the pain penetrated her eyes like dark-black mist that cast a shadow over once burning passion.

Misha breathed deeply into the open window. He turned toward her and smiled for the first time since his return. She returned his smile weakly. She seemed pleased they were still able to smile at one another. Thank you. She thought without uttering a sound, afraid it would dispel the magic of the moment.

"You must forgive me for behaving so abominably in the past," Misha said, as he crouched down on the floor close to her again. "It was unfair of me to allow my private problems get the better of me, intrude into our lives, when you were the one putting up with your own crisis alone and abandoned." He stretched out his legs under the coffee table and leaned his head back in a mode of relaxation. He seemed determined to exonerate himself and put her at ease.

"You don't have to apologize, Misha. And you don't need to make amends." Alida gazed at him with much gentleness and the typical subservience that had been inculcated into her mindset early on during her adolescence by both her mother and grand-mother: "To keep a husband happy and satisfied in every way at all times the wife ought to be one step ahead of his innermost wishes in order to accommodate him." She remembered those vital instructions well.

"It is I who owe you an apology for having rejected your attempts at reconciliation. It was so utterly thoughtless of me." She spoke now, and she knew those were Carla's words not hers. It was her mother who spoke, of necessity, in conciliatory terms. She continued: "It was just that I would get up in the morning and sit there staring into space. All alone. Not angry, just not knowing what to do. Where did I fail you, dear Misha?"

"Please, dearest Alida, There is no need for remorse now. It was I who had failed you." He said, trying to thwart her sudden confession. But she went on in a monotone voice, as if thinking out loud to herself. She ignored his attempts to assuage her fears and put her at ease.

"I'm no longer awash with grief, my dear Misha, no longer insane and a danger to myself and others. I have traveled deep inside my self, walked the empty beaches of my native island and stared into the shark-infested ocean. I have argued with the white-bellied ospreys and the great blue night herons. They are all such good listeners." Here, Alida paused, as if ready to make an all-important confession. She glanced at Misha obliquely. She felt herself blushing unexpectedly, and her heart missed a beat. She looked away quickly, lest he discovers her glance, not to lose the flow of her thoughts.

"Well, I'm certainly not going to bore you with my problems today," Misha said gently. "Some things must take time; they come gradually." He readied to get up from his crouching position, but she detained him with a resolute gesture of her hand. "Things are going to be different from now on!" He almost exclaimed, his face aglow.

"Yes, my dear Misha, they will." She agreed. Before she went on, she observed Misha thoughtfully. She found in him every quality she most admired and respected in men. His exceptional intellect and his worldliness were a constant revelation to her. Physically, too, his large blue eyes were widely set and lucent; his handsome face bore great distinction and grace, and she knew full well how some of these qualities were the roots of attraction and admiration women held for him. How sad, she thought, was his vulnerability; unable to resist their adulation. He was victim and seducer all in one.

"Nickel for your thoughts," Misha interrupted, watching her intently, fully conscious of her introspection. Alida reacted, startled from her daydream, seemingly embarrassed at being caught off guard. "I was just putting my thoughts in order," she said. And before he could say anything, she continued, now more animated than before.

"When, in my solitude, I looked into my soul, I was full of affection and forgiveness. I accepted your acts of infidelity. A beloved friend doesn't panic with fear of abandonment when you walk out the door. A beloved friend can watch calmly as you leave for days or even weeks and months. A beloved friend," she repeated with emphasis, "must learn to trust." A faint smile played on her lips. "After all, no one wants to be alone. Mutual abandonment in marriage is fertile ground for all sorts of presentiments. They breed all kinds of demons. They are quick to raise their ugly heads and sow irreparable mischief."

"Please, my darling," he tried in vain to put a stop to her philosophical outpourings. He was awed at her introspection. She resisted sharply, silencing him with a meaningful gesture of her hand.

"Now, I must make it all up to you, my dear Misha. The only way I can. In payment for all I've put you through. But you must also understand, my dear. After surgery, I'd felt as if I had been violated and my husband rejected me instead of a show of understanding and compassion I had expected from him. It was then I had understood that our relationship was purely sexual..." Alida paused, seemed very remote. He was silent, shocked at the radical turn in her attitude. He knew she was incapable of cynicism. Not his Alida, though he had given her ample opportunity to embrace it. He heard her distant voice, hollow in its solemnity: "One after another, Xin-Xin...Susanna...yes...and the others of lesser duration. That's why I moved away and into my own world of solitude..." Misha was in shock, now aware of his blindness and utter stupidity. His attention peaked, and he tried to interrupt the flow of her thoughts and speak his remorseful mind.

"Alida, my dearest Alida..." He repeated. He moved closer, tried to put his arm round her shoulder, but she motioned him away. It was obvious she had used the last reserve of her will power with which to rebuke him.

"No...not yet...you must hear me out completely." She said, but she kept silent for the longest moment, keeping him on the very edge of his patience. Clearly, there was much on her mind, but she seemed at a loss for words to convey these thoughts to him. Finally, she spoke:

"In your absence, some more letters arrived from Germany. Here..." she reached into her night-table drawer and produced a bundle, neatly tied with a ribbon, "you can have them now. I took the liberty of having some of them translated at the university. I'd felt there was urgency in her pleas. You'll see when you read them yourself..."

"No, Alida, it won't be necessary. I've made up my mind..." he interrupted her. "I know what I shall do now..."

"And so do I, my dear Misha..." she reflected for a moment. "You must be aware of the child..." she hesitated, "the son this woman had given you. Aren't you? Don't you feel responsible at all? He must be now, what, about six years old, maybe seven? Aren't you in the least curious?" She waited for him to respond, but he was silent, stunned.

Suddenly, a lifetime of deceit passed through his mind, and he was reliving each instance with bitter awareness, racked with feelings of guilt and the need of self-flagellation. It had occurred to him that it has been some time since he had confessed his love for this lovely woman before him. No degree of repentance was adequate now. His omissions were all she knew of a lifetime they'd spent with one another. How well he recalled his mother's last admonishment. Her last words were etched in his conscious mind forever: "You must not love anyone before they have first declared their love for you." True to that dictum, each time that situation developed, he'd lose interest in the other; withdraw into himself with nowhere to go, into a total void.

Those days were gone now; he made a mental promise. The days when he was safe and protected by his mother's vigilance were only a memory. As a child, he saw everything as magical; the sun shining onto the billowing clouds; the evening sky with its infinite distance that implied mystery in the impenetrable darkness from which sparkling stars shone onto his universe. As time went on, he'd lost interest in universal phenomena, as they were supplanted by other, more pragmatic pursuits. Life itself became less fascinating, its riddles unworthy of being solved. How he wished he'd been able to return to the childish games they played together. Misha and Alida, children both. But in the rush of time, the games were forgotten, innocence gone. And now, he was at a loss about playing the reassuring adult, sharing thoughts and insights, comforting the woman he'd married and loved because he thought and knew full well they were made for each other. Instead, he sat mute, tried to conserve his energy flow lest it be spent on trivial talk rather than on reconciling with his great losses.

Misha knew that Alida's eyes were glossy with tears, even though she turned her head from him. "I can't believe my ears," he muttered. He was glad she didn't wear her mascara else her face would have surely been stained with streaks of tears. He realized, too, that he had never before been compelled to stop her flow of tears. And her gentle sobbing at the moment seemed only natural for her to continue. If only they could return to the moment of their beginnings together. He wished. Only then, maybe, he could have hoped to share and abate all her hidden fears. Restore a semblance of trust between them once again. For the moment, all hope was gone, and the inevitable question remained very much alive and present: What to do with Susanna?

Before all this happened, hadn't he offered to take Susanna with him to the States, and she refused? The security of her position at the Children's Institute in Heidelberg, and the presence of her loving parents persuaded her to remain in Germany. Only when she was with his child, did she experience the urgency of being with him, amply demonstrated by the flow of letters.

"Do you realize, dear Misha, that you haven't once mentioned our darling son?" Alida's words startled him. "Not once, have you visited little Albert's graveside. Not even once." It was his turn now to remain mute. Not with grief, but with a sense of deep shame and remorse for his oversight. "Do you think little Albert is in heaven?" Alida asked suddenly.

It was an awkward question. Difficult enough to answer under relaxed circumstances, but impossible when he was preoccupied with his present and more urgent problems. She asked it honestly, as an expression of hope, even though he had expressed to her his agnosticism on numerous occasions in the past. Now, as if against his will and absentmindedly, his voice said clearly and loudly "yes, I believe he's in heaven." As he had done so often in the past, Misha used specific moments to dress up his life. With clarity to himself, he had become aware that telling white lies was his camouflage, a way of life; lies needed no embellishment from him; others would enrich his sketches to suit their own imagination as the need called for.

"Thank you, Misha," Alida said and got up, ready to leave. "When Susanna arrives, she will share your bed." Alida spoke without a trace of emotion in her voice. "You'll have what you need most, so long as I'll remain your wife. Do we understand each other?" She seemed fully rational in her proposal, more like demand. At that moment, Misha realized that their paths have completely diverged and would not meet again.

Suddenly, their roles have reversed; Alida seemed strong and peaceful, in full command of her emotions, but he was the one crying inwardly. She was firm in the face of her losses, with a steely resolve of a grownup. He found himself unable to cope with the situation he had created. What had taken place was that Alida had brushed herself off and marched on without him, while he was temporarily overwhelmed by his inability to cope; the price he paid for his inability in all those years to truly love her. And all he was able to say, as he held back his tears, was "I'm so sorry...so very sorry, darling."

"It's okay," she replied, in her half effort to console him, "we'll manage."

He lost count of the many times he silently repeated Alida's name during those sleepless nights. Hours of contradictory thoughts and vain regrets had passed, when he welcomed the first hint of the rising sun. Suddenly, he was awake, and the illusions of yesterday had all but vanished. It would not be morning for another hour or so, but he got up, showered, and made ready to face the day.

# 21.

WHEN HER SUPERIOR, *Herr* Dr. Isidor Fleischmann, summoned Susanna to his office in an "urgent matter," she was certain it was another of his many attempts to lure her into the sack. Her boss was one of her many suitors—the most persistent by far—and everyone in the office knew it.

The way to Fleischmann's office led through a labyrinth of desks, and Susanna was painfully aware of the derisive stares behind her back and the subdued whispers and chuckles, which sounded more like suppressed coughs. In the past, she had been promoted ahead of some of her senior co-workers several times and, for those who cared to deliberate why that had taken place, the reason was quite obvious to all those who lived by malice of forethought. Wag their tongues they did and backstab to boot. Susanna was the boss' favorite mistress.

Now, like many times before when she was summoned, she stood outside her boss' office, about to turn the door knob. Was it going to be another of his vulgar propositions? She wondered. If so, she would put him in his place once and for all. Even at the expense of her job. Damn! At the mere thought of losing the job she liked and was good at, just because she wouldn't accommodate Fleischmann's lecheries, her entire being rebelled. She would have informed his wife long ago, if she were sure it would yield the desired results. Mrs. Fleischmann herself was no innocent lamb. Her husband's pursuits of the "weaker" sex had made it all the easier for her to pursue her own path of iniquity. Okay. So be it. Susanna thought intensely. This was the end of the line for her.

"*Herr Hauptrechnungsführer,*" Susanna addressed her boss with deference due his position as Chief Accountant, "you sent for me?"

"Why so formal, *Liebchen?*" Her boss smiled, and his puffy, bulldog-like, face assumed the form of a painful grimace, the closely set pointy eyes devouring the object of his desires. His appearance was nothing to boast about. In his late middle age, he was much overweight for his five feet seven inches frame and, as he got up to offer his visitor a chair, the enormous beer belly was evident by the strain of his shirt buttons that almost burst with each step he took. The resulting cracks in his shirt lay to view an abundance of kinky hair, which had found its way to his belly on down from the burly chest. His balding head was sparsely covered by the few remaining strands of hair, which he had let grow from the nape of his neck, and combed, amply gelatinized and lustrous, onto his forehead. "Come, sit down," he offered a chair.

"Thank you, sir," she said and took the seat.

"Aren't we formal," he mocked her.

"I prefer it this way," she avoided his eyes.

He came around her chair, and the tips of his thick fingers touched Susanna's shoulder with a lightness of which she thought him incapable. Still, she sat quietly, motionless, with the rigidity of a porcelain vase ready to burst into shards in response to the least provocative force.

He chuckled awkwardly. "Relax, my dear," he said, thinking it would soften her tense features and attitude.

"I wish you wouldn't take up my time and yours on such trivialities, *Herr* Fleischmann." Susanna pleaded meekly. "Haven't I made myself abundantly clear that I'm not interested in your pursuits? You should know by now that your efforts in that direction are all totally in vain. Give it up, *Herr* Fleischmann. Please." Her conscience screamed to let him know how repulsive he was to her, but reason dictated caution.

He stepped away from her, walked behind his desk, and sat down in the leather-upholstered chair with a heavy sigh. Feeling safe, Susanna raised her head, and their eyes met. Hers were defiant. His bore a mysterious smile that puzzled her. To be sure, he had something up his sleeve. Though she had by now grown accustomed to his devious nature, she could not contain her curiosity. She knew, he would let her know when he was ready. They sat in silence for a long moment. Then, he picked up an airmail envelope from his desk and held it up for her to see.

"This came for you over the weekend, as I happened to be in the office on Saturday morning." He grinned. "It was addressed to you, in care of our firm." He paused, squinted his eyes, as if he had tried to penetrate her thoughts. She showed no reaction, and it took all the will power she possessed. "Since it bore the name of the firm as addressee, I took the liberty to..."

"How dare you?" She wanted to heap insults at him. More than that, she had a strong urge to strike at the barrel chest with all the force in her. But she used the wisdom of restraint. After all, he had already read the contents of the letter, and no amount of outrage would give her the satisfaction she had sought.

"May I have it now? Or do you wish to tell me its contents?" She could not contain her sarcasm as she held out her hand. He came from behind the desk toward her, his thick fingers turning the envelope playfully, drops of sweat rolling down his huge nose onto his lips. He licked them meaningfully.

"What? No gratitude?" He taunted. "I act the faithful mailman to deliver an important letter from America and what do I get in return? Gratitude? No. I get bitter sarcasm, my dear Susanna. And to think of all I had done for you the time you've been with us. Is your behavior warranted?"

He went on in his manner, reminding her of the benefits she had reaped from his infatuation, for which he had received not a hint of gratitude, etc., etc... But Susanna did not hear his chatter. America! She thought silently. Misha! All these years she'd been waiting to leave, endured the insults of this animal and the indignities of his behavior as well as those of her co-workers. She sustained them all stoically. The promise of impending liberation softened her features.

"I'm sorry to have offended you, *Herr* Fleischmann," she said almost in a whisper. "I didn't mean to be fresh." She held out her hand. Now, please, may I have *my* letter?" She laid emphasis on the pronoun *my*. He placed the envelope in her hand, not without a light squeeze of her palm in the process. She withdrew her hand quickly and readied to leave. Even then, he blocked her way to the door with his massive frame. "Think carefully, *Liebchen*," he grinned exposing his cigar-stained teeth. "Here you will always have a great future. I could be good to you...and the boy." He added quickly, knowing her weakness. "Consider your career."

She used all of her athletic dexterity to maneuver her way past him and out the door. She could see heads disappearing in the cubicles behind the flimsy partitions. But she knew their eyes were pealed on Dr. Fleischmann's office while she was inside, imagining less than complimentary thoughts about the boss and his "mistress". Suddenly, it was of little concern to her what was on their minds. People usually believe what they want to believe. She knew.

In her own cubicle of an office, she spread the letter before her on the desk. It was written in longhand. Indisputably, it was Misha's character. She knew it so well. He always wrote to her in longhand when he tried to convey warmth and sympathy.

*Dearest Susanna!*

*Wonderful news! Just as soon as you can put your things in order, pack up and catch a plane for America. If it comes to you as a surprise, I want you to know that it startled me as well when, all of a sudden, Alida made the suggestion. God knows what had gotten into her. It must be some kind of Latin tradition. If the woman can't please a man, she'll get him another or something like that. Shortly after she had undergone radical hysterectomy, she also underwent a gradual change of character. In fact, she moved her things to another bedroom, slept there ever since. We have had no contact other than a polite "good morning" and, before bedtime "good night." No telling what the future holds. Meanwhile, I'm terribly lonely and would like nothing better than having you and Rudi here with me. Isn't that what you had wanted all along? Don't delay, wire your arrival time. Love, Misha*

*PS. The enclosed cashier's check is to defray expenses.*

For the longest time, Susanna sat motionless, stunned by the contents of the letter. How was she to interpret Misha's request? Is his Alida out of her mind? Dear God! How can anyone attempt to understand the roots of human behavior? As for herself, she had to weigh all possible options. She had made one big mistake already, and it nearly broke her heart. Were it not for little Rudi, it would have. How many major errors was one allowed in the course of a lifetime? How many could a person survive and still function rationally? Questions such as these would have normally preoccupied her mind. At this time, however, there were other issues to be resolved; more practical questions that overshadowed those rooted in philosophy.

How would Rudi adjust to the change? His schooling? A new language for both of them? True, she had been learning classroom English for some time, but could she function professionally in that new environment. Would Rudi, transplanted so abruptly, miss his friends? But then, there was one huge reason for leaving: to escape *Herr* Dr. Fleischmann's pursuits and be with her Misha in the process.

Throughout the day and restless night of tossing in her sleep, she battled the demons of assertiveness and negation, weighed her options. And when morning came, exhausted from lack of sleep, Susanna had reached her decision. Now, she prayed it would not become her life's second worst error.

It had taken two weeks to put all things in order: pay due bills, cancel apartment lease, and renew the old passport she had never used. These things accomplished, she arrived at the hardest task of all; saying good-bye to family and friends. Hard to believe, for a fairly well educated person, this was to be Susanna's first long journey to anywhere, and she was quite apprehensive.

The seven-year-old Rudi peppered his mother with questions. They stemmed more from a child's curiosity than anything else. Are we going to see daddy? Will he bring me presents? What if daddy doesn't like me? Susanna tried to answer each of them, though sometimes she found it hard to make her replies sound realistic. The child sensed his mother's doubts, but continued his game without letting on he knew. Only when they boarded the plane did Rudi allow his mother to immerse herself in her own thoughts, while he kept himself busy with the colored drawings of jungle animals and the soft drink and some snacks provided by the flight attendant.

Susanna let out a sigh of relief. She needed time to reflect; do some soul searching. Now, 35,000 feet above sea level, all of her preoccupations seemed as minuscule as the antlike objects making their tedious way on the surface below. Things seemed quite clear and laid out in proper perspective. It seemed all of her earthly, mundane, problems became distant and less significant, the great rivers that wound their way through the countryside appeared alike small creeks meandering toward nowhere in particular; the super highways carrying all those microscopic vehicles seemed insignificant from her vantage. Would she be able to achieve such objectivity now that she flew above her problems?

Never before had she felt so profoundly at peace with herself as she did now in this zone of time suspension. She closed her eyes and saw herself being carried to some distant, exotic place; one with ripe fruits and healthy, nimble bodies. Or, perhaps, she fancied remaining there, suspended high above the clouds. Yes, there was a sun high above the clouds, forever free. And there was peace above the turbulence of the volatile elements. She imagined herself dying there one day, above the troubling spheres of human toil and sorrow, and she found a measure of solace in that thought. But at this very moment she could only think of life and living. She glanced at Rudi from the corner of her eye, and he had fallen asleep after having exhausted his fascination for coloring. They were flying over the Channel onto the Atlantic, and the immensity of the great Ocean waters below had proven all too monotonous and put the boy to sleep.

The very nature of the trip was such that Susanna experienced a feeling of escape immediately upon boarding the plane. She would concentrate on the future from this moment on. She had finally caught up with her life and would not let go. Suddenly, the frustrations of yesterday, so firmly locked inside her self, seemed to dissolve as did the web of presentiments that had spun a tangle inside her mind. She was glad they had left Germany before dawn and would spend the crossing over the North Pole at dusk. She looked forward to the spectacle the Captain had promised the passengers on takeoff. It was to be that awesome moment, when the sun almost kisses the moon over the North Pole. She remembered the old jazz hit made popular in the fifties by the French crooner Charles Trenet titled *Le Soleil avait un rendez-vous avec la Lune*. A droll little tune, which tells the story about the two heavenly, spheres never being quite able to meet as planned; the arrival of one always signals the departure of the other. It has been their song; hers and Misha's. She gazed out her window onto the vast expanse below and wandered whether those days of "missing out" on life would now come to an end at last. The sky was azure and rich blue, in sharp contrast to the dark waters that swirled below. Uncomplicated and clear as the sky presented itself, it stood in stark contrast with the dark mystery of the Ocean's depth. Separated by the immensity of space between them, these fundamental elements seemed to melt into one another on the distant horizon; two lovers in a passionate embrace. Only a slight, thin line remained barely visible as evidence of their union.

Susanna glanced at Rudi, still fast asleep, undisturbed by the chatter of the passengers and the loud humming of the powerful engines. Barely seven years old, he was the essence of her life up till now. She had no need to lie to him about the absence of his father. And she placed no illusions in his fragile psyche regarding their future prospects. He had the intuitive wisdom not to ask those hard-to-answer questions. And though they've experienced some significant obstacles—it wasn't easy for a single working mother to provide the care the child demanded—he had from infancy that inherent sense so few children demonstrate to become a helper rather than a hindrance. A child of his mental capacity is a blessing to his parent.

Susanna closed her eyes. They had good times together, she and Misha. Has he changed? Was he trustworthy? She wondered, and she'd hoped he was. Would he be able to accept her as the mother of his son? How would motherhood affect their relationship? All her friends cautioned her not to burn her bridges. "Just in case." They said. Her parents, too, expressed anxiety over her radical departure from "common sense," as they called her decision to leave a life of tranquility and a secure future. But, then, they weren't informed about *Herr* Dr. Isidor Fleischmann. Were they? She was aware of an illusory reality that the life she had built for herself and her child was ablaze. All of the essentials that she had always taken for granted were engulfed in a fire. Suddenly, she became keenly cognizant of their absence, though now without much alarm.

Flying, too, was a new sensation for Susanna. She leaned back in her seat; a pillow comfortably supported her neck, her eyes closed though she had no intention of falling asleep neither was she capable under the circumstances of doing so. Was it a question of anxiety? Oh, well, you have to place your trust in someone, strangers though they be. "Children," she thought, glancing imperceptibly at her little boy in deep slumber, "have no worry and lack the adulthood acquired fears." An attendant approached with the beverage and snack cart down the aisle, politely reminding passengers to remove their legs from the walkway. Her pleasant sounding voice reminded Susanna that, as a young woman, she entertained the thought of becoming a flight attendant. It had maintained for her a certain measure of adventure and romance. She hadn't chosen it for several reasons. One of which was that the job did not require a high school diploma, and another her doubts about the ability to overcome the fear of flying.

But the idea of unlimited travel was appealing. It was as if life would go on indefinitely, and if a destination did not meet her expectations, there was always another horizon to be conquered at the end of the runway. She imagined sitting on the coast of the French Riviera, basking in the hot sun alongside many, cooled by the pleasant breezes of the Mediterranean. She thought momentarily that she would rather be in that place than anywhere else. But she realized that it was no different from any other place. It would be filled with so many people who were obsessed with common concerns about what they saw and what kind of gourmet food they'd consumed the previous day. What they planned to experience next that would surpass their previous experiences.

"Your first journey to America?" The man leaning toward her from the opposite aisle brought her back from her reverie. His resonant voice penetrated the prevailing noises. It was deep and masculine. His question startled her. He was a young man perhaps in his late thirties, his wavy-black hair graying sparsely at the temples, which lent him the appearance of maturity, perhaps distinction. His lively, brown eyes smiled at her and, somehow, gained her confidence. The sculpted square jaw lent him a semblance of possessing a firm character.

"Patrick O'Malley," he introduced himself with his hand reaching out across the aisle. She forced an almost imperceptible smile but did not offer a handshake. He waited patiently with his outstretched hand. His smile affected two of the deepest dimples she'd ever seen on a man's cheeks. She was about to offer her handshake, when he withdrew his hand, still smiling: "I guess, after all, it isn't safe nowadays to shake just anybody's hand. With all of the..."

"Oh, no, not at all," she hastened to assure him. "It's just... well...I..." she was unable to find the right words to define her hesitation, but he proved helpful.

"Not to worry," he laughed. "I can see you're a stranger in a strange place, with added responsibility." He nodded toward little Rudi. "Son?" He asked.

"Yes," Susanna said, "he's almost seven years old." The words issued forth, her hesitation gone, and she wondered why she confided so swiftly in a total stranger.

"And a fine young man he is," the man paused, "bet you're a proud mother."

"My name's Susanna...Susanna Flossberg. Nice meeting you." She used the best classroom English she was able to muster.

"Germany?" He asked. He detected the characteristic accent of her nationality.

"Yes," Susanna responded, "from Nuremberg. Ever been there?"

"No," Patrick said, lowering his eyes, as if apologizing for that omission, "though I've been to a conference not far from there, at the University of Augsburg."

"Oh? On business?" She inquired.

"Not really." He said, now looking into her blue eyes with such intensity it made her blush to the roots of her fiery red hair. He noticed, pleased. "Some might call a conference on recent archeological findings a sort of business, but as far as I'm concerned, it was a pleasure trip."

"You teach?" She asked, and he didn't seem to mind her inquisitiveness.

"Yes, tenured professor of archeology at the University of Illinois, Urbana."

Longer than a moment, Susanna observed the man, eyes widened with amused astonishment, her lips pursed to speak, yet unable to say a word. He sensed the impression his revelation must have made on her and was quick to add: "If you have a special aversion for this kind of profession, I will renounce it at once!" He laughed and made her feel at ease. She, too, burst out in a carefree giggle.

"No! Not at all!" She assured him. "This is quite a coincidence," she went on, "I'm on my way to your city, to meet…" She stopped there, not sure she wanted to divulge further details of her private life to a total stranger.

He was discreet, didn't pry. "I'm sure you'll like it there," he hastened to assure her. "It's a university community with great cultural outlets, music, the arts in general, visiting speakers, you name it." He paused to elicit some comments, but none were forthcoming, and he continued playfully. "And, besides, in addition to all that, you'll find me there, too." He handed her his business card. She regarded the dainty, elegantly embossed print carefully. It read: "Patrick O'Malley, Ph.D., Professor of Anthropology and Ancient History." "That's quite impressive." She stated simply, without raising her eyes. "Really." He smiled.

"And you?" He asked, and his probing eyes met hers. "What will you be doing there?"

"I'm a steno-typist by profession," she said, and she lowered her eyes in an attempt to avoid his, "of course, I realize that secretarial work has its fundamental differences in America from the work I did in Germany; the most radical being the language itself. Why, it even differs from the British English I'd studied at school."

"Don't let that worry you, Susanna." He addressed her by her first name, and she liked the sound of his voice enunciating the three soft syllables comprising her name, though in her native society such familiarity was reserved for intimate friends no casual acquaintances. "Besides," he continued, "you're needlessly modest. You speak our language quite well. I only wish my knowledge of German equaled that, and I might have been able to deliver my recent guest lecture in German instead of having to use an interpreter's services."

"Uh," she blushed again, "I try my best, but I still find it hard to express myself in American English with ease."

"It'll improve just as soon as you'll step on American soil." He assured her. "It's a matter of getting used to the idiom." He paused, and she was able to anticipate that certain playfulness in his voice.

"And, besides, if you should encounter any obstacles whatsoever," he controlled his desire to laugh, "then, you have only to pick up the phone and dial my number. I'll be there for you, day or night," he assured her boldly. "You can count on it." His forward behavior was puzzling. She wandered silently whether his was the accepted norm in the American culture. None of her English teachers had touched on the differences in social behavior or cultural topics. The urgency and haste in acquiring rudimentary survival English competence did not allow such interesting diversion.

# 22.

LATELY, MISHA'S STRUGGLE to produce a decent bowel movement had increased markedly. Was it the prison food or his gnawing preoccupation with the impending decision of the judges? He couldn't tell. There were moments when he was totally fed up with the ongoing interrogation; he wanted to end it in his desperation by signing a full confession. But the faint glimmer of hope that he might yet succeed in proving his innocence kept him going. Like the legendary Sisyphus, he pushed the weighty burden of proving his innocence in an up-hill manner, hoping against hope. The daily god-like scrutiny of the judges served only to temper his failing morale. Yet, throughout his great tribulations during the ongoing ordeal, he was gradually able to emerge victorious from the hollow man he had been. He understood for the first time, perhaps, that he had lived the life of a man without feelings of compassion and lacking the ability to love another.

He took another deep breath and then pushed downward with all his might. Nothing happened. He was almost able to partially grasp a woman's great and selfless struggle during pregnancy and labor. Another attempt at discharging, and then another, had all proven futile. While he concentrated on his temporarily vital concern, he hadn't noticed the black-clad, ominous, figure of the prison Chaplain standing before him.

"Are you prepared for your communion now, my son?" The visitor said with the beneficent smile of the kind to which only the saints are privy. Both of priest's vein-less hands held on to an open prayer book. To the uninitiated observer, this lent the cleric a grotesquely superficial aspect in the midst of a less than pious environment. An embroidered shawl that reached both his knees was slung round his slender shoulders, and the Eucharist in a small basket rested on the floor in front of the laboring inmate, whose reddened countenance did nothing to mark a desired readiness for spiritual endeavor. Nevertheless, the cleric's eager eyes were pealed on the lips of the prospective confessor as if in expectation of a minor miracle.

"This is neither the right time nor the place to conduct such solemn function, father. Don't you think?" Misha spoke with the greatest of efforts, fatigued as he was due to his struggle with his obstinate intestines. Suddenly, and with astonishing swiftness, an internal dam was removed, and his rectal opening almost burst with violent successive eruptions, as the viscous substance was released through the colon onto the commode. He smiled sheepishly at the priest's inscrutable face, speechless and embarrassed. Subsequent periodic, only loudly vulgar, rectal explosions disturbed the ensuing silence. This lasted only a few moments but what seemed an eternity to Misha. A faint and distant smile appeared in the priest's eyes.

"Shall we commence?" His voice echoed as if from a great expanse of time, and Misha knew nothing short of a natural disaster would dissuade the cleric from his assigned duties.

"Oh, okay," Misha said, "give me the host and be quick about it. I want to continue my crap in peace."

The priest opened the prayer book on a previously marked page with a bureaucrat's meticulous industry. His facial lines turned well nigh angelic, and a triumphant smile rested on his face all the way to the completion of the ritual. Misha listened to the admixture of Latin and English vernacular as it issued forth from the priest's lips during the strange incantation. On occasions, the cleric would stop for a brief moment to glance expectantly in Misha's direction. The inmate surmised that this was the time he should echo a soft "amen" in concert with the elegy, which was, to his great consternation, occasionally accompanied by his gaseous releases. The sheepish smile that appeared on Misha's face was more as a response to his relieved bowels than in gratitude for the priest's supplications in behalf of the absolution of his sins.

"My son, you ought to be more respectful of the Holy Sacraments," the priest commented.

"Why, I can't help it, father," Misha spoke laboriously, "the gasses just keep on coming.

"It isn't that I'm referring to, my son," the priest smiled mysteriously. "It isn't that at all."

"Yes, and what exactly is it I should be respectful of?" Misha asked in a manner of challenge.

"Well, how should I say..." the priest hesitated.

"Go on...go on padre!" Misha's impatience grew.

"Well, the other day, this little Chinese lady came to see you, and they turned her away." The priest looked at Misha concerned.

"Xin Xin? She came to see me? What an angel! Nobody had told me!" Misha exclaimed in agony. "Why didn't they tell me?!"

"Only family has visitation privileges, you know, and counsel," the priest said in his monotone delivery.

"That's not fair, not fair at all," Misha lamented.

"I'm doing my best to remedy the situation, my son, and my very best." The prison Chaplain grew suddenly pensive and distant...

...She was so beautiful in her agony. The prison Chaplain noticed her consternation. "Can I be of any help?" He asked.

Xin Xin wiped a tear from her cheek. "Only family and legal counsel may be admitted to visit my Misha," she regarded the priest with a guarded but not admittedly adverse attitude. "Just for that reason, I'd marry him."

"We can discuss it, my child," the priest broached cautiously. "I've been his confessor all along."

"Would he marry me?" She looked at the priest, her eyes pleading.

"That can be arranged, my child," the Chaplain said. "See me in my office tomorrow at nine in the morning."

The priest's solemn promise of aid disarmed her intuitive suspicion toward strangers. She arrived at the appointed hour the following morning. The priest's study smelled of incense, a sweet and nauseous aroma not unlike that of her experience with pot. She smiled, and she wasn't quite sure he saw her through the haze of daylight cracking in through the closed shutters.

"Come closer, daughter," the priest beckoned from behind the desk, and she stepped forward until she reached the chair near him. "Sit down, my child," he pointed to the chair, and she sat down. Her dress fit tightly, and sat right about round her thighs as she folded her legs. She wasn't sure the priest's eyes had focused on her, as he held his face in the palms of his hands, and his eyes were almost shut in pious meditation. He informed her that she was there for reasons of conversion, which would enable her to marry Misha.

"How soon will that be?" She asked.

"Well, that depends, my child." The priest said in a whispered tone.

"Depends...on what?" She persisted in her native curiosity.

"On your ability and attitude, my child." He said. He explained about the rigors of communion and serious study. She listened attentively, and only occasionally changed the position of her legs and adjusted her dress round her thighs. Her movements did not escape his vigilant eyes.

It was the third day of instruction and the prison Chaplain informed Xin Xin in a kindly voice: "You must kneel my child," he sat before her and she went down on her knees, her hands folded as ordinary people do in prayerful contemplation. Her blouse was only a thin veil of modesty, as it revealed the full contours of her heaving breasts.

"Is this quite necessary, father?" She asked, blushing.

"You ask why, and I shall explain, my child," the priest answered. "As you bare your heart and soul to the Holy Communion, so must you bare your body. It helps to purge you completely of your sins. When you are cleansed, you become one with the Holy Spirit." His mind wandered to his earlier students of the same nature. A Priest's life is a lonely existence. The vows of celibacy are hard to follow for all those who are wed to the Church, which remains impervious to the desires of the flesh. The restraints were extreme in the case of the Prison Chaplain. He remedied them as well he could, and considered his occasional trysts into the realm of the real world under the guise of piety as ample recompense the Church tacitly approved.

Xin Xin complied. She now stood before the priest in her naked exotic beauty and without knowing what to expect next. Suddenly, the priest knelt before her, his arms round her buttocks, his face buried in her pubic region. He inhaled deeply, intoxicated, as it seemed, by the aroma. His action caught her completely off guard. His grip was too strong for her feeble attempts at disengagement. He moaned as he covered her body with passionate kisses. His fingers deftly manipulated her vagina and melted the weak albeit irresolute resistance she'd intended to offer.

Quickly, they lay on the sofa, and he entered her as he had done in the past with his other "confessional" conquests. She was astonished at his ability to manipulate his member to his advantage, and the act was not without some pleasure to her as well. They both screamed with passion simultaneously, and he instantly withdrew to make sure there was no danger of impregnation. She lay still, and the priest sat in his chair behind the desk. "You have been with other men?" He asked rhetorically.

"You didn't think you were the first, padre?" She giggled. He wasn't amused. He looked sternly at his confessor. "You will have to refrain from having sex for the period of your conversion." He counseled. She smiled.

"Only with you, padre?" She said coquettishly.

"Yes, only with me." He answered. "You may dress now, my child."

She dressed silently and left the chapel office. From that day on, she returned there repeatedly to "study" and ultimately receive the holy sacraments. The chaplain informed Xin Xin that she was worthy of her newfound faith…

…Misha's mind labored with great effort to keep apace with the intestines. Only yesterday, Dr. Ferrucci informed the prisoner for the first time since his incarceration about the circumstances of Susanna's reappearance…

"Police divers had located her body in the waters of a small pond near Lake Michigan." His social worker had informed him. "A suitcase full of your research papers, heavy reference books, and her personal letters and sundry clothing items, was tied to her feet. Though her dress was in tatters, it must have been one of her finest, pure silk. It looked as if she was on her way to meeting someone important and wanted to look her best."

Misha let out a loud shriek, and Ferrucci was not sure whether it was astonishment or joy. Neither was Misha, for that matter. He was unable to sort things out, due to his mixed feelings. Was he now closer to convincing the tribunal of his innocence?

"If anything, this is evidence I didn't kill her!" He exclaimed. "Are the letters legible? May I have a look?" He asked, and his anxiety was evident.

"How do you figure that?" Ferrucci asked. "The autopsy revealed she was four months into pregnancy. Could it have been yours?" Ferrucci asked, but Misha momentarily ignored her question obsessed with the one thought that spoke in his favor. "And, yes, the letters were tightly wrapped in plastic and recovered completely dry. I'll see what I can do to have them released to your scrutiny."

"Thank you, counselor." He said. "The authorities ought to know that no scholar by his right mind would sacrifice his research material in such a manner. Not even to…"

In his enthusiasm, Misha wanted to continue, but Ferrucci decided to play the devil's advocate. "They might think you did that to throw off suspicion, dear Misha, when you had discovered the baby was on its way." She said with a shrewd smile. "Did you want another baby?"

"I…I…" he stammered, not knowing what to say next…He was ready now. The priest waited patiently, while Misha got up from the commode and pulled up his trousers. "Sorry, padre," he apologized. "Is there anything further?"

"Yes, my son," the priest answered. "Your young lady, Xin Xin, is ready for you to wed."

"She may be, padre, but I'm not." Misha said defiantly.

"She has gone through communion for you, Misha." The priest said. "Just so she could see you before…"

"…Before you recommend me to my Maker?" Misha was angry and the priest stood up ready to leave. "Besides, I should have been consulted!" Misha shouted at the departing Chaplain.

"There was no time for that, my son," the priest said in parting, "what's done is done now. Accept it and be grateful…"

…Misha welcomed Susanna warmly on her arrival at O'Hare, however with apparent though unintended reserve. God knows, he had planned it to be far more cordial. Now, facing his hapless concubine, feelings of apprehension surged inside him he hadn't anticipated. It turned the welcoming act, an anticipated joyful reunion fit to be celebrated with uninhibited spontaneity, into a fidgety situation of a half smile on his tense lips and awkward, forced politeness.

A peculiar thought occurred to Misha, while his mind labored to overcome the frustration in the awareness of hypocrisy: had they been dogs, they'd surely circle one another in ever decreasing spirals, until their snouts touched, sniffing, each emitting a familiar growl, fierce at first, gradually softer, more like sounds of courtship than aggression. He glanced at the small boy attached to Susanna's side. A pleasant astonishment stirred Misha's soul, for he was sure to have glimpsed a reflection of his own boyhood's self. It expressed puzzlement and wonder at those strange acts, totally out of a child's reach, in which grownups seem to indulge habitually. They were acts that, to his thinking, bordered on the bizarre, puzzling, and incomprehensible. The boy stood almost motionless at his mother's side, as if waiting to be instructed, patient beyond his age.

"My dear Susanna!" Misha's trembling arms enfolded her with tenderness.

"Misha...Misha..." She whispered faintly in his ear, returning his embrace. The boy hid behind his mother's skirt, as if to protect his eyes from this unexpected demonstration of tenderness.

"And...this young man...must be..." Misha turned toward Rudi who was still hiding behind his mother.

"...*Your* son, Rudi..." Susanna hastened to complete Misha's sentence, with an emphasis on the pronoun your.

"Ah, so he is." Misha bent over toward the little one who showed reluctance to be drawn into the ritual of greetings. "Come, give us a big hug." Misha said in German, their native tongue. The boy hesitated.

"Come, *Schatzi*," Susanna addressed the child, "give daddy a big hug." Still hesitant, Rudi came forward and put his arms around the kneeling Misha's neck, though lacking in genuine enthusiasm.

"My name is Rudi," he said slowly, in well-tutored English, "and I am happy to meet you, papá." He smiled. It was a smile of accomplishment, for they had rehearsed these few pleasantries for some time with his mother. He knew she was proud of him now, and this brought a feeling of warmth inside him such as he felt only on occasions when he knew he had done the right thing. But before Misha was able to respond to the boy's labored elocution, Patrick O'Malley came briskly toward them, his hand extended toward Misha.

"Well, hello there, Misha, what a nice surprise!" He exclaimed, shaking the latter's hand vigorously, though his eyes were focused on Susanna.

"How nice to see you, Patrick," Misha responded. "You must be returning from your conference in Augsburg, are you?"

"Indeed, I am." Patrick smiled, while he threw another furtive glance in Susanna's direction. Her cheeks reddened with embarrassment, though she feigned intensified preoccupation with her son.

"Hope it was a resounding success," Misha said, trying to return to his main interest, but Patrick was not to be dismissed easily.

"This must be Ms. Susanna Flossberg," he nodded in Susanna's direction. Her eyes to the floor, she blushed from ear to ear, for she was caught off guard by Patrick's unexpected boldness.

"You've met?" Misha's icy voice betrayed a challenge that echoed an admixture of paranoia.

"In a way, we have." Patrick's honesty was disarming, though Susanna's eyes pleaded for mercy, unsure of Misha's reaction.

"Uh? You didn't tell me." Now Misha addressed Susanna. His lips quivered without letting out another sound. She was at a loss for words. What to tell? What would be pleasing to Misha? When, suddenly, Patrick came to her aid. A smile on his handsome face, he seemed to enchant through his cheerfulness. He spoke with the facility of a professional, as though he needed no rehearsal saying what was on his mind. Locking in on Misha's suspicious eyes, he uttered his words slowly, without hesitation:

"Really, my good man," he addressed Misha, "what's there to tell? It was just an insignificant me, sitting across the aisle of an enchanting young lady, and making idle conversation to kill the monotony of a long and dreary journey."

"No need to go into details, my dear Patrick," Misha interrupted, feigning nonchalance, "in a way, I'm glad you've met. It saves us the formality of a future introduction." He paused. "Yes, this is Susanna and her son Rudi, whom you've most likely met on the plane as well." They all laughed, Patrick shook Susanna's hand and Rudi's, picked up his luggage and was on his way. He held Susanna's hand in his far longer than the customary handshake, and she had the feeling, when their eyes met, that he was a man that could be put to the test when the time came. Why she felt this way, she could not tell, she only knew the thought was there for her to ponder.

Even as Patrick disappeared around the ticket counter, Susanna's mind was rushing so fast she feared Misha would somehow be able to detect the dynamics of emotional turbulence. She felt as if she'd wanted to sit right there and cry. So many mixed, conflicting, feelings pounded through her racing heart. This was a dream come true. She knew she was here in the U.S. with Misha, but she thought of the family she had left behind. She knew how much she owed them for their support and encouragement, and she remembered her friends and their prayers. When would she see them again? If ever?

As they walked toward the exit and into the parking lot, it suddenly struck her how things and events she had heard about would talk to her on this strange soil. She was ready for whatever comes her way. There was always a preliminary adjustment to the new scale of size and abundance. Along with the snacks and beverages the Lufthansa stewardesses served, they should have handed out an Alice 'Drink-Me' potion that would expand one's internal environment adapter. That would surely help cope with the prodigal space allotted to each American in his home. It might have explained the average American's journeys through the immense landscape. They were formidable, to say the least; as were the number of Kleenex boxes, toilets, and TV programs. These came in color at any hour through the night, given the many sets to watch them on. It would also explain what the quantities of wire hangers were all about, the kitchen gadgets, an array of body sprays, and wash-and-wear shirts in the countless closets and drawers. The quantities of food heaped on each plate in a restaurant boggled the imagination. The dizzying choices available in the supermarkets and convenience stores that were open 24 hours seven days a week, spelled revolutions, utopias, hopes and an emerging envy for the have-nots. And then there were those many kinds of cheeses: cottage cheese alone, large curd, small curd, creamed, fat free, salt free, pineapple added, cranberry added, blueberries added…She was forewarned that no place in the world can match American abundance. As little Rudi would say, when she enumerated all of America's advantages: "It must be really quite gross."

She had brought music with her, mostly pop of a few years back, which she was going to listen to in her free time. Would it be considered "bad" music here? Why worry about things before they occur? She reminded herself: "Just look at what you've got to do, don't worry about anything else. And the rest of the times, if things get overwhelming, or seem so, try not to get hung up on a lot of details and dilemmas. Don't sweat the small stuff."

She knew. It was easier said than done. Meanwhile, she needed to conserve energy for the bigger, more important things. She glanced at Rudi. She knew he was bursting with curiosity, wanting to ask his many questions. But he sat in the back seat of the car, observing the countryside as they traveled southward.

On his part, Patrick was unable to shake Susanna's image from his memory. To the contrary, he was impressed by some very intense thoughts about her. Even as he boarded the Greyhound bus for Urbana, his thoughts were with the shapely red head he'd met on the plane. He remembered the color of her eyes. They seemed like the wings of a bird and they barely concealed her dreams. He gave in to the impulse, as he did when he had watched over Xin Xin's sleep. Yes, Patrick felt proud to have taken her from Misha. The little vixen owned an uncanny talent for alienating her occasional lovers.

Now, surrendering to his daydreams, Patrick remembered staring at Xin Xin's narrow eyelids and trying to penetrate her inner secrets by counting the rapid movements of her eyes beneath them. He loved the danger, when he thought of the girl waking and seeing him there. She might scream at the lurid look in his eyes, the revelation of his lecherous desires. But he took the chance, his breath almost touching her delicate features, his fingers probing the contours of her subtle skin.

Inexorably drawn to the temptations of her body's curvatures, Patrick would probe, until he'd arrive at the delicate texture of her pubic region. The hairs so fine, they resembled the soft strands of silk, of Asiatic origin, to be sure. Was it instinct? Had he pressed too hard? On that, Xin Xin would sigh and wake and they would make passionate love, indulging senses he'd never known existed, even in his imaginary musings.

And when they lay side by side, exhausted, breathing heavily, he sweating from every pore on his body, she nearly as cool as a "cucumber"—another Asiatic characteristic—he would pop that inevitable question: "Was he as good as I?" He meant Misha, and she always knew what to say to make him feel an accomplished lover, a man. She would press her body to his and say: "You're different. He's different." And he puzzled over her response, never knowing whether the word "different" meant better or worse, higher or lower in intensity, more or less satisfying. At such times, when she was so inscrutably stoic, he wished he could have walked away or become like her. But he hated to abandon a good thing, which Xin Xin was indeed, a damned good thing. And he had taken her away from Misha. How he relished that thought.

Patrick opened his eyes. The bus seemed motionless, while the countryside was passing rapidly by. He closed his eyes again, and his thoughts traveled to Susanna. Was she thinking about him as well? He wandered. He had a feeling their paths would cross. When? From the venue of an archeologist's temperament, time was immaterial and irrelevant. He was nicknamed "patience" for good reason by those who knew him intimately. He would wait, and he was going to sniff her out no matter how long it took. Sniff like a dog sniffs his bitch, and measure the time when she's in heat. Misha's self-destructive nature would ultimately prove beneficial in Patrick's new quest. He was almost certain, judging from the latter's track record in these matters. Why should it be different now?

He leaned back and closed his eyes. He looked forward to winning Susanna for himself, and the mere thought of victory made him want to howl like a mad triumphant, coyote. "Wahoo... Wahoo...Wahoo..." In his mind's ear, he was able to hear the echo of the howling creature's melody. He listened carefully. He was almost certain he heard her responding howl. He heard the howl of a bitch in heat.

Their journey south on Route 57 to Champaign/Urbana seemed rather uneventful from the moment Misha placed the luggage in the car's trunk at the airport parking lot. Approximately one hundred miles of flat countryside stretched before them across the seemingly limitless horizon. Rural settlements disappeared into the vast landscape behind the fast moving vehicle before the curious traveler was able to decipher their strange names. Susanna sat silently in the passenger seat of the Ford convertible, while Rudi, curiosity in his eyes, occupied the small, and somewhat uncomfortable "rumble" seat, which had never been manufactured with the thought of passenger comfort in the first place. She turned to him often and smiled a mother's reassuring smile, but to no avail. The boy did not respond; neither affirmatively nor negatively. That was how her Rudi behaved when other children pouted.

Who is this man behind the wheel? Rudi's eyes met hers questioningly. Where has this stranger been all of my life? When I needed him most? He asked mutely. How can I call him 'papá' when I hardly know him as a person? I won't let him near me. I won't. I won't.

Susanna's eyes beseeched the little one: Let's not fret, my love. He did sent word for us to come. Forget the past. Look forward to our future together. We're in America, the Promised Land.

Rudi resisted. It was easy for her to talk all of this nonsense of the future and a good life. How does she know he'll not abandon us again like he did before? If he did it once, he can do it again. Wasn't that a proven rule in life? The best I can do not to hate him is to ignore him now like he ignored us in the past.

The son did not have to bare his thoughts audibly to his mother. His deep, intense, dark eyes spoke to her eloquently. She regarded her son distressed.

Talk to me, dearest Rudi, please say something, Susanna pleaded silently with her eyes. Rudi ignored his mother's pleas and kept his obstinate silence. "It will be just like it used to be." She whispered anxiously, in afterthought, under her breath. Rudi smiled sadly. "As if it could be, dear mama. As if it could be." He responded in a thin whisper. Misha was unaware of the exchange between mother and son, both silent and vocal. The former had escaped his attention, for it was unspoken. The latter had been drowned out by the roar of the engine, which he gunned impatiently and in an ungentle manner in his desire to cover the distance before nightfall.

Misha was aware of Alida's habit to retire early, and he so wanted her to meet the new arrivals before daybreak. After all, it was all her idea to begin with. Still, he sought her approval before the first night he'd spend with his concubine and his bastard son under the same roof. Soon, bored with the monotony of the flatland, Rudi was sound asleep. Misha observed the boy in the rear-view mirror. He marveled at the synthesizing power of creation, which takes so many strands of genes and weaves them into a miraculously coherent, engaging whole, in his own image, his own son-child, and a result of the Y chromosome. Misha was proud of his fragmented dabbling in the sciences.

Only a few months ago, Misha was ready to give up—"end-it-all," as he put it—resigned to cash in his chips. Abandoned by Alida, and Xin Xin, his latest clandestine lover, he showed little enthusiasm for living. Life has dealt him severe losses and, like the gambler he was, losing carried with it the penalty of disillusionment. After all, true to his nature, he suddenly considered himself suffering along with Jesus. He was unjustly taking on the burdens of life and the wicked universe. His erstwhile friends mocked him—ridiculed behind his back—he was abandoned by his students or as he referred to them, disciples, who once used to adore every word he had uttered. He was scorned by the envious scribes and peers who questioned his motives incessantly and, lo, the fickle mob of his academic community eagerly awaiting his crucifixion.

Driven by self-pity, Misha reacted by heightening the dramatic element of his own passion. It had never been his custom to proceed with caution. Striking back was most appropriate to his thinking. Most importantly, he wanted to hit back at those who had hurt him, betrayed their sworn loyalty to him. Now, his passion had combined the elements that were quite absent from all Gospel texts, which he had privately long considered a banal display of sentimental religiosity, overt superstition and, well nigh, obstinate stupidity.

How great, then, was his astonishment when—almost as Christ on the cross—by Alida's own design, he was resurrected. Passion would, once again, become his playing field, everything from the chase to the conquest and an ultimate abandonment of the innocent victim. He saw himself now as Herod, backed by a bevy of high-stepping drag queens, who enjoyed the prerogative of choice without restraint or trepidation. Penitence was for the arrogant; the meek would inherit the kingdom of heaven, he remembered, as it was written somewhere. No longer was he self-conscious, afraid to be struck by someone from the spectator crowd, like Jesus; chased by the horrid grumble and chirp of that hateful back-chatter that made his blood run cold. Rather, he would say to them, alike what Jesus had said to his companions on the cross: "Today you will be with me in paradise," which, to him, expressed a new exuberance for life and sonority of existence. For now, he decided to abandon his wanton past.

Another glance at the young boy's serene, almost angelic, features. Does his exterior countenance resemble the true mettle of a boy abandoned by his father in infancy? Was he the type of kid capable of saying: "Hey! Look at the bright side!" Or are there deeply concealed scars left by a pressured childhood? Would he have been better off had I stayed with him then and exposed the child prematurely to a domineering father, much like my own? Misha thought silently. Would I have been an ideal father to an ideal son? He mused on. Even now, with the intention to make good, the boy was forced to abandon his country of birth, family and friends that had all been there for him when Misha failed to nurture him through tough times. Would Rudi, also, like Misha before him, be forced from here on in to carry his pain deeply concealed by an outward steeliness and subdued anger? But all of that was too difficult to guess at best.

Misha's own mutilated childhood, fragmented though it was, appeared vividly before his mind's eye. After years of serving as his stepfather's punching bag—the boy occasionally shielded his mother for whom the blows had been intended and not vice versa—Misha fled home at age sixteen. His escape was not so much the fear of killing the villainous *Herr Doktor* Schweinfurt or avoiding his fists, as it was an earnest attempt at rescue of whatever vestiges of humanity he still possessed. "It was killing the kid in me," he would later tell his intimate friends of his childhood ordeal.

Susanna glanced at Misha from the corner of her eye. She no longer liked to be blocked out of his thoughts. It created in her the fear of being unloved; feelings of powerlessness and helplessness. She knew those feelings well, for they had been her constant companions for some time now. They had instilled in her incapacity to control all aspects of living and caused her agonizing pain and depression. They frequently led to her irrational behavior toward Rudi and promoted insecurity within her own self.

After all, she was entitled to a rational love. She was capable of giving of herself, of thinking carefully, logically. She wanted to be loved, as she loved, without restraint, unselfishly; focus on truly important aspects of life. It wasn't that she wanted love to dominate their every thought. All she desired was an enduring relationship; being together with the one she loved because of mutual need and fulfillment. It was time for Misha to think *we* for a change, instead of his *me* attitude, as he had done in the past. She wanted him to give, without having to demand; to please her as she would please him with total abandon. She longed for love that would endure unconditionally and unrestrained. She wanted their love to be rooted in truth from which it would derive its strength.

While these thoughts lingered, there followed an ineffable feeling of wellness as it permeated her entire being. She smiled. Misha glanced at her from above the steering wheel, puzzled. He returned her smile. Their smiles interlocked and enfolded them both in a strong embrace. They shared that moment of union and serenity without caring to know the "whys" of it all.

"Are you happy?" He asked in a whisper, as if afraid to startle.

"Yes, my dear Misha, very." She responded likewise in a whisper.

"It'll all be okay," he assured her, hoping he wasn't lying.

"I know it will," she said hesitantly, as if trying to reassure herself.

"What would you do at this moment, if you could do whatever comes to your mind?" He asked. She looked at his profile carefully. He was serious. She was again hesitant. "I would kiss you, Misha! Passionately!"

"Right at this moment? Dangerous, you know." He said, chuckling happily. He feigned fear playfully.

"I know. I want to live dangerously." She defied him. Challenged him. He put his arm round her shoulder, then lowered his open palm to her waist—but not before a searching squeeze of her full breasts—and pulled her toward him. She didn't resist. He positioned her head in front of him so as not to loose sight of the road, and they kissed. It was their first, passion-filled kiss since their reunion. Their tongues entwined playfully, he felt the promise of tomorrow. No, more like of that very night…

"Good news, Misha!" Ferrucci announced. "Here are Susanna's letters the Court permitted you to examine." She produced a modest bundle of letters neatly tied with a ribbon inside a plastic pouch. He could wait no longer. With the eagerness of a condemned man, he opened the first letter. It was undated…

*My dearest Misha,*

*Everything is absolute in my life. That's my way of thinking, my opinion of the whole* Weltanshauung, *world view…Now is too late for me to change. I don't want to go to bed with a new husband and he should know that I am damaged goods, no longer a virgin, and that's why I am giving myself to you. I know all you ever wanted was my body. That is very cruel.*

"It's human," *Misha couldn't help but muse, and if being human is cruel, I admit to being cruel." He continued reading.*

*You took advantage of me, a stupid small town girl. That was wrong. You were almost twice my age and you knew what was going to happen and you didn't tell me. That was wrong, too.*

"No one can foresee the future," *Misha reasoned.*

*You were experienced, and you could have enlightened me, but in your selfishness, you didn't. I want you to know that I hold this against you. You always speak out for your situation, but you can't live mine. When you talk to me, you don't have the feeling that you are steeling someone's happiness. But when I speak with you, I am guilt ridden about robbing someone…*

*You give the easy solutions where there aren't any. But I can't follow because I have a battle between the heart and the mind. I fight myself to the point when I can't stand any more. When you remind me at times that your family or your wife are after you, giving you pressure, my mind goes out completely. I have to do something or I'll collapse.*

*I was pretty stupid to let myself fall in love with a man that wasn't able to offer anything. You love your wife too much. That's all right. But they have the power over you, not over me. I don't have to accept your problem and make it mine. Your wife owns you and I have nothing of you.*

*Perhaps the best way would be if you stay with her. Then you won't have to lie to her. She has to have a good reason to permit you out of the house to come to see me.*

*What do you think about the fact that you make love to me and then you walk out on me, leave me? That's very cruel, and you do that because you're afraid of her. That hurts me. I try to smile, but it hurts. That's maybe why I'm afraid to make love to you. It makes me old. It terrifies me and destroys my youth. I give myself to you too easy. You take, but you don't appreciate.*

*You're not the one to give me help. Help is very important, very big. You can't even give me love and care. How could you give me help? It's only me now; me and your son Rudi. I'll have to try. If I can't do it now, no one will do it for me. I'm stupid, worse than stupid...getting deeper...deeper...don't know how to control my feelings.*

*No one can.*

*I won't see you again, dear Misha. I give you back to your family, your wife, so she won't have to be afraid there's another woman. I don't like to do that to anyone. I'm not that kind of woman. I won't allow myself to do such a thing anymore. I now release you. Hope you can be happy.*

*At least I won't have happiness, but I won't have guilt either. Being with you, I don't have happiness but I have guilt. You never understood me. Yes, I understood you well...no you can't...You haven't made love to anyone else's wife and you don't have the guilt to your parents, to people you're a good person; you're innocent in their eyes. You're not in my situation. All I got is worry. Worry that the mask will fall off my face that my parents will find out the truth. Your wife might find out the truth. My friends will find out the truth. It's all very bad…sigh…*

*You know what, Misha? I'm not sorry for anything I've done. I've done it with love, much love. And no one should be sorry for that. I know that your guilt shall destroy you some day. That's the biggest problem you had, no, still have. I knew it, and I couldn't stop it. As you can see, it drove you all the way to this, and even in this, you won't find happiness…*

*I have never known what happiness is…*

*It's not true. Mine was never real. It was something you just borrow from other people, from your wife, your family, my friends, always a liar. Never had anything of my own. Happiness is too short, so now I can't have happiness and I won't have the guilt and won't hate them anymore for standing in my way…*

*Tears flooded his face. His hands trembled and his fingers loosened their hold of the assorted letters; the ramblings of an utterly miserable mind. He was astonished at the simplicity of her utterances, but it all made good sense. Now fear entered his heart lest those of the prosecution who read these innocent declarations of love and loneliness come to see in them evidence of ill doings.*

…In his mind's eye, Misha saw Susanna in the dim light of their bedroom, the curtains drawn tightly so as to keep out the daylight. She stepped out of her clothes. Her back was red in the mirror, and she inched toward him. Her rather oversized breasts were firm, and he observed those succulent, pencil eraser-like, nipples that he yearned to enfold with his hungry lips. What he could not guess was Susanna's sudden flashbacks to her erstwhile neighbor who had died of chicken pox at thirty-five years of age. She didn't particularly care for the man, but he had been a divine lover all those years of Misha's absence, and he should not have died such a horrible death. She glanced back at the mirror. This rash will go away soon, she mused to her reflection, for it must be altogether something entirely different from that of her lover's affliction. She will no doubt recover quickly.

Susanna wanted to excuse herself—"need to go the restroom" excuse—because of her nudity. She was embarrassed as well as profoundly fearful, considering that awful patch of redness that appeared as if it were a plague on her back. And, oh, God! What if it's contagious? But she didn't think so, after all. With the idea of chicken pox dispelled from her mind, she figured the worst was eliminated from the realm of possibility. She even managed a faint smile.

Misha, too, had by now shed his clothes and lay on the bed in full sight of his approaching lover. She was reminded that one can distract oneself from pain, but one always comes back to it. Susanna felt as though her muscle tissue was melting underneath her skin. Staring at the ceiling, as she lay on the bed next to Misha, both of them in awkward expectation, she swore that she saw ancient philosophical models that have transformed themselves into complex mathematical equations on her visit to the bathroom. Misha, however, felt again as though death was approaching. And if it were, he would do best to hurry out of the room.

He raised himself up from the pillow: "I've got to do some errands. Be right back." He dressed quickly and hurried toward the door. She grimaced, but said nothing, and he was gone without fully knowing why.

Outside, shop windows glistened in the brightness of the neon signs, and he squinted to see through them. He had forgotten who or what he was looking for. Everything had an orange tint, as if the lights had set things ablaze. Even that old man who approached him the next instant and offered him beads without having uttered one word. Misha could have sworn the old man resembled Motele, his father's deep-set eyes stared at him out of that timeworn face distorted by an ugly grimace. The specter disappeared almost as quickly as it had appeared, and Misha knew Motele's victims had begun to have effect on his father's conscience, if he had one. He now held the beads close to his eyes. They were multicolored and transparent like those children would play with. What was the sense of wearing those silly beads? Love? As if wearing them around the neck would change things suddenly. Why would that despicable man care about love when he'd never before known its meaning?

Would he turn into a prince charming? Would he come galloping out of a forest on a white charger to seek out his fair damsel or wander through the countryside aimlessly?

Further along, around the corner, there was a coffee shop, and Misha peered inside. The old man was seated at one of the tables as if awaiting Misha's arrival. He was reading the paper, giggling to himself. "Come! Sit!" The man beckoned. Misha wished he could sit, but he had to run. He'd explain to the man later, if he lived to see him again. Turning to go, he caught a glimpse of the headline the old man held up for him to read: "Nazi criminal dead by his own hand at age 73!"

He was intrigued and approached the table, only to find the paper spread out on top of it and the old man gone once again. Motele Vino, a.k.a. Winograd, Polish Jew and Nazi collaborator, was found hanging from the toilet flushing chain… The story went on to relate Motele's duplicity even to his last moments: "Under the guise of Holocaust survivorship, the Nazi criminal claimed reparations not only from the German government but also a handsome pension from the Polish authorities…"

"Good riddance," Misha whispered under his breath, "the hangman's noose would have been a merciful demise for you. I hope you'll fry in h…" He stopped himself in mid-sentence. Why should he believe this newspaper nonsense? He wished the man to live. And if he lived to see him again—he must see him again—if only as an answer to the prayer he recites every day. Part of the prayer that he recites to himself even now, be it the one his mother taught him as a small boy, that gives reference to the hateful man they both despised. He was the one who asked God to keep everyone together. Misha has never outgrown its comfort. But in the midst of his silent mantra, he envisioned Motele's limp body dangling slowly from the toilet flushing chain, like the marionette he was in his lifetime. "Let his victims forgive him. It's not my task. Not now. Not ever."

The thought broke his rhythm and he lost his place in the prayer. That was of little concern to him now, for it was all but certain that he would someday be with Motele again. And his love did not depend on a string of absurd beads. That much was certain.

Light drizzle had started despite the continued strength of the morning sun's rays. In the distance Misha saw a faint rainbow forming. "It is a good omen." He whispered. But through the precipitation he imagined Susanna's lips as they formed the words: "You're mine...all mine!" A rugged individualist that he was, no one would own Misha. The mere thought of anyone claiming his individuality set him into a rage. "Don't you ever!" He screamed into the void, even though deep down he knew she wasn't going to hear his reprimand. With his mother's last words echoing in his mind, he turned to return where he had come from. Would the lethal case of an adult chicken pox still be there on his return or was it also imagined?

...There she stood in her nudity before him, but the rash had cleared up from her back. Misha was glad he had left to give it a chance to heal. He even felt a bit awkward, if not downright guilty, to have run out on Susanna when she really needed his support. That pattern had settled into granite rock. He grimaced lamely in the hope she wouldn't be able to read his thoughts. Once again, his mother's words echoed from the distance. He repeated them faithfully in silence: "You must not love anyone before they have first declared their love for you." It went several times through his mind, while he acknowledged the adoration in Susanna's eyes.

Then she spoke: "I love you, Misha."

He didn't reciprocate in kind. He would wait, to be sure. After all, there'll be ample opportunity to make amends for time lost. He will try to be the father Rudi has been denied all these years, though he knew there were no quick courses given on the intricate art of fatherhood. As for Susanna, he'd hoped to give her the affection she craved.

The following week, Misha purchased a compact used car for Susanna. She was overjoyed. Hugs and kisses followed. Behind the wheel of her car, she felt a surge of a hitherto foreign feeling of a kind of unusual energy; a sense of being emancipated. She would now be able to drop Rudi off at school in the mornings, pick him up at school day's end and take him to his piano lessons in the afternoon.

# 23.

UNABLE TO CONTINUE his testimony, Misha looked toward his social worker, Dr. Ferrucci, in a silent plea.

"Anything you wish to tell me in private?" She asked.

"May I?" He countered.

"Well, we'll have to ask the court's permission." Dr. Ferrucci informed him. Then, as if on second thought, she whispered: "What is it? Why can't you go on?" She looked at him inquisitively.

"It's sort of...private...if you know what I mean?" He said with his eyes lowered.

"This is a court of law, Misha. And you're not at liberty to decide what is and isn't private." She informed him again.

"But...you know..." He whispered. "The three of us together... Alida, Susanna and myself, and a very young boy in the same apartment..." Misha was hesitant again, not knowing whether to continue.

"The court will hear your testimony now, Misha." Dr. Ferrucci turned toward the Justices, who witnessed patiently the hushed exchange between the defendant and his medical counsel. The Presiding Judge nodded toward her. "The doctor may advise the defendant to continue." He said, without a smile. She nodded first in the judge's direction then at Misha.

*Misha began to wander within the padded cell of this madhouse— in spite of his being so completely harmless—why he felt like a fugitive with a price tag on his head. Nevertheless, when called on by the presiding judge, he attempted to testify in his own behalf with zest and dramatic energy. However, his situation was gradually aggravated because of his continued isolation. And no matter how he had intended to impress the judges, he was frustrated by his inability to articulate coherently at the arrival of his testimony. In addition, he was concerned about the complete absence of communication from his companion in the adjacent cell. What could have happened to the man? Will I be next? Please, God, let me speak slowly and think clearly, to make them understand…he prayed…*

…Several hours and countless billboards later, they arrived after nightfall in Champaign/Urbana. It was as Misha had expected, and Alida had retired for the night. He cautioned Susanna and the boy to move about quietly. "She's a light sleeper," he said with concern, "and the slightest disturbance will wake her." Susanna repeated his warning in German to the boy, and Rudi nodded understanding. Misha wondered why he hadn't addressed the boy in their native language himself, but he decided not to, tempting though it was.

To Misha's great surprise, Alida had attended to all their needs in making his bedroom ready to accommodate the three of them. A small cot in the corner of the room was waiting for the boy, and Misha's king-size bed was made up with fresh linen; an aromatic candle, its fire flickering happily in the dark room, stood in a glass container on the night table.

Misha glanced toward Susanna, while she busied herself with Rudi, but he wasn't able to see the expression in her face. What must she be thinking about this curious "arrangement?" he thought silently. Did she have a problem with her present "status?"

No sooner did Rudi's head touch the pillow, than he fell into a deep sleep, Susanna turned toward Misha quizzically. And his stomach grew sudden holes, for he understood the meaning of her silent inquiry. They lay quietly in a tight embrace, though still lacking in the necessary passion. He felt her soft skin, her body pulsating warmth as she pressed against him. His trembling member emitted spasmodic bursts of energy in response to her nimble fingers. But her efforts to cause an erection proved futile. He continued to caress her full breasts, and his lips hungrily devoured their ripe nipples. Emboldened, he placed his hand on the moist orifice, throbbing with desire. He savored the now familiar reaction to the delight of Susanna's violent heaves, murmurs and impassioned moans.

"*Was ist los, Schatzi?* What's the matter, love?" She said in both languages, as if to reassure herself that he understood. He was silent, unable to find the proper response. "Am I not the same as I was then?" She pressed.

"Oh, no, *Liebchen*, don't even think these thoughts, honey," he whispered into her ear. "I want you more than ever." He added. "It's the excitement. And…maybe…I'm trying too hard…and…" She interrupted him in mid-sentence.

"…Maybe we should get a good night's rest," she completed his thoughts. "There'll be lots of time to pick up where we left off…" She paused. "We'll do it when we're ready. Okay, *Schatzi?*" She added anxiously.

"Okay," he replied faintly and kissed her on the lips. Then he turned on his side and was asleep before he could hear her soft whisper of "I love you, Misha…"

It was late morning when they awakened. They entered the kitchen, and Alida was at the kitchen table, having breakfast. She heard them, but did not look up from her activity, nor did she show intention to greet the newcomers.

Misha approached her, leaned toward her from behind and kissed the back of her head. "Hello, dear." He started. "I want you to meet Susanna." Alida raised her head and scrutinized the newly arrived woman and her son.

"Ah? Susanna, my slave woman." She said, obviously alluding to her Biblical precedents of Sara and Rachel; both barren wives who selflessly supplied their husbands, Abraham and Jacob respectively, with concubines. Her voice sounded firm, almost resolute. "And who might that be?" A nod in the boy's direction.

"This is Rudi, Susanna's son." Misha hastened to inform her.

"And yours, I presume." Alida added without the slightest hint of rancor or implied cynicism in her voice.

"Yes," Misha murmured sheepishly, "and mine."

"Did you enjoy the journey? You must be terribly fatigued after the ordeal." Alida asked with genuine concern. Susanna did not respond instantly. It wasn't clear whether her hesitancy was language oriented or lack of familiarity with American customs. She observed Alida for a long moment, as if asking herself: "What kind of woman invites another to cohabit with her husband, while she keeps on living under the same roof?" At that moment, she was unable to make up her mind whether or not to hate or love this woman. That she would not love her was almost certain.

Problems and frustrations beset Misha all along the way. He stumbled over forgotten—though well-rehearsed—statements, stammered incoherent expressions, only to go helplessly mute in the end. Time and again, his mother's wisdom echoed in the far recesses of his memory; if only he had paid more careful attention when they were uttered, he made a mental reprimand. But, then, parental wisdom, even when accepted, does not provide instant motivation in the young.

He looked back, alas too late, at his years in the university classrooms and could not readily think with satisfaction of having made one genuine contribution to his many students. Had he added to their understanding of the real world? Not even.

What of his own opportunities? Had they been readily available, he might have taken a shot at one or another. But even there, he stumbled over inveterate professors whose posture was fixed in the light of past glory, and who did not willingly move aside to make room for livelier, more imaginative people with fresh approaches. Shielded by tenure, and buoyed by an obstinate sense of pride, they held on—though dead weight and lacking in creative energy—while those inchoate fledglings were fated to go intellectually hungry, and eventually starve; their spirit dead for lack of stimulus.

It was at such moments of introspection that Misha regretted rejecting his stepfather's repeated demands that he follow in his footsteps. "The medical profession will afford you excellent earnings and respect in the community." *Herr Doktor* admonished the recalcitrant youth.

Thoughts of taking his own life had now recurred in view of a hopeless situation. The medical profession would have provided autonomy. How much easier would it have been for him than for most of the others, for he could have found relief through a hypodermic needle. It was better than to suffer the indignities of academic life; after all, he belonged to the educated class not the common riff-raff that by dint of their background had always carried the stigma of subservience and passive acquiescence to inequities.

Day after day, surrounded by secretly rejoicing and laughing colleagues, he was made to go down on his knees and scrub away for hours at the hopeless salaciousness of civility to the roaring delight of the onlookers.

Susanna's and Rudi's arrival lent him renewed energy to pursue his goals. In a manner of speaking, he was now where he had been years ago when they first met as young students at the university. He displayed a youthful bounce in his step, and his eyes did not wander when a pretty coed was passing by. After all, he was contented with his sex life at home, no need to crave for more of the same elsewhere.

He stopped playing his customary game. He decided to make an honest effort in trying to turn inwardly, to exorcise the blackness which had previously enveloped him. Far ahead, he was now able to make out a smattering of light. He tried to get his mind off the thoughts imbedded in his past; tried to wish their weight away. Yet in spite of all that, in his heart there was a presentiment of a kind, and he couldn't put the mark on it. Alida, yes she was all too easy about the circumstances prevailing in the household. He would have never presumed her sudden change of character. Was it the drugs she was taking? Would they make this much of a difference? He couldn't tell. His cynical, suspicious, mind was playing tricks on him again. He must put a stop to that kind of mental attitude, though it would be against his character. Still, come what may, Misha remained keenly aware of his good fortune and thankful for it.

He'd always wanted to learn how to fly, for he felt it was the best and easiest way to escape mundane reality. It was a favorite escape route for all gravity-ridden creatures. He knew. He also knew that he would be comfortable with the experience. He would not grip the armrest on take-off and descent, and he would not avoid looking down at the dizzying view of the miniature world beneath him to see the crawling insect-like human creatures.

When all his problems would pile up weighing heavily upon his shoulders like rocks, he would cast them off in flight. He could use that subterfuge now. His greatest concern by far was how to accommodate Susanna and Rudi in their strange new environment. She would take driving lessons not only to refresh her mechanical skills but also to study the American guidelines for the upcoming driver's license test. Only then would he feel secure about the purchase he had made of the pre-owned vehicle for her. How else was she to commute to work? Yes, work. Would they be able to find a job with her qualifications? It isn't going to be an easy task, what with her lack of everyday English.

"Americans are pretty lenient when it comes to their language," she'd say with a mischievous chuckle, "they hardly speak faultless English themselves, you know."

"Ah, but it's different when it comes to the work place." He warned.

"I'll learn on the job." She assured him.

"There is an interview before the job." He informed her.

"That's all right," she assured Misha coquettishly, "I'll cross my legs…"

He was astonished at her bold suggestion. She did have a pair of slim, shapely, legs to compliment the beautiful torso, but to use them as an asset in the job market! Well! She will learn soon about its hazards. Sure enough! Physical attributes cannot replace necessary experience. Or can they?

Susanna's job search came as a total surprise for both of them. The university Office of Human Resources ran the following announcement in the *Illini Weekly*: Position Open—effective immediately, Departmental Secretary—Archeology—beginning salary commensurate with qualifications and length of typing skill and shorthand experience—job description—filing, assisting faculty and chairperson in correspondence, etc.

Susanna spread the page before him. "Take a look, Misha!" She pointed at the ad "You think I could qualify?"

"It's up to a selection committee, I suppose," Misha said without much enthusiasm. "I'm sure they'll have a wide range of candidates."

"Didn't you say Patrick O'Malley teaches archeology?"

"What's that got to do with the job?" Misha's voice sounded alarm. He suddenly realized his old nemesis Patrick would indirectly become one of Susanna's bosses. "You'll have as good a chance as any, Susanna. Go for it." He was glad he didn't betray his feelings of apprehension. After all, the department might still reject her. He hoped. Meanwhile, he had broken enough walls with his head. Why try another?

Contrary to his personal expectations, Susanna was hired. She returned from the interview the following day triumphant. "I got it! I got it!" She yelled, to Misha's astonishment and utter, though reluctant, disillusionment.

"How do you know, you got the job?" Misha inquired, still hoping for the contrary. "Are you absolutely sure?"

"Sure, I'm sure." She smiled. "Patrick told me so himself!"

"Uh, Patrick? Not again?" Susanna looked at Misha, anxiety in her eyes.

"Yes…he happened to be one of the interviewers." She said. "One of three." She added quickly to allay Misha's apparent concern. "He was very courteous." As soon as those words resounded, Susanna knew she should have withheld the last remark.

"I see…so he was…yes…I would think the least he could have done was be cordial." Misha's eyes turned from her, and Susanna was unable to read the emotions running through his mind.

"I believe he helped me more in deference to your friendship than for my benefit." She breathed heavily. "I don't think he had ulterior motives."

"Men just don't do things for women without ulterior motives." He replied with the tone of an obstinate child. Susanna did not expect Misha's disconcerting reaction toward her first triumph in the New World. Didn't he know he was the man she adored unconditionally? Knowing Misha as well as she did, she didn't expect him to be ecstatic about her new job, but neither did she expect his overreaction to the contrary.

"I thought…you wanted me to get a job. Didn't you?" She barely whispered. He could feel the hurt in the tone of her voice.

"Of course, I did." He replied, again avoiding her inquisitive eyes. "I would have told you otherwise."

"Is anything wrong?" She insisted.

"No, nothing." He assured her, although he hated himself for not being honest in revealing his gnawing presentiments about Patrick. Should he warn her, tell her about Patrick's womanizing and tell her about Xin Xin? Would this knowledge increase her fascination with Patrick's desirability? Would his own involvement with the latter come into the open by sheer coincidence? He thought for a moment and decided he had better wait for a more suitable occasion.

The following week, Misha purchased a compact used car for Susanna. She was overjoyed. Hugs and kisses. Behind the wheel, she sensed a surge of an unusual degree of zest and dramatic energy, a feeling of emancipation. She would now go places with the boy, unrestricted by Misha's busy schedule. He, too, tried to forget his petty concerns about Patrick's alleged designs regarding Susanna. He was now more worried about explaining to Alida why he had not offered as yet a means of transportation during the years of their marriage. These thoughts brought on a huge increase in Misha's feelings of guilt. Inasmuch as he felt a genuine satisfaction in having made a positive contribution to Susanna's progress, he was equally uneasy about his neglect of Alida's in the past.

Was he being punished for his father's sins? He mused, as his sense of festering guilt spilled over into his present life. But he was quick to reject these thoughts of self-deprecation. A just and loving God will not let a son suffer for his father's sins. This is how it is supposed to be, he was taught since his early youth.

Only things don't always turn out the way they're supposed to. Misha looked worn. It was obvious; worry had hit its mark. His eyes were blood-shot most of the time from lack of sleep, and there were dark, puffy circles beneath them. His once well-groomed hair was in neglect. The erstwhile meticulously dressed professor wore a pair of rumpled trousers, and the shirttails hung down below his buttocks. His manner had also suffered from the events of the past weeks. He was irritable, and his friends and acquaintances seemed to have sealed his fate. At least, that's what he truly believed had happened. Thus he began to fear the people who had known him by his given name. Anonymity seemed desirable now. For the first time in his memory, he would seek advice, but there was no one willing to offer it.

Quite the contrary, Susanna appeared to enjoy her newly acquired job and the environment it had offered. On numerous occasions, Patrick was there to brief her about the duties that came with her job description. In Misha's absence, he had become her occasional companion and mentor.

"How was your lunch?" Misha would ask on her return home. "Nice, very nice." Susanna was non-committal.

"That's all? Nice?" He pressed.

"Yes, very nice." She added, and he was visibly perplexed. He couldn't believe it was happening to him. Jealousy? Misha? No. It couldn't be. There has never been a jealous bone in his body, and this was not the time to acquire one. He was the one of whom others were jealous; not the reverse. And Patrick should not be considered serious competition. On occasions, Misha would allow him to enjoy a morsel, like in Xin Xin's case, of which he, himself, had grown tired. Yes, that's how it was. And he was always aware of his commanding post.

He would not relinquish Susanna. She was still in his "stable." He hadn't grown tired of her and given anyone reason to believe that she was public domain, open to their propositions and designs.

"If you feel uncomfortable with it," she hesitated, "I'll let Patrick know. But it would be a pity, because he's been a great help to me."

"No, not at all," Misha hastened to assure her. "I don't mind him taking you to lunch." He turned his face away, as was his customary manner when he had wished to hide his emotional state. It was a daily occurrence during those horrendous paddling meted out by his stepfather, the good Dr. Schweinfurt. He refused to break down, grant victory to the foe, to reveal his hidden weakness. So it was to be now. Misha's eyes met hers. He regarded Susanna with great intensity. Taking more than his usual time, he spoke: "As long as there are no complications." He paused. "I will not accept complications."

"Complications?" She asked surprised.

"You know what I mean." He reflected. "Like your former boss; the fat bastard in Germany who was eager to sniff your underpants every time he laid his eyes on you." Misha spoke rapid fire, as if he'd wanted to get the words out before they would suffocate him.

"I don't know what you're talking about, Misha." Her patience was being severely tested. "After all, he didn't get anywhere." She studied his face. "Besides, that was Germany, and this is America. I'm a free person here. Free to quit if things get out of hand."

"That's precisely what I'm trying to prevent." He said. "Things getting out of hand." He paused. "We've just merely gotten a green card for you, haven't we?" There was a veiled threat behind his last statement, and she felt it deep in her gut.

That evening, before turning in, Susanna took her diary into the bathroom, as she had done on many occasions, and wrote:

*Dear Diary,*

*I couldn't believe my own ears. Misha was jealous of my relationship with Patrick. I don't know what has gotten into him to feel suddenly threatened. He had always seemed so self-assured and adequate. My friendship with Patrick has absolutely no bearing upon our relationship. I want to write a letter to Misha. I would most likely just break down and cry if I wanted to express it in words to him. So, it would be better to write.*

*My darling Misha, I would say, I love you more than you seem to realize. I guess, since I can't fall asleep, I shouldn't waste the time, and write what I feel, so that I can clarify it to you and to myself as well. Your obvious objection to my friendship with your colleague Patrick took me entirely by surprise. Why should you object when such relationship is motivated purely by kindness?*

*Each time we touch on this topic, you seem so harsh in your reference to him. I don't want to be the one to defend Patrick. This would only add to your feelings of suspicion. Surely, you don't think he's after me? I know, you have explained the basis of man-woman relationships in the U.S. being based entirely on sex. Could there be no exception? I feel there is in Patrick's case, for his interest is purely platonic.*

*I cannot find peace within me when I feel that this issue remains unresolved, just like our talk this evening. You seemed so cold. How*

*can you change your attitude toward me so abruptly? It's scary when
I think you could cut me out of your heart on a simple turn of your
mood. On previous occasions, when we had such talks, you turned
away from me in bed, and I lay next to you all night sleepless, tears
wetting my pillow.*

*At one point, you mentioned that you seem to "encourage" me to seek
Patrick's company with your behavior. But every time I try to convince
you to the contrary, your suspicious nature prevents you from believing
in me. If this were so, then I'd rather find out about your attitude right
now, before it's too late. You can't seem to understand that it hurts me
very much when I hear you speak such ugly things about a friend. And
I hate to take Patrick's side, for fear you will misunderstand my intentions again. I want you to know that my relationship with him is as
impersonal as it is with my other co-workers.*

*But you can't seem to accept that. So it seems you're holding on to
your anger against an imaginary rival. If this is true, then it seems
very simple to me, to admit your feelings openly and follow your heart.
This is my sincere opinion. If you wish to put this whole thing to rest
once and for all, do so, and I am willing to listen to what you have
to say.*

*In order for our relationship to succeed, we ought to be truthful
with one another and gain each other's trust. We can only achieve this,
if we act in good faith and on equal terms. Equal is the key word here.
Speak to me, with me. Love me as I have always loved you. We are
supposed to be one happy family. Aren't we?*

Susanna finished her entry. She read and reread it. She
changed nothing.

I think, my dear diary, some day, I'll mail this letter to him.
Some day. She closed the diary and tucked it into the hiding
place above the towel rack.

Until next time, she thought on her way to the bedroom. She
could hear Misha's loud snoring when she entered the bedroom.
His back was turned to her. She would not wake him, as she care-

fully slipped under the covers. Open-eyed, she lay for a long time, deep in thought and filled with anxiety and fear.

Gradually, Misha's pride in his profession eroded. It grew into feelings of guilt and inadequacy when he was informed of his being denied tenure by the Promotion Committee. Promotion and tenure were expected routinely in the academic ranks as recognition for scholarly output of some significance. He had much to his credit, more than the average, and the committee's denial of his promotion was a putdown. The note only stated: "Due to circumstances beyond our control, we will be unable to consider your application for promotion at this time..." He did not read on. After all, his once fierce belief in a sincere pride and satisfaction by making a genuine contribution to society through teaching had eroded even before the present rejection.

It occurred the moment he had realized that the American academe sheltered tenured personnel lacking creative productivity. Sadly, it impeded every ambition of academic dynamics and encouraged an arrogance of seniority. It even caused inertia among students, who regarded education merely as job preparation and showed little or no interest in exploring ideas. Once, all this was part of the intellectual challenge. Though at the inception of his endeavor as an academic, he did not conceptualize his visions immediately, or even in their complete shape, he had strongly believed that persistence, energy and tact, would enable him to begin something important and see it grow. But that was not to be.

Now, his erstwhile optimism has all but vanished. With the growing illusions about Susanna's infidelity, feelings of impotence rampant, his once self-assured personality was damaged. An insurmountable obstacle was anchored in his inability to love someone unconditionally. Most of the time, he felt lonely in his solitude; a kind of loneliness that carried with it a deep sense of betrayal and the urge to compete. The more deeply he was to feel his solitude, the less he was able to rely on his own feelings more profoundly, and to recognize his own singular humanity. He was distancing himself from the only woman who really cared about his wellness. In doing this, he began to doubt his direction as he aimlessly floated forward.

Susanna despaired. Misha's mute rejection of her efforts to reach him had led her to invoke God's interference: "Dear Jesus in heaven, "she prayed; "only you know what there is to be done. Please guide me in this hour of need." And when her calls went unanswered, she turned to the only acquaintance that held the promise of providing guidance and some comfort.

Patrick regarded Susanna quietly. Unlike the decorum dictated during his counseling sessions with his students, he chose to sit on the sofa next to the dismayed woman. She wept quietly, and he offered a box of tissues. "Come, Susanna, wipe those tears," he hesitated, not knowing whether to attack Misha's behavior directly or choose the "patient" route. He chose the latter, wisely.

"After all, there must be an explanation to Misha's peculiar behavior." He put emphasis on the word "peculiar," while he cast glances at her long legs and, upward, to the shapely thighs and well-formed breasts that he had admired secretly ever since he had laid eyes on her during their flight crossing the Atlantic. She wiped her tears away and blew her nose loudly.

"I've never seen Misha this depressed," she said softly. She paused. "And for this long." She added as if wanting to inform further.

"It will pass," he patted her knee gently, cautiously. "He's just going through difficult times." Patrick looked away, afraid he'd betray his glee. "What with being rejected in his quest for tenure..."

"...But that isn't the reason." She interrupted. "He's been acting weird even before the tenure issue came up." She assured him.

"Uh? Is that so?" Patrick acted surprised, though no one could claim better knowledge of Misha's self-destructiveness than he.

"I'm sure he's still the good old Misha." He praised his colleague. Always speak well of the one you want to dislodge. Patrick followed an age-old dictum he had borrowed from Brutus' treachery against his old friend Caesar. Nothing works better than flattery before the kill or after. He recalled his conquest of Xin Xin. "And he'll come around in good time." He added as if after reflection.

"You…really…think so…?" Susanna looked at Patrick through tearful eyes.

"I'm sure." Patrick assured her.

"I hope you're right." She repeated as if in a daze, readying to go.

"I know, I am." His hand on her thigh, he gently detained her. "Stay, please," he advised. "I don't want you leaving this office with tear-shot eyes." She remained seated. Emboldened by her apparent dependency, Patrick's arm reached over Susanna's shoulder. She didn't react. He withdrew his arm; his predatory instinct had warned he was advancing too rapidly.

"I want you to know, Patrick; I appreciate your listening to me. I know you have little time for this kind of thing."

"Don't you worry about time, Susanna," Patrick assured her, "remember my promise at the airport?" He paused for greater effect. "I'll be here for you. No matter what." He chuckled inwardly. Would she swallow the line? "Remember the old saying? What are…"

"friends for?" She completed the banal aphorism with a smile of relief. Patrick smiled, too. This was different than advising students in their selection of electives. It was not a matter concerning philosophy, psychology, or aesthetics, as second choices for some errant student. This was more like dealing in alienation and inability to communicate. He burst out with a hearty laugh, and Susanna had a puzzled look on her face. She was about to question Patrick, but she didn't feel confident to express herself fully. She just looked at his smiling face and felt restricted as if she were straining to shout in a padded cell. But looking at him didn't get feedback. She was thinking what to do next, and she stood up from the sofa, ready to leave. He didn't try to restrain her.

"Leaving so soon?" He asked.

"I've overstayed my welcome," she said, her eyes lowered. "Besides, they must need me at my desk."

"Come see me whenever you need to talk." He encouraged.

"Thanks, Patrick, you're a dear." She stood stiffly in his sudden embrace.

"Think nothing of it." He answered, letting go. This whole business of treachery is complicated. Patrick thought. You rattle your brains and offend your ethical being. If there ever is one in the first place. His conscience added for him. Anyway, boldness and insensitivity are a great help. He mused silently. What happened to the once decent and straightforward approach?

"I appreciate what you do for me," Susanna said in leaving.

"Any time, my dear." Patrick responded with a smile. "Any time at all." He closed the door behind her and let out a triumphant "yes!" Doubling his right fist, he threw his arm into the air and his feet left the floor.

# 24.

THEY ALL KNEW it was bound to happen one of those days...
or nights. They only wondered why. For some mysterious reason,
the inevitable hadn't happened sooner. The prevailing elements
set the appropriate atmosphere. A mighty storm raged outside,
and rain fell in streams. Nature provided the orchestration, so
it was quite normal to assume that humans would dance to her
rhythm. It was around 3:20 a.m. when Alida walked in on them.
And to think it was one of their rare nocturnal encounters Misha
and Susanna were in the process of testing.

Alida's eyes were half closed. She hummed softly one of those
Cuban tunes they had listened to on their vacations while on
her native island. She stumbled over the wardrobe chair. It fell
to the floor with a sudden noise that startled all of them. Alida
opened her eyes wide as Misha and Susanna attempted to hide
their nudity under the covers; too late.

During that brief moment of surprise and indecision, Alida
was able to witness the macabre dance of the two bodies entwined,
engaged in a frenzied continuity of fluid motion. Susanna's long
legs seemingly rested on Misha's shoulders, allowing her torso to
be centered on his belly, beneath which, and upon whose member
she was impaled. Her eyes were completely shut, and she emitted
sounds not unlike an animal in heat. On his part, Misha labored
supported on both arms, penetrating his member fiercely into
her pliant womb, all along breathing heavily, and frothing at the
mouth. Where one would expect harmony, there sounded a dissonant kind of music. Susanna's melody centered on conveying

an ecstatic abandon: soft sighs, painful moans denoting supreme pleasure, and occasional gutturally centered expressions of an approaching climax; *le petit mort*, as the French call it. His were the sounds of physical exertion as they attempted to intermingle with vocal expressions of pleasure. What resulted was a chorus of multiple voices in dissonant competition rather than complementing harmony.

An awesome sight it must have been, for Alida stood transfixed longer than discretion and decorum might have permitted. Her eyes were wide open now, and she seemed terrified. Her lips moved in silent motion.

"Alida!!" Misha was first to grasp the circumstances. "What in God's name are you doing here?" Quickly, he catapulted himself out of bed, pulled up his pajamas above the hips and turned rather violently to face the stunned woman. Alida continued silent in view of the challenge.

"Uh...my goodness...please...excuse this...intrusion..." Was all she was able to stammer. Misha approached her with the intention of showing her the way out. Susanna, now partly dressed and composed, had mistaken Misha's gesture as a threat to Alida's safety. She positioned herself between the two, her arms extended full length toward Misha, pleadingly.

"Please, honey, please don't strike her. I beg you."

"I had no intention of doing any such thing," he assured her.

"Let her stay, Misha." Susanna continued. "I don't mind her presence. She's family, after all." Susanna took Alida by the hand and led her toward the bed. The latter followed, childlike. She did so in complete silence, compliant, for events had taken place on that night that would have seemed strange to anyone unacquainted with the players' past.

Quietly, Alida sat on the edge of the bed, while Susanna knelt before her. The latter spoke softly, endearingly to her erstwhile antagonist as if to soothe her fears. Alida's eyes were now completely closed, while Susanna commenced to caress the tender parts of her thighs. Her hands traveled upward toward Alida's now exposed torso. She rested there for a brief moment, as if to test Alida's resolve. The latter sat passively, without apparent resistance, only a few quick, disrupted, breaths. Encouraged, Susanna continued her journey, now her tongue engaged in a circular motion, Alida's breasts engulfed in rapture, her face almost crimson with emotion. Choked plaintive sounds, seemingly straining to shout, issued forth form Alida's throat. No longer able to contain herself, she placed both hands forcefully in the back of Susanna's head. Alarmed, the latter ceased her activity, hesitant.

"Oh...oooh..." Alida sighed.

"It's all right, my dear Alida. It's all right." Susanna massaged Alida's plump arms from her shoulders down, then up and downward again. Alida sat seemingly emotionless, her face turned toward the open window. "You can lie down now, my dear." Susanna held Alida's shoulders and gently pushed her downward. "Lie down and relax now, dear." Susanna repeated. Alida complied without the least resistance.

Now, it was Susanna's turn to lie beside Alida. Both women shared one pillow, facing each other. Misha stood aghast at the spectacle, while Susanna caressed Alida's breasts with both her hands and whispered inarticulate words he could scarcely hear and even if he did, he did not understand.

Misha experienced what seemed to him heat waves enter his skull and settle there for the longest time. The two women lay before him, their arms entwined in a loving embrace. Alida's lips whispered into Susanna's ears. He knelt close to them, to listen, to hear what his ex had to tell that so engrossed Susanna. He listened with incredulity.

"Don't you ever trust Misha," he heard Alida's evolving narrative, "for as long as he can use someone, he'll show interest. But, even while the object of his desire starts to become less attractive, he'll look elsewhere, search for new conquests." She went on in a relentless monotone, and Susanna didn't interrupt.

Misha was aghast. Suddenly, he did the unexpected. He lay down on the bed behind Susanna. There was no reaction on her part. He reached out and softly touched first Susanna, then Alida. Emboldened by their passive acceptance of his presence, he quickly shed his pajamas. He now raised his body over Susanna and positioned himself between both women.

"God, what am I doing?" He thought to himself. "What would mother say? Why, barely eighteen year olds do such radical things." She would say. He also knew what his father Motele would say. He'd say, as the Jew, not as the Nazi he was: "Screw them and leave them." And didn't he act according to this dictum even though he did so as an SS-man and not a Jew? Mom, on the contrary, would sound a warning: "You're beginning to resemble both your father's, dearest Misha; Motele, the sleazy scoundrel; and your step-dad, the sadistic oaf that he was."

Strange as it seemed, both women proceeded eagerly to seek out his private parts. Their heavy sighs intermingled. He rewarded them, while turning to one and then to the other. He caressed every inch of their bodies and his eager hand ventured boldly into their pubic triangles. He sucked their hardened nipples intermittently till they voiced their delight, and then allowed them to handle his erect member with their nimble fingers. The strange triad continued until he mounted Alida, and Susanna eagerly caressed the latter's breasts. Misha reached out to Susanna's orifice, inserted his middlefinger—the way to her liking—and she moaned and let out guttural sounds, while she reached a paroxysm of an orgasm jointly with Alida's shouts of ecstatic fulfillment.

The three lay exhausted and exhilarated beside each other for the longest time. A merging of bodies, such as neither of them had experienced before, occurred. It seemed they would then remain happily in after play, but Alida was the first to break up he threesome. She got up, put on her nightgown, and left the bedroom without uttering a word. Misha regarded his ex with mixed feelings, and then he glanced at the clock on the night table. The time was 4:30 a.m., and there was still a little sleep left him before he would meet his first class. A picture of Alida's smiling face as she labored beneath him in his mind's eye, he fell into deep slumber.

It seemed unnatural, even perverse, that he should spend the rest of that night in the company of Motele, his father. What developed here was a dialogue with a dead man. He was going to forget it at waking but it was nevertheless anguishing. *"Is this going to be another thousand year nightmare?"* Misha thought even in his sleep. *"Am I destined to spend the next thousand years in the bastard's company?"*

*"Is that the right way to think about your daddy?"* Motele mocked.

*"Who invited you into my life?"* Misha's belligerence was evident.

*"Hey...hey...someone must have invited me. I'm here, am I not?"* Motele knew how to annoy his son.

*"It wasn't me, pop."* Misha addressed his father in a manner most distasteful to the pedantic Nazi accustomed to respectful subservience.

*"Don't they teach you respect in your New World?"* Motele asked.

*"They do. But not toward your ilk."* Misha was merciless.

*"I guess you're right."* Motele smiled derisively. *"After all, you're my kind of people. Aren't you?"* He was about to escape into the dark of the night, when Misha called back to the man he'd keep hating eternally: *"You can rot in hell forever before I address you respectfully!"*

*"Look who is talking,"* Motele laughed sardonically, *"the man who just made love to his ex while his shickse whore looked on."* He giggled with great glee.

*"I must have inherited your sense of humor, dear pop."* Misha was relentless. Motele was also silent for a few embarrassing moments.

*"Forgive your old man,"* he started softly, *"if I have half hoped you'd grow up not to be like me."* He paused, as if to weigh his words carefully. *"But I can see, as they say, 'the apple falls close to the tree...'"*

*"...Doesn't fall far from the tree..."* Misha corrected Motele.
*"Anyway, you know what I mean."* Motele chuckled gleefully.
*"I'm glad we can agree in principle."*
*"Don't flatter yourself, pop,"* Misha's eyes sparked with hatred, *"I'm as far removed from you as can be."*
*"Now, now, boy..."* Motele knew how much Misha abhorred being called boy, *"...don't let your hatred speak for you. Emotions can lead reason astray."* The old man philosophized. *"Besides, I've paid for the awful things I did. Amply. Don't you think?"*
*"If you pay with a millennium in hell, it wouldn't be enough, pop!"* Misha almost screamed. *"Isn't that what your Führer promised? A thousand year Reich?"*
*"He...he...don't be too severe on yourself. If I suffer, you suffer."* The old man was readying to leave again.
*"Why can't you admit you were wrong, old man?"* Misha called after the departing Motele. *"Why can't you say you're sorry for what you have done?"* His fists hit against his temples, Misha cried loudly, without shame.
*"Believe me, dear Misha, I've tried."* Motele turned, facing Misha once again, *"but they're so unrelenting...those Jews...they don't want to forgive our kind..."* He reflected for a brief moment. *"Could anyone? I try to put myself into their shoes. So much suffering. So much killing. Such anguish. How can anyone forgive? Even God cannot forgive such acts of pure evil. If God forgave, it would be His admission of collective sin. Wouldn't it be?"* Motele's image had begun to fade, when Misha stopped him. *"Not so fast, pop."* He spoke with deliberate slowness. *"God had no part in your mischief. You'd like to have a co-conspirator in high places, wouldn't you? But it won't work. Not this time..."*
*"...But...but...I only did my d..."* Motele stammered.
*"...Put the blame on your confounded duty, will you?"* Misha cut in. *"Listen to me, pop. Wish you'd hear me out. And try not to interrupt. That's what you've always done. In all of your days on this earth, you never listened. You interrupted. Now, you are the one on*

*the receiving end. And you must admit the ugly part you played in the Nazi drama. I can't say that my heart is with you. It never was, never will be."*

*"You, too, my son, must forgive yourself,"* Motele said in leaving. *"And though it never was, my heart is with you now."* With that, Motele's image faded and, gradually disappeared from view. Misha wanted to shout after his father, but he was gone. *"Go to where you came from,"* Misha murmured, *"here you cause too much harm."*

His mother's last words of counsel strutted frivolously in Misha's subconscious chronologically filed and, therefore remembered verbatim. Try as he did, he was unable to shake the specter of those fateful nights of fear and presentiment. Needless to say, his sleep was terribly disturbing and his waking bode ill to his daily endeavors.

Misha woke with a start. He glanced at the clock on the night table. It was well past his first class period. The class he'd missed most often. Susanna was gone, and so was little Rudi. "Damn," Misha seethed, "why didn't she wake me?" This will be the second time in one week he'd given his class a walk. No wonder the committee of his peers refused to grant him tenure. He knew full well that his errant behavior couldn't lead to anything constructive.

Slowly, he picked himself out of bed. He would not eat breakfast. His appetite was gone. He recalled the details of last night's events. "Alida! Merciful God! What have I done?!" Went through his laboring mind. He looked into her bedroom. She, too, was gone. He remembered her doctor's appointment at 9:30 this morning. Good thing, too. He didn't know how he'd face her. He'd only exchanged a few polite words with her during the past year and hadn't laid a hand on her body. And now this. A sex orgy? A threesome?! What degenerate behavior! Where will this lead?! Questions crowded his mind without answers. Radical actions demanded like reactions.

Suddenly, the door opened and Alida stood before him. "I cancelled the appointment so that we could talk undisturbed," she regarded Misha with a familiar look of determination. He was unable to sustain her burning eyes and stood there sheepishly allowing his own to survey the floor. "You don't have to feel guilty about last night." She stated with a candor he'd expected from her on all issues but those regarding sex. "Does it surprise you?" She read his mind.

"Uh...no...uh...I don't think you understand, Alida..." He stammered.

"Well, all I meant to tell you is that you shouldn't feel remorse." She seemed to delight in his embarrassment. "It is now time to make a few changes around here."

"Changes?" He inquired meekly.

"Yes, my dear Misha." She spoke with a deliberate slowness, and he didn't dare to interrupt. "You see, my dear husband," she placed an especial emphasis on that word she hadn't used for so long; "you're still my husband, aren't you?"

"Indeed, I am." He admitted.

"Well, then, as your wife, I must admit to having made an error in judgment by inviting this...this..." she searched for the right word, but was unable to pin it down exactly to her liking... "Let's call her, in the manner of the ancients, a concubine." She smiled, and he was certain she was the joyful Alida once again. Could it be? He wondered silently. What's gotten into her? He listened, and her words sounded as if they were coming out of an endless tunnel of time, from the bosom of Sarah, the wife of the patriarch Abraham...

*...She must be sent from here, away she must go, for I am your rightful wife, and this is my wish. And I shall bear you a son, to become the heir to your estate. And our son will be the firstborn and not her bastard son. Proceed now, swiftly, for I have seen the truth, and the truth is in our marriage. And it will be a blessing...*

Misha stood mute and dumbfounded, struggling to understand Alida's words. "Is it true?" He asked. "You will bear a child again?"

"Yes, my dear Misha, I shall bear a child." She assured him.

"But...but...how is this possible?" He expressed his doubts.

"You must trust me in that, Misha." She repeated. "You must have faith, and it will happen."

"There is more than faith involved here, isn't there?" He asked. She smiled unperturbed by his questioning.

"I know what you think, dear Misha. I don't blame you for doubting my words." Alida's smile disappeared from her face. "Look at me, Misha." She demanded. "Do you think I am capable of joking in this manner?"

Joking. Joke. Wasn't Sarah's son named *Isaac*; in Hebrew it meant "laughter" or "joke," for no one believed she could bear a child at her ripe age of seventy-three. But she did, and...

"...Now you must tell her to leave, Misha. She has overstayed her welcome here." Alida completed Misha's thoughts. She issued her statement forcefully, in a manner he had never before experienced.

"It was you who invited her in the first place. Didn't you?" He argued meekly.

"So it must be me who will have to evict her." Alida responded. "Is that what you mean?"

"Well, not exactly..." He hesitated. "You can't all of a sudden force changes on people on a whim. Can you?"

"I thought about this for some time now. My decision isn't based on a momentary caprice." Alida was adamant.

"Still, I believe we should give her some time to adjust her thoughts on this. I'm sure; our decision will have a radical and adverse effect on her." Misha tried to persuade Alida to reconsider. "It isn't fair. Neither to her nor to the boy."

"They're not my responsibility." Alida insisted. "You'll have to deal with it in your own way." She paused. "Haven't you always?"

She added and that certain smile he was so well familiar with curled her lips. He could well imagine the inference.

"I'll try." He said meekly.

"You'll do better than try." Alida's tone was steel hard. He had never heard her speak this harshly. It was a tone of foreboding he wouldn't dare challenge. What happened to the sweet little girl with whom he once fell in love? Where is the innocence of their first meeting?

"I'll speak with Susanna as soon as opportunity offers itself," he promised.

"Let it happen this evening." Alida insisted.

"So be it," he sounded tired and resigned.

Evening came, but Susanna had not returned from work. Rudi was dropped off by one of his schoolmate's mother. In the hope that the boy knew Susanna's whereabouts Misha inquired: "Have you any idea where your mother might be?" He asked in German in Alida's presence.

"*Nein,*" the boy replied. He left the living room to fetch a glass of milk from the fridge.

"I guess it will have to wait till morning," Misha informed Alida. "The boy has no idea where his mother might be."

"You can stay up for her," Alida was relentless.

"Okay, I shall." Misha complied. "I've got some papers to grade."

"That's good of you, Misha." Alida's was uncompromising.

Through the night, Misha agonized over Alida's demand. In addition, Susanna's nocturnal absences had made him feel uneasy and betrayed. His anguish and the fear of losing another lover were by no means new experiences. He remembered the time Xin Xin had left him for Patrick, and he dreaded a repeat. Xin Xin was a reject and therefore fair game. Susanna was as yet an undeclared entity. But lately she has been absent when he needed her. "So much work to do at the office and not enough time to do it in," was her ordinary excuse. And she had left Rudi's daily fate up to Misha's care. He wasn't ready to assume the role of 'Mr. Mom.'

His suspicious, agonizing mind labored overtime. Was Patrick at it again? He tried to guess. No, it couldn't be. Was he using his paranoia as a cop out? Did he owe Susanna an explanation? He thought he did. After all, she had answered his desperate request and traversed the Ocean to be with him. For once, he would level with her. What if mother was wrong after all? He thought. Could he afford another major error at this crucial point in his life? He heard the sounds of the front door opening. Quickly, he turned toward the wall, pretending to be asleep.

Susanna tiptoed into the bedroom. Even if he hadn't felt her presence, he would have been aware of it by the scent of her cologne that filled his nostrils: *Faberge*. After all, he had given her the very first carafe of that precious essence the day after their reunion, and made it a repeat gift on its anniversary from then on. She wore it for him alone. He had hoped.

The time she had taken to undress and change into her nightgown seemed endless. He shrunk into his side of the bed. At last, he felt the mattress give under her weight, and he knew she had settled near enough to touch. Had he still wished to resurrect their love, he might enfold her in his arms, cover her body with kisses. He hesitated. The damage has been done. His pretense of being asleep was a way to punish her for the infidelity he had imagined she has committed. It was a lethal kick to her most vulnerable self, an ill-intended knockout. But she seemed to land gracefully as a cat on her feet and disappeared into the shadows of sleep. He would have to wait till morning for the showdown.

And morning came without fail. This time, she wasn't going to leave before him. He would make sure it didn't happen. And he would contain his temper. For him this was going to be a gravity-defying leap, as he would try to blend emotion with rational thought.

"You've been working so very late, Susanna," he began, while she was applying her facial makeup, "they should be paying you overtime."

"Uh?" She seemed startled. "It's only that there are so many things that have to be done." She said, while concentrating on her eyebrow tone in front of the mirror. "If I let it go, I'd have to come in on weekends."

"You have gone to the office on weekends, Susanna." He smiled sadly, "or haven't you noticed?"

She knew she was cornered. "You haven't shown any interest in my work in the past; nothing that even approaches the ordinary." She knew if she were to match him in this contest of words, she would have to revert to a bold offense. He looked at her puzzled.

"I knew not to interfere." He said softly. "You would have put me in my place for being too inquisitive."

"I've made new friends. Don't I have the right to have friends?" She had learned how to mix apples with oranges. It always worked in the past. Why shouldn't it work now?

"Did you say friends, in the plural?" He asked, and she detected a note of sarcasm.

"Friend…friends, what's the difference?" She was challenging. But Misha would not back off.

"In the past, I've made it a point to introduce you to all of my friends. Aren't my friends yours as well?" She realized where he was going with his arguments. She looked at him intensely.

"Well, yes," she replied softly, "we do have common friends. But it's not like the world should end there. Or should it?"

"You don't seem to understand, Susanna," he said in a steely tone of voice that barely disguised his pain. What surprised him was that at moments like these his rational self would give way to memories of a childhood plagued by relentless prodding and mental abuse. Had his parents nurtured his self-confidence, he might surely react in an altogether different manner to momentary setbacks. Occasionally, miracles can be made to happen. By dint of hard work and sheer force of will he might have been able to transcend his youthful obstacles. But this was not to be, for he lacked both industry and the strength of conviction that forge a strong will power. He had understandably reached adulthood riven by psychic scars. He hesitated. He lacked the resolve to continue for fear he might seal his losses irrevocably.

Susanna was now staring at Misha in his indecisiveness. Was this the man for whom she had abandoned her native country, family and friends, traversed thousands of miles? "You do not understand what it is to lose your country and your loved ones." She whispered as if to herself. "Have you ever loved?"

"Yes," Misha replied, "I understand, and I…"

"…How can you understand?" She cried, interrupting him in mid-sentence. Tears had always worked for her under similar circumstances, she remembered. He turned away from her and walked over to the window and stood there looking out. It was a dreary September afternoon, and across the street he could see the bleak mist that gathered between the dense trees and a few isolated pedestrians and cyclists. Soon, he knew, huge raindrops would come splashing onto the red rooftops of the adjacent houses.

"What is it you want, Susanna?" He asked.

"What I want is not the issue here." She said without looking at him. "It's what you want that matters. It always has." With these words, she turned to go, but he stopped her before she reached the door.

"Alida wants you to leave this place immediately." He blurted out in one breath. "She wants back into our marriage." He knew this was not the way to express the things he wanted to convey to her, but he was angry and spiteful. As soon as he had realized his error in judgment, he would have given anything to retract his words and place them on hold temporarily. But it was too late.

Susanna stood stiffly, unable to utter a word. Alida's message had caught her by surprise. But it was the messenger's delivery that had a devastating effect. Still, she kept silent, as though weighing her options carefully. "We ought to have moved out long ago, when I asked you to do so, Misha." She said without apparent emotion. "This could have been foreseen. After all, none of us has water running though our veins."

"I'll talk with her," he promised, "try to give us some time."

"Time's one thing I haven't got, dear Misha." She said with sadness in her voice. "The other night I found Rudi in the bathroom, snorting coke and rolling some marijuana tobacco." She looked at Misha who stood speechless only shaking his head. "If that's what this country does to the children, I don't want any part of it."

"Why haven't you told me sooner?" Misha asked, his eyes glazing over, remorse in his voice.

"You're always so busy with yourself, Misha. It has been difficult to get your attention most of the time." He tried to touch her shoulder endearingly, but she stepped back and out of his reach. "And that night, the three of us in bed together, the boy saw our grotesque performance." She wept bitterly. "What do you think were his thoughts then?"

"Dear Lord, Susanna, I'm sorry, so very sorry." He whimpered sadly. "I didn't know...I didn't know."

"Of course you didn't, dear Misha." She spoke slowly, without rancor. "And now it's irreversible. It can't be helped. I'm certain there is something inherent in this country's culture of the superfluous and amoral arrogance that causes children to die in this terrible manner."

"That is nonsense, Susanna." He tried vainly to argue. "This country is no different from any other. We are part of a global culture, my dear."

"Do you know what my father said to me before I embarked on my journey to America? Are you curious?" She asked. "You've never asked."

"I know you'll tell me even if I don't ask." He replied.

"Still the arrogant Misha, yes?" She looked at him defiantly. "My father said, and his words still ring vividly in my mind, as if I could hear him right at this moment: 'Children in America are strong in body but weak in spirit.' He said that, and I rejected his warning because I believed in you. In due time, you proved him right, Misha."

"Your father spoke in stereotypes, Susanna." Misha bristled. "Like mine, he was steeped in old Nazi propaganda. Couldn't help but parade the old lies even when he knew they were only lies."

She came very close to him, put her face squarely into his view as though she were examining a tiny insect, and she said, "All I am saying is why couldn't you have been a better specimen. That's all I'm saying." Misha did not know how or what to answer.

"Please, Susanna, don't think about it now." He pleaded.

"What would you have me think about?" She asked.

"I would want you to think about us right now." He started. "Put our relationship to the test, shouldn't we?" He asked, and he didn't wait for her to answer but continued: "Let's give it a new start. The right one this time, can we?" He pleaded.

She didn't answer.

"A year from now we will look back and laugh at all this." His voice carried the sound of desperate hope.

"I don't know. I'm not sure."

"Give me another chance." He begged.

"I thought this was your other chance, Misha."

"Be serious."

"I am serious." She insisted.

"What does that mean?" He was at a loss for argument. "I promise you it will be different this time. You would be wrong not to believe me."

"I believed you once. Where has it gotten me?" Susanna was unyielding.

"Let's reflect on it together."

"Nothing left to reflect on." She readied to leave. He stood there, swept away by a paroxysm of emotion, not knowing whether to make another attempt at stopping her. That moment was perhaps the first time he had realized that the mysteries of joy and suffering cannot be intellectualized—they can only be understood with the heart.—Resigned, he stepped aside and yielded the passage for her to exit.

To Misha's great surprise, Susanna returned that evening earlier than usual from work. Immediately, she began to pack hers and Rudi's belongings; a hard look of determination in her eyes. Misha stood by with vague feelings stirring in his heart. Should he try to convince her to stay and wait till they can both leave? He wondered. He finally spoke: "Do you know where you're going to stay?"

"Haven't decided as yet." She answered without facing him.

"You'll let me know, as soon as you get settled, yes?" He inquired.

"I might." Again a curt reply.

"It'll only be for a short while." He assured her without conviction.

"Sure, it will." She continued packing.

"You must believe." He pleaded.

"I believe you, Misha." She said and lifted her eyes toward him for the first time since she had begun her meticulous activity. "Haven't I always believed you?" She added.

"And you must continue, darling." He implored knowing full well that words of endearment did not sound less hypocritical than on previous critical occasions. Still, he harbored hope that he could go on with the deception. Susanna did not react to his latest assertion. Neither did she interrupt her activity. It was best this way, and she would not engage in this useless small talk. "A bastard will always remain a bastard," she must have thought silently. Rudi busied himself, helping when it came to packing his meager belongings. They were ready.

Mother and son did not feel like wasting time in prolonged farewells that night. The very moment they stepped out onto the street and the door shut behind them, the night had become darker. Heavy clouds gathered above them. Susanna's heart stopped a beat and fear was foremost in her thoughts. "Where shall we go? Sweet Jesus, where?" She implored God the only way she knew how; through His favorite Son. She felt Rudi's innocent eyes peeled on her. Though he was silent, concern about seeking shelter reflected in his inquisitive expression. She promised herself not to panic. Now she knelt on the bare pavement and hugged Rudi in a strong embrace. "Dear God, show me the way." She prayed. The answer was swift.

Rudi looked at his mother with an expression of utter bewilderment. He has never seen her in such a state of helplessness. She gazed deep into the boy's eyes now, and she saw no fear in them. Would she hear fear in his voice when he addressed her? She wondered.

"Why don't we visit Uncle Patrick? Surely, he will think of something." Susanna was moved, though startled, by her son's mature manner. He was another example of a child turned adult in time of crisis. She thought silently. "Well, mama?" He prodded.

The idea of calling on Patrick unannounced and asking for help seemed a bit strange to her, but on second thought she felt it to be a good albeit temporary solution to their problem. "Yes, darling," she said, "we'll try and see how things work out." Although she tried to sound carefree, a still small voice in her subconscious sounded a warning. Shouldn't she learn from her past experiences of seeking favors from men? Their demand for repayment had invariably caused her much grief.

But the street looked oddly abandoned at that time of night, what with the stars and the moon invisible to the eye because of the heavy cloud cover. In addition, Susanna felt a few large drops of rain collide with the soft spots on her face, and lightning struck a nearby garbage bin. The profound rumble of thunder followed. "Let's go!" She urged Rudi, and they stepped lively into the dark and threatening night in their search for shelter. Meanwhile the few wispy clouds had turned into a deep cover of darkness. Nature's mood reflected Susanna's deepest presentiments.

She remembered Patrick's address. She chose not to phone him for fear he might change his mind and "not be there" for her and little Rudi as he had promised on many occasions. "123 Lake Street," she instructed the cabby. Soon, suitcase in one hand and Rudi holding a strong grip on the other, she stood in front of apartment number 21's door. She let go of Rudi's hand and rang the bell. "Who's there?" She heard Patrick's voice approaching the door, and momentarily she felt an eye pealed on her face through the peeping hole.

"It's me and Rudi," Susanna responded. There was a long moment of silence, and her heart beat faster. Soon, Patrick's voice sounded unusually cheerful under the circumstances as he called out: "I'll be a minute!" There was silence, and she could not guess what it indicated. "Hold on." She heard him undo the security chain and the door opened revealing Patrick clad in a bathing towel and a big grin on his friendly face.

"Hum…hum…pardon me, dear, I didn't expect company at this hour." He said cheerfully. "Come inside, please, step out of the rain." He took hold of her suitcase and carried it inside the small hallway.

"I didn't mean to inconvenience you, Patrick." She was apologetic and somewhat embarrassed as she glanced at Rudi's reaction to Patrick's half nakedness. "If it's inconvenient, we can come another time." She added hastily. Patrick glanced at her, then at Rudi and at their luggage, and he understood.

"You've been evicted, huh?" He smiled. "And your visit happens in as good a time as ever." Just then, a female voice resounded from the direction of the bathroom" Who is it, Patrick dear? Did we expect guests tonight?" Susanna could have sworn she'd heard this voice before. At that very moment Susanna recalled the tone of the voice as well as its unique rhythm. Xin Xin appeared in the hallway also wrapped in a bath towel. Patrick was quick to defuse the situation.

"You'll have to pardon me, dear Susanna." He started, and the grin has not left his lips. "What you see here is, simply, that I am entertaining an old friend." He looked at both women, especially Susanna, to see their reaction. The only reaction he received from Xin Xin, she uttered softly: "Did you say 'old'?"

And he was quick to correct himself with all of the charm at his disposal: "You know old in the sense that we have known each other for some time." He paused. "You know, like we would say, 'dearest friends'." Xin Xin smiled.

"Oh, silly man," Xin Xin carried on. "No need to take it so seriously. Besides, Susanna and I are well acquainted." She smiled mischievously. "In fact, we've enjoyed something in common or should I say someone? Our common interest has been carried on long enough to make us, how should I say, almost blood related." She burst out with a loud, vulgar laugh.

Patrick's apology and Xin Xin's inappropriate remark did nothing to allay Susanna's fear and apprehension lest she and her Rudi disturbed the couple during an inopportune time. Before Susanna was able to respond to Xin Xin's frivolous remarks, Patrick, once again, used his personal charm in suggesting: "Say, let's prepare the bed for Rudi or he will fall asleep standing up." He took the boy by the hand and led him into the adjacent guest bedroom. "After we have enjoyed a glass of wine and some challenging conversation, you may join your son." He addressed Susanna with some concern in his voice. "You've had enough excitement for one night, I think."

"We are intruding, Patrick, aren't we?" Susanna repeatedly insisted, though she would be at a loss had he agreed with her.

"No, not at all," Patrick assured her. "I want you to feel at home. Yes, you must remember what I have said to you on your arrival to our friendly country." He paused. "I only wish I could provide you both with a more comfortable environment." He said as he reappeared from the guest room. "I trust Rudi will know where to find his pajamas and enjoy a good night's rest. And, please, Susanna, do feel at home." He repeated.

"Oh, you shouldn't worry about the boy." Susanna studied intermittently Xin Xin's and Patrick's faces for any sign of discomfort. "He'll be asleep as soon as his head rests on the pillow." She remembered Rudi asking the inevitable question in the cab on the way to Patrick's place. "Do we stay this time or leave again to wander aimlessly, mama?" She excused herself to go and check on Rudi. He was in deep sleep. She sat on the edge of the bed, her hands folded in her lap. She stroked the boy's wavy dark brown hair, part hers and part Misha's inheritance. And she admired the beauty of this small creature, breathing deeply, seemingly without the slightest worry in the world. As she bent over him to plant a kiss on his forehead, a tear fell onto his reddened cheek and he stirred without awakening from his sleep. "Are we leaving, mama? Don't cry, mama. I'll take care of you from now on. Don't cry."

She looked into his bright blue eyes, quite unusual for him, since the color should have been a mixture of both parents, a light hazel brown. She ceased crying instantly, kissed her son on both cheeks and said: "My dearest Rudi, I am happy that you promise to take care of me. See? I stopped crying already." She suddenly realized what great measure of maturity her "little" son had displayed in this time of great crisis. She felt shame at showing distress when she should have been supportive of his needs. How could she behave so dismally weak? "As long as I have you with me, darling, nothing bad is going to happen to us. We will look out for one another. Won't we?"

"Yes, mama, we will." The boy yawned, turned on his side and, before sleep took over, said: "We sure will, mama. We sure will."

Sitting comfortably on the living room sofa as she faced Xin Xin and Patrick opposite her, conversation did not flow as they may have wished for. They could hear the storm raging outside. Rain was now mercilessly splashing on the pavement and beating violently at the door and the windowpanes to the accompaniment of thunder and lightning. Whatever polite thoughts Susanna may have harbored about retreating to someplace other than Patrick's hospitality, they were quickly dissolved by the inclement weather outside before she had had a chance to express them.

Xin Xin had taken the opportunity to dress in the bedroom, leaving the others to themselves. Patrick now wore a sleeveless nylon shirt and a pair of well-tailored trousers. Susanna couldn't help but admire his muscle tone fairly visible through his clothes' texture.

With Susanna's and Rudi's arrival, Patrick's relationship with Xin Xin had cooled considerably. There were occasional phone calls from and to Xin Xin, but Patrick handled them casually without commitment of any kind and without stress. He was not about to endanger his promising relationship with Susanna. He considered it a God sent. His behavior toward the latter was exemplary: only an occasional hug and a furtive kiss on the cheek at greetings and goodbyes. These were not indicative of his long range intentions. It has now been three months since Susanna's arrival at his doorstep.

"At the final bell, I find myself looking forward to spending some quality time with you and little Rudi," he confessed at dinner time. He composed his words carefully so as not to arouse suspicion. Rudi remained quiet during those exchanges. In spite of his tender age, he had understood intuitively the direction of the verbal intercourse. Susanna glanced anxiously at her son, and her responses were as veiled as were those of Patrick's at communicating his feelings. His attempts at putting Rudi to bed early have failed; the boy was true to his pledge given his mother to stand by her.

"It's time to go to bed, young man." Patrick suggested on occasions.

"Don't tell me what to do, you're not my father." The boy responded.

Susanna did not reprimand her son, thankful for the reprieve. Her thoughts were still with Misha. She fantasized during her waking hours and dreamt through the night of reuniting with the love of her life. That hope was her way of resisting Patrick's continuous attempts. But the more she rejected his amorous advances, the more challenging his task was becoming. He was in no hurry. An opportunity would offer itself, he was sure.

With Rudi asleep, Susanna retired early as well. The night was dark and moonless. With all the courage he was able to muster, Patrick entered Susana's bedroom. He sat down on the edge of her bed, not wanting to wake her from the first sleep to startle her needlessly. What was it he wanted to achieve? He silently examined his motives and their chances of success. Meanwhile, he felt his desires mounting as he sat mute admiring her feminine contours outlined through the flimsy linen. He was hesitant and perplexed.

Unable to arrive at a bold decision, he got up and left the room as quietly as he had entered. The confirmed bachelor experienced feelings hitherto unknown to him. Was he falling in love? Not a chance, he averred silently though he made his nocturnal visits to Susanna's bedroom frequently. Did he know Susanna was aware of his presence every time?

On her part, Susanna was at a loss whether to sit up and confront the intruder or let the situation continue for as long as there was no physical contact. He had gradually realized something his nature refused to admit: Susanna was unlike any of his past conquests. Her traditional adherence to the ethic of fealty and a moral abhorrence of the betrayal of her loved one prevailed throughout. He considered the challenge, but he was going to persist in his attempts with patience.

The tranquility of the night was suddenly interrupted by celestial fury. He woke to the sound of thunder. Flashes of lightning multiplied frenetically, brightly illuminating the countryside. It seemed a foreboding of some sinister events. Would they be caused by an act of wicked sexual perversity? Patrick wondered, not without some strange elation pervading his psyche.

He sat up in his bed and remained immobile for what seemed to him an eternity. His mind labored with great intensity trying to come to terms with his next move. Tonight, he felt, offered the opportunity. The elements presented themselves as unwitting partners in his designs. He could not accept being passive. Seeing her every day only served to increase his desires to the point of obsession. He wanted to touch her, to caress her, to make her his own. When he occasionally wavered and postponed his plans for some strange reason never experienced before, his indignant ego had told him that this was his fair due. Hadn't he cared for the two of them ever since they arrived at his doorstep?

His hand slid under her flimsy cover and touched the warmth of her thigh. Susanna responded in her slumber with a soft moan and a whisper: "Misha...Misha...my love..." Patrick withdrew his hand but remained seated on her bed's edge. She stirred and turned away from his reach. Tears welled up in Patrick's eyes. Tears were definitely not written into his character. Once again, his left hand slid under the covers. Now, the right hand followed and both of them softly massaged her private parts. For a brief moment she seemed to respond murmuring some incoherent words. Suddenly, she sat up in the bed and turned on the lamp on the night table.

"Patrick!" She exclaimed, wide eyed and frightened. "What in heaven's are you doing?" He withdrew both hands.

"I...I'm here beside you...loving you..." He stammered embarrassed. This too was a new experience for him. Ordinarily, it was the opposite gender that showed a lack of composure when in his predatory company. Not Patrick. Not he. He was always the master of his emotions.

"You had better leave now, Patrick." Susanna was calm but forceful. She glanced anxiously in the direction of the adjacent room as she listened to Rudi's rhythmic breathing with an admixture of soft child's snoring. "He might wake." She warned. "That won't be good." She added smiling.

"We need to talk, Susanna." He pleaded. "I'm trying to sort out some things here, and you'll have to help me." He regarded her with teary eyes. "The last thing I wanted you to think is that I would harm you or the little one." He stood now at her bedside, his arms folded on his chest. He was waiting for her to say something, anything favorable to lend a glimmer of hope to support his designs. She remained silent while he probed for her reaction, read into her mind, for anything that might help him win her over. Breaking the silence, she spoke: "There is no reason for you to do this sort of thing, coming in here in the middle of the night and scaring me out of my wits."

Meanwhile the storm had subsided and another day was ushered in by the dim streaks of light entering through the window shutters. She squinted into the faint traces of morning sunshine. "Besides, dear Patrick, when have I ever given you reason to assume the right to invade my privacy?"

He felt like shouting at her, enumerate the many favors he had performed for her since her arrival. Wasn't he the perfect host for the two of them? And he felt like confessing his love for her, thought it was lust he really felt. But he was speechless the first time for as far back as he could remember. His emotions were under control when he spoke: "I'm dying inside in my desire to please you and Rudi in order to win your affection, dear Susanna. The fire inside me flares brightly when I know you are only a thin wall away from me each night, yet so very distant in reality." He breathed heavily. "Tell me, please, what am I to do?"

"Will it help if I start looking for another place?"

"That's really not the thing I have in mind, my dear." He assured her. "You can stay as long as you wish."

"And you will be tormented by the thought of not obtaining the permission to sleep with me?" Susanna slowly emerged from under the covers and started toward the bath room. He stood rooted to the spot and watched the graceful movement of her shapely limbs through the sheer negligee. She closed the bath room door and called to him from inside: "It's time for us to get ready, don't you think? We'll continue to discuss this issue on our return form work this evening!"

He barely murmured a "yes", but she did not respond further and he assumed she'd heard him.

# 25.

MISHA WOKE TO THE violent knocking at the door. Still rubbing the sleep from his eyes, he put on his house robe and opened the door. A couple of stern looking civilians, brandishing police badges into his face, burst noisily into the apartment followed by several uniformed policemen. One of the uniformed persons handed him a warrant and recited him his rights while cuffing Misha's hands behind his back: "You have the right to remain silent...etc...etc...."

Overwhelmed, and dumbfounded, Misha stammered, "W...h...a...t...?" He felt the cold steel of handcuffs on his wrists and agonized under the initial pain as they pressed onto his skin and beneath to the bone. "When was the last time you saw your...uh...friend, Ms. Susanna Flossberg?"

"Why...about three months ago...she had left me...has taken the boy with her..." Misha related. "Haven't seen her since."

"Where were you the night before last between midnight and 4 a.m.?"

"Most likely at home in bed." Misha answered.

"Was anyone with you?"

"No, my wife and I are separated." He knew it wasn't quite true, but he had no way to reverse himself.

"Anyone else who could testify to that?"

"There isn't anyone."

"Mr., you had better get yourself a lawyer."

"Am I under arrest?" Misha trembled uncontrollably.

"This is to serve you notice that you are being detained relative to the death of Ms. Susanna Flossberg."

"Death?!" Misha felt his legs give way beneath him. A severe pain entered the pit of his stomach, such as he had not experienced ever before. Were it not for the support of the two uniformed officers, he might have crushed to the floor. "What do you mean death?" Misha asked. "When she left me several months ago, she was very much alive and well. I don't know anything about this... this alleged death."

"All we can tell you at this time is that her submerged body was found at the bottom of a remote pond by two young boys. When they called us to the scene, she was still anchored there."

"Anchored? How?" Misha interrupted. The detective ignored Misha's inquiry. But, on momentary reflection, he decided to explain.

"Your...uh...former girlfriend...was anchored at the bottom of the pond at its deep end. There was a heavy briefcase...yours... filled with your research papers...some books...tied to her ankles with a pair of panty-hose."

"My briefcase? Papers? Panty hose?" Misha repeated in a whisper, his eyes focused on some distant point. "And I've been looking for them all this time..."

"Looking for what? The panty-hose?" Asked the detective.

"My research notes, Sir." Misha's eyes exhibited a spark of life and his voice became animated. "I've been doing some original research on the life of a seventeen century German author. Here...let me show you the publishing contract..." Misha motioned toward his desk. "Let me show you..."

"There'll be plenty of time for that in the courtroom, Mr. Winograd." The detective interrupted. "You'd best discuss it with your lawyer. You have a lawyer? Don't you?"

"A lawyer?" Misha still didn't seem to understand why he would need a lawyer. "I'm telling the truth, I swear." He assured the detective.

"All in good time, Mr. Winograd. All in good time." The detective was unperturbed. "And now, would you, please, come with us."

"Can't we wait for my wife, please?" Misha pleaded. "I'd like her to know what's going on."

"We'll notify her from down town, as soon as we get there." The man assured Misha, while the officers accompanied him to the squad car.

Clad in his housecoat and slippers, Misha was fingerprinted, given a pair of trousers and a drab UPD (the "U" stood for Urbana), marked jail shirt to wear while in detention there. He seemed completely disoriented as he was placed in solitary to await his arraignment. More questions followed.

Unsavory thoughts raged mercilessly in his mind and carved deep crevices in his psyche. His temporarily erratic cognizance was painfully aware of the fact that Susanna has been murdered. He also surmised that the police was trying to tie him to the crime. Misha was deluged with absurd questions, such as: "Did you plan it? Why did you do it? Confess and the law will go easy on you. Is the child yours?" And he kept his replies brief: "No comment." They recruited his former students and some faculty to testify regarding his character. Why all that futile effort? He agonized. Detained for the night, he panicked.

The arresting officer read to him the customary disquieting litany of police jargon: "You have the right to remain silent...as all you say can be held against you in the court of law..." It was followed by: "You have the privilege of one phone call..."

The police had no hard evidence to indict him for Susanna's murder. He was picked up and, subsequently, arraigned on suspicion of conspiracy to murder. Of course, they needed "probable cause," and they produced one since he was their closest possible suspect; one who may have been trying to rid himself of an illicit relationship at any cost. Though some from within the university community were summoned to testify, not one has been able to produce evidence of Misha's tendency to physical violence. Needles to say, the university community was riveted by a developing legal drama they had never before experienced.

The following morning, Misha made his customary phone call to his friend and colleague Pedro Pamies. The latter was devastated by the news. He looked at his friend on the other side of the glass partition, as they spoke by phone.

"Misha, you'll need an attorney," Pedro said.

"I don't know about things like that,"Misha seemed disoriented.

"You must keep a clear mind, my friend," Pedro spoke softly. "It will all turn out well." He paused to reflect. "I am convinced you couldn't have done this…this terrible thing."

"I'm really frightened, Pedro," Misha wept. "I know they will turn the evidence against me. I don't dare believe it, but they will. What can I do?"

Slowly, Pedro turned his head and looked straight into the depth of Misha's frightened eyes. "Don't do anything stupid, Misha. A friend of mine, Diana Ferrucci, is a social worker, often assigned to cases like yours. I'll prevail on her to see you as soon as possible. Think positive, my friend."

"Thanks, Pedro," Misha whispered almost inaudibly into the phone, "I'm sorry to burden you this way, but I had no one else to turn to."

"Alida?" Pedro asked. "How's she taking it?"

"I don't know." Misha turned away, and Pedro was unable to study his face. "She hasn't come to see me yet. Well, maybe it's still too early."

"I'll look in on her," Pedro offered. "Poor thing, she must be devastated."

"Incredible as it may seem, she hasn't even inquired about me." Misha said, now staring at Pedro with a kind of supplicating look. Pedro hung up, took a couple of quick paces away from the partition. He then turned back, as if he had forgotten something, picked up the receiver and spoke: "There has been a lot of grief here for both of you, Misha." He paused, reflected for a brief moment, and went on. "I'd like to see if some semblance of civility can be salvaged, or whether it is worth salvaging, if at all possible. For our friendship's sake."

Misha was bewildered and stricken with immense grief. He was weeping now, and great sobs were shaking his entire body. He moved closer to the glass partition and placed his left palm on its surface. "Be good to her, my friend, as I have failed to do my part. Please, it's very important to me."

Pedro placed his right palm, his fingers spread and fitting those of Misha's, he pushed them forward surreptitiously till his finger tips were white. "Rest assured, my dear friend, I'll do my best for you." With that he turned away from the booth and walked slowly toward the guarded exit door.

As promised, Dr. Diana Ferrucci arrived in the company of the court appointed lawyer, Anton Berg. She wore a pantsuit, the jacket of which was colorful, injecting some measure of life into the dark surroundings of the penitentiary. Anton was of average height and of stocky built. His receding, dusty-looking, short-cropped chestnut hairline lent him a mature appearance beyond his age. His deep, blue eyes inspired confidence. The informality of his attire, a beige sweater and the absence of a coat, added to the lawyer's youthful looks. Misha regarded the youthful counselor, feverishly trying to guess his age and, by the same token, the range of experience. After the customary exchange of superficial question and answer items, Anton went directly to the heart of the matter with a legal notepad in his hand.

"You must tell me all you can recall about the events of the recent past, as well as anything in your background that might bear on them, Misha." He looked intensely at the accused. "Don't hold back. Every detail is important," he spoke slowly for emphasis, "even things you may take for granted or hold of little importance may be very significant in the courtroom."

"I'll tell you all I know." Misha assured his counsel. "Every bit of it.

"I'll need complete honesty from you." The lawyer said, "Trust me, and you can expect total candor on my part."

"May I ask a question?" Misha hesitated.

"Go right ahead," Anton encouraged.

"You don't seem old enough to have the experience in criminal law." He paused. "How long is it since you've been accepted to the bar?"

"Well, now, Misha," Anton smiled, "you've made a statement and asked a question." He giggled happily. "I'll try to address both to your complete satisfaction."

"Sorry, if I have offended you, counselor." Misha showed genuine contrition. "But my head is on the block, and I'd like to consider my chances." He added.

"Despite my youthful appearance, I'm well into the mid-thirties." The lawyer went on. "I was admitted to the bar in the State of Illinois in 1978, and served as an Assistant District Attorney for three years, mostly trying criminal cases. I've been in private practice the last five years. With much success, I might add." He looked at Misha inquiringly. "Is there anything else you'd like to know?"

"This is...then...your first defense of someone like me accused of murder, is it not?" Misha forced a grin.

"Yes, it is." Anton replied with a broad grin.

"Then...then...do you think...?" Misha hesitated again.

"...that I can do you justice?" Anton finished the sentence.

"Well, yes..." Misha admitted his doubts.

"Okay, Misha...let me put it this way." Anton's smile disappeared. "We can say with a certainty that I have more experience in the courtroom than you in doing what you're accused of having done. Are we in agreement on that score?"

Misha was silent for a long moment. "Yes, I guess we are." Misha knew that his future was at the mercy of this man-child's skill as a lawyer.

"I'm glad we can see eye-to-eye on that issue, Misha." Anton said with a somewhat triumphant smirk on his oval face. "And now, we'll move for a trial date to be set by the preliminary judges." He glanced toward Diana who had been silently observing the encounter. "Wouldn't you say, the earlier the better?" He asked her.

"Yes, by all means, Anton." Diana nodded. "I believe Misha has been locked up in his cell long enough, don't you?"

"I fully agree." He smiled. "I'll be moving for bail to be set. Let's get Misha out of this miserable hole to some place where he can live and behave like a human being." He stood up from his chair and approached Misha, his hand extended. Misha shook the lawyer's hand enthusiastically. None of the law-enforcement types had offered him a cordial hand thus far, as if to humiliate and disorient the defendant even before the final verdict. Misha felt human for the moment. The young attorney had by now gained his full confidence.

Bail was set at $300,000, and Misha was released to the custody of his young lawyer. Breathing the air unfettered by prison walls was a new experience. His clothing hung loosely on his lean body, but Misha didn't mind. A shave and a long bath would be just what he needed. Alida was visiting Claudia in Ft. Lauderdale at the moment, and he had the apartment all to himself. Little Rudi had become a ward of the State until the outcome of the trial. Misha missed the little guy, but that couldn't be helped. Patience.

"Why couldn't he stay with me?" Misha asked.

"The boy may have information relating to the trial. That's why the State will hold him for the duration." The lawyer explained.

"Will a nine-year-old boy be a valid source of information in a court of law?" Misha asked.

"You'd be surprised how much you can get out of a young boy, Misha." Anton shook his head meaningfully. "Most have a keen sense of awareness and keen observation, at times more acute than that of a grownup."

"That wouldn't surprise me at all," Misha smiled sadly. "Just look at me. What's the degree of my cognitive perceptions?" He said almost in a whisper. "Lord, what a mess I've gotten myself into!" He was about to wallow in self pity, when Anton interrupted:

"We'll have a chance to cross examine any of the State's witnesses." He assured Misha. "That includes Rudi."

"Hasn't the boy suffered enough?" Misha protested.

"Regretfully, he has," Anton agreed, "but if he should hold some facts that might shed light on this sad episode, the pain is well justified."

"No pain is ever justified," Misha insisted. "And why should Alida have chosen this time to visit with her mother? Why now?" He questioned.

"Not to worry about trivialities, Misha," Anton pacified his client. "She will be subpoenaed when the time comes, and she will testify."

"What if she becomes a witness for the prosecution?" Misha was in a speculative mood.

"Do you have reason to believe that?" Anton asked.

"Well, not really," Misha was evasive. "But, what if?"

"We'll cross that bridge when..." Anton caught himself in mid-cliché, and he abhorred clichés. "Well, anyhow, as I was saying, witnesses can be used both ways; for the prosecution and the defense."

As if on a sudden impulse, about to leave, Anton turned to Misha: "No matter what the outcome, I want you to know it will be a privilege to serve as your defense attorney." He paused. "And you should be content to have lived a very exciting and eventful young life."

Misha did not expect such outpouring of admiration from his lawyer. He looked somewhat sheepishly into the void and asked the only logical question that came to mind: "Why did you say 'young life'?"

"Well, it's just a matter of rhetoric," Anton explained, "and you mustn't allow it to affect your confidence in our relationship." That said, Anton turned on his heel and left his client open-mouthed and utterly baffled.

Misha Winograd's trial stirred the emotions of the faculty and student body alike. Those who came early had filled the court chambers to capacity. His colleagues, most of them, were there to lend him moral support. Others came to gloat over his misfortune. Students would not miss the opportunity to see their favorite literature Prof. on trial for the murder of his latest object of a torrid love affair. They knew him as a philanderer and notorious womanizer; but one who could commit murder, even as a most bizarre fantasy, he was not. Nevertheless, this was genuine life drama, entertainment at its best, not some fictitious substance delivered in a mystery novel. The opportunity to witness the proceeding first hand excited them to the core of their beings. After all, they were the public, and the public had become accustomed to lend an aura of mystery and empathy for perpetrators of heinous deeds, not to their victims.

The verbal dueling had begun early on with the jury selection. Some of the candidates did not meet with the approval of the prosecution. Others were rejected for one reason or another by the defense. At last, after two long sessions of wrangling, twelve jurors have been put in place; five men and seven women.

Anton was elated. "We must appeal to the women's sense of being the underdog in any heterosexual relationship. Play the male versus the feminine mystique." He told Misha during one of their strategy sessions. "This way we can effectively split the vote; a hung jury. Go for mistrial. Get a dismissal." He spoke in half sentences in his great excitement.

The morning of the first trial day, Misha kept looking over his shoulder into the audience. He saw many familiar faces, but the one he was looking for wasn't there. Anton had told him of the subpoena the court had issued for Alida's appearance. If she had by now returned from her visit with Claudia, there was no indication of her presence in the courtroom.

"Could it be she left the country?" Misha whispered anxiously into his lawyer's ear.

"Not a chance," Anton whispered back, "the immigration authorities have been alerted."

"They won't cause her any trouble, will they?" Misha asked.

"Not if she complies with the letter of the law," Anton smiled.

"Lord, I want to see the end of this...this...circus." Misha thought to himself. As much as he looked forward to Alida testifying in his behalf, he was worried about the havoc this trial might wreak on her already weak mental state. In fact, he wasn't sure any more that her presence was such a good idea. She might break down and go the opposite direction. But Anton thought he could handle whatever problems might arise with her delicate condition in regard to Misha, and insisted on hearing her testimony.

It was on the second day of the hearings that Alida finally appeared. As a potential witness, she was seated in the first row of the gallery from which all of the forthcoming testimony would be derived. Misha cracked a weary smile in her direction, but she seemed not to notice and looked vacantly into space. "I need you now more than ever," Misha thought silently, "give me a small sign at least that you are with me." His silent supplications received no response. He had no way of guessing her thoughts, though his own mind concentrated with all its intensity on some ever so slight sign from Alida.

In its opening statement to the jury, the prosecution made a compelling case on behalf of the state. The usual "...we will endeavor to show without a reasonable doubt...etc...etc..." assertions indicating their intent to convict Misha of murder in the first degree. The attorney for the defense countered with an appeal of its own, which ended with the usual promise to demonstrate its client's innocence "...beyond the shadow of a doubt..." strategy. This promise had made it clear which was the direction Anton would take to extricate his client from a difficult and obviously compromising situation.

The initial cross examinations, those of the public safety officials who had recovered Susanna's body from the depth of the pond, went rather routinely. They responded to the questions put to them by both legal adversaries without hesitation, straightforwardly. At times, they were compelled to elaborate on the technical aspects of their activity, which they did expertly.

The forensics expert from the City Morgue lab was next on the witness stand. While you could hear some subdued whispers in the spectator ranks during the cross-examination of the police officers, there was an eerie silence in the courtroom, as everyone in the gallery hung on he responses to questions pertaining to the autopsy.

"State your name and profession, Sir." The prosecutor requested.

"My name is Horace Xavier. I'm the City Coroner." The witness stated matter-of-factly in a tone of voice which betrayed great confidence and experience in matters of legal proceedings.

"In your professional opinion, Dr. Xavier," the prosecutor took extra time to emphasize the importance of his question, "what was the cause of the victim's death?"

The pathologist smiled self-assuredly. "Suffocation, Sir." He was not a man of many words, but those he had spoken brimmed with professionalism.

"By drowning?" The prosecutor hedged.

"No, Sir," the coroner assured the prosecutor, "by strangulation." A collective gasp resounded throughout the gallery. The judge rapped his gavel.

"Silence in the court!" He bellowed.

"How did you arrive at such a conclusion?" The prosecutor pressed on.

"There were distinct bruises around the victim's neck." Was the reply. "Bruises caused by some sort of material, like that of pantyhose." Dr. Xavier elaborated. The prosecutor lifted "exhibit 1" for the people, Susanna's alleged pantyhose, and waved it in front of the coroner's face. "Something like this?" He asked.

"Yes, Sir, exactly." The coroner nodded.

"What else led you to this conclusion?"

"There was no water in the lungs, Sir." The coroner said. "The victim was strangled before she was tossed into the pond."

"No further questions for the moment, your Honor." The prosecutor yielded with a triumphant look in the direction of the jury. Anton stood up and approached the witness stand.

"Now, Dr. Xavier, are you absolutely certain the victim was dumped into the pond after having been strangled?" Anton weighed his words carefully. "Could there be an element of error in your diagnosis? Could the death be due to drowning after all?"

"Absolutely not, Sir." Dr. Xavier responded with equanimity. "You see, Sir, when rigor mortis sets in, the lungs cease functioning, and with it all of the body tissues and organs. The coroner used the Latin expression for "state of rigidity caused by death."

"Could you tell the court how long the diseased was dead before entering water?" Anton asked.

"Judging from the partial deterioration of the victim's skin tissue, I'd say approximately forty-eight hours; give and take an hour." The coroner's reply did not leave Anton with further questions.

"I'm done with this witness for the time being, your Honor," he said.

"You may step down, Sir," the Judge instructed the witness. "The court will recess for lunch," he announced. "We will reconvene at 1300 hours." He rose from the bench.

"All rise!" The bailiff called out. The audience stood respectfully as the judge exited the courtroom into his chambers.

"How are we doing thus far?" Misha asked.

"It's too early to tell," Anton answered.

"When will we know for sure?" Misha pressed.

"For sure?" Anton smiled. "You won't know for sure until the moment the jury reaches a verdict."

"And when will that be?"

"When we have exhausted all of the testimony, Misha." Anton fought to keep his composure. "It takes patience and perseverance, my friend." He repeated, nodding his head. "You must learn that."

"This might be the hardest lesson for me to learn," Misha said meekly.

They had little time for lunch. The deli around the corner offered fast food at the counter. Misha practically swallowed his sandwich without chewing its contents. He washed it down with a cup of coffee. By then it was time to return to the court room.

It was hard for him to put Susanna's last moments out of his thoughts. Misha speculated about the events that led to her death. His now weakened sense of reality, aided by a feeble imagination, ran amok. He thought the worst. Could he have done it in a fit of passion followed by a total black out of consciousness? He had heard of such cases before, where the perpetrator passes out and suffers complete loss of memory upon waking caused by a deep sense of guilt and shame. What if Alida, of all people he could think of, killed her rival and set him up to make him seem he was the killer? She had ample motives to rid herself of both Susanna and him in one bold move. Here, his fantasy carried him to the limits of reality, as he envisioned…

…As usual during the morning hours, Alida was having her second cup of coffee when Susanna entered. Alida seemed unperturbed about her rival's presence, even though she had been the cause of Susanna's banishment.

"What brings you here at this early hour?" She asked.

"I'm here to make some sense out of this whole mess, Alida." Susanna seemed conciliatory. "First, I come to the US on your invitation, and then it's you who tells me to leave for some Biblical reasons. I've come to ask you to reconsider."

"Reconsider? How, may I ask, do I do that?" Alida feigned ignorance.

"Misha means nothing to you now, Alida." Susanna argued. "To me, he means everything. Can you understand?"

"Yes, my dear Susanna, I can understand." Alida responded without a sign of resentment at Susanna's claim. "So, what do you expect me to do?"

"Let him live with me and our son for one year, Alida." Susanna said, her eyes lowered to the floor. "If it doesn't work out, I'll send him back to you."

"Uhu...hmm...yes." Alida seemed amenable to the proposition. She rose from the kitchen table and walked over to the stove where the teapot emitted whistling sounds. "Let's think about it." She turned to Susanna. "Will you have a cup of tea with me?"

Though Susanna would have preferred coffee, she was agreeable to tea for fear of offending her hostess. "I don't mind, thank you."

Alida emptied a vile of potent barbiturates into the empty cup, after which she placed the tea sac into the scolding water. All blended evenly and without a trace of odor or hue. She handed Susanna the cup, taking one herself, and both drank the beverage while chatting on. Alida observed her guest for a while. Susanna's eyelids were becoming gradually heavier. Her arm hung limply to her side, and her knees became weak and rubbery. At last, she was unable to sit erect and slumped onto the edge of the table.

Alida helped Susanna to her feet. "Come, my dear Susanna. We must go." She said and led the passive woman to her car in the parking lot. No one saw them leaving. Besides, no one would question the two of them being together at that early hour of the day. With the strength of determination rather than an ordinary physical force, Alida placed her victim inside the passenger seat.

She was quickly behind the wheel, and it had taken them less than half an hour to reach the small pond near the lakeshore.

It was there that the most difficult task awaited the former ballerina. She virtually carried the now limp body of the dazed Susanna to the abandoned boat house. There being no one present at that time, Alida placed Susanna in one of the rental boats. She returned briefly to her car to fetch the briefcase full of Misha's research material. It also contained a pair of Susanna's pantyhose and the plastic envelope containing the daily prayers, all items the latter had left in their apartment among other negligible belongings.

Alida proceeded to paddle the boat onto the deep of the lake. There, she tied the briefcase to both ankles of the soundlessly asleep Susanna. Alida's powerful hands encircled her victim's slender throat and her piano trained fingers placed enormous pressure on the carotid arteries. She could feel the great arteries pulsate through the silkiness of the gloves. As if wakened by the sudden threat to her life, the dazed victim responded faintly as she tried to push away her assailant. She did not succeed and soon exhaled her last breath of life. With the energy of purpose, Alida tossed the briefcase into the water, and while it weighed down the side of the boat slightly, she pushed her hapless victim after the weight into the deep Alida watched them disappear into the murky water. She waited the customary 15 minutes for the body to float to the surface. It didn't, and she was satisfied with a job well done.

Alida paddled the boat to the shore without looking back. Quickly in her car, undetected, she was in her kitchen sipping coffee before anyone was able to miss her...

It was time to return to the courtroom. Heavy hearted, Misha followed his attorney to the defendant's table. He felt all eyes on him throughout the entire afternoon. The scenario he had dreamed up of an alleged perpetrator had not left his thought, and he realized soon that it could be attributed to almost anyone.

Pedro Pamies was Misha's character witness. Anton had intended to call on some more of Misha's colleagues as friendly references when the usual name identification has been completed, Anton proceeded with the interrogation.

"How long have you known the defendant?"

"Ever since he had arrived in the US," Pedro replied.

"Have you ever had reason to doubt his integrity?"

"Object to this line of questioning, your Honor." The prosecutor interjected. "Defense is coaching the witness."

"Just trying to get a line on the defendant's character, your Honor," Anton responded. "After all, he is on trial for allegedly committing a violent crime."

"I'll overrule." The judge declared. "Counsel may continue."

"Thank you, your Honor." A slight grimace appeared on Anton's face, as if in reaction to his first, if only small victory over the objections of the prosecution.

"And, professor, would you say the defendant was inclined to frequent bouts of violent temper?" Anton played carefully with his words. He stepped up to the balustrade separating the jury from the courtroom floor. He relaxed both his hands upon the polished wood. His upper body leaned over the balustrade as he continued to keep eye contact with the jurors while he queried Pedro. "Do you consider the defendant, Dr. Misha Winograd capable of committing the act of which he stands indicted?" Even before responding to Anton's question, Pedro shook his head in negation.

"Object! Leading the witness!" The prosecutor almost shouted.

"I withdraw the question," Anton responded quickly, although the jury has been able meanwhile to read the expression of denial in Pedro's face and study his body language. "Let me rephrase: Do you believe Misha Winograd murdered Susanna Flossberg?"

"Objection! Your Honor!" The prosecutor jumped up from his seat.

"I withdraw the question." Anton quickly defused the situation, and before he could dismiss his witness, the jury saw a stunned Pedro shake his head in forceful negation to the lawyer's question. "No more questions." Anton returned to his seat.

"Prosecution may cross-examine." The judge said.

"I have only one question, your Honor," the prosecution announced.

"Go ahead, counselor." The judge nodded.

"Dr. Pamies, are you by profession a psychiatrist?"

"No, Sir, I'm a professor of literature." Pedro replied.

"Thank you, no further questions." The prosecutor regarded the jury with that meaningful look of confidence that could only be taken one way. He had proven that Pedro's viewpoint was that of a lay person much like their own would be, and should not be construed to render important expert testimony. It was now the prosecution's turn to produce the next witness. The prosecutor, a seasoned trial lawyer, knew the significance of diminishing credibility. He handed the bailiff a note with the next witness's name on it.

"Miss Xin Xin Lee," the bailiff called into the gallery. She stood up, and for the second time the audience allowed itself a murmur of surprise. There was silence before the judge could admonish. Xin Xin wore a stunning Oriental dress that complemented her native beauty. Its satin sheen was a perfect fit. The colorful material enveloped her shapely body. It was in stark contrast to her alabaster skin. She walked slowly toward the jury stand, and all eyes were on her shapely legs and the graceful sway of her exterior. No telling how many men in the audience had wished they could possess this exquisite woman. Misha alone could tell the passion of fear mixed with envy and hate in the eyes of the women present. By the time Xin Xin had reached the witness stand, everyone was able to form a strong, though biased opinion about her worth as a witness for the prosecution.

Misha's heart leaped to his throat. His eyes focused on Alida's face, and he knew what was going through her mind. "What's she doing here?" He asked his lawyer with an anxiety bordering on hysterics. Anton placed his hand on Misha's trembling shoulder in an attempt to quiet him.

"It was expected, Misha." He whispered. "The prosecution will dredge out as many of your extra-marital affairs as possible to show what an immoral rake you really are." He paused. "And it will be our task to repair the damage they may have done. That's the name of the game, Misha." He smiled with that reassuring smile of his profession, and Misha leaned back in his chair somewhat calmed. Following the introductory remarks, the prosecution drilled Xin Xin with the perseverance of a pit bull. Finally, he had reached the salient issue of her affair with Misha.

"How would you describe your relationship with the defendant?"

"What do you mean, Sir, by relationship?" She asked.

"You know, was it casual? Intense?" The prosecutor indicated he sought some specifics.

"Oh, intense, very intense!" Xin Xin assured the court. Some sporadic giggling resounded from the back of the gallery. The judge tapped his gavel. Voices silenced. Misha glanced back at Alida who sat rigidly in her chair. He was unable to read the expression in her eyes, as they were turned away from him. But he had seen her assume this rigid state before, and he now felt a heavy weight in the pit of his stomach. He readied his response to the dark foreboding of things to come. The prosecutor resumed his interrogation.

"Did you know Mr. Winograd was a married man during your relationship?" Misha was brought back to reality by the prosecutor's question.

"Of course, I did." She responded with that mischievous smile of hers. "We were candid with each other. Isn't that the first rule of any relationship?" She asked.

The prosecutor disregarded Xin Xin's question. Now Misha tried to read the reaction of the jury to this turn of events. The men and women charged with the responsibility of passing judgment on his guilt or innocence sat in their seats quasi expressionless. Inasmuch as he had considered himself to be a good judge of human character, he was baffled by the inscrutability of the jurors' behavior.

"And it didn't bother you in the least to..." the prosecutor searched for the proper expression, "...sleep with the defendant?"

"Oh, no, not the least bit, your Honor," Xin Xin responded in the direction of the judge. "And it didn't bother him either," she continued, "we had awesome sex together." Once again, there could be heard soft giggles in the audience, followed by the rapping of the judge's gavel.

"There will be silence in the courtroom!" The judge declared, "else we shall vacate the courtroom!" Silence ensued.

"Did you continue your relationship with the defendant after the arrival of the deceased, Ms. Flossberg?" The prosecutor asked.

"Yes, off and on, we would...uh...have sex..." Misha felt the lid of the coffin closing over him and he heard the hammering of the nails. How could she? He thought silently. Why was she doing this to him? Who was behind it? Questions crowded his busy brain, but he was unable to determine her purpose. Did someone put her up to this?

"Your witness." The prosecutor yielded to the defense.

"Now, Ms Lee," Anton began slowly, "did the defendant force himself on you at any time?"

"No, he didn't."

"Then, it was simply consensual sex between two adults, wasn't it?"

"Well, yes...it was." Xin Xin hesitated, unable to determine where Anton was leading with his questions.

"Consensual or not," the attorney went on, "does it make it less adulterous, does it?"

The question stunned Xin Xin momentarily. "Well, if you put it this way, Sir, it doesn't." She lowered her eyes to avoid his.

"In fact, you were his student. And wasn't it you who seduced the defendant, Dr. Winograd?" Anton asked. "Did you not pursue him with the intent to seduce the man?" He paused briefly. "As you have done quite often with others," he added marginally.

For a brief moment Xin Xin sat silent, the smile gone from her eyes. As if reaching an important decision, she looked at Misha, then at Anton, to whom she directed her response: "Well, it's hard to tell who was after whom. All I can say is that each of us…" she hesitated briefly, "well, we both did what came naturally. There's no need to speculate on who was first to make the move on the other." This time there was complete silence. Was it because of the judge's threat or the seriousness of her response, nobody knew. Fact was, Anton had proven his point. Misha would not be portrayed as a womanizer. He was as vulnerable to a beautiful woman's seductive charms as the next man. There were five men on the jury. Any one of them could hang the jury merely out of empathy for the defendant. Misha let out a sigh of relief for the first time since the trial had begun. One annoying boulder has been lifted from his shoulders. How many more were there to be removed?

Misha has never been a sentimentalist who would gush over any of his many conquests. Clearly, his only interest and fascination in the pursuit lay in the sexual act. He attributed his successes to his seduction techniques and an inherent love and romantic triggering device to which women were genetically programmed. That powerful code behavior removed their resistance to the point of following the seducer's plan willingly. Always searching for new encounters, he would lose interest in partners who had not provided sensations unaccounted for in his previous "amorous" trysts. Oftentimes, Misha would seek satisfaction not in the act itself but in visual and tactile experience. He was fascinated by the contours of a woman's body when he ran his fingers greedily up and down the dune-like mounds until they met with the irresistible texture of her sparsely-haired pinkish shaft. He lingered on its warmth for a moment before allowing for a deeper probe than the extended digits of the hand.

He was awakened from his rather pleasant reverie by the sound of the gavel issuing the terse indication of recess.

The court recessed until the next morning. "Let's take a walk," Misha suggested. Anton nodded. They walked together through the well groomed municipal park. At first, each one was deepened in his own thoughts. The afternoon air was pleasant, sunny but cool. The trees were still in full foliage, and the multicolored flowers gave out a pleasant scent, which was carried aloft by a slight breeze. In a few days, fall would arrive, and a multitude of golden and rusty-brown leaves would cover the streets. Winter would follow in its severity, though it offered a welcome respite until the arrival of spring, the time of renewal. Misha mused, as he contemplated life's ordinary cycles. Would he, too, be given another chance? Soon, the silence was broken. Anton was first to speak.

"You're a good man, Misha," he spoke softly. "I'm not sure I'd have held up under pressure like you did." Misha was invigorated from root to leaf by the lawyer's statement. "Wish it were all I will have to endure," Misha barely moved his lips.

"So do I." Anton gripped Misha's shoulder in a friendly gesture. "So do I." He repeated. "But so far we have only touched the tip of the iceberg in presenting witnesses." He paused to reflect. "I'm sure prosecution will put your ex on the witness stand..."

"...oh, no," Misha interrupted. "She'll break down, I'm sure."

"Still and all, they'll do it, and we can't prevent it from happening." Anton's voice expressed sadness, for he was contemplating an attorney's conflict of interest when it came to represent two opposing parties. After all, Alida was still his client's spouse and, at the same time a prosecution witness.

Needless to say, it was a restless night for Misha. During the intervals of sleep, he saw repeatedly the vision of his biological father Motele, as he had seen him on his visit to Poland. At first, he was unable to determine the nature of the strange language in which Motele addressed him. Was it Polish? Misha strained his ears. It wasn't. He listened again. The sounds seemed almost German, yes; it was German with a slight nuance that transformed it into Yiddish. Motele must have grown weary of the *Führer's* harsh tongue and took refuge to the jargon. Misha had soon gotten accustomed to its peculiar sound and understood what the hated man said.

"*You're in a bad situation, my son.*" *Motele said.* "*I know how hard it is for you to face your accusers. I was there once, you know.*"

"*Don't you compare your murderous acts to the false accusations I'm facing!*" *Misha shouted at the hated image.*

"*Now, now, son, you shouldn't lose your composure so easily,*" *Motele grimaced, intending it for a smile.* "*I can see you are following in your father's footsteps, temper and all.*" *Motele chuckled nervously.*

"*Don't flatter yourself. A murderer I'm not.*" *Misha assured him.*

"*Don't be so bitter, Misha, and stop hating with such a great passion.*" *Motele cautioned him.* "*It can only harm you in the long run.*"

"*Look at who is moralizing,*" *Misha mocked the old man.* "*Wish you'd get out of my life for good.*"

"*If I knew you meant it, I'd leave you in a heartbeat.*" *Motele said.*

"*Yes, you would,*" *Misha said bitterly,* "*if you only had one.*"

"*I'm leaving, son,*" *Motele's image faded from Misha's view,* "*but I'll watch from there.*" *The voice came from a distance now.* "*It's my legacy, and you will carry it with you whether you like it or not...*"

"*No! I won't! I won't redeem you! Damn you! You must pay the price to cleanse your dark soul...!*"

Misha woke with a start; his body shook uncontrollably, small drops of cold sweat filtered down from his forehead to moisten his cheeks as it traveled to his chest. He glanced at the clock on the dresser. It was almost 4:30 a.m., and he didn't feel like sleeping. He got up, poured himself a strong cup of coffee and picked up the book which lay open on his desk. It was Oswald

Spengler's monumental work, the two volumes of *Der Untergang des Abendlandes*, (The Decline of the West). It had struck him with a sudden horror that he hadn't read at all during the months of waiting for the trial to begin. And he remembered that he was in the midst of an exciting discussion in his class dealing with the History of Civilization at the time of his incarceration.

The chapter he hadn't finished reading dealt with the advent of decadence in the New World. Spengler viewed it as the ninth cycle, the last cycle of a vanishing Western world. "What a pity." He could hear the author sigh. "And only an infant compared to her predecessors." Now it was Misha's turn to let out a moribund sound from the depth of his inards. He, too, was a true son of that vanishing, decadent, culture. And, as such, he was not to be considered an anomaly by acting in concert with its dictates. No man, he thought, can live unscathed in such circumstances. Following the erstwhile, long forgotten, moral and ethical codex would truly be an anomaly. How could the artificial decorum of society expect him to be a paragon of virtue when his character was forged in his whore/mother's womb and his derelict father's skewed mindset? Misha agonized silently.

Are we truly doomed? He deliberated silently. Is my own behavior a sampling of the decline Spengler had envisioned so long ago? He had seen as the salient cause of that gradual decline in society's abuses of the aged and the handicapped; its worship of physical prowess, an inherent infatuation with entertainment as perceived in "gladiatorial" performance; and the rebellion of the young against all traditional convention as well as a gross neglect of education's rigors. Why wasn't I able to see the signposts of this great turmoil in the making? He wondered. Perhaps because I was also blind to my own transgressions as well as of those of my errant parents? He reasoned.

Misha was unable to shake the image of his father's specter during the ensuing trial days. That mocking, defiant person kept on appearing in his mind's eye during restless sleep and in waking hours. He thought, at times, it was his own madness that had placed that demon inside him. Was it a sign of an awakening moral consciousness in a person hitherto immune to things decent? He was tormented by these and countless other questions.

Here he was once again—as so many times in the past in his young life—betrayed by his inability to judge human character and values. There must have been a deep psychological necessity which drove Misha to follow this course. He saw only now the full extent of that betrayal as evidenced by the testimonies of those who he had counted on being merciful. They compromised their promises and voided their loyalty. At last, they threw off the mask of sincerity.

What was left him was now his indomitable faith in justice and the courage to pursue it. He was imbued with a flaming conviction of *his* truth and the victory of his cause. Yet he was somehow doubtful even then whether he would be given a chance to seek and find the answer to the question he so passionately posed: "Why would anyone want to pin on him the title of *murderer?* And another one: "What had they to gain from it?"

There had been much deceit and lies expressed in an attempt to spare his feelings in an attempt to break gently the news of the impending arrival of a first degree murder verdict. He was dazed and mentally paralyzed by the sheer treachery of his alleged friends. Befogged and bewildered, forbidden by routine penitentiary regimen to speak without being first spoken to, Misha was like some great mastiff muzzled and chained, subjected to the incessant yapping of a large and unfettered terrier. He had lost momentarily all initiative to free himself. He spent his idle days and sleepless nights clearly out of touch with reality and thoroughly downcast.

# 26.

"THE COURT CALLS Patrick O'Malley to the witness stand," the prosecutor announced. Patrick sat in the front row of the gallery, ready to oblige. He rose from his seat, and with slow but firm steps, followed the bailiff to the stand. Standing, he touched the Bible with the left and raised the other hand high. "Do you swear to tell the truth and nothing but the truth?" The Bailiff asked. "I do." The witness replied. He sat down in the witness chair, adjusted the mike closer to his face, and confidently regarded the prosecutor and the entire courtroom with a slight, self-confident, smirk playing at the corners of his mouth. In the front row sat some of the most prominent leaders of the academic community. Patrick seemed to enjoy his role as a witness, being the focus of everyone's attention. "State your name, please." The prosecutor instructed. With a clear, loud voice, Patrick responded for all to hear:

"John Patrick O'Malley Ph.D." He paused for effect. "Everyone calls me Pat for short." He added.

"You're a colleague of the defendant?"

"That I am." Patrick replied.

"What is your field of expertise?" The prosecutor asked.

"Anthropology."

"Hence you and Dr. Winograd are not members of the same section or, as you might call it, department. Am I correct?"

"Indeed, you are." Patrick replied with a nod.

"Have you known the defendant for a long period of time?"

"I have. Since his arrival at the university in the fall of 1966."

"To your knowledge, Dr. O'Malley, was the defendant often taken to fits of violence?" The prosecutor asked.

"Well, um, not really..." Patrick hedged, "Misha was fairly... um...how shall I put it...in control." He hesitated briefly.

"But, on occasions, he was capable of severe fits of temper. Wasn't he?" The prosecutor asked.

"Objection!" Anton intoned in the judge's direction. "Prosecution leads witness to speculate."

"We are trying to determine character, your Honor," the prosecutor defended his line of questioning.

"I'll let it go this time," the judge said, "but see to it that you arrive at some results quickly." He instructed the interrogator.

"Thank you, your Honor;" the prosecutor acknowledged the judge's admonition, "I'll be brief." He turned toward Patrick. "You were saying, the defendant was known to have his moments of uncontrollable anger, yes?"

"That is a fact, Sir." Patrick agreed without hesitation.

"No further questions." The prosecutor relinquished the witness.

"You may question the witness," the judge nodded toward Anton.

"Thank you, your Honor." Anton acknowledged the judge's directive. He turned toward Patrick. "Now, Dr. O'Malley, as you have earlier stated, you were quite friendly with the defendant... and for a great length of time, at that. Am I correct?"

"True, we were good friends." Patrick replied.

"By saying 'were,' are you implying that you no longer are?" Anton asked the witness.

"Well, yes...no...I'm..." Patrick hedged.

"Which is it? Yes or no?" Anton feigned impatience.

"Not as close as we once were, I might say." Patrick's cheeks reddened. "At some point, our friendship cooled."

"And what was that point?" Anton pursued his line of questioning.

"Well, what with our heavy share of teaching and research work, it got so we weren't able to keep company as often as we had in the past."

"And, to your knowledge, that was the only reason?" Anton asked.

"Yes, so far as I know." Patrick replied in a whisper.

"Could you speak into the mike, Dr. O'Malley?" Anton inquired, "I doubt the jury was able to hear you.

"Yes, it was because of our enormous workload that we were not able to see one another as often as we would have wished." Patrick affirmed in one breath.

"Dr. O'Malley, may I caution you, you're still under oath." Anton reminded the witness. "Was there anything else you might remember that has caused you to distance yourself from Dr. Winograd?"

"Well...no...um...I can't tell there was..." Patrick was hesitant.

"May I refresh your memory, Dr. O'Malley?" Anton asked.

"If you wish." Patrick avoided the lawyer's eyes.

"Wasn't it, in fact, your involvement with the defendant's girlfriend, one Ms. Xin Xin Lee?"

"Uh? Well...I don't know about that." Patrick was defensive. "Dr. Winograd had terminated his relationship with the person in question long before my involvement with her."

"In fact," Anton pressed, "the defendant made his closure with the lady *after*, not before you had become involved with her romantically? Isn't that so, doctor?" Anton placed emphasis on the word "after."

"I may have temporarily forgotten the sequence of circumstances relating to the relationship in question." Patrick betrayed for the first time some strange form of apprehension. He lowered his eyes so as to avoid eye contact with those inquisitive eyes directed at him. Blood had reached his temples, as was evident in the swelling of the temporal veins.

"Are there any other details or facts you may have forgotten, doctor?"

"I don't think so, Sir." Patrick took his eyes off the floor and let them rest for a moment on the jury, then Misha and, finally he looked straight in Alida's direction.

"Isn't it true you've been a rival of the defendant where women are concerned?" Anton paused, but continued before Patrick was able to respond. "And wasn't Ms. Lee up to her ears in love with you even before she had left your good friend, Dr. Winograd?"

"That's absolutely false." Patrick nearly rose from his seat.

"We are not in a classroom setting, Dr. O'Malley, playing 'true' or 'false' charades." Anton admonished the witness. "This is a court of law and, may I remind you that you are testifying under oath." Anton's eyes now penetrated into the depth of Patrick's, and the latter lowered his to the floor again.

"Well, uh, perhaps I am slightly off with the chronology of events here," he said in a whisper, but audible enough for the listeners.

"Furthermore, Dr. O'Malley, didn't you, in fact, gain favor with the diseased, Susanna Flossberg, even before she had begun work at your department?" Misha was startled by this latest revelation. He had not suspected Patrick's involvement with Susanna. His eyes bored holes into Patrick's skull, but the latter relented and let his eyes wonder all over the courtroom. "I couldn't hear your reply, doctor." Anton insisted, but Patrick drifted off into a recapitulation of recent events...

...From the moment they had met aloft the trans-Atlantic flight, Patrick was taken with Susanna's demeanor. When he had told her "call on me whenever you'll need me," he meant it literally. It wasn't one of those politically correct invitations that weren't missed when unrealized. He wanted her to call on him; more than that, he wanted her. She occupied his thoughts when he was in company or alone; between waking and sleeping.

Problem was, once again, he coveted someone who was committed to his friend and colleague Misha.

Susanna was not to become another temporary conquest; like the brief affair he had engaged in with Xin Xin. The latter he had considered just a good conquest. A relationship that was basically physical. Funny, he even pronounced her name Sin Sin. That made him chuckle, as he relished the idea surreptitiously. His feelings for her were vague, for he knew they had nothing in common, and he felt uneasy about their relationship. But when he had at last slept with the beautiful Asian, he realized that, after all, sex was just, well, sex. The passion of the conquest embellished at first the physical enjoyment, but that done, the act appeared mechanical and desensitized to mere subtleties. He concluded with absolute certainty that to relish the act of sexual fulfillment, one ingredient is absolutely necessary in a relationship; and that is love.

From the moment he saw Susanna, Patrick imagined himself in love with her inner beauty. Her body was secondary. That, he reasoned, would come in due time. He would do whatever necessary to posses her completely. Patrick was not one to waste time in idle talk. What about Misha? To hell with Misha. He was incapable to love anyone. He had told him so himself. And Patrick was glad to have learned Misha's cardinal rule: "Don't ever tell anyone you love them when they did not first declared their love for you." Besides, Patrick reasoned, Misha wouldn't notice the loss.

It seemed a coincidence they had met at the shopping mall. Susanna was alone, and Patrick mustered all of his courage to approach her. "What a nice surprise!" He exclaimed. At first, she appeared distant and wanted to dismiss him with a slight nod. But he was undeterred by her indifference. "Is that a way one greets an old friend?" He asked, smiling.

"More like a casual acquaintance." She corrected him.

"I was afraid you'd say that. Am I to be blamed for this insignificant technical discrepancy?" He flirted.

"Please, Dr. O'Malley, I must be going." She walked past him, and he followed her into one of the department stores. She was visibly embarrassed but couldn't help feeling flattered. Misha had been busy lately with his research. He spent his evening hours in his library carrel behind the stacks, and she rarely got to see him. She felt neglected, and the attention she was presently receiving was reassuring.

"Why so formal?" He smiled broadly. "We were on first name terms, if you recall?" He reached out and touched her hand. "Let me buy you a drink."

"Oh, I wouldn't think of it," she resisted, "it's much too early for that." Her subconscious dictated a bit less coyness.

"Is it too early in the day or in our relationship?" He asked with a roguish wink.

"Both." She answered tersely.

"Then, perhaps, a soda will do for now?" His tall frame towered over her, though she was considered quite tall herself at her six feet plus on high heels.

"All right, a soda," she said, "I did work up a thirst walking the mall."

They sat opposite each other in an intimate corner booth. Soon, each told the other precisely what had been happening in their lives during the past months. From a mere narrative, confidence grew and conversation was transformed into confessional confidentiality. Asking "May I?" he sat down next to her and placed his arm round her shoulder. She did not protest. On the contrary, it seemed she had welcomed it and it emboldened him.

"I regret few things of my past," he carried on, "but I will mostly regret not having been with you all this time…to help." He added quickly.

She smiled embarrassed, she knew he was coming on to her strongly, but she did nothing to stop him. She accepted his advances in grateful silence. It felt good to be wanted again. The element of random adoration was missing in her life with Misha. Missing was also a sense of truly belonging.

"Do you...really... ...?" She asked shyly.

"How can you doubt it?" He asked, and he gave her the all adoring look none of his past conquests were able to resist. Patrick seemed to be privy to some magical, fail-safe scientific method that triggered love and romance in women. It worked for him every time because, he figured, women were genetically programmed hot-wired to fall for a man if he was familiar with their triggering devices. Patrick knew them all too well.

He chuckled inwardly at the mere thought that women were helpless against his treacherous behavior. Even when they resisted at first, their resistance soon crumbled. They would get moist and began to fantasize about him. Susanna was no exception to his rule. Simply said, his technique was based on the assumption that women responded to his advances due to the millions of years of biological gene behavior. They just could not help themselves in his presence.

"I've been alone and I miss good company. It's a miserable feeling." He confessed his loneliness to her. It had worked before, and he knew from experience women had a weak spot in their hearts toward the 'lonely' and 'helpless' guy. It was part of his ruse. From that moment on, her resolve to caution melted away and she had placed herself at his mercy without even knowing why.

"I must see you very soon," he said with an urgency of a caring person in the tone of his voice.

"I don't know if I can." Susanna hesitated. "He might notice." They had now become co-conspirators, and Patrick rushed to ensure his success.

"I wouldn't worry about that small detail," he assured her, "Misha's too busy doing his thing to notice others, even those around him." He knew right away that he spoke disparagingly about his rival, a strategy unacceptable as a rule, but it was too late. She noticed his sudden hesitancy and grew suspicious. His hand reached to her knee, the fingers squeezed slightly, disarming her with that gesture of intimacy she had craved vainly in her relationship with Misha.

"I'll think about it," she promised.

"You know where you can reach me, Susanna." He squeezed her hand gently. She did not withdraw.

"Thank you, Patrick," she addressed him informally for the first time that evening. He was pleased.

"Tomorrow, then?" He pressed.

"Tomorrow...uh...I guess..." she said hesitatingly. She held out her hand and he kissed it gallantly. She withdrew it quickly, afraid someone might notice, and left the premises.

"By the way, I have a job opportunity for you," Patrick couldn't contain his joy in telling Susanna about the opening for the secretarial position at his department.

"Misha won't like that, I'm afraid." She said sadly. "You know how he feels about you."

"Never mind Misha," blood rushed to Patrick's temples, "make the decisions concerning your own life without his input." He feigned anger. She hasn't seen Patrick in this light before, even in her imaginings about him.

"I'll see...maybe...I should work..." she thought aloud.

"Of course, you ought to have a job," he assured her. "Think of what it would mean for you and little Rudi," he struck a sensitive cord by placing Rudi into the picture. "Think of yourself as an independent woman, Susanna. Assert yourself."

"I've been hesitant for too long," she whispered, "to take a risk in seeking emancipation."

"Sooner or later, you'll have to make that decision," Patrick argued, "besides I haven't seen him proposing marriage lately." He knew how to hit low.

Patrick's last argument was convincing. On her part, she had been waiting for Misha to make up his mind about their status.

She feared to broach him about the promises of marriage he had made in all those letters he'd written to her. All that had changed after her arrival to the US. Misha found ways to invent novel excuses. Sometimes it was the simple question of inappropriate timing: "It's too early, dear." And frequently, it was: "Alida isn't ready for separation, maybe even to sign a divorce decree. Wish I'd know how to convince her to the contrary." Another time he had used an even more incomprehensible alibi: "It'll be a messy affair, what with Alida contesting on the basis of adultery."

Things were going to be different now. She was determined to sound an ultimatum, something she had dreaded, as one would in a situation without given alternatives. She knew Misha didn't like for her to surprise him at the office, but she took the chance. He was with a student, and Susanna waited for the secretary to announce her. It took only a few moments, and a pretty coed emerged from Misha's office. With a brief "sorry" and a smile toward Susanna, the girl discretely departed. Susanna regarded her with hidden envy. Her walking bounce reminded her of those university days when her youthful gait could attract the whistles of her male colleagues.

"In a way, I'm glad you stopped by, my dear," Misha seemed cordial.

"Oh?" She was somewhat astonished at his cordiality, though she knew how annoyed he has been with her occasional surprise visits.

"I meant to see you about this urgent matter before, but, somehow, you haven't been readily available." She prefaced the purpose of her visit.

"I'm available and attentive right now." He motioned her to sit. "And I also have something to share with you." He paused. "You go first."

"Well, Misha, I have been idle long enough, more like bored, and I decided to get a job." She blurted it all out rapidly, in one sentence, afraid she would lack the courage if she hesitated. He looked at her for a long while.

"Sure it was your very own idea?" His skepticism had in its very tone of voice a flair of annoyance. But she was determined not to show her discomfort to him. She begrudged him his small victory.

"What could you mean by that?" She wasn't going to let him bait her into submission, as was his way on many occasions.

"Well? Did anyone in particular help you on the way?" He smiled.

"Not really." She showed uncommon composure. "I feel so inert with nothing to do but wait for you all my days and attend to domestic chores."

"What else do you imagine?" He was edgy, challenging. "You expect me to help with the chores perhaps?"

"Not really, Misha, I just want to earn my own support for now," she avoided his inquiring eyes.

"Well, good," he saw the opportunity to reveal his surprise to her. "In a way, I'm glad you came up with the idea of independence, my dear." He paused. "It so happens that Alida wants you look for a place and move out as soon as possible. She seems to think that you have overstayed your welcome."

"Even after what had happened the other night? The threesome?" Susanna was surprised by Alida's sudden demand.

"That was a mistake, she says," Misha smiled sadly. "She wants to avoid repetition." He hesitated. "Besides, Alida wants a baby of her own."

"But it was she who had convinced you to make me come to the US in the first place," Susanna argued unabated; "doesn't she acknowledge that? Is she capable of bearing a child? It's contrary to what you had told me, Misha."

"Some inner voice had told her she could expect motherhood again."

"She must believe in miracles," Susanna grinned.

"She had a change of mind. She says she's entitled. She wants to try." Misha replied. "And we shouldn't underestimate the power of faith." Misha suddenly grew pensive. "This may have been the breakthrough of the greatest magnitude for Alida." He smiled. "Only time will reveal the consequences of her decision." Susanna wanted to interrupt, but he wouldn't let her into his musings. "I've tried to dissuade her, but I failed, and I'm so terribly sorry. She's resolute in her demand." Misha sighed with great relief, as if a major burden had been lifted from his shoulders. Susanna knew not to argue her case. It would be to no avail, for Misha had broken under pressure. He had run out of excuses. None of them would work, he knew.

Alida's demand struck Susanna like a bolt of lightning. She winced under the burden of its suddenness and apparent illogic. Why would the woman who had invited her to become her husband's concubine no longer tolerate hers and her son's presence under the same roof with her? She questioned in silence.

Suddenly, resolute, she rose to leave and addressed Misha: "Surely, she'll give us a couple of days to hunt for an apartment, won't she?"

"I've thought of that already and made some inquiries with the school's housing department." He assured her. "We'll take a look at some of the vacancies they have. Okay?" Misha's anxiety was evident.

"I'd rather do it myself, if you don't mind." She wouldn't let him off the proverbial hook so easily and enjoyed seeing him cringe under stress." I'll be out of Alida's place as soon as I find something to our liking." She left him open-mouthed in his puzzlement at finding her so fearless and resolute. Could there be more to her self-assertiveness than met the eye? Suspicion and sudden feelings of jealousy (none that he would ever admit to himself), entered his soul.

The following day, Susanna found a small place in the graduate apartment facility. It was ideal for the two of them. Rudi had meanwhile learned not to ask too many questions. He'd realized in time that even though he would ask, answers weren't forthcoming. He helped with the chores of packing.

As it turned out, Patrick made good on his promise. He was there for her and the boy, helpful in their hour of need. He consoled her, helped her find useful employment, and became a daily companion. Soon their relationship had become nocturnal, *sans* sexual activity. He was not one to make his amorous progress too quickly. On occasions, he drove Rudi to school. The boy grew accustomed to his mother's new boyfriend. He even grew to like Patrick in his attempt to please his mother and called him "Uncle Pat."

Soon, evening visits had turned into nightly stayovers; with frequent sex. Rudi spent some sleepless nights at first. He would listen to the lovers' moans, sighs, and whispers that carried through the fragile wall of his room. He would wake up worn and sleepy the next morning. He didn't complain. It wasn't in his nature to complain. Besides, boyfriends have come and gone in the past. He was sure this one would be history soon as well. He had learned to be patient beyond his age and allow time to work its magic. But he was by now an observant young man. Watching his mother's facial expression had become an art. He was able to sense her moments of happiness and those of sadness. She was happy with an eager anticipation of Patrick's visitations. She seemed lost in his absence.

Back to the courtroom.

"You haven't answered my question, Dr. O'Malley." Anton's high-pitched voice brought Patrick back to reality.

"Would you mind repeating it?" Patrick played for time.

"Were you having an affair with the deceased Ms. Flossberg?"

"Well...now...we were dear friends..." Patrick hesitated, "if you can call that as having an affair."

"Would you consider sleeping with the lady night after night as having an affair?" Anton addressed his question more to the jury than to the witness.

"Well...I...don't know about that..." Patrick loosened his tie and the first button of his shirt. His Adam's apple performed a rhythmic dance.

"May I inform you, doctor, that based on thorough investigation, my associates have established a precise time table of your visitations at the deceased's apartment. Give or take a night, you spent a minimum of five nights weekly with her." His mention of "associates" was an exaggeration, since he has not as yet hired a competent PI to aid him in his endeavor of defense. Anton's eyes searched the reaction of the jurors.

"Sure, I visited Ms. Flossberg on many occasions." Patrick regained his composure. "Does that mean I was having an affair? Can't a person have an ongoing friendship with another without getting romantically involved?" He caught Anton with the surprise question.

"Please, limit yourself to answers, doctor." Anton leafed through his notes for a long moment. "I will ask the questions."

Patrick hesitated. "God knows, I'm trying my best here."

"Leave God out of it, doctor," Anton was aware that the witness was playing the moral martyr for the benefit of the jury. He deliberated in silence. His next point better be a winner, else the momentum might well swing in favor of the good doctor. He knew.

"I didn't mean to offend anyone, counselor," Patrick added. He seemed to have realized he had gained the upper hand in the exchange.

"No offense taken," Anton said, "I, myself, am a God-fearing man." He smiled toward the jury box. Suddenly, he pivoted, his eyes peeled on the witness. He pronounced each word carefully: "There is still the unresolved matter of the autopsy..." He rifled through the paper folder in a manner of a man accustomed to think things out and present his case in a precise way.

"Autopsy?" Patrick asked.

"Yes, my investigator had brought the document to my attention just moments ago," Anton held up a letterhead stationery for the jury to see. "May I enter this document as exhibit 'A', your Honor?" The judge nodded, "so be it entered."

"Have you been made aware, Dr. O'Malley, of the deceased condition at the time she was murdered?"

"Murdered?" Patrick asked with an expression of horror on his face.

"Yes, murdered mercilessly, pregnant with child."

"Pregnant?" Once again, there was an expression of incredulity on the witness' face.

"You were not aware of Ms. Flossberg's condition, Dr. O'Malley?" Anton asked.

"Not in the least." Patrick replied.

"Not even that it might have been caused during all those nights of cohabitation and sex play?" Anton addressed his words to the jury.

"We were aware of the possibilities, and we took precautions." Patrick responded without flinching.

"What was your reaction when the deceased informed you about her delicate condition, doctor?" Anton pressed further.

"Your Honor," the prosecutor objected, "counsel is harassing the witness. Dr. O'Malley is not on trial here."

"Prosecution's objection is well taken," the judge remarked, "defense counsel will, hopefully, show where all this is leading." The judge said with a tone of reprimand.

"That I shall, your Honor," Anton smiled faintly, "in due time." He added, and then, as if on second thought, "you may cross-examine," he said, nodding toward the prosecution. "I reserve the right to recall witness."

"Thank you, no questions at this time," the prosecutor declined the offer. "Witness may step down," the judge addressed Patrick. "May I remind you, doctor, you are still under oath, available until the end of this trial?"

"I understand, your Honor." Patrick stepped out of the witness stand and walked over to the first row of the gallery, where he sat down two seats away from Alida. The judge rapped his gavel. "The court will recess for a brief lunch," he said, "we will resume at 1400 hours sharp." Everyone rose as the judge walked into his chambers.

The courtroom was filled to capacity even before it reconvened after lunch. There prevailed an atmosphere of suspense, as if everyone knew things were going to open up toward the approaching trial's end. Misha had no idea his trial was approaching its end. He had taken advantage of the court's recess to take a short nap. As he drifted into a deep slumber, he felt such an awesome chill all over his body as he'd never known before…

…His eyes fell open now, and he gazed into the face of death. *"Go away," he said to the dark shadow which hovered above him, "my time hasn't come as yet." The shadow distanced himself slowly from him, hesitant and silent, arms stretched out wide, as if to enfold Misha in an embrace.*

*"Please," Misha begged the strange figure before him that bore an uncanny resemblance to Motele, "I want to live, and I haven't begun yet." His halted, quivering voice broke into sobs. The great dark shadow hovered for what seemed an eternity but lasted mere mini seconds. A booming voice came to him from a great distance: "You've been given many chances, son, and you managed to bungle them all. Now, you might have run out of options altogether."*

*"One more, please. Give me one more chance." Misha pleaded.*

*"It's…it's not up to me…" A distant voice replied.*

*"For her sake, then," Misha wept, "for Blanche's sake, Father. Let me off the hook one more time."*

*The ghostly figure raised his hands to his face, as if to shield it from an unwanted intrusion. The shadow swayed to and fro and was as suddenly gone from Misha's sight as quickly as it had appeared.*

Misha rose from the couch with a start. He looked at his wristwatch. It was time to return to the courtroom. On the way there, he deliberated whether he would share his bizarre mid-day experience with his lawyer. He then decided against it. At best, it might be received by the uninitiated with justifiable skepticism. At worst, his sanity might be questioned.

# 27.

"KEEP YOUR COMPOSURE, Misha," Anton said with a nondescript smile. "This is the big day. We await testimony from Alida and your son, Rudi."

"Oh, my God!" Was all Misha was able to utter.

"No need to worry. Let's see what they've got to say." Anton was an expert in displaying artificial cheerfulness. Misha looked intensely at his lawyer, still unable to place complete confidence in the latter's courtroom skills. But there were no options left him. His entire body shook in horror, remembering the apparition's departing words.

From the moment she was called to the witness stand, Alida had shown the unease with which she had regarded the proceedings. She had always carried an intense dislike at having strangers intrude into what she considered her own intimate affair. In a court of law, personal matters come to be revealed in public, for all to see and hear. It reminded her of the title the great poet Baudelaire lent his candid, autobiographical tome of poetry. He called it *Mon Coeur mis a nu*. In English it meant more or less "My Heart Laid Bare." And Alida wasn't ready to lay her heart and soul bare, least of all in the public's view. The mere prospect of such occurrence caused her immeasurable anguish with the initial steps taken by the prosecution to establish the rudiments of her identity. Followed by the sacred oath, the prosecution proceeded with the routine of questioning:

"Mrs. Winograd, how long have you been married to the defendant?"

"As far as I know, I am still his wife." Alida responded.

"Let me rephrase the question, Mrs. Winograd." The prosecutor smiled at the puzzled Alida. "What I had meant to ask was about the state of your marriage. That is, how long have you carried on a proper marital relationship with the defendant, Dr. Winograd? I did not mean to imply that it is no longer in effect."

"Uh...I misunderstood...sorry..." Alida hesitated briefly. Then, as if she had reached an important decision, she sat up straight in her chair, looked the prosecutor squarely in the eyes, and responded: "We've had a good marriage...until...until..." Alida was close to tears.

"Until what?" The prosecutor pressed.

"Until my surgery...you know...radical hysterectomy, Sir."

"Why is that?"

"I...I...sort of..." Alida wiped her eyes with one of the tissues she carried in her purse, "...well, I distanced myself from all things physical." It was evident for all who were present that such confession had taken a great toll of Alida's emotions. She slumped in her chair once again, visibly a defeated person. The prosecutor allowed the pause to linger for Alida to compose herself. He then continued his probing.

"How do you mean that?" He asked. "Please explain."

"Well, I had no longer the desire for physical gratification. What with the doctor prescribed medication after my surgery and my mental state..."

"...What have you done then?" The prosecutor's line of questioning had assumed a personal nature.

"I...moved out of our shared bedroom." She answered.

"For how long?"

"As I recall, it was over a period of a year and a half."

"And during that year and a half you had no sex whatsoever with your husband? And you lived under the same roof all of that time?"

"No, we had no physical contact at all during that time. And, yes, we lived under the same roof all that time."

"You mean to say, that you felt no urgency for sexual gratification?" The prosecutor addressed his question at Alida while his eyes were directed at the two rows of jurors.

"No, I felt no need." Alida answered.

"In what manner did Dr. Winograd acquiesce to this arrangement?"

"Well, he has been known to look for extra-marital outlets," Alida hesitated then, after a brief pause, added, as if in passing, "even before my situation had called for it."

"Yes, I dare say he has." The prosecutor smiled triumphantly toward the jury. "No further questions, your Honor."

"Does the defense wish to cross examine?" The judge asked.

"Thank you, your Honor," Anton responded. "I shall only take a few minutes." He turned toward Alida. "Mrs. Winograd, you were aware of the relationship between your husband...uh...the defendant and the deceased, were you not?"

"Yes, indeed, I was."

"And you tolerated this relationship for quite some time, did you not?"

"I did so, for as long as it was at a distance."

"Explain what you mean by that, please."

"The deceased...uh...Susanna...was in Germany, and we were here in America. They were writing letters to one another and occasionally talking long distance. I did not think that was in any way harmful to our marriage."

"But, didn't you, in fact, throw fits of jealousy on occasions of having read some of the correspondence?" Anton was at his best, probing, taunting, and driving a point across.

"At times, I must admit." Alida paused. "It was only because..."

"Please, Mrs. Winograd, don't elaborate. Just answer my questions 'yes' or 'no'."

Alida went into a sudden coughing spell. With the tissue close to her lips, she murmured: "May I be excused for a few minutes, please?"

"Will the bailiff help the lady back to her seat?" The judge ordered. "And hand her a glass of water."

"Yes, your Honor," the bailiff complied. He led the coughing Alida back to her seat in the first row of the gallery. Moments after, he handed her the requested glass of iced water. Alida sipped the cold water slowly, and it seemed to have relieved the coughing spell.

"Recall your witness, please." The judge addressed Anton.

Back on the stand, Alida steadied herself in anticipation of some hard questions. Anton had taken advantage of the brief pause to study, once again, the list of interrogatives on his agenda. He was quite ready to refute the prosecution's foregone allegations.

"Now, Mrs. Winograd, let me remind you that you're still under oath," he said before commencing. Alida nodded compliantly. "Now, let's see, we were talking about the letters your husband had been receiving from Ms. Flossberg, the deceased, weren't we?"

"Yes, we were." Alida replied.

"And I had asked whether you've read those letters on occasions, right?" He pursued his line of questioning.

"I admitted having read them…" Alida paused briefly "…on few occasions, that is." She promptly added.

"On few occasions," Anton repeated, "on few occasions you've read those letters that weren't meant for your eyes. Is that right, Mrs. Winograd?" He paused. "Would you explain to the court how you've managed to *read* those letters written in the German language with which you are not familiar?"

"Yes, that is right, counselor," Alida responded with amazing coolness. "They weren't meant for me." She paused. "In Misha's absence, I persuaded a friend of ours at the university to translate them for me. There may have been some urgency in them, I figured."

Were you enraged?" Anton asked, and quickly added: "Do you suppose there might have been some inadvertent loss in translation?"

"No, I don't think so, being that the translator in question was a professor of German literature."

"So, anyway, did you resent these letters?"

"Yes, at first, I was appalled." Alida replied, eyes downcast.

"Why, only at first?" Anton asked.

"As time wore on, I realized I wasn't much good to Misha after all." She spoke softly, apologetically, now her eyes on the jury. "It was at that time I even suggested to my husband that he might send for his…his…" She was hesitant, choking, and unable to go on. Everyone in the courtroom was on the edge of their seat, aware of the inner struggle Alida was experiencing.

"Please continue, Mrs. Winograd." Anton urged. "You were saying?"

"I insisted that he send for Susanna and their son." Alida answered, and her voice was firm, without a trace of hesitancy.

"What was the purpose of this arrangement?" Anton probed.

"It was the only way I could stay married to my husband. The only way his needs would be satisfied." Alida explained. "I was of no practical use to Misha, my husband…uh…the defendant… after my surgery."

"So, you became the Biblical Sarah to your husband's Abraham, didn't you?" Anton addressed himself to Alida, though his eyes were now also directed at the jury.

"It was so, in a manner of speaking, yes." Alida replied.

"Did the arrangement work?"

"It did, for a while."

"You mean you've changed your mind? Or did they?" Anton asked.

"At one point, the relationship had become too strained…"

"Too strained? What do you mean by that?"

"Well, the apartment had become too small for the three of us in it."

"By too small, you mean..." Anton did not get a chance to continue.

"...I mean I could hear what was going on in their bedroom, and..."

"...You decided that you wanted to be a part of those goings on?" Anton was aiming at the central point of his interrogation, but the prosecution objected vigorously: "Your Honor, the counsel is harassing the witness. We see no purpose in this exchange at all. The witness is not on trial here."

"I will overrule at this time, but I'd like to see where this line of questioning is leading up to. And make it quick, counselor." The judge addressed Anton. The latter smiled triumphantly. "Yes, your Honor." He said. "I'm trying to establish a sequel of events whose purpose will become obvious." He turned toward Alida. She observed the exchange between prosecutor and judge quietly, unable to figure out its consequences. Anton's next question made it obvious.

"Was it the renewed desire for sexual gratification that made you change your mind regarding your husband's concubine, Mrs. Winograd?"

"I...I...don't know..." Alida was in tears once again, unable to answer the question put to her. "No further questions at this time." Anton returned to his seat. "We reserve the right to recall this witness."

"So noted," the judge responded to Anton's statement. "Does the prosecution wish to reexamine?"

"Not at this time, your Honor." The prosecutor said. "However, we wish to call a new witness." Anton looked puzzled. He stood up, looked around, and his eyes fell on Rudi's small figure. Was he to be next? Went through his mind. "Your Honor, may we approach the bench?" He addressed the judge. The latter nodded approval. Both attorneys approached, and the judge covered up the mike.

"Who is your next witness?" Anton asked the prosecutor.

"Of course, the deceased's son." The prosecutor replied.

"Why wasn't I informed?" Anton asked. "The boy isn't a material witness, is he?"

"On the contrary." The prosecutor smiled. "Quite material."

"Stop the haggling, both of you." The judge urged. "Let's get on with it. Hopefully, we can finalize the issue soon."

"As far as I'm concerned, it may go to the jury today." The prosecutor assured the judge.

"And you, counselor?" The judge addressed Anton.

"I have no quarrel with that, your Honor." Anton assured the judge.

"I should hope not," the judge said. "Let's get on with it." The two men returned to their places, and the bailiff asked Rudi to follow him to the witness stand. The boy's slender frame was in stark contrast with the adult world he had entered on that day. He seemed tranquil, though no one could have guessed the turmoil inside that vulnerable soul. Thoughts ran through his mind ranging from his secure childhood in the midst of family and friends to the time of his arrival among these strange people whose culture he was as yet unable to absorb.

Though he had matured beyond his age quite rapidly, the events he had witnessed in recent weeks had been too much of an emotional stress for him to comprehend. His mother had always been a question mark in his mind. Now, with her gone out of his life in a most unusual manner, he was more confused than ever about some of the things she had meant to him as a mom. The strange people around him since her death, and those weird questions they kept asking, seemed like an entirely different world than the one he had dreamed about and imagined for himself.

The prosecutor was choosing his words carefully, lest he alienate the youthful witness. Rudi sat silently, his eyes fixed on his interrogator. He said "I do," after being told to tell "the truth and nothing but the truth."

"Did you like the idea of coming to the US to live with your dad?" The prosecutor broke the ice by asking a general question. He knew full well the boy's opinion held little or no importance to the case.

"I was too young then to form an idea about that." Rudi said, and there was no visible emotion in his facial expression. "But I always obeyed my mom." A hushed admiration swept the courtroom.

"Uh...yes...I see," the prosecutor taxed his mind in search of a proper continuation. He smiled. "Can you tell me what you think of it now?" He was hopeful the boy understood the gist of the inquiry.

"All I know is that my mom would still be alive if we had stayed away in Germany where we belonged." Rudi responded to everyone's astonishment.

"Did your mom get along with your dad?"

"You mean him?" Rudi pointed at Misha.

"Yes...uh...your dad." The prosecutor repeated.

"Well, not always," Rudi paused, "they had their good times and their bad times."

"Like most people?"

"I don't really know," Rudi looked the prosecutor in the eye. "I can't speak for most people." Again a hushed murmur and occasional giggle swept through the gallery.

"How about fights? Did they fight a lot?"

"They had their share of fighting," Rudi answered.

"Did the fights ever become violent?"

"Objection!" Anton rose quickly from his seat. "The prosecution is leading the witness."

"We'll allow for now," the judge ruled. "And we hope counsel will show the relevance of this questioning."

"I shall, your Honor," the prosecutor smiled.

"Now, young man, you may answer the question," the judge instructed the boy.

"Yes, a few times dad would hit mom," Rudi answered. "He didn't hit her too hard, and he was sorry right after and apologized."

Misha listened to his son's testimony in disbelief. Now he really felt as if the lid of his coffin was being lowered on top of him, and his own son held the hammer and the nails. He looked at Anton, as if he'd wanted to read his chances in the lawyer's eyes. But there were no clues there. "What now?" Misha whispered.

"Patience," Anton smiled reassuringly.

"I'm at my own funeral, and you ask me to show patience." Misha whispered and paused briefly. "Please don't let me down;" he implored his lawyer, "I'd never before felt as dependent on your skill as I do now." Anton nodded.

"I understand your concern, Misha," Anton's lips barely moved, "and I don't intend to fail you now and as the case may develop."

"No further questions," the prosecutor's bass voice interrupted their exchange.

"You may step down, young man," the judge instructed Rudi. "We'll adjourn and resume at 2 p.m. tomorrow." The judge rapped her gavel. She rose and all in the courtroom did, too, at the bailiff's instruction: "all rise."

That night, Misha slept the uneasy sleep of those nearly condemned. He shook haltingly; a cold shiver of death's mantle enveloped him. "*Mamá! Mamá!*" He called out, but it was in vain. Instead of his mother's vision, the specter of his father appeared once again. "*Let your mother rest,*" Motele admonished, "*you've caused her enough grief already.*"

"*You're not the right person to preach to me about my mother's grief,*" Misha said bitterly.

"*Let us not argue about moot things, son,*" Motele was in a conciliatory mood, "*what I'm here for is to talk about your fate at the hands of this kangaroo court.*" He paused. Misha was frightened. How did the old man know? What did he mean by "*kangaroo court?*"

As if able to read his son's thoughts, Motele continued: *"You might as well know the whole truth. They've already decided your guilt or innocence. So you had better prepare yourself for the worst, just in case."* He couldn't refrain from a mischievous chuckle. Obviously, the monster has retained his dark sense of humor. Misha thought silently. *"Besides, should you receive the maximum sentence, it'll still be beneficial to you,"* Motele added as if on second thought. *"You may as well know, take it from one who's been there, if you haven't died, you'll never know what it means to be alive."* That said the shadow faded slowly from Misha's view. Not a moment too soon.

Misha was irritated at Motele's indifference toward his mother. He remembered well the anguish he had caused her with his absence. Even at the end of the war, it was Blanche who initiated the search, while Motele had already married for the second time and moved back to Poland. Neither did his father feign the slightest interest in the fate of the son he had never even tried to find. Indeed, it was Misha's inherent curiosity that had compelled him to venture out on a journey to seek out his counterfeit father.

Now, that he was laid to a restless grave, Motele frequently interfered with Misha's fate and knocked his gavel of guilt before him like a regular preacher on the church pulpit. Where was he when I needed him? Misha agonized silently. He felt that Motele's past indifference had denied him fatherly love as well as the filial adoration of his paternal role model; both being the essential nutrients to an early upbringing. It was the love he had craved often during the darkest nights alone and at the mercy of the world. Despair had led him to wish for his father's death. Strange as it seemed, Misha had gradually adopted his father's legacy of indifference as a means of self-preservation. Only Blanche was able to spark a faint flicker of affection in Misha's heart. When she finally succumbed to her illness, she had taken that glimmer of emotion with her, and from that day on, he was seldom able to articulate true love for another.

Now, Motele's frequent and annoying nocturnal visitations had become a thorn in Misha's still vulnerable psyche. He likened these sinister messages to terse telegrams from hell. He wished for some sensitive love letters of which he knew little but for the obscene remarks they contained. As a young man he was unable to determine why he had always tended to magnify his many negative qualities while he would diminish and make coarse those rare good ones he still possessed.

Misha got up and approached the window. He sensed Motele's shadow lurking behind him. It was a cool autumn night. *"I'm freezing."* He remarked as if to himself. He pulled the cover off his bed and threw it over his shoulder. He returned to the window and leaned out on its edge. *"I need some fresh air."* Misha said. *"And all you can provide is putrid."*

Suddenly, the dark shadow of his father reappeared. He stretched out its skeletal hand toward Misha. *"I won't let you go."* The hollow voice thundered. Misha laughed sardonically. *"It seems like everyone wants a piece of me nowadays."* He said with apparent bitterness. *"You've arrived too late, dear papá."* The shadow was silent. Were he still holding an option, Misha might have contemplated a bullet through his father's and his own skull. But he was neither an assassin nor an innate suicide material. In the first instance, he was too cowardly. In the second, he had harbored an overpowering amount of self love. Anyhow, he recognized the futility of an attempted run at his own destiny, for it now lay in the hands of total strangers.

On his part, there were moments when Misha could sense a resurgence of moral qualities he knew not existed within his self. In a sudden surge of remorse, he wished to keep that elusive thread of moral fabric intact and became especially resourceful in adapting to ever-changing situations, though he began to demonstrate a rapid decline of self-confidence. Every so often, he would admonish himself not to dwell on his defeats, but under the prevailing circumstances it was well nigh impossible to push them aside.

As a last resort, he was led to believe that he was haunted by the mark of Cain; his fatal birth defect. A sudden emotion overcame him, of which he had hitherto considered himself incapable. It came at the thought that he had spent half the night with his father without having betrayed his emerging feelings regarding their relationship; without having let on that there still was a corner in his heart, ever so minuscule and well nigh dormant, which belonged to the old thief and assassin. That he was not, as the saying goes, "bad to the bone." Try as he did, that dormant whisper of a strange emotion refused to fall dead silent, to become extinguished altogether.

The hour had come. It was time to return to the courtroom. He must be present for the customary summations and the jury's deliberations. He must look his best. He knew he was a wreck of a human being, but he was determined to persist in the belief that he was still capable of loving, and he wanted the world to know it. On his way to the courthouse, steeped in thought, the fatal words resounded in his subconscious: "I must silence you! Fry in hell, murderer! Betrayer of innocence! Thief…thief…thief!" It was the desperate sarcasm of a betrayed son's despair.

Events progressed rapidly that afternoon. The prosecution presented its "irrefutable facts," and asked for the ultimate penalty for "a most singular act of heinous proportions." In his rebuttal, Anton presented an impassioned plea for his client's vindication, since most of the facts presented "were at best murky" and at worst "could be considered circumstantial evidence." From an impartial observer's view, the jury's verdict could go either way.

By day's end, the jurors returned to their places. Everyone sat on pins and needles. Eyes were peeled on the jury's foreperson, and when she stood up in response to the judge's "did the jury reach its verdict?" The tension could be felt in the total silence that ensued.

"We have, your Honor," the woman responded.

"What say you?" The judge asked.

"In the matter of murder in the first degree, the jury was unanimous in its decision of ..."

Before the foreperson was able to finish her sentence, Misha fell into what had seemed a deep faint, while the press hastily filed out of the courtroom to announce the news of the "guilty" verdict to the world. "Help me here, will you, please?" Anton called for the bailiff's aid, and both tried to revive Misha. He slowly came to his senses and sat in his chair, eyes blurred, as if in a trance. He did not hear the latter part of the verdict. He was convicted on the basis of "compelling evidence" that pointed at him to be, "beyond a reasonable doubt," the perpetrator of the murder. It was to be recorded by the press as the "most heinous crime in the annals of the twin city Urbana-Champaign."

"What happened?" Misha asked his mind still in a semi-haze.

"The jury found you guilty as charged." Anton informed him, while holding fast to Misha's midriff. The latter stood on his faltering legs beneath him, ready to be led away by the eager bailiff.

"What?" Misha exclaimed with incredulity that betrayed his lasting hope for the jury's benign decision.

"Calm yourself, Misha." Anton followed him to the exit. "Don't give up."

Misha stopped with his eyes cast toward the departing judge. "You're holding me for a murder I didn't do!" He shouted. The bailiff tugged at his elbow forcefully. The judge rapped her gavel and, seemingly, without paying attention to Misha's agonizing cry, she left the premises.

The hysterical prisoner was cuffed and led away to be transported to Joliet's maximum security death row facility. A crowd of hundreds of students and curiosity seeking townspeople lined the courthouse steps. They jeered and shrieked "Murderer! Murderer!" as he was led to the prison cruiser which was to carry him to his destination. Anton's reassuring handshake and a cheerful "keep the faith, we'll appeal," did little to inspire hope in the one who had given up long ago his self-esteem in favor of self-deprecation.

Alienation and inability to communicate with the outside world contributed to Misha's agony. It has been long since he had heard himself burst out with a hearty laugh. But there was no reason to laugh. Was there?

Misha no longer felt confident to express himself fully even when given that chance. It seemed to him as though he was straining to shout in a padded cell, but the response was muted, lacking proper feedback. The survivor in him dictated resistance, but he was racking his brains, as he sought a way to cope. The whole legal business was immensely complicated and well nigh impossible for him to understand. They told him there were no books available on death row. They might have as well denied him the means to breathe. The world of ideas he had found in reading had been the essential part of his existence for as long as he could remember. Not being able to pursue this vital function, his intellect would surely atrophy gradually.

He began to wonder how long it would take to render him intellectually mute. Most of all, in order to go on in his present environment, boldness and insensitivity were vital. He had given both up for lost long ago.

On his part, Anton had planned to launch a vigorous appeal in the 214th Circuit Court. He intended to hire a private P.I., now clearly aware that help was essential facing the magnitude of labor in the task of gathering evidence in order to disprove the prosecution's contention of "irrefutable proof" of Misha's guilt. The sound of the frightfully eloquent vehemence in Misha's parting outcry resonated in Anton's memory. On his initial meeting of the defendant, and even during the course of the trial, Anton was not one hundred percent convinced of Misha's innocence. At long last, after the verdict fell, he had made a mental pledge to free Misha who he believed was wrongfully indicted. His own life and that of Misha's were now inextricably intertwined. He knew he would pursue his quest in behalf of the convicted death row inmate even through the Illinois Supreme Court, if it came to it, and on to higher federal entities. If his appeals could not help him there, then he reasoned that there was really something fundamentally wrong with the justice system. He was determined to seek the truth at his own expense if necessary.

Anton's first visit to death row was a tough emotional ride for both of them. Misha broke into hysterical sobs and Anton consoled the hapless inmate through the transparent bullet-proof plastic window separating them. He would have preferred to give the prisoner a strong, encouraging, bear hug. "Don't, Misha, please, compose yourself." Anton pleaded. "I haven't given up, and you mustn't either. Now, more than ever, we need each other's support."

"It's easier said than done," Misha spoke haltingly, choking off and on, and Anton strained to hear him as he pressed his ear to the receiver. "You're on the outside looking in, and I'm inside counting the hours for the hangman's noose." He concluded.

"Keep the faith, Misha," Anton placed his hand on the partition in leaving, "we'll make it right." He remained fiercely optimistic. "I have filed a motion for continuance." Misha grinned. The lawyer's assurances injected him with renewed hope.

Misha pressed his fingers opposite Anton's. With a faint smile along his taught quivering lips and a glimmer of hope in his dried eyes he said: "I believe in you, my friend. I believe in you." He repeated, and it sounded as if he had tried to convince himself and was successful in doing so. It was the first time he had called Anton "friend." The lawyer was pleased. His client's expression of trust has been the ultimate reason to convince his attorney that there was no basis to regard him as a depraved, coldhearted criminal, allegedly unable to feel empathy or guilt, depicted in the court files and by the judgmental media eagerly true to follow a tendency that leaned toward sensationalism digging for the least sign of a scandal.

Misha was seemingly one of those rare characters who would survive adversity and, in the end, triumph over life itself. Yet lately thoughts of self-doubt began to filter in through the hard outer core. Was it a weakness caused by the terrible trauma he had experienced as the only witness to his innocence? Anton stood up ready to leave the premises. He raised his thumb to his lips that made a smacking gesture simulating a kiss. Misha responded likewise.

# 28.

CRAIG NELSON, THE PRIVATE INVESTIGATOR, whose services Anton had solicited, was a man in his early fifties, but his blond hair, an irrepressible smile on his cherubic face as well as his energetic bearing, made him look more like a recent college grad. He came highly recommended as a professional of great skill when it came to doing his job of sleuthing.

Several weeks had lapsed, and there was no breakthrough. Though frustrated by the impasse, Craig pursued his task with the determination of a bulldog. In fact, because of the roundness of his face and the jowls that jutted out forward in a fierce characteristic manner, he betrayed unmistakably the canine inside him. Luckily, the 214th Circuit Court, due to its heavily overburdened docket, had been unable to set a definite date to schedule a preliminary hearing. Anton was encouraged with the delay, in the hope that new evidence might surface in the meantime which will aid him in his efforts to exonerate his client Misha.

Has he exhausted the opportunity to comb through the testimony of the fourteen-year-old son of the victim? Anton probed his mind. Should he have laid aside his concern for the witness' tender age? Did his action deny Misha vital evidence in support of his innocence? These and, indeed, other salient questions weighed heavily on Anton's conscience as he plodded patiently in his endeavor to shed light upon the prevailing obscurity.

On his part, Craig spent many hours at the pond looking for clues that had not been presented in evidence before. After all, the autopsy had determined that the victim's death had happened prior to the drowning. He had examined the recovered suitcase which had been held at the police pound. There were neither fingerprints found on the frame, nor did the police record traces of blood. Could there have been residues of the attacker's skin tissue under Susanna's fingernails? Craig hastened to the morgue.

The forensic expert at the County Morgue, Dr. Xavier, was helpful. The victim was kept in the original state at the morgue's refrigerated "out-cooler," and access to the specimen was available pending the appeal.

"Let's have another look," Craig requested, "under the fingernails."

The two men leaned over the dead body. The coroner probed patiently. Soon, it was evident that further pursuit in that direction was in vain. Craig needed another approach desperately.

"The water," the coroner spoke softly as if to himself. "The water will have washed away whatever traces were under the fingernails." He mused. "That is, *if* there was anything there to begin with." He placed emphasis on the "if". "I wonder."

"Is it too late to examine the fetus, Dr. Xavier?" Craig inquired.

"It's never too late," the pathologist replied.

"Then, let's go for it," Craig smiled, "we might hit pay-dirt."

"It'll take a while," Dr. Xavier warned, "with much patience."

"Patience is my middle name," Craig chuckled.

Patience was long worn off in Misha's delicate condition. Nothing had caused more damage than the destructive nature of continuing isolation. He looked for sustenance in that utterly rejecting place of confinement called "death row." Night after night, in his restless sleep nowadays instead of confronting the specter of his old nemesis, Motele his derelict father, he saw visions of Susanna. Once he had seen her rise from the narrow confines of the morgue's out-cooler, as the body storage is commonly called.

*"You mustn't feel guilty, dear Misha,"* she addressed him; *"all of this was none of your doing. I brought it all on myself."* She looked at

him with great concern, he thought. He had reached out toward the unreachable.

*"I know now that I should have gone with you when you'd left us to be on your own,"* he lamented. *"I should have, but I didn't."* He wept bitterly.

*"Don't be so hard on yourself, my dear Misha,"* she spoke with tenderness in her voice he hadn't heard for so long it had the sound of a strange, almost alien occurrence. *"You have followed your conscience, Misha, and I did the rest."* Her voice had begun to fade into the distance, and her image with it. He implored her to remain a while longer.

*"Stay, dearest Susanna, please, don't leave me, I beg you."* He talked fast, desperate, as he had tried to prevent her impending disappearance. *"I must know, who..."*

*"...did this to me..?"* She did not permit him to continue.

"Yes, my dear, you must tell me before you go...you must, my dearest Susanna."

He wept aloud. *"Please tell me who'd committed this foul deed for which I must pay with my life."*

*"Do not despair, dear Misha,* she assured him, *"I'll reveal the murderer...all in good time...I'll give testimony on your behalf..."*

Her voice faded completely, and the apparition had followed the sound beyond the depth of the unknown. There appeared a kaleidoscope of images in Misha's feverish psyche. He stepped cautiously into the spot where the apparition stood only seconds ago and stopped there. In the momentary surge of his accelerated pulse, he had felt as he experienced an infusion of Susanna's spirit into his own self. Though he was not of religious persuasion, a sudden sense of the supernatural compelled him to get on his knees, his hands folded into prayer. He felt the coolness of the hard, forbidding, floor beneath him. It was a sobering feeling, and his lips moved soundlessly, eyes peeled on the elusive void.

"I'm at the end of my rope," he whispered to himself, and the word "rope" bored a persistent imprint into his agonizing psyche. "It's no use, no use at all..." He concluded. "I must end the torment...I must end..." He looked around in his cell, searching for the necessary tools to implement his plan. All he saw were naked walls, a thin mattress on the floor in the room beneath the Spartan sink adjacent to the commode.

Suddenly, he heard approaching steps. Was it time? He thought. No, it couldn't be. The door to his cell opened with the characteristic squeak of dry metal friction.

"Follow me, you've got a visitor." The jailer uttered hoarsely. Misha did as told.

To his elation, it was Anton. They greeted each other through the glass partition, smiled, and expressed mute amenities.

"I have good news, Misha," the lawyer said.

"You must know that the only good news is my exoneration, Anton." Misha said with sadness in his voice.

"We've got a hearing to decide on the appeal." Anton ignored Misha's remark. "There's a good chance a new trial will be granted." Misha did not react immediately, though his eyes showed a faint glimmer of hope.

"Well, aren't you going to say something?" Anton prodded his client.

"What can I say?" Misha asked. "Wish I could share your optimism, Anton," he paused. "But whatever joy I'd want to build on hope get's beaten to the ground by our track record thus far. There are always provisions that dominate my fate within these walls."

"Things are going to change," Anton assured his despairing client. "Mark my words, Misha. Things will turn for the better," He placed his hands on the glass, which signified his impending departure.

"Please, Anton, don't leave yet, Anton," Misha implored. "I... saw...Susanna..." He whispered into the speaker.

"What?" Anton showed astonishment, although he had tried to temper himself against surprises as far as Misha was concerned. "Susanna?!" He almost yelled out loud disregarding the jailer's presence. "First it's your old man you see, and now…"

"Sorry I mentioned her, Anton," Misha expressed genuine concern. "I shouldn't subject you to my hallucinations, and I ought to keep my demons to myself." Misha placed now his hand on the glass partition onto Anton's and readied to leave.

"Okay, okay, Misha," Anton hastened to keep his client a moment longer. "I believe you've seen Susanna. So? What's the point?"

"As clear as I can see you now, Anton." Misha's voice turned into a near whisper.

"So? So? Go on." Anton's impatience was evident. For the first time of his many visits with Misha, he regretted the absence of Diana. After all, she was the shrink on the case, not he. Now, more than ever, he'd wanted Misha to keep his rational mind together. The moment of truth was near, and the least screw-up might jeopardize the case. The prosecution would have a field day with Misha's nocturnal hallucinatory tales of ghosts and demons. "Okay, Misha, okay." Anton humored Misha's volatility. "What was it about Susanna's visit that impressed you?"

"It's quite simple, Anton." Misha displayed a measure of self-control. "She assured me of my innocence." Now Misha lost his composure and wept unabashed. Tears rolled down his cheeks. "She implored me to stop worrying."

"You see?" Anton picked up on Misha's narrative. "Why don't you listen to her, even if you refuse to listen to me?" Anton reproached the weeping friend and client. "Wish you leave the worrying to me, Misha. That's my job; to worry." Anton paused. "And stop your whining. Let's take the things on the come. OK?" Once again Anton placed his hand on the glass plate, and Misha did likewise. "Good bye for now, Misha." He said. "I want you to concentrate on the positive, do you hear me?" Misha's face was turned from the partition and the mike. "Can you hear me?!" Anton shouted into the phone, afraid it had malfunctioned.

"I hear you," Misha replied without turning his head. Only I wish I could be doing it on the outside, and not in here. This place is so...it's so hard to..."

"...I know...I know..." Anton interrupted. "I'll get you out of there very soon for the new trial. Sit tight till then, okay?" As soon as the words left his lips, he was sorry it sounded as it did. Misha caught the gist.

"Sure I'll sit tight." The sound of irony was evident. "What else can I do under the circumstances?"

"Quite true, my friend," Anton mused out loud, "quite true, indeed."

"What can I say?" Misha asked. "Wish I could share your optimism, Anton," he paused. "There are always provisos that dominate my fate within these walls." Misha stared at his attorney with countless unvoiced questions on his mind. Subliminally, he would attempt, now and again, to answer half of them, but his responses seemed totally absurd and he rejected them out of hand. Anton had tried on occasions to engage him in trivial conversation, perhaps to melt the ice, and induce some semblance of relief from his client's morose but silent denial and his repressive behavior. He had, perhaps, hoped to encourage some loud rumination, all to no avail. Misha seemed to have no interest in such interchange which, in his view, offered little or no substance. What he had sought was answers not inconsequential chitchat.

Anton withdrew his hand from the glass partition and left the premises with a bitter-sweet grin on his face. Misha stopped to glance at his lawyer, hesitant, and then he felt the tap of the jailer's hand on his shoulder. He turned obediently and followed the man to his cell.

"Interesting!" Anton exclaimed excitedly at the sight of the small, neatly wrapped, packet. Craig handed it to his employer. "Boy oh boy, you're damned good! Where in tarnation did you find it?" Anton did all but a joyful jig to express his satisfaction.

"Not far from where it had happened," the investigator replied, a sly smile on his boyish face. "A small ravine some distance from the pond. The cops don't seem to sniff for clues beyond the yellow line." He chuckled.

"Good for you...good for you..." Anton repeated, while his trembling fingers struggled with the knotted wrapper. "Damned thing won't unravel!" He uttered through his clenched teeth. "If any good comes out of it, you've got a big bonus coming."

"That's music to my ears, Anton." Craig smiled, "and the little lady and the kids always know how to spend it."

"Finally!" Anton threw the stubborn wrappings onto the floor. He saw before him the partly weather-worn pages of Susanna's diary. Neatly written on lined letter-paper were the last words of the only eye-witness capable to shed light on her own fatal end.

"*I think I'm falling in love with Patrick,*" Anton read out loud with great fascination as Craig listened attentively for any clues. "*He has been such a great help with the move, kind to me and Rudi. I really couldn't have done it without him during those difficult hours.*" Anton let out a long, shrill whistle through his teeth.

"Damn! And to listen to the good professor in the courtroom you'd think their relationship was nothing but casual!" He leafed through the dainty pages. "Aha! Here we are. Now we're getting warmer!" He exclaimed and began reading again.

"*I know he'll ask me again. It's been two months since my move, and I know I won't be able to refuse him. What shall I do? We have had a good and peaceful relationship up to now, except for the occasional fights as a result of my refusal to let him into my bedroom.*"

"Fights! Did you hear that? She's been fighting him off, and all along he wanted to sleep with her. Now we're getting somewhere." Anton's face was flushed with excitement. Craig listened fascinated as the narrative continued.

"*I must say, dear diary, it isn't altogether unpleasant. Patrick has come to dinner and bought a fine bottle of wine. We closed the door to Rudi's bedroom and put on some nice music. We danced. He pressed me close to himself, and I could feel his excitement. My pulse quickened. He must have noticed my arousal, for he leaned over and pressed a passionate kiss on my bare shoulder. I didn't think to resist. He reached with his free hand and squeezed my breast; first one, then the other. I felt my nipples harden. The last of my resistance was melting in his strong embrace...*" Anton paused, reached into his pocket and drew a handkerchief. He wiped the large pearls of sweat from his brow.

"Hey, Anton, please don't stop not while my curiosity is at its highest. It's like viewing an X-rated flick! Come on now, just when it's getting real hot! If you can't stand to read it, let me do it!" He pleaded. Anton threw a meaningful glance in Craig's direction, as if to say "for God's sake calm yourself." Then, with a gesture of disgust, he handed the loose-leafed diary to his assistant.

"Okay, read out loud. That'll be your just punishment for your lascivious soul."

"I'm only doing it to gather empirical evidence, you know." Craig said with a mischievous smile, and Anton glanced at him quizzically, like saying "where did he get this word *empirical?*"

"There's nothing else on my mind but criminal science." Craig repeated. On saying that, he began to read:

*"And all along he continued to caress me to the point of seduction, and he whispered into my ear words of love and caring. He assured me that he would care for little Rudi as much and as sincerely as his own father would. That said, he suggested that we turn in for the night. He took me by the hand and led me into the bedroom. I was too weak to resist and followed him, though I knew where it would lead."*

"Wow!" Craig exclaimed. "This guy is smooth!"

"I'd say he is," Anton agreed. "Still we haven't got anything seriously incriminating to present to the jury." He paused with a lovable smile. "You must know, this is clear and simple a case of two mutually consenting adults ready to rock and roll in the hay...or...bed. Anton reflected for another silent moment. Then, with a mischievous grimace on his face, he said, "At least, everything up to now seems commonplace. But let's continue our reading session."

"Okay, Anton, I'm ready. Let's dig some more, and we might strike gold." Craig leafed through some of the pages in silence. Suddenly, he stopped. "Wait, we might have something here." He continued to read silently, but his shining eyes followed the lines eagerly. He stopped and looked at Anton. "I think we found what we have been looking for." He commenced to read out loud an entry dated several months later than the initial date. He read slowly, with a certain sense of sadness in his voice:

*"Oh, my dear diary! What has come over him? He lost his temper right after dinner. It was something about Rudy not wanting to go to sleep. He shouted at my boy to get going. Rudy pouted and didn't move fast enough for him and he raised his hand as if to strike my son. I came between them and his fist struck my shoulder with a loud, cracking sound.*

*"He was sorry it happened. I saw that right away. He tried to make up and was apologetic. It hurt my sense of pride more than it did my shoulder, and I refused to speak to him. He yelled insults at me and Rudy. Terrible words came out of his mouth. I don't dare remember what he said. It was something that sounded like 'I could kill the little bastard!' and 'I wouldn't want you to try to stop me!'*

*"I can't go on like this, dear diary. He might bring harm to both of us."*

"Well, what do you think of that?"

Craig continued perusing the fragile pages. Suddenly he exclaimed: "Hold on, Anton, it gets even better here." He examined the narrative with an especial scrutiny. "Listen to this, Anton. There were further developments."

*"Two months ago we left his place and rented a modest apartment not far from the campus. On a Friday he appeared at the door. "Hi, I've missed you. I have a peace offering. He fixed his eyes on mine. At that point my resolve had left me. He hesitated. "Sulima is performing tonight as usual for the faculty and students." He breathed*

*deeply. "Would you both join me?" I knew he was referring to Igor Stravinsky's son, and I had always looked forward to these intimate concerts the son presented of his father's music. "Well? Please join me." He smiled.*

*He seemed sincere and contrite. I hesitated, unable to refuse, though I sensed trouble. I knew that ultimately the three of us would enjoy the concert.*

*"After the concert I'll prepare a deluxe gourmet dinner." He stopped. "No strings attached. Deal?" That seductive smile appeared on his face again. He knew that his women would fall for it every time. "Besides, I have it through the grapevine that you are...well...with child. The meal will be prepared with this in mind. I promise."*

*The concert was delightful. But throughout I was troubled by his last utterance. How do I tell him whose it is? I wondered in silence. Little Rudi seemed entranced by the music. During the intermission we chatted about various topics. He was amusing as ever and the baby topic never came up.*

*He prepared a meal fit for a queen. His motives were transparent. There was little that was more effective in impressing a woman than a man's ability to demonstrate his "feminine" characteristics. The apex of these was his culinary skill. The aroma lingered throughout. I was impressed by the many aromatic candles he had placed in a proper setting. The table was elegantly set and Händel's* Wassermusik *emitted its soothing sounds. "Wasn't it the great Goethe who recommended these sounds for perfect digestion?" He asked me to show off his wide knowledge of German culture.*

*"Yes, it was he." I responded astonished. I was caught unawares by his intimacy with our habits. Most of all it was his familiarity with Goethe's famous novel* Die Wahlverwandschaften. *"You have done your homework." I added.*

"Where are you going with all of this culinary crap, Craig?" Anton interrupted impatiently.

"I'll come to the point instantly, if you allow me."

"I wish you'd hurry it up a bit." Anton was not one to waste time on trivia. Craig read on.

*The table cloth was of the finest crochet linen with dainty pink frizzles running down in its sides. There was an uncorked bottle of the prestigious Baroncini red wine in the midst of silverware and exceptional* Meissen *China. The food was meant to impress. Unable to produce a typical German* Eintopf, *he traveled back to his roots in preparing a traditional Irish stew.*

*"It went under the Gaelic name of 'bally maloe' or 'stobhach gaelach'." He informed us. Its main ingredients were lamb or mouton, potatoes, onions, and parsley. He apparently made an effort to choose only neck bones or shanks. The pot had simmered long enough to have rendered the desired product; a hearty bowl of Irish stew.*

*Already at the entrance, I was able to inhale the intoxicating aroma of the assorted spices: turnips, parsley, and carrots. He regarded us with that typical smile of confidence. He must have detected in my astonished eyes a promise of enjoyment during the ensuing night.*

*Needless to say, we enjoyed the evening. When the time came to depart, He whisked off the yawning Rudi and put him to bed. "Let's have a nightcap." He suggested. Before I had a chance to refuse, he had served me another glass and filled his own. "To us!" He made a toast. I did not reciprocate. I experienced an uneasy sensation in my stomach after swallowing the rest of another glass of wine. I remember resting my head against the table. My eyelids felt heavy and I remember making an effort to keep my eyes open and my mind alert. It was all to no avail. Vibrant colors danced in my head as I listened to Händel's music and felt lifted onto his bed…"*

"Well? What do you think of them apples now, Anton?" Craig asked.

Anton remained silent for what seemed a long moment. He slowly nodded and, as if he'd arrived at an important decision, he addressed the detective: "I think we have cause for an appeal here. If need be, all the way to the Supreme Court!" He chuckled with glee. "I do, strongly, believe we've found what's been missing." He concluded with a broad grin on his face. "Right now, our urgent task is to determine how we must launch our investigation into the alleged 'evidence' the prosecution has that we need to rebut with viable proof to the contrary." Anton reflected for a brief moment. "Precisely, we've got to identify the source of the allegations they had presented thus far and put doubt into their validity."

"You mean, who set up the nice professor, and on what grounds he'd landed in the cooler?" Craig put it in the characteristic jargon of his trade.

"I couldn't have put it any better." Anton intoned. "They've got something pretty strong, and we must put it to the test. I've got a feeling there's somewhere a crack to be found in their armor, and now is the time to test it."

"All I can say, I'll try."

"'Try' won't cut it, Craig." Anton was serious, almost taciturn. "There are deadlines we've got to meet. The D.A. is convinced he's got a sure conviction here. His fledgling political career demands it. The burden of proving his theory false lies squarely on our shoulders."

"Hum…Hum…" Was all Craig Nelson was willing to utter under his breath with a broad smile on his face. He snapped his fingers. "I'll have it done in a jiffy, just like a big detective agency." He declared with a tinge of hidden sarcasm that did not sit well with the lawyer.

"Come on, Craig. Be serious. If I'd wanted a big agency, I would have hired one." Anton locked his eyes with Craig's and its intensity intended to emphasize the seriousness of the situation. "That's why I selected someone like you, a local with an intimate knowledge of every bit of gossip circulating in this tightly nit university community."

"Haven't the police done the work you ask of me?" Craig asked, smiling.

"You might come up with some ideas they haven't thought of yet." Anton was insistent.

"But you've got to know that I can't put in the hours single-handedly on this case as the U.I.P.D. can." Craig argued. "What with my other clients…"

"…I'm not asking you to do exclusive work for me." Anton interrupted, aware of Craig's manipulative bargaining chips "The greedy bastard." He thought silently.

"Even so, you can't expect me to compete with the U.I.P.D., can you?" Craig was getting ready to leave. "All arguments aside, to begin with, I'll need a retainer."

"We haven't discussed the fees as yet." Anton was evasive.

"Well now, my regular fees are seventy-five an hour. The advance will count into the totals."

"What numbers are we talking about regarding the retainer?"

"I guess…eleven hundred dollars will cover it for a starter." Craig paused. "And I'll get to work right away."

"Who do I write the check to?"

"Make it out to *Craig Investigations*, okay?"

Anton hastily scribbled the necessary entries onto the check and handed it to the P.I.'s outstretched hand. "Will that do?" He inquired, and the P.I. nodded.

"Quite. I hope I won't disappoint you, counselor." He pocketed the check securely into his billfold. "My clients have always been satisfied with the results of my work." He paused. "Some were to a greater and others to a lesser extent. But overall, coming up empty-handed is not in my nature." He smiled.

"A man's life depends on *our* work." Anton placed emphasis on the collective pronoun where it belonged. "Let's hope your search will yield called for results. He readied to leave.

"You'll have a report soon." Craig assured the lawyer, "just as soon as is humanly possible. Trust me."

"It had better be so." Anton added from the exit. Those two frequently uttered words have been commonly used by politicians and proffered charlatans, and they did not sit well with him and the legal vocabulary. He cringed, while whispering to himself, "Where have I heard these words before, where indeed?"

With his sight fixed on one of his two visitors, then on the other, Misha approached the glass partition. He was eager to hear about new developments whatever they might bring. Unable to read their facial expressions, he picked up the receiver on his end. "Have mercy, Anton," he addressed his lawyer, "give me some good news; whatever it may be." Anton smiled.

"We found...uh...Craig found Susanna's diary not far from the...lake," Anton hesitated. At that moment, Craig decided to fill Misha in on the discovery he'd made. He stepped up to the glass plate and picked up the second phone.

"I found her diary near where she had drowned. It lay in some brush, as if she had intended it to be found there." He looked at Anton. "Do you want to tell him the rest?" He asked the lawyer.

"Well, if it's what we think it is, we can take it to court and ask for a hearing. But..."

"...what do you mean by 'if it is what we think it is...?'" Misha interrupted.

"As I was saying," Anton continued, "there may be evidence in what Susanna says that Patrick was on occasions violent with the boy. Maybe even with her." Anton looked at Misha intensely. "But she only uses the pronoun 'he', when she refers to the occurrence." Anton's eyes burned into the mind of his client. "Was it you, Misha? Did you ever strike the boy or Susanna?" Misha's eyes expressed surprise, and Anton continued. "It could have been in anger, and you might have forgotten by now. Try to remember, Misha. This is extremely important if it's to stand up in the Appellate Court for us."

"This is all so confusing." Misha whispered into the receiver. "I can't believe you're asking such a question at this late hour."

"Face it, Misha, you either talk to me or you'll have to answer the prosecutor in court." He glanced at Craig. "Tell him what it was about. You read the thing. Was it clear who Susanna was talking about, Patrick or Misha?"

"It wasn't clear to me, Anton." Craig lowered his eyes. "If they agree with what we understand she says, then we're okay. But if they take it the other way, we're in deep shit."

"What do you mean?" Misha had regained his voice, realizing his life once more hung on semantics. "What do you mean 'the other way'?" He choked.

"Well, she could have been referring to you." Anton interjected.

"To me?" Misha shouted into the phone. "I have never..."

"Hold it, Misha," Anton interrupted his client, "think carefully before you make statements that may be attacked as inaccurate in the court of law." He paused. "Prosecution would have a field day with these allegations." He paused to study Misha's facial response to his questioning. "Trust me; they will doubt your word. It's their job. They'll try every trick in the book to break your spirit. And it's my duty and mandate to warn you about their intentions." Anton added with a mischievous twinkle in his eyes.

Anton's pseudo-rejection of Misha's assurances regarding his innocence put him on the defensive. "I'm surprised," he said, "I didn't expect you to doubt my word at this point of the game." He paused. "If that is so, then I'm really fried." He used a word he'd seldom used before. In desperation he wanted to shock. But both Anton and Craig sat silent. They wanted stronger evidence than the defendant's assurances. Their cynical expressions boded ill for him, and he wondered how the system expected a jailed person to vindicate himself from behind a locked, isolated cell on death row. He was about to hang up his receiver, when Anton spoke:

"I don't want you to jump to your hasty conclusions." Misha listened attentively. So all this cynicism and baiting was only a sham designed to test his resolve. They are clever, these lawyers and their handymen eh? "We're going to appeal." Anton continued. I wouldn't be here if I didn't believe you; believed *in* you. You've got to trust me now more than ever. Everything depends

on mutual trust and a sincere belief in the success of our mission."
Misha was silent. "Is that okay with you?"

"Uh...I guess so..." Misha mumbled confused. "I guess it's
okay." His face froze to stone. Without further exchanges, Misha
replaced the receiver and left his guests in a state of puzzlement
as he walked out of the visitation room without his usual inquiry
as to their follow up visit.

# 29.

ONLY ONE WEEK to Misha's rendezvous with destiny, Anton's petition to plead the case before the Appellate Court was granted. Misha entered the packed courtroom by a side door, un-cuffed, and followed by the ever-present deputy marshal. The spectators and the press fell silent. The defense attorney shuffled through some of his files, as did the public prosecutor. Misha's appeal in his capital murder trial was about to begin. The courtroom drama became almost as emotionally charged as the mystery that surrounded its circumstances.

"I understand the defense has some new evidence to present which might exonerate the defendant." The judge opened the session. "Do we have the facts?" He added, directing his question at Anton.

"Yes, your Honor, we have." Anton replied.

"Is that acceptable to the prosecution?" The prosecutor nodded.

"Then, let us begin." The judge rapped his gavel.

"I have here, what seem to be pages from the deceased's diary," Anton raised the pages high above his head to render them visible to all concerned. He approached the court clerk. "May the court mark this exhibit one," he handed the evidence to the clerk and the judge nodded approval: "May it be so entered."

The prosecutor interrupted with a comment of his own. "May we approach the bench, your Honor?" The judge nodded. Both parties stepped up to the judge's mike, and the latter shielded it so as to prevent the audience from listening in on their off the record exchange. The three whispered briefly among themselves.

"Your Honor, I fail to see the relevance of exhibit one." The prosecutor whispered almost inaudibly. Anton smiled in silence. The judge turned to him.

"Has the defense discussed the issue with the prosecution?" He asked.

"Haven't had the chance as yet," Anton held his smile. "Things had been moving so rapidly..."

"Rapidly or not," the judge interrupted, "defense should have made certain we were all informed." It was meant as a reprimand.

"May it please the court," Anton's smile vanished, "we will explain in due course."

"I wish defense would explain now," the prosecutor hissed.

"I presume, prosecution refers to the indefinite nature of the third person pronoun 'he', as it is used by the deceased in her designation of her son's alleged assailant."

"Indeed, I do." The prosecutor agreed.

"The very fact that it could designate almost anyone as the assailant is reason to grant a stay." Anton looked intensely at the judge. "Based on this assumption, we wish to petition an indefinite stay of execution for our client, your Honor."

"I'm inclined to give it some thought," the judge said. He signaled the prosecution. "How do the people feel about that?"

"Well, I don't know..." The prosecutor hesitated. Anton smiled again.

"We shall adjourn and give the prosecution time to examine. Will that suffice?"

"We see no problem with that." The prosecutor replied.

"Let's return to your places, gentlemen." The judge ordered. Both men slowly returned to their seats, weariness evident on both sides. The judge pulled the mike closer to his lips. He addressed those present in the courtroom. "Ladies and gentlemen, Thank you for your patience. Harrumph," he cleared his throat, "due to some...let us say...rather strange but relevant developments, it is the court's decision to grant a temporary stay to the defendant,

Misha Winograd. The court will convene at such time when all matter has been resolved to the satisfaction of all parties concerned." He rapped his gavel. "This court is adjourned."

The press and TV crews spilled out of the courtroom ahead of everyone. On the steps leading to the courthouse, they formed a veritable barricade through which everyone exiting had to pass. There, they lay in wait for the two court adversaries: the defense and the prosecutor.

Anton appeared on the steps ahead of the prosecutor. Craig's muscular, towering frame served as a kind of respectable barrier between his boss and the media types. There were all sorts of questions directed at Anton all at once. They pressed mikes into his face and stood tightly, encircling him. The prosecutor stood aloof, waiting his turn. "What's in the new evidence!? Who else is implicated?! What are the new findings?!" There were as many questions as there were media people milling around. Anton regarded them amused. One could tell he relished the attention.

"In due time…all in due time, ladies and gentlemen of the press…" Anton smiled at the crowd. There was no doubt he relished his moment of their undivided attention. "We need some time to sort it all out." He pointed to the prosecutor who stood closer now. "The prosecution might want to answer a few of your pressing questions. Mr. Prosecutor?"

"I concur with the gentleman of the defense." The prosecutor said. He, too, basked in the spotlight of opportunity to display his skill. One never knows when a little public exposure might do a politician some good. He must be careful, though, not to fall into a media trap. Go gently now. "The evidence in question is still not for public consumption. As soon as we sort out the details, you will be the first to hear about it. At this moment, however, the judge felt, it would be imprudent and counter-productive to due process. Therefore the court imposed a moratorium on news." There was a brief silence. Before any of those present pressed further, he added. "We hope you'll indulge us a bit. Have patience."

"You ought to ask the man on death row to have patience!" Someone in the crowd shouted.

"Now, now," Anton admonished the speaker, "we're doing all we can to keep the situation calm. Please don't let your imagination run amuck."

"How's about the little boy?" Someone asked. "Has anyone come forward with adoption papers?"

"No need to worry about the boy at this time." Anton hastened to assure the speaker. "His father is still among us. We're doing all we can to ensure their reunion."

"What if you don't succeed? Will he become a ward of the state?"

"We'll jump over that hurdle when we come to it," Anton was beginning to feel annoyed. "That's all for now, ladies and gentlemen. I have nothing further to add." He turned to the prosecutor. "You, Sir? Do you wish to enlarge?"

"Thank you, there's no more than we've already given you."

"What about the deceased's relatives?"

"Has anyone notified them? Her parents?"

"Was there a will?"

"Will the boy testify again?"

The media mob hurled relentless inquiries at Anton and the prosecutor. Cameras clicked, bulbs flashed, and mikes followed the two to the very point of their swift departure in their respective cars. "Well, get a load of that!" Craig exclaimed while accelerating their getaway car. Anton was silent for a long moment. "You'd think we were on trial." Craig added laughingly.

"As far as the media go, we *are* on trial," Anton said softly. "They're the public's eyes and ears. Apparently, we haven't done a complete job here." He paused. "Something's missing, Craig. Something we haven't as yet brought to the table. And we should have. Something vital."

"Oh, yeah?" Craig wondered. "And what can that be?"

"I can't put my finger on that missing clue as yet, Craig," Anton said. "But I have long felt that some detail has eluded us. It is obviously something very simple, real, right in front of our eyes and we can't see it."

"What makes you think that, Anton?"

"It's all those questions they threw at us over at the courthouse. That's what makes me think there's something missing." Anton paused again, as if reflecting on what he was going to say next. "You see, we're deep inside the circle of events here. The media, they're on the outside, looking in." He smiled. "And all they see is an incomplete picture. They want all the pieces of the puzzle to be in place, to fit and to make sense. Then they can do their job and bring it to the public. Isn't that how it's supposed to be? Isn't it what this is all about? They're doing their job, that's all. And they want us to complete ours as well, so they can likewise do theirs."

He finished what seemed to Craig a soliloquy, a kind of self inquiry. It was, indeed, an exercise in self evaluation, for he did not expect any kind of feedback from Craig, the gumshoe. Detectives do what you ask them to do when you hire them. You do not pay them for speculation. The latter is the purview of lawyers. But they demand hard facts from their helpers. The P.I. is not always at liberty to use autonomy, though it is initiative and imagination that often separates the professional from the amateur.

The attorney and his hired investigator traveled the rest of the way together immersed in an introspective silence. Craig dropped Anton off at his hotel, while he had decided to stop over at a local pub for a drink and maybe some female company. His self esteem dictated some rest and recreation. In his coat pocket he held a good portion of Susanna's diary—minus those entered as court exhibit—which Anton had entrusted to his care. He felt uneasy about the inconsequential advantage these pages had brought his employer. He had expected greater returns and was clearly disappointed. So what now? Something had to be done. He had to find a way to profitably exploit his efforts. Why not bend a few rules of law to let justice prevail? He chuckled devilishly. He reached into his pocket, though he knew this was neither the place nor the time to indulge his curiosity. A waitress approached.

"What'll it be, handsome?" She asked with a smile. Quickly, he covered the diary pages with his hands, guided by an intuitive professional distrust toward everything and everyone unknown.

"Well, now, let me think," he deliberated for a moment in his attempt to cover up his secretive behavior, "I'll have a double martini." He smiled, and the waitress lingered as if awaiting further instructions. "Make it extra dry," Craig added, and she said "okay" and turned toward the bar to fill his order. Craig let out a sigh of relief. He looked around. He didn't see anyone suspicious close by, but at the bar there sat one of the reporters he'd seen on the steps of the courthouse. Craig remembered her for her slim figure and the genuine blond, teased, hair that embraced a rather striking oval face. In its center were two of the bluest eyes he'd ever seen and a pair of full, sensuous lips that managed to remain closed throughout the commotion. He had a sudden idea. "Why not?" He whispered to himself, smiling satisfied.

"Will there be anything else?" The waitress asked. She placed the martini on the table in front of him.

"See that lady over there?" Craig pointed at the blonde.

"Yes, what of it?" The waitress was hesitant.

"Here's a five," Craig handed her a five dollar bill. "In five minutes, get her another one of what she's having. My compliments. And keep the change." "Okay," said the waitress "will do."

Craig found the important sentences in the diary easily. Fortunately, Susanna's meticulously sweeping handwriting provided ample space in which one was able to insert additional monosyllabic words or just a single letter here and there. He searched out the crucial pronoun "he." There were several. Most importantly, there was the scene where Susanna described Rudi's alleged assailant. Craig put his pen to work quickly. It was done.

He looked over his shoulder toward the reporter at the bar, and their eyes locked. She smiled, savoring her second martini. He smiled back. Carefully, Craig made his corrections. The 'h' in 'he' was now "corrected" into the initial 'P' for the scene describing the alleged violence. There, it was done. He glanced toward the bar again. Slowly, he began to stuff the pages back into his inside coat pocket. The blonde left her barstool and walked slowly toward him. He had hoped she had noticed his strange, clandestine activities at the table. Curiosity was her professional virtue, and material for good copy didn't come easy.

Glass in hand, the reporter remarked over his shoulder. "May I join you?" She giggled. "Or have I come too soon."

"My pleasure," Craig stood up and pulled up a chair. She extended her dainty hand toward him. "You can call me Smiley." She giggled again.

"How very appropriate," he remarked. "I'm Craig." They both laughed happily. By then the last of the diary pages had disappeared into his pocket.

"Hope I haven't intruded into some hush-hush conspiracy. Have I? Really, allow me to correct myself. I *do* hope I have!" Her whispered voice was pleasant and sensuous. He admired her adroitness and played for time, seemingly lost for an answer.

"Uh...no...uh...not at all," Craig hesitated long enough to arouse her innate curiosity. "Why would you think such sinister thoughts?" He asked.

"I couldn't help noticing you at the attorney's side on the courthouse steps. You're some kind of body guard?" She smiled broadly.

"Gee, you do have a good memory for faces, haven't you?"

"That goes with the beat, you know."

"What paper do you represent?" He asked.

"None. I prefer to freelance." She paused. "Now, that I revealed you mine, will you reveal yours to me?" She teased.

"Oh, well, why not," Craig was glad she'd been hooked. Now he could manipulate her curiosity to his advantage. "Private investigator," he said with a degree of nonchalance, "presently in the employ of the defense attorney."

"Tell me more about your work," she encouraged him. Craig smiled through his martini. "What do you mean?" He teased, knowing full well what his companion had in mind. They're just as anxious to meddle in people's affairs as some nosy social workers. He thought silently.

"Well, uh, I find your work fascinating…somewhat related to what I am all about." She lifted her glass to his. "Cheers." He responded with his own "cheers," and they both sipped deep from their respective glasses.

"So, what you mean is…uh…that we're…uh, soul brothers… uh…sorry about that…" he let out with an uproarious laugh, "Freudian slip…I meant, more like soul brother and sister. Eh?"

"Exactly," she prodded, "now, do tell your sister about some of the exciting and mysterious things you've done lately." She studied his smiling face. "Must be a real challenge working on a murder case, uh?"

She swallowed the bait. He chuckled inwardly. Craig was trained to keep his distance professionally. But not this time, he wouldn't. He was going to have it his way. "I've got an exclusive, Smiley," he whispered, as he leaned over closer, "for the record." He paused to observe her eyes. They were searching his, too. He took his time. The longer she waits the better. He knew from experience. He reached into his inside coat pocket. "Hey, for the record, is Smiley really you name?"

"Does it matter?" She asked coquettishly.

"It does if we are to do business together," he said, readying to put the diary back into his pocket.

"No, wait, wait," she was anxious; "the name I go by is Francis Hunt."

"Wow!" He whistled softly. "Good name, catchy, especially for one of your…uh…" he smiled, "well…ability. Francis Hunt has a good sound to it. Very appropriate."

"Now can I have a look?" She showed impatience.

"How can I be sure you'll print it?" He knew he was tormenting her and he enjoyed it.

"You'll just have to trust me, Craig." She was resolute, and he detected some anger building up. He'd better not try her patience any longer.

"Here it is," he whispered, and he placed copies of those crucial pages on the table before her. Francis restrained her enthusiasm, though Craig noticed a slight tremor of her hand as she reached for the material he laid out for her.

"May I?" She asked, likewise in a whisper.

"By all means, dear, be my guest." He coaxed. She caressed the fragile pages of notebook; her eyes darted from one to the next rapidly.

"Has anyone seen this?" She asked.

"Only three pairs of eyes." He smiled.

"Three?"

"Yes, Anton, the lawyer, me and, now, you." He was triumphant. His plan was going to work. It took all his will power to restrain his euphoria.

"So, it's an exclusive?" She wanted to make sure.

"Only if you agree to print it verbatim," he cautioned, "nothing left out, no editorializing. What you see will be what the public will read. Agreed?"

"I'll take a shot at it." She cautioned. "You know, of course, I'll have to sell it to the editor. He might not buy it in its present form." She noticed his quizzical look, and she added quickly, "all of it, as it is, understand?"

"I'm counting on your powers of persuasion, Francis," he took the liberty to place his hand on her shoulder and squeeze it lightly. "After all, you talked me into letting you have an exclusive. I'm sure others would jump at such an opportunity. Eh?"

"I said I'm going to try my level best to have a great editorial in the Sunday edition. That's day after tomorrow. Okay?"

"Okay, partner, it's a deal." He made sure to call her by the confidential "partner," and she put the papers into her brief-case. He knew the risk he took in entrusting the diary to a perfect stranger. In her hands, the pages were now "hot." In his possession and without his "editorial" they were useless. If his plan was to work he had to take risks. That was inherent in his kind of work. Beaming with confidence and a feeling of accomplishment, Fannie was about to leave. He held her hand.

"What's the hurry, dear? Let's have another; to celebrate the partnership. Huh?" He offered. She declined politely.

"Not if you want me to do my work, Craig," she gently pulled her hand from his grip "Besides, I'm driving. It wouldn't be wise to see me in a headline: *Reporter arrested for DWI*, would it?" She laughed loudly.

"Definitely bad for credibility," he joined in her laughter.

# 30.

7 MARCH 1984 WAS A DAY none of them would be able to forget. It was Friday. Almost an entire year had gone by since Misha's arrest and subsequent due process of trials. The day of the final hearing for the dismissal of charges in the Appellate court was scheduled for 9:00 a.m. sharp.

Judge Norman C. Harrow of the 73rd District Court of Appeals kept closing his eyes off and on in order to afford himself better concentration. The uninitiated might have taken it as a sign of boredom or fatigue. However, with little or no self-awareness, he represented the epitome of the well known adage that claimed "justice to be blind." He listened patiently to both of the attorneys' arguments. Someone unfamiliar with the proceedings might have assumed that this justice was not only blind but also dozing off.

"May it please the court," Anton produced the pages of the diary, "the pronoun 'he' does not point in the direction of the defendant." He read the crucial passage aloud, for everyone to hear.

"Neither does it indicate anyone else, your Honor," the prosecutor interjected. "May it please the court," he continued "this is getting us nowhere. I respectfully submit, defense continues to engage in vain attempts at delaying the process." He seemed irritated. "This entire exercise is a waste of the taxpayer's money. I, therefore move that these proceedings cease."

"Does the defense wish to respond?" The judge asked.

"Indeed, I do," Anton began. "If, as my learned colleague claims, the pronoun 'he' may be assumed to signify any given individual, then it would in and by itself be evidence of inconclusive proof against my client." He stopped for a breath. "Thus the burden of proof beyond a reasonable doubt rests with the prosecution. That proof in the case of the State vs. Dr. Misha Winograd has as yet to be submitted to this court."

"The defense engages in speculation, your Honor." The prosecutor objected to Anton's argument.

"So does the prosecution," Anton responded, "and if all we are doing here is speculating with a man's life on the line, then I move the charges be dismissed."

"I wish to remind his Honor that said defendant has been tried in the court of law. He was found guilty of the charges brought before that court by an impartial jury of citizens. The verdict must stand."

"I am inclined to go with the prosecution in this case," the judge said. "In the absence of further concrete and irrefutable evidence to the contrary, this court has to deny the defendant's petition." The judge's gavel sounded much like a hammer driving nails into Misha's coffin. Anton listened silently.

No amount of eloquence was able to persuade the court to reconsider its decision. The matter of the ambiguity the pronoun 'he' Susanna used in her diary implied was not sufficient cause to stay the progress of implementing the court's established verdict. Neither was the prosecution inclined to argue further in reference to Anton's motion for a reduction of the charges to second degree homicide. Anton kept looking over his shoulder toward the courtroom entrance in the hope that Craig might walk in any minute with some new findings which might shed some light hitherto obscured by inadvertent negligence. But that was not to happen. He stood alone, resigned to his now secondary role of a mediator in pleading another stay of execution. It was a sad day for the defense. It was a day of reappraisal and regret.

The prosecution was adamant and unyielding. "What would be the reason for postponement, now that all things have been resolved?" He asked.

"May it please the court," Anton argued, "if we are to send an innocent man to the gallows, isn't it worth some caution?"

"He has been tried by a court of law," the prosecutor emphasized his point; "a jury of twelve citizens have listened to all of the arguments and delivered the guilty verdict." He brushed the hair out of his forehead in a gesture of impatience. "The defense is stretching our sense of fairness."

"Begging the court's indulgence," Anton wet his lips with the tip of his tongue, a trait which had often plagued him during bouts of anxiety. "What if there is something we have overlooked? It may have been a material witness that hasn't come forward? Was it perhaps an inconspicuous piece of evidence that hasn't surfaced?" He smiled sheepishly, for he knew he was grasping at straws. "Wouldn't that be worth another slight delay?" Both the judge and the prosecutor kept their silence for a long moment. Anton's eyes darted from one to the other, but he was unable to determine their trend of thought. Suddenly, the judge spoke:

"The court has deliberated on this issue long enough, counselor. We have taken all eventualities into consideration, given the circumstances." He paused, as if to gather his thoughts. "We've traveled every possible path, and we conclude that all of them lead to the defendant." He sighed deeply. "With a heavy heart and a profound sense of responsibility, I must deny the plea for another stay. In the opinion of this court, your findings are inconclusive. Therefore, it is our decision to proceed setting the date for the execution of defendant's verdict. The sentence will be carried out three days from this hearing. So be it for the record." Judge Harrow stated his final judicial position and rapped his wooden gavel with unmistakable authority. Anton experienced an eerie sense of having witnessed the nailing of the coffin's lid.

The court clerk continued his transcription of the judge's final decree until the last words were spoken. Having done that, Judge Harrow rose from his seat. He shook the hand of the prosecutor, then Anton's. With a sad smile on his face, the judge addressed them: "You are both to be commended for a job well done. The law has been served to the letter. God help us and have mercy on the defendant's soul."

Anton kept calling Craig's number, but to no avail. The phone rang continuously throughout the rest of the morning without result. He was not looking forward to carry the adverse news to his client alone; to let him know that they have run out of options. Maybe call Diana? Pedro? Or maybe ask both of them to accompany him? Yes, he would ask the two loyal friends to come along on his last journey to death row.

When Anton explained what he had in mind, both Diana Ferrucci and Pedro Pamies agreed to accompany him on his difficult mission. How were they to explain to Misha that all resources for saving his life have failed? What would be the best way to tell an innocent man, for they each believed in Misha's innocence, that he must die for someone else's crime?

As he stepped into the visitation lobby and saw the three people on the opposite side of the glass partition, Misha knew. He knew that all efforts in his behalf had failed. The helplessness of his situation depressed and struck him with the suddenness of brutal reality. His last hope was crushed by society's insensitivity toward his assertions of innocence. Though he had clung to life for as long as he had seen a glimmer of hope, Misha's passion had now turned to thoughts of a dignified form of death. That moment has arrived when all the tenacity with which he had fought the odds had surrendered to a quiet resignation. He understood, perhaps for the first time during his ordeal, that life is only worth pursuing when there is no price to pay for its shortcomings. His price seemed now too steep.

Naturally, his attorney had come to inform the client. He was expected to speak but the words didn't come easy. Pedro and Diana stood hesitant, not knowing what to do or say. They looked at Anton expectantly, while he stared into the void. Somehow, Anton had felt a strange sort of sympathy for Misha. As a rule, lawyers aren't supposed to experience such sentimentalities regarding their clients. But he couldn't help it under the circumstances. After all, nearly a year has gone by, while they were involved in a common cause. Even a lawyer's objectivity, some could call it callousness, might have softened to make a client seem more like family than a client.

"Alida?" Misha's utterance was meant as an inquiry to her absence.

"Gone," Pedro summoned all his strength to inform Misha about her departure for Cuba, "to stay with her mother in Havana. Sorry."

"Misha..." Anton swallowed hard, "I'm so sorry..."

"You did all you could, Anton," Misha seemed composed. "I have only myself to blame."

"There's no blame," Diana interjected, "no need for that at all."

"I want to thank all of you, my dear friends, for your loyalty," Misha talked through the intercom. He readied to leave. They listened attentively. None had the courage to speak, for they knew it was his last goodbye. "Oh, yes, Pedro, my dear friend," Misha suddenly addressed his old friend and colleague, "would you tell Xin Xin I'd love to see her before..." here, his voice broke and he put his hanky to his mouth in order to suppress the sobs he felt were about to issue forth. They looked on silently as the door closed behind him. Unabashed, Diana cried bitterly. Anton's sad face reflected his thoughts, and Pedro's defiant stance pointed to his stubborn belief in Misha's innocence and disdain for the bum rap he had got from the American system of justice. "It couldn't have happened in Cuba," they barely heard him whisper as they shuffled out of the visitation room. Only Anton wore a nondescript smile, more like a smirk, which meant to say "yeah, right," in response to Pedro's defiant remark. Absurdities are not easily argued.

It was later that afternoon Pedro returned with Xin Xin. She wore her favorite attire, a tight fitting dress cut above her knees, and no pantyhose to detract from the slender shape of her legs. Heavy makeup and a colorful scarf around her neck completed her wardrobe. Much too garish for a visit to a man about to spend his last two days on death row.

As soon as he stepped through the door, Misha smiled all the way to the partition, his eyes peeled on Xin Xin's enchanting whole. She, too, was happy to see him. Discretely, as befitting a Latin gentleman, Pedro withdrew to wait in the hall. She picked up the receiver. So did Misha.

"Good of you to come," he said happily. For him, the most evocative memories of their relationship were those of the many kindnesses they have received from one another. Now, when so many who might still be in his debt stayed discretely away, the one he had least counted on was by his side.

"Wouldn't have missed it for the world," Xin Xin's face was radiant. "I would have been here sooner, tried it, but they wouldn't let me in. Family and legal assist only, they told me, have the right for visitation."

"I know, I know," he assured her hastily as if to let her know he was now able to transcend such mundane worries. So many memories went through his feverish mind. Only now he came to realize how happy he'd been with her. In her typically Asian manner, she was always self-effacing; never making demands on him that would strain their relationship. Her only wish was to satisfy his hunger for her beauty. She shared willingly, unstintingly, and he took abundantly. Did he give as well as he had taken? He asked himself silently.

"How have you been?" She asked only to break the silence.

"Uh…as can be expected…not too good, not too bad." He smiled sadly. "I want you to know how much I appreciated your court testimony," he whispered. "I thought it would be incriminating evidence, instead you were kind to leave out the gory details."

She giggled happily. "Why should I tell all those strangers about our most intimate pleasures?" She asked a rhetorical question. "Those moments are forever etched in here," she placed her dainty fist to her chest, and he could see her full breasts through the low-cut dress heave with excitement.

Contrary to his expectations, he was now able to admire her simple beauty without the usual lusting in his mind. If he only could, he would enfold her into a very tender embrace, caress her jet-black hair and whisper loving words softly into her ear. He would tell her the many things he had failed to tell her during those torrid, love making nights they had spend together.

"There is a special place in my heart for you, Xin Xin," he spoke into the receiver. "I want you to remember that when I'm no longer…"

"…of course, I'll remember," she interrupted his sad elocution, knowing what he'd say next. "And you must know that you occupy a major part of mine." She added, smiling.

"I…" he had the intention to let her know that he loved her in spite of all that had transpired, but he stopped short. Instead, he continued, "…want you to know that I didn't do it. I didn't kill Susanna. You must believe me, I didn't."

"Oh, you don't have to tell me that, my dear Misha," she smiled. "A bad lover you were sometimes, but a bad person, never." They exchanged fond glances. "Besides, you were always too busy thinking about your work, and lovemaking came second. Where would you have the time to plan an honest to goodness murder?" She giggled and he grimaced.

"Thank you, darling," he placed his palm on the partition, and she put her diminutive hand on it. "Think well of me."

"Always." She assured him.

"Thank you, Xin Xin." Just then, he'd become aware of his 'Zin' and no longer the former 'Sin' in the sound of her name. "Good bye, sweet woman." He said in her native Chinese. Just then, she wanted to tell him the story about her aborted conversion to his faith and the subsequent seduction by the prison chaplain. She studied his anguished face. How was she to tell him that the priest is no longer a man of the cloth but a lay person soon to be her husband? What good would that revelation do? She smiled a bitter-sweet smile of farewell, and he sensed some hidden meaning in that smile. Yet he preferred not to pursue the course of senseless inquiry at that juncture.

"Good bye. Thank you for letting me come here." She responded likewise in her native tongue. Xin Xin was glad to have withheld the news of her impending matrimony with the defrocked padre. She wasn't any good at playing Herodias's daughter Salome to this martyred John the Baptist. She turned to leave, and Misha watched her shapely back, the swiveling hips, and he smiled happily. "I'll see you in heaven, my angel." He whispered under his breath.

The approaching steps sounded unfamiliar. Unmistakably a jail chaplain's shuffling gait, but not that of the padre he had grown accustomed to seeing. This one was a middle aged, stout man, his weather worn face carried signs of habitual worry. Misha wasn't going to ask for reasons of this change. It mattered little at this point. For the first time since his incarceration, Misha welcomed the person of the cloth. He recalled his strange initial encounter with the prison chaplain during the time he'd suffered a heavy bout of diarrhea. Luckily, he was in a much better shape now, and the occasion demanded some soul searching. "I called for you, Padre, I'm ready. Bless me, Father, for I have sinned."

The chaplain made the sign of the cross over Misha's bowed head. "May your sins be forgiven, my son." He said in the solemn tone of the pious. He then extended the small crucifix toward the contrite confessor, and Misha imprinted his lips on its cold surface.

"I have many sins on my conscience, Father," Misha began in a soft voice, "but the sin for which I must give my mortal life I didn't commit." The chaplain's face resembled a stone mask. Most of the confessors on death row maintained their innocence. Was this one any different? Did he wonder? If Misha's assertion impressed him, you couldn't tell from the sight of his immobile features.

"God, the Father forgives all sins, large and small, my son," the priest intoned as though he hadn't heard Misha's assertion.

"Did you hear me, Father? I'm innocent of the crime for which I must give my life. You hear?" Misha raised his voice slightly.

"It is not my station here to judge one way or another, my son," the priest said in the monotone of a friar celebrating mass, "I must prepare you for the high court in heaven."

"You don't understand, Father," Misha insisted, "I'm going to die for a crime I have not committed." He looked insistently at the priest who avoided the condemned man's eyes. "Isn't there anything you could do? Talk to the warden? Call the governor? Anything?" Misha pleaded as if he were facing a tribunal of last resort.

"It is not my station to…"

"…I know, you don't have to repeat it, padre," Misha interrupted, "…judge one way or another…" he mimicked the priest's words. Suddenly, as if he had made up his mind to some sort of action, he stood in front of the Chaplain. "You must leave me now, padre." He said. "You've done your part, and I have no further need of your ministering here."

"Bless you, my son, *in nomine patri et filli et spiritu sancti, amen.*" The chaplain chanted his parting words, as he made the sign of the cross.

# 31.

THE HEADLINE IN SUNDAY'S Urbana-Champaign Express could be heard on every corner of the city's down-town area. Kids, hawking the afternoon daily, shouted it for all passers-by to hear: "READ ALL ABOUT IT! THE MYSTERY OF THE GHASTLY MURDER! READ ALL ABOUT IT!" Local TV news programs subsequently aired the story in every detail available to them. The news release appeared during the mid-day and the 5:00 pm news programs and, again, during prime time at 7:00 and 10:00 pm. In fact, even the talk shows had reaped the harvest of second hand, digested, news turned gossip. Callers jammed their phone lines all day long with all sorts of suggestions and theories as to the alleged assassin and the method of his craft. It was tragedy turned amusement and, in the final analysis, into entertainment for the masses. It turned out to bring a financial boon for the media.

The public snapped up copies of the paper faster than the vendors could recite the headline. Frances Hunt had done her job well. By late afternoon, the paper was a complete sellout.

In the solitude of his isolation, Misha contemplated his approaching final hours. Tomorrow at dawn he would face the State Executioner. Though he wasn't familiar with the intricacies of administering an execution, the very prospect of becoming a public spectacle revolted him. A kaleidoscope of memories flooded his feverish mind.

In his youth, Misha was able to enchant others through his cheerful nature. Now, as a mature individual, he tried his best to impress through his melancholy disposition. Either way, he knew it wasn't effective. Above all, he attempted to become his own self; to shed the weight of his mother's last words. A sudden awareness pervaded his melancholy mood; that of having been *in love* with his mother for as long as he could remember. Yet he did not understand why it was so, for he had no assurance that his love was reciprocated. He agonized that loving her was a contradiction in terms and an obvious rebellion against her legacy: her last words.

Suddenly, like a flash of light, in his self-awareness his conscience dictated that she be removed from him, though he would always remain an integral part of her existence. She had given him life, but only through him was she able to transcend time. He listened to an endless tide of voices that rushed in a steady, monotone flux, like a surge of symphonic cantos intoned at a special Great Mass for the departed. "Mother...dear mother...what have you done? Oh, mamá *Schatzi*, what have you wrought?" He murmured to himself over and over again.

Spurred on by the memory of his mother, Misha began to fashion a makeshift rope. He tore strips of his shirt and tied them together in knots. He was astonished to see that one shirt would make into a rope almost three meters in length. He tightened the knots carefully and tested their endurance by trying to pull them apart with all the force he was able to muster. They wouldn't give. He was pleased, yet he knew that the ultimate test of their strength would soon come unbeknownst to him.

High above the Spartan wash basin in the corner of the small cell was a tiny light fixture. Up until now it had remained lit during the night and served as a sort of surveillance. Propped up on his bunk bed, he removed the wire mesh and unscrewed the light bulb. He wiggled the remaining part of the fixture. It was rigid. He tied the "rope" to the light bulb receptacle and tested how it held. Again, he was satisfied it would serve its purpose. Now, he was ready for the moment of truth. He thought silently.

Strange, the one regretful thought that appeared to him at this crucial moment was that he had discarded all of those lovely letters Susanna had sent him from Germany, while she had collected many years' worth of his correspondence neatly packaged in chronological order. Hers would have brought a measure of solace to him during his dark moments.

With a solemn prayer asking forgiveness for his sins and a last shout for his maa…má…maa…má…! He tied a noose and placed it over his head onto his neck. He tightened the noose until he struggled for breath. "That's okay." He whispered. With a violent leap from his bunk, he jerked the full weight of his six feet two inches frame onto the rope.

With the last trace of consciousness, Misha felt the whole of his blood supply explode to the top of his brain. It kept a steady flow and with it one sweep of a horrible pressure. Suddenly, there was nothing, a profound void, and an all pervading lightness he only perceived subliminally. He kept falling into an unending abyss, he heard voices, notably that of his father Motele calling from a great distance, and then there was silence. Brightness turned dark, and he was carried upward on the wings of a strange weightlessness.

Sunday Patrick slept late. After all, early lectures didn't afford him that luxury during week days. It was almost noon when he got up and put on the coffee pot on the gas stove. He measured out two teaspoons full of extra fine ground coffee to make his morning cup strong. Much has happened in the last few months, and he hasn't slept too well. This would be a special weekend. Monday would mark a significant date for him; one that would end his current preoccupation. He smiled wearily. His thoughts traveled to Misha's solitary existence and his own, self-imposed, solitude during these last few months. His most evocative memories rested with Susanna and their fledgling relationship.

Patrick recalled that time. A little over a year ago, as expected, Misha's self-destructive behavior had helped Patrick in his conquest of yet another woman. He could still see her soft reddish hair as its waves followed immediately behind the graceful downward movement of her head. He was fascinated by the deep blue of her eyes, but most of all he admired her intelligence and quick wit. They had a lot of fun together. It might have been complete bliss, were it not for Susanna's son, Rudi, who was bent on wrecking it all. The initial moments, during which they had been together, the boy was able to monopolize his mother's time completely. Patrick had almost succeeded in seducing her, save for the presence of the spoilt brat. How he'd grown to hate the little bastard. Like a shadow, he would follow his mother wherever she went. It was ultimately the boy who had caused him all this trouble.

"Get him out of here!" He shouted at Susanna.

"Get yourself out of here," the boy responded, "you don't live here."

That was the remark that caused him to strike the boy in anger. Patrick was not a violent man, but he took the boy's remark to be a sign of rebellion and arrogance which couldn't go unpunished. He had intended to strike the boy again, but Susanna came between them, and he struck her instead.

Immediate remorse overcame him, but the damage was already done. Susanna asked him to leave, and her attitude toward him underwent a complete turn. He pleaded, even begged her to return, all to no avail.

"What shall I do?" He asked. "How can I convince you I've changed? What I did was wrong, and I ask forgiveness." His remorse was genuine.

"It's not that, Patrick," Susanna explained patiently. "Rudi's not yours to strike, and if you did it once in anger, you'd do it again. I want to spare us future grief." She paused to collect her thoughts. "Rudi stays, you go." She added resolutely.

He stood staring sheepishly at the floor. Being rejected was a first for Dr. Patrick O'Malley. It was not so much that he was desperately in need of female companionship. No woman should dare to humiliate this handsome intellectual. He lamented in private. Besides, it galled him that Susanna's behavior had proven more elegant and refined than his; his appeared rather provincial and crude in comparison. Only at the moment of parting did he notice that she was endowed with a deeper sense of worldliness as well as cognizance of human character. That combination has lent her that rare second upbringing which was superior to his; one that makes for a consummate individual.

"Don't I deserve another chance?" He asked.

"Oh, Christ," she said exasperatedly, "as if another chance would all of a sudden make you over, Patrick." She looked into his eyes intensely, "you are what you are."

"I'm so sorry." He stared into the void. "I'll leave you alone, Susanna." He kissed her on the cheek, and she received his affection stiffly. He walked to the door alone, and she stood watching him close the door behind him.

He was badly shaken. The experience left him completely demoralized and he knew he had to react to that defeat in a manner worthy of his track record to regain his self-esteem and confidence. He was always buoyed by women who showered him with attention. He craved it; was addicted to it.

Her presence in the departmental office didn't help matters. Most of the time, they exchanged a polite "hello" and "bye" only in passing. Not a word beyond the common amenities. He was tormented to the point of losing his appetite and having a hard time falling asleep after a hard day's work. He knew full well that he could not go on like that. It would destroy him both physically and spiritually. He went to confession and tried to make sense of the priest's gentle advice. It had gotten so critical he feared to face his colleagues for their caustic comments. At times, he felt their eyes on him, their imagined gossip grinding into his psyche.

Several weeks went by. On occasions, he would try to engage Susanna in conversation. "We're leaving for Germany in two weeks," she announced, "father insists." I miss the family. He was stunned. For this rare moment in his professional life, he was tongue-tied. Suddenly, an idea occurred to him.

"Under the circumstances, you know what would be nice?" He asked.

"No, tell me." She seemed genuinely curious.

"This coming Sunday, we could go on a picnic, eh?"

"It's no use, Patrick," she tried to dissuade him; "we would only come away from it sadder that we already are."

"I'd like to take that risk, Susanna." He pressed. "Trust me; I know what I'm doing. You'll both love it."

"Rudi has to attend an all weekend catechism workshop in our church, and I have to be there with him." It was a last resort attempt to reject Patrick's invitation. "It's important for both of us."

"Just this once, let someone take him to church." He pleaded. "He'll be okay, I'm sure. And this would give us a chance to be alone before your departure the following week." She wavered, and he sensed her indecision. "So, it's done? I'll pick you up early. There's a lovely spot not far from town. I'll show you. You won't regret."

Even as they talked and planned their little picnic, he had made up his mind he wouldn't let her go. It was going to be her last chance to return into his fold. There was no question in his mind. Susanna belonged exclusively to him. His only concern now was the manner in which to accomplish the task he had in mind and throw no suspicion whatsoever toward him. With a smile and a nod, he left.

He grew pensive. It was at that very moment that he realized what he had to do and he weighed the consequences of his action for all concerned. There was a time, not so long ago, when Susanna meant everything to him without whom he could not think of a viable existence. Recent events only strengthened his resolve not to allow his imagined bliss to slip through his fingers.

He stopped over at the nearby wine store and bought a bottle of vintage Cabernet Sauvignon, Chilean no less, he knew was her favorite. He would chill it well for their planned excursion. In the picnic basket he laid two of the finest wine glasses wrapped in soft cloth. Susanna would not drink wine from a paper cup. He knew her habits. There would be sandwiches made of rye bread and an assortment of cold cuts and fine cheese. Ah, and yes, he mustn't forget the rohypnol; the antidepressant that always worked for him when mixed with alcohol. He was making notes so as to remember every detail of his plan...

...Suddenly, a knock at the door startled him out of his reverie. Patrick was leery of people calling unannounced. "Even on Sunday, they won't let you enjoy breakfast in solitude." He murmured annoyed.

He opened the door. It was the area paper girl who came to collect the monthly dues. She handed him both the bill and the Sunday's paper. Hastily, he took care of the business, eager to peruse the daily. Surely, there'll be something about tomorrow's... "Damn!" He exclaimed through his clenched teeth. The headline stared at him in big bold print. "Whoa?" His eyes read the article twice, unbelieving. "God...oh...dear Lord..." He kept repeating in a whisper as if afraid someone would overhear. "Now, don't panic." He was calm again. "This is all speculation...conjecture...don't let them trap you, Patrick." He talked with himself. But, what if? He grimaced. "What if they have hard evidence?" He whispered under his breath. "Nah", he quickly dismissed that assumption. He knew the cops would have knocked at his door even before the paper girl came by. He reassured himself. Curiosity got the better of him and he immersed himself in Frances Hunt's lengthy headline article: a story line that proved to be part conjecture and part speculation. His critical nature marveled at some of the detailed analysis of the unfolding events. "Damn, she's good!" He shuddered at the very thought...

*...P. checked his picnic basket once again. All items were in place, and he was satisfied. Now he was ready for the last detail. He removed the suitcase from his closet. It was full of Misha's research papers and reference books Alida had entrusted to him for safekeeping before her departure for Cuba. "I'm sure he'll want to go on with his work, once he is exonerated and freed." She told P. "I have no use for them where I'm going, and you're his colleague and friend." "I'll take good care of his research material." He assured her. "I'm confident he'll want to go on with his work after..." She didn't hear the end of the sentence, for he was out the doorway when he muttered something under his breath that sounded like: "The hell he will, if I have anything to do with it."*

*Now, as he hauled the heavy piece of luggage full of research paper and reference books into the trunk of his car, he couldn't help but marvel at the coincidence of its usefulness. Since he had no use for it, he would let Susanna take it with her to Germany; a legacy for Rudi from his father. That, he was sure, would please her.*

*Susanna was resigned to that last rendezvous with P. She even felt good about giving it a chance to chat and explain herself and her actions to the man she once thought of marrying. After all, she was pregnant with his child, albeit unbeknownst to him. Would it be prudent to tell him? She asked herself silently. No, she had better not reveal her pregnancy. They have some strange laws in this wonderful country that give both parties certain rights of parenting. It might prevent her departure. Let's not tell him. Definitely not. She was satisfied with her decision when the door bell rang.*

*"I see you're ready," he greeted her, smiling.*

*"I have been, in more than one way, for some time." She smiled, and he realized how difficult it will be to go through with his plans. "Oh? Am I late? Again?" He helped her into her coat. "It's a bit chilly out there." He said. "The lake breeze, you know."*

*"Thank you," she squeezed his hand tenderly without knowing why. He withdrew his quickly. This is no time for tenderness. He thought silently. They sat in the car without talking at first, and he drove in the direction that led toward Lake Michigan.*

*"Tell me, now, where are you taking me?" She asked.*

*"It's a wonderful place. Trust me. Don't let's spoil the surprise." He* kept the mystery alive.

*"Oh, okay,"* she was playful; *"you can have your surprise, if it means that much to you."*

*"I appreciate your forbearance,"* he turned on the car radio, and they had no need to talk for the next few minutes. Susanna shifted her weight toward the door. As the side of her coat brushed against the doorknob, she felt something hard in her right pocket. It was the small notebook she has been using as a diary. Last she'd remembered, she had taken it to work with her and forgot to empty her coat pocket on returning home. *"Oh, my Lord,"* she panicked in silence, *"he mustn't get his hands on it. He'd find out everything."* She put her hand in her pocket and clutched the little booklet convulsively; afraid it might fall out into the open.

P. was whistling a familiar tune along with the sound of the radio broadcast; at times he even repeated the words. He seemed in a good mood, and she didn't want to ruin his hour. The road ahead was narrow now, a typical country two lane.

*"Are we almost there?"* Susanna asked.

*"Not very much longer. A little more patience, dear."* He smiled.

*"It's so peaceful out here in the countryside."* She said earnestly.

*"See? I knew you'd like it. I knew it."* He was triumphant. *"There! Look ahead!"* He almost shouted. *"There it is. There's my little lake, well, it's more like a large pond."* He looked at her from the corner of his eye. She smiled. He was pleased.

He parked the car on a low bluff a small distance from the pond. One was able to see, judging by the darkness of the water, how surprisingly deep the pond was at the point closest to their picnic area. P. carried the blankets and the basket full of provisions to a nearby spot, sheltered by high shrubs and a few low lying trees. Susanna took the opportunity to dispose of her diary while He was busy with the chores. She helped spread the blanket and uncorked the wine bottle. Glasses ready, P. poured a sampling into his, sipped and allowed the liquid to roll on his tongue. *"Perfect."* He said. She held out her glass, and he poured a fair portion for her and then for himself. He raised his glass toward her.

*"Well, here's to your journey home. I wish you all the best."*

*"And the very best to you."* She toasted him.

They ate their sandwiches and chatted about things, all very trivial, none touched on the more personal issues. Suddenly, Susanna gazed at him over her glass with an expression of pity. *"You'll no doubt suffer terribly over all this, as will I."* She said, now looking away. He shrugged his shoulders with resignation. *"It cannot be helped,"* he said softly, *"though I shall try to think of you with loving kindness and remember the happy moments we've experienced together."*

*"So will I,"* she concurred. *"Would you let me share the expenses for this splendid outing?"* She asked.

He shook his head. *"Don't you worry about a thing, dear. Go ahead and explore the environment. Enjoy. Relax, and I'll take care of the rest."* He insisted.

She got up glad she would be able to waste a little time on a walk toward the shore. She soon came upon a tract of swampy land adjacent to the pond, and she turned to call for him. In her momentary absence, P. filled their glasses anew, and managed to carefully empty the contents of rohypnol into Susanna's. *"There's a marsh here, look!"* She called out to him, *"and a boat moored not far from the shore!"*

*"Yes, I know!"* He responded. *"We'll explore in a moment,"* he spoke calmly as she approached. *"Let's have another toast."*

*"What would you have me drink to?"* She asked playfully.

*"Oh, to everything and nothing,"* he replied. He was now so close to her she could smell his breath. They emptied the bottle and sat near each other just talking. His hands wouldn't stay idle either. He tried to pull her to him and was about to kiss her when she pushed him from herself with all her might. *"Stop! Please! This was not in my plans!"* She resisted desperately, only the more to challenge his inhibitions. In the end, she was no match for him. The drug had begun to take effect and played havoc with her senses. *"Please, be a dear...no...nooo...!"*

*She resisted with the feeble strength still left her. His hands worked feverishly and he seemed obsessed with the task he had undertaken. "You're hurting me... stop...don't ...It's not funny...you're raping me..." Her voice faded into the great expanse.*

*Disregarding her pleas, he ripped off her pantyhose and underpants and proceeded to wedge his legs between hers. All the while he kept muttering inarticulately, more to himself than to his intended victim: "You must forgive me. Dear, dear Susanna, I don't mean to hurt you. But it has to be this way. The only way I know how to keep you." She struggled bravely, but now his strong fingers encircled her throat and applied great pressure on the carotid arteries. He entered her with a desperate thrust and emitted a groan not unlike a wild, primordial, beast. She tried vainly to fight her way to freedom. But her strength left her with her last breath.*

*Unable to loosen his grip, Susanna wanted to scream for help, but was able to emit only a weak whisper: "H...e...l...p...me...somebody...help..." And then there was no sound. She lay silent and limp beneath the weight of his body, and he realized he was violating a lifeless woman.*

*At first, he panicked. It wasn't his intention to go that far. He brought the drug along to have some fun; to laugh a bit and to make love without inhibitions. But this? How did it become so violent? He thought feverishly. Did it really happen? He put his ear to her lips. There was no breath. Only now he became aware of the gravity of the situation. He looked around, listened to the sound of approaching cars on the road. No one was coming. He felt some relief. Now think. Think how to salvage whatever future he had. Great fear reached up to seize him at his throat. Has he gone too far? He knew he has, and he felt remorse, but things couldn't be undone. He was who he was, and now he had to come up with a plan to make a virtue out of this great fault of his.*

*Her limp body was heavier he'd expected, now that she was no longer alive and vibrant, and he would carry her to the bedroom on those many joyous occasions. He saw the boat in the distance, and his walk became heavier once he reached the marshes. At last, to his hips in water, he reached the boat and deposited Susanna's body inside with great care not to capsize it. For a brief moment, he regarded her now pale features with great affection. Tears welled up in his eyes, and his lips quivered with emotion. "Dear God, dear God, what have I done?" His eyes toward the heavens, he muttered. "You must forgive me, Susanna, darling." He repeated several times, as he stroked her red hair. Just then, he noticed her wide open eyes directed at him. His hand trembling, he pulled her eyelids downward. "How can I ever be a happy person again?" He whispered sadly.*

*Only then, it came to him that he must complete what he had started. He tidied up the picnic area, removed all traces of their presence. Susanna's panties in his trouser pocket, the pantyhose ready to do the chore. He carried the suitcase on board the boat. Once aboard, he grabbed the oars and began to paddle furiously, frothing at the mouth. In the deep end of the pond, he tied one pantyhose leg round his victim's ankles, the other to the suitcase's grip. For a moment, he thought of the undergarment in his pocket. Should he put her panties on her before going on? No, time was of the essence and, besides, the prospect of dressing her and all that... His nerves were not up to it.*

*He rolled the lifeless body into the murky water. It floated on the surface for a while, which to him felt like eternity. Laboriously, he pushed the suitcase overboard after his lifeless victim. Submerging slowly, the suitcase's weight pulled the lifeless body of the woman down into the darkness of the deep. He watched their slow descent. Soon, there was no trace of them...*

Unbelieving, Patrick read the long editorial several times with incredulity. He was looking for some clues of evidence pointing toward him. The letter 'P' was quite obviously meant to denote a name. His name. And there was a diary? He didn't see any diary on that fateful day at the pond. Did Susanna conceal it somewhere in the vicinity of their last encounter? Must have. Why didn't she tell him of her pregnancy? It was his child. "Oh, Lord have mercy on my soul! I killed two people. The one I loved most and another yet unborn I would have surely loved." He prayed in a whisper, then talked inarticulately and walked over to his TV set and turned on the noon hour news.

There he was on the TV screen. His photo and that of Misha displayed by one of the news anchors, while the other commented on both: "Professor Misha Winograd is temporarily confined to sick bay at the maximum security prison with a minor head concussion after an attempted suicide. He is to face the executioner tomorrow morning at 9:00 a.m. sharp for the murder of his former live-in friend and mother of his son Rudi, Susanna Flossberg." The announcer nodded in the direction of his partner. She took up where he left off.

"New developments, however, give rise to speculation that there may have been another person implicated in the murder, and frantic appeals for a stay are in the process. Partial diary of the murder victim has been recovered by a private investigator. In it the victim identifies someone with the initial 'P' alleging the involvement of a second party with possible motives.

"The man on the right is Professor Patrick O'Malley who was known to have been romantically involved with the victim shortly after her breakup with his colleague Dr. Misha Winograd. Authorities are in the process of..."

Patrick turned off the TV. He has heard enough. Slowly, a defeated man, he walked toward the corner closet where he'd always kept the loaded 9mm Browning. He took it from the shelf and regarded it almost with a certain degree of affection. He had bought the weapon as a security measure at a time when he was receiving threatening phone calls from former students disenchanted with his grading practices. He'd never suspected it would someday become the instrument to rectify his transgressions and failures. At his desk again, he composed a brief confessional statement, with the meticulousness characteristic of his archeologist's background. It started with the words: "I, Patrick O'Malley, being of sound mind, confess to the murder of..." details of the account followed, and ended with: "...my conscience does not permit me to make an innocent man pay the penalty for..."

He walked serenely into the bathroom, his hand caressing the cocked handgun. One hand held the newspaper, which he began to read out loud and with great emphasis. He let the water run till it filled the bathtub to the rim. This done, Patrick undressed and placed the pajamas neatly on the stool. He climbed into the hot, running water. Once inside the bathtub, his head completely submerged, he inserted the barrel of the pistol into his mouth and pulled the trigger. The water was now overflowing from the bathtub onto the floor, tainted crimson, with loud, continuous splashes.

# 32.

MISHA WOKE UP with a terrific headache and a sprained ankle as a result of his fall during his suicide attempt. His vision was still a bit hazy, but he was able to distinguish familiar faces; those of Anton and Diana, Pedro and Alida who had stood around his bed, concern written on their faces. A trustee medic was taking Misha's temperature and a nurse was in the process of changing the bandages on his bruised temple.

"He's awake!" Alida exclaimed joyfully. "Misha! Misha! My darling!" She held his hand in hers and wouldn't let go. Surprised to the degree of shock at the sight of Alida's presence, Misha's attempt at producing a smile was muted by a painful grimace. Yet he was aware that he wasn't dreaming. The last reality he remembered before falling to his cell floor was the feel of being carried airborne in a manner so strange he attributed it to supernatural intervention. But here he was, alive, among his friends and in the presence of his Alida.

"Alida...Anton...Pedro...Diana...my friends...what has happened?" He tried to collect his thoughts, his voice tremulous with excitement at seeing his dear companions.

"You've been out for the last four days," Alida said with a happy smile on her tanned face. "Tried to kill yourself. Thank God you're a pretty clumsy when it comes to tying knots."

"You fell and knocked yourself out," Diana interjected.

"You're a free man, Misha," Anton informed him, "as soon as you're able to get out of bed, you're free to go."

"You mean? I'm not...?"

"...you're not going to be executed for someone else's crime." Pedro could not resist announcing.

"You'll never believe it, darling," Alida chimed in, "who did it to her. Never in a thousand years will you guess." She carried on.

"Anyone we know? Who was it?" Misha asked.

"It was our friend and colleague, Patrick." Pedro announced sadly.

"He left a note exonerating you before he blew his brains out ..." Anton informed his client. "The landlord called the police when the water in the bathroom overflowed into the apartment below. Patrick didn't answer the door and police had to make a forceful entry into the bathroom. They found his body immersed in bloody water, weapon still in his cramped fingers. The authorities accepted his handwritten confession, which he left on his desk, as a valid proof of your innocence."

"Patrick? But why?" Misha's countenance expressed great pity. His own miraculous rebirth as well as Patrick's bitter end in suicide affected him greatly. "Patrick?" He repeated. He tried to sit up, but fell back unable to lift his head. "But why?" He repeated.

"Who can tell?" Diana always the social worker injected a note of concern for a person's mental well being. "Who is to judge?"

"Anyway," Anton interrupted with uncharacteristic cheerfulness, "the State has dropped all charges, and my job here is done." He said his good-byes on his way out of the sick bay. It would have been redundant to explain Craig's part in the ruse that undid Patrick. Anton chuckled inwardly. They would learn about that soon enough. He knew that acts of that nature rarely remain unknown.

Barely out of the gate, was Anton met by TV cameras and hordes of media people shouting questions he didn't feel obliged to answer.

"I'm pressed for time, ladies and gentlemen," he begged off, "but should you wish to interview either one of us, me or the defendant, please contact my office," he paused with a wicked smile in his bright eyes, "during office hours, mind you." With those words, he boarded the waiting limo and hastened on his way.

"I have yet to thank the good lawyer," Misha remarked in Anton's absence. "I must admit, there were times I had my doubts." They shouted with joy at the understatement. Only then, Misha noticed Alida's radiant expression and her delicate situation, for she was over four months with his child, and it was clearly evident due to her diminutive height.

Without further inquiries, he pulled Alida toward him into a tight embrace "Alida, honey, it has come true. It's really happening." He exalted, the tone of his voice expressing incredulity. "How? What?" He sought answers.

"It did, indeed, my darling," she kissed him on the cheek, blushing, "a miracle of modern medical science. Will explain later, not now, have patience." All present broke into a happy applause.

Expecting some rational answers that would explain those series of bizarre circumstances, Misha began his first press conference, disbelieving his own ears. He stood silent, transfixed by his recollections of the recent past. Amidst soft murmurs of the eager reporters and his heart's increased activity, Misha said, "Well then, let's hear it from you, Ladies and Gentlemen. I'm open to questions."

"Are there any future plans?" A petite blonde reporter asked smilingly. She represented the *Urbana Daily Journal*, and Misha remembered her presence during his indictment. After some reflection, he reacted strangely to the question:

"To be honest, I haven't a clue." He smiled. "My present priority is to try and sort out my own questions in view of the recent happenings; the 'what to do' and 'how to deal' with it all." It was obvious to the assembled that his memories had stirred a good measure of sadness. "I'm hopeful that in due time I might be able to solve part of the puzzle and I'll be thankful to leave it at that." He uttered the last sentence rather abruptly, indicating that the interview has reached the end. As he had begun to walk away, he turned once more to face the throng, and their faces wore expressions beyond the power of description. "Let us all reflect on those circumstances before we meet again." Those were his parting words.

It had taken some time before Misha was able to meet the press again. This time accompanied by his able attorney. Would he be able to tell his story without overflowing with emotion? He promised himself he would stand before a group of his peers and tell the story of his miraculous survival...

"...and now, regarding my plans." He glanced at Alida and then continued: "Let me respond to your many questions briefly. I wish to assure you that my dear wife Alida stood by me during the entire ordeal. Were it not for her steadfast support I might have surely succumbed to self-pity and depression. It was she who has defrayed the legal as well as investigative costs which exonerated me in the end." Misha paused. He breathed heavily before continuing. The slight animation among the assembled was testimony to their genuine interest in his fate. Certainly, there was a human interest story in his overcoming of his ordeal. But each of them seemed to also glimpse a sense of genuine personal tragedy and eventual triumph in the forthcoming revelations. Misha gave a sigh and slight smile appeared on his still weary face. It was a good feeling to know himself vindicated. "There exists rational thought after all." He thought to himself gratified. Now that the sensational aspect had quieted down, emotion was subdued and logic prevailed. "What had transpired was my destiny." He said, and his voice quivered imperceptibly. "Now I have a date with a more tempered future." The small university conference pavilion resounded with subdued applause.

"Will you continue your tenure at the University?" The question was quite appropriate being that on his arrest he was publicly tried by his erstwhile friends and former colleagues. "Or will you seek accountability for the injustices you have endured?"

Misha pondered the response longer than he had thought necessary. "I haven't had the time to arrive at a definitive course of action since my release. Sadly, what is most perplexing is the discovery how a fickle public can hold a simultaneous fascination for the frightening and the entertaining. Most people will try and commit a person in that spirit." Misha measured his words with great care. "I can assure you that it isn't in my nature to seek revenge on or reparations from those who had brought injury to my professional reputation and in the process disrupted my life." He studied the individual expression on the assembled. "Still, the thought of quitting my post has not occurred to me as yet."

Alida's strong fingers gripped his arm tightly and tears welled up in her eyes. Several moments passed before Misha was able to continue. "Above all, I'm happy to have been exonerated and that I owe in large measure to those few who believed in my innocence." His smiling eyes met those of Anton's and Alida's. "And I also owe a great deal of gratitude to my loyal friend and colleague Pedro as well as the professional integrity of Diana Ferrucci." He nodded in their direction returning their smiles of acknowledgment. "They are all exemplary individuals and, no doubt, I am forever indebted to them. They have acted in concert with their conscience despite social pressure, and I want to thank them again, now as a free man." There was the sound of applause and repeated cameras flashing in bright explosive sequence.

# Epilogue

IT WAS A TIME of decision-making. Misha knew this was his final reprieve, a chance to seize the opportunity and transcend all worldly trivialities. His resolve was a sign from above. Call it God, the awesome universal energy of which he considered himself an integral part.

He gave it a lot of thought, now able to communicate without straining to shout in a padded cell; without alienation and the inability to receive feedback. It had become clear to him now that he had to devote his life to something other than self-gratification. The whole business of change was going to be difficult for him. All his adult life he had been accustomed to boldness and insensitivity toward others. That was his *raison d'être*, his way of life. It was also in keeping with his mother's legacy; no longer now.

His greatest asset was his youth and his steadfast resolve. Both he and Alida stood ready to make a fresh start wherever life might lead them. Above all, they concluded that in order to ensure success in their partnership they must share all that matters to them; even thoughts and acts of the most sensitive nature. They hoped that fate would favor them with a more benign atmosphere eventually. He was now Abraham trading through Babylon's and Egypt's deserts; he was an erstwhile captive of the Roman Empire, a slave resulting from their sacking of Jerusalem. He was a refugee from the Spanish Inquisition that had condemned all of the faithful of heresy and forced them to wander eternally in exile. How much has he wandered since that hapless moment of his arrest and incarceration for a crime he has not committed? How many others share his fate? Worse yet, how many forfeit their lives innocently prejudged?

He found himself standing on a riverbank waiting to cross the current, since there was an absence of a bridge. A soft voice urged him to swim across, but he didn't know how to stay afloat. Suddenly, a stranger came by on a motorcycle equipped with a side car and invited him to come along. After having covered some territory, the cycle stopped and Misha disembarked. He arrived among friends who congratulated him for his many successes.

Was that too only a dream? Misha wondered.

Rudi was very much on Misha's and Alida's mind now. Would the motherless boy want to accept them as his parents? Misha was willing to face the challenge and struggle for his son's well being and, at the same time, his own. For he understood that to lose the boy now meant to lose Susanna forever. He would feel her great loss, and the pain of its recurrence would not permit him to contain his grieving in his waking and sleeping hours. Oftentimes he burst out crying like a child in his nightly episodes to be awakened by Alida's tender embrace. He wanted to communicate his views openly with her; begin to achieve an inner peace he was so desperately seeking. He needed her now more than ever. Would she stand by him in the future as she has done in his hour of need? Misha has come to a final awareness of his tragic and destructive ways which he has treated for as long as his memory could take him. He fantasized about his future, but it was all in the realm of dreams and speculation.

Suddenly, thanks to the irony of notoriety turned fame, he was able to acquire plenty of money for travel and the comforts of the good life he was hitherto unaware existed. Things had quieted down a bit. He was suddenly the darling of the 'high' social circles. He was now ceaselessly hounded by literary agents and publishers for the rights to his 'story' with six digit offers. It was society's passionate hunger to explore its many vices rather than its precious few virtues. Magazines and newspapers vied for articles, and Misha was tempted to sacrifice his newly found karma on the altar of material wealth. His pockets were empty, and he was not above exploiting society's gluttony by enriching his coffers. In any event, it was comforting to know that, if the need arose, they could always count on the insatiable greed of the business establishment. Thoughts of the irretrievable time he had wasted during his incarceration kept returning, but he had resolved not to give in to negative impulses. He focused on the tangible future instead.

"I want you to share my life with me, Alida," Misha held her hand in his and looked enamored into her eyes.

"I'm willing to give it a try," she replied, and there was an expression of great joy in Misha's loud giggle.

"I promise to make us happy," he declared.

"I'm glad you said 'us', because I couldn't be happy without you."

The first order of business was to wrest Rudi from the foster authorities and to do it with the now young man's tacit approval. That was not as difficult as Misha assumed. Rudi was now a mature teen, fully aware of the prevailing circumstances. There was no need for Misha to spend energy on explaining the past. The past was overshadowed by the present.

"And you'll be okay with the new baby brother...or sister, Rudi?" Misha asked.

"Why should I object, dad?" Rudi's candor was disarming. "I've always liked this woman," he added, smiling, as he put his arm round Alida's waist. "May I call you 'mom'?" he asked. "Of course," Alida replied, though she knew it wasn't often strangers took other strangers into their hearts.

"I hope you'll get to love her in time," Misha mused. "No one can replace your birth mom, I know, but I'm sure Alida will try her best to be a loyal friend and companion."

The agony of the past had turned to joyful anticipation toward their future. They have emerged from a dark tunnel into a world of light. Their hearts have grown mutually stronger and purer in their love for each other in particular and people around them in general. Misha had signed a book contract with a major publisher, and the advance alone provided them with comfort and extensive travel possibility.

Though he did not voice his concern immediately, Misha was really mostly preoccupied about his career. The need to reform lay dormant within a fatty tissue of the newly found contentment. Deep down, however, he believed in being aware of his surroundings and capable of solving the problems facing him. His self-confidence grew gradually. Fortunately, it didn't seem necessary to tackle all of the questions at once. First, he wanted to find the proper place where he would find direction and, above all, his true identity.

"Let's visit Israel and Poland," Misha suggested. "There are unfinished issues for me in both places," he added.

"And maybe Cuba?" Alida chimed in.

"And Germany and France?" Rudi smiled faintly. "I want mom's ashes to be buried in Israel, and reacquaint myself with my roots."

The three of them reached a stage of mutual trust wherein they could dispense with offense-defense and communicate with a fair degree of candor.

"I have no quarrel with that," Misha smiled and, as he looked over Rudi's shoulder, he spied Motele's face, grimacing, as if to say, "you're okay now. Just don't go back to your old ways." Misha seemed content with himself. It was up to him now.

On the eve of their departure for the Middle East, they were invited to attend Xin Xin's and the Padre's informal wedding at the *Won Ton* Chinese restaurant. The ceremony was simple. The bride was resplendent in native traditional dress, colorful and exotic. The bridegroom, unburdened from the constraints of the cloth, seemed relaxed and cordial in the presence of his former prison confessor. "How nice of you to come." He extended a cordial welcome. "And also you, dear lady," he addressed Alida.

"We are happy for you, now that the ordeal is over." Xin Xin hugged them both and left a kiss on Rudi's blushing cheek. "And, by the way, the Padre has changed my name to *Agape*, so that he would not continue to pronounce my name Sin Sin." She smiled happily.

"And so we are also very happy for you," Misha said. "We wish you much happiness and many children."

They were served a sumptuous dinner of many exquisite Dim Sum culinary creations: shrimp stuffing sealed in a tapioca flour dough skin and steamed. This was followed by a serving of Lai Wong Bau—steamed wheat buns filled with sweet, thick egg yolk custard.—Dishes followed one another in rapid succession. There was Gin Doil, sweet lotus seed paste and Fun Kwok, dumplings filled with shrimp and many other dishes they have heard of in the past but never tasted. Of course, a steaming hot pot of tea continually replenished served to wash down the tasty delights. It was a most appropriate farewell to Urbana-Champaign. They would all remember it, especially Rudi who had experienced such great treats for the first time in his young life.

Their spirits soared. A further traditional touch arrived toward the dessert being served in the form of fortune cookies. Misha opened his and read the tiny print of the aphorism it contained for all to hear: "Listen to your mother's exhortations more." He regarded the minuscule writing on the tiny strip of paper and smiled sadly. He understood the tragic consequences of his mother's final admonishment. Alida regarded her husband with concern. On a sudden impulse, Misha crumpled the cookie's 'fortune' in the palm of his hand and let it drop onto his empty plate.

"Rest easy, mama," he whispered inaudibly, "I must follow my own and altogether different drummer from this moment on."

Unencumbered from the demons stemming from maternal and paternal anxieties, Misha would change into an open, easy-going adult and probe candidly into his and his parents' lives. He would keep his opinions and emotions about his own world well guarded. He was now motivated almost entirely by concerns for his family. He understood that one doesn't examine life objectively until middle age, and yet some of the most crucial decisions must be taken during the fleeting moments of youth. Perhaps free choice even at his age was an illusory concept; weighty deliberations served merely to rationalize situations arrived at emotionally or through some mysterious subconscious process.

All in all, each of them was simply involved and happy in their own doings. There was no motivation or the need to influence or manipulate the other. There was nothing else that particularly attracted them.

The excitement reached crescendo as they boarded the El Al 747 jet. The pilot gunned the motor at the startup of the runway. They looked at each other, smiling. It was their first journey together. There would be many more, of that Misha was certain. Soon they were aloft. The stars filled the infinite horizon, on their dreamy night voyage. Sparkling sunlight burst on them above a solid white cloud high above the North Pole. Misha closed his eyes, and opium visions of fish-like, iridescent clouds appeared, swimming in a colored glass atmosphere at dawn somewhere over Iceland. The stars sparkled all around on a dreamy night's journey. But the dawn of light burst on him above a solid white cloud high above the North Pole.

Misha reached inside the seat pouch for the airline magazine. On its brightly colored cover was the map of the globe. He turned the page. Inside, there was a full-page photograph of a female model airline hostess. "How curious," he thought, "if I were to tear up the human model, it would also destroy the wholeness of the globe. As long as one remains intact, so does the other. They're as interdependent as the Yin and Yang." The harmony of the universe was neatly mapped out. For him there were no more problems. Everything seemed under control.

Israel's coastline was visible on the far horizon above the blue Mediterranean waters. Misha's hands trembled with excitement as he held Alida's hand in one and Rudi's in the other in a tender squeeze. Everything about their experience filled him with an inner satisfaction. Without speaking a single word, they somehow connected. They needed each other and that is all that mattered for now and the future. Gracefully, the huge ship touched the Lod International Airport runway.

Misha smiled at Rudi and then at Alida. In silence, he asked himself that inevitable question regarding Blanche, his beloved mother, "Would this idyllic picture of her grandson showered by the love of his father and his new step-mom, have made up for the pain she had suffered in missing her own son and never knowing her grandson?" After all, psychologists have always maintained that youth is better off on its own. Now, Misha concluded, it may be that parents are too.

***

# About the Author

William Samelson, PhD., Professor Emeritus, Foreign Languages, Holocaust & Genocide Studies, English as a Second Language, and International Relations.

Born in Poland, he lived there until the age of eleven when he was interned in various ghettoes, Nazi labor & concentration camps throughout Poland and the Third Reich. He spent three and a half years in the Buchenwald concentration camp and its satellite Colditz. Liberated by the US Army on 1 May 1945; he immigrated to the US in 1948.

Dr. Samelson holds a PhD degree from the University of Texas at Austin, Texas. He has taught at Kent State University, the University of Illinois at Champaign-Urbana, the University of Texas at Austin, San Antonio College, from which he is Emeritus Professor. He has taught as a Visiting Professor at Trinity University and University of Texas, both in San Antonio. Dr. Samelson has published extensively on the Holocaust and other literary genres. He has lectured globally on a variety of topics. He has conducted lecture discussion/workshops throughout the US and in numerous foreign countries.

The Federal Republic of Germany honored Dr. William Samelson for his contribution to German letters and culture. He has served as ESL (English as a Second Language) Consultant in the Dominican Republic. His texts are used in colleges and universities throughout the world. He was Contributing Editor of The Voice of Piotrków Survivors.

Dr. Samelson was awarded the Piper Professorship as the outstanding teacher of Texas Colleges and Universities. He has been honored with an Honorary Citizenship of Texas and appointed Admiral of the Texas Navy by the Texas Legislature and Governor John Connally. He is listed in numerous publications, and his credits include "The Directory of American Scholars'" "Men of Achievement Award," as well as many "Who's Who" publications.

# A Mother's Last Words

Teaser:

*A powerful, riveting story, based on historical events and characters taken from authentic persons entangled in the web of war and its consequences. The story has a compelling fascination in its narrative that speaks to the heart of human anguish and resonates with the restorative spirit emanating from Divine Grace. God's purpose seems clear, on the one hand, but it challenges human imagination clouding all in the proverbial mystery.*